BOB UECKER feels more fortunate than most former big leaguers, because he has no feelings of frustration, of promise unfulfilled. He knows he got the most out of his talent—and it wasn't much. This is from the man whose greatest thrill in baseball was watching a guy fall out of the upper deck in Philadelphia—who loved being in the minor leagues, and who once shagged fly balls with a tuba. What he lacked in talent, Uecker made up in high jinks. His stories are hilarious, his insights keen, and his heart is as big as a diamond . . .

"An engagingly droll journeyman's view of the national pastime."

—KIRKUS REVIEWS

MICKEY HERSKOWITZ is a broadcaster for Houston's KPRC-TV and a nationally syndicated sports columnist.

CATCHER IN THE WRY

Bob Uecker
and Mickey Herskowitz

A JOVE BOOK

Baseball cards from the collection of Larry Fritsch, 735 Old Wausau Road, Stevens Point, WI 54481. All interior photographs not otherwise credited are from Bob Uecker's personal collection.

Cover photo courtesy of Lite Beer from the Miller Brewing Company of Milwaukee, WI.

This Jove book contains the complete text of the original hardcover edition. It has been completely reset in a typeface designed for easy reading, and was printed from new film.

CATCHER IN THE WRY

A Jove Book / published by arrangement with the authors

PRINTING HISTORY
G. P. Putnam's Sons edition / August 1982
Jove edition / May 1983

ISBN: 0-515-07254-0

Jove books are published by Jove Publications, Inc., 200 Madison Avenue, New York, N.Y. 10016. The words "A JOVE BOOK" and the "J" with sunburst are trademarks belonging to Jove Publications, Inc.
PRINTED IN THE UNITED STATES OF AMERICA

Acknowledgments

When people ask who made me a broadcaster, or a baseball humorist, I give them the names of a dozen pitchers in the National League.

But I also want to express my thanks to Merle Harmon, who talked me into doing an audition with ABC; to Alan (Bud) Selig, who gave me my first opportunity in broadcasting with the Brewers; and Al Hirt, for letting me try out my brand of comedy on the stage of his nightclub. I just recited the highlights of my career and the audience thought it was hilarious.

The efforts of many people went into the making of this book, but a special debt is owed to Mark Stillwell, the president (retired) of the Bob Uecker Fan Club (also retired).

To Gus, my father,
who was never surprised
when I struck out.
He would have seen the humor
in all the good it did me.

Contents

PART IV—Short Subjects

PART V—Touching Some Extra Bases

APPENDIX—The Record 215

Introduction

MOST OF WHAT I have written here is true, especially those descriptions and examples of how I struggled to become a lifetime .200 hitter in the major leagues.

Some of what I have written might have happened, but didn't, and some could only have happened in the dark corners of my own imagination. I have not used any arrows, cartoon balloons or parenthetical asides to tell you which is which.

Those who love baseball as a game, the way I love it, will know the difference, and they are the ones for whom this book was written.

Preface

THIS IS BILL LEE, the rather unconventional pitcher for the Montreal Expos, on the subject of catchers:

"Catchers anticipate. They try to receive vibrations, waves. Catchers have to be very sensitive. Their attention wanders a lot. So you have to stop, shake them, get all the screws back in the right place. If my catcher wants to come out to the mound and tell me how bad I am, I'll say, 'You're right, so what shall we do about it?' I give everybody their own space."

When Bob Uecker was asked if he would like to select a friend, perhaps a former teammate, to say a few words about him and possibly provide an insight for his book, he said he would take his chances with Tim McCarver. It was an interesting choice, the obvious conclusion being that one catcher understands another. Certainly, these two do.

Uecker was McCarver's backup at St. Louis in 1964, the year the Cardinals won the pennant in a four-team pileup. Tim retired at the end of the 1980 season after a remarkable career that spanned twenty-one years. He was the first modern catcher to play for four decades, in most years a splendid performer, always a hard-nosed one.

He recalls catching a rookie lefthander named Steve Carlton in the spring of 1965, then having the young man approach him in the clubhouse and say, earnestly, "Hey, hey, you've got to call more breaking pitches when we're behind the hitter."

By then McCarver was moving into his sixth season, having established himself in the World Series as a coming star. He backed up the startled pitcher against a wall and screamed at him, "You sonofabitch! You got a lot of guts telling me that. What credentials do *you* have?"

That, as Tim describes it, was the beginning of a long and beautiful friendship, tight enough that the Phillies would bring him out of one retirement just to catch Carlton.

Between Uecker and McCarver—one catcher to another—there was never any pugnacity. When Tim became a broadcaster in Philadelphia, Bob was among his well-wishers. He knew McCarver would have to make it the hard way. There is not much comic material in a baseball career as solid as that one.

Perceptive and direct, McCarver may blow a few of the covers Uecker has created for himself, but here he is:

When I roomed with Uke in 1964, people were always saying to me, "I'll bet that's a zany room." It wasn't zany at all. You'd go down to the lobby or out to the parking lot and there'd be a string of guys telling one Uecker story after another. But he isn't one of those people who has to be *on* all the time. When he wanted to relax, he got away from people. I guess that's one of the ironies of his life. Maybe it's true of any humorist.

The thing is, you never knew what was going to come out of that imagination. Once he invented something called the Ugly Card Game. He had a friend who was a police detective in Philadelphia, who kept sending him pictures of prisoners, until he had collected fifty-two of them. We would deal them out and play a version of War. You put three cards down and one face-up. The ugliest won the hand. I was the judge in case of a tie and each guy would challenge.

There was one woman's picture in the deck. I'll never forget her. She wore a wide-brimmed hat with a feather in the back that did a kind of corkscrew. She had Coke-bottle glasses, and a half-moon scar that curled right under her nose up to one eye. She was ugly. It isn't often that you can look at someone straight on and see into their nostrils.

Uke saved that card, had it whittled down to wallet size, and would just wait for someone to come up and ask about his family. He'd say, "Doin' great. My wife just sent me a recent picture," and he'd whip out his wallet. All small talk around Uke went right down the tube.

I used to wonder at what went on in his mind. All those army sergeant routines. None of it was written down. You'd think the guy had rehearsed for years. He'd be a platoon leader, demanding to know who filled the motor pool with water. When they were thinking of making him a coach, in Atlanta, he walked around like he had a pocket watch, timing everybody. He picked up all the bullshit clichés.

He and Ray Sadecki used to broadcast the news in the clubhouse. They bought a metal frog with a key in its back, and they'd wind up the frog and have it clacking in the background. That was their tape. They'd set it up on a bench and read stories out of the paper . . . Dateline: Tel Aviv . . . and there was no way to ignore them.

I know he played for some managers who didn't understand him. I think Johnny Keane did. John was a serious man, but I think he appreciated Bob, his sense of humor.

Uke really did have some talent. The first thing you looked at was his defensive ability. His throwing arm and glove. I haven't an envious bone in my body, but I envied his arm. His relaxed, quick hands.

It's strange about catchers. They really root for each other. There isn't the kind of envy you find among pitchers. You see a guy on the mound and there is always someone in the bullpen thinking, "If he fails, I may get a shot." Catchers don't have that. I guess we got banged up too much to be jealous.

One thing about Uke, he would fight anybody. He was a docile guy, but he'd come to the front very quickly. He didn't like to call knockdown pitches, and Gene Mauch called them all the time with the Phillies. But if there was a guy you wanted next to you in a fight, it was Uecker.

Bob used to make up nicknames. He called me T-bone. He was one of those people who had a knack for immediately becoming your friend just by the way he spoke your name. T-bone. Timmy. A very affectionate thing. Not too many people are caring enough to cultivate a trait like that.

I remember listening to him talk about his dad, after his dad had his operation. It was touching, and funny. He's so comfortable that you don't feel bad laughing. Uke is so outlandish that if you missed a little, you missed a lot.

—Mickey Herskowitz

CATCHER IN THE WRY

PART I

The Bob Uecker Story

In which a poor but honest smartass from a small beer town in the Midwest goes off to win fame and fortune in baseball, and is never heard from again. . . .

"I was the first hometown boy to sign with, and play for, the Milwaukee Braves. Technically, I wasn't born in Milwaukee. My folks were on an oleo run to Chicago, and my mother was due any day. On Highway 41, just out of town, she got the pains. My old man swung the car off the exit ramp and she dropped me in a mangerlike area. There were three wise men standing under an exit light . . . one had oleo, one carried butter, the third was a baseball scout."

Weeks later, my mother took me off milk and fed me beef jerky to toughen me for the Cinderella story that was to follow.

1. A Funny Thing Happened on My Way to Cooperstown

IN JUNE AND JULY of every year I go through the same ritual—an ordeal, really—of waiting for the telephone to ring. I am waiting to be told that the dream of my lifetime has come true.

I am waiting to be told that I, Robert George Uecker, known as "Mr. Baseball" to a generation that never saw me play, have been elected to baseball's Hall of Fame.

But the call doesn't come. And I realize there is no point in getting nervous or uptight. My record speaks for itself, and the fans, at least, haven't forgotten me. I go to the Old-Timers' games now and I know I haven't lost a thing. I sit in the bullpen and let people throw garbage at me, just like in the old days.

Actually, given the way things work now in our National Pastime, and were I just a few years younger, I too could be the object of a bidding war. I would play out my option, declare myself a free agent and twenty-six teams would be drooling. I would probably have to take my phone off the hook. Can you imagine what the market would be today for a defensive catcher who had a career lifetime average of .200?

And I mean on the nose. Not .201 or .199. A cool .200, lifetime. A lot of retired players joke about being a career .200 hitter, but I was the real article. Modestly, I'd say I could command a salary today of one hundred fifty thousand dollars per annum as a backup playing sixty games. Of course, if the team I signed with was deep in catching and only needed me for thirty games, I'd be worth two hundred thousand. The fewer games they needed me for, the higher the minimum bidding would go.

Of course I'm not a few years younger, and bidding wars or not, I can't but feel a warm glow of nostalgia when I think back over my years in the big leagues. I played with three teams, in four cities, under six managers. My teammates included four Hall of Famers: Henry Aaron, Eddie Mathews, Warren Spahn, Bob Gibson.

In my heart of hearts, I believe my accomplishments were as great as theirs. What did it mean for Aaron or Mathews to hit their .350 or their forty homers? Anybody with ability can play in the big leagues. To last as long as I did with the skills I had, with the numbers I produced, was a triumph of the human spirit. I played thirteen years of pro ball, and remember all but the last six clearly. Up to the very end of my career, I was still being judged on my "potential."

Many times I have been asked how a player knows when he is washed up, through, at the end of the line. Willie Pep, the former boxing champion, once said that you could look for three signs: "First your legs go. Then your reflexes go. Then your friends go." My friends went first.

In baseball the clues were more subtle. In my case, I began to get the hint when my bubble gum card came out and there was a blank space where the picture was supposed to be. Sporting goods companies offered to pay me *not* to endorse their products. I got to the park for what the manager had announced would be a night game, and found out they'd started at 1:00 P.M. I came to bat in the bottom of the ninth, two out, the bases loaded, my team trailing by a run, and looked over at the other dugout and saw them already in their street clothes.

When a player is sold or traded, he may feel a certain rejection. But when he gets cut, well, the news is traumatic. He is face to face with that moment of final truth, that he will never put on a big league uniform again. Nor is it easy on the manager who has to break the news. How do you tell a man that his career is over, that the only life he had ever known is behind him?

I'll never forget how it happened to me. I went to spring training with Atlanta in 1968. The manager was Luman Harris. I opened the door to the clubhouse and Luman looked up and said calmly, "No visitors allowed."

I suppose it is safe to say that my sense of humor caused me to reach the big leagues at least a year late, and my sense of mischief drove me out a few years too soon. But I hung around long enough to prove that my first manager was wrong, the one who sent me back to the minors with the warning, "There is no room in this game for a clown."

There was, and is, a place for Bob Uecker, it pleases me to report. Actually, I still have the view I always had—from behind home plate. Today I'm just a few tiers

higher than field level, as a broadcaster for the Milwaukee Brewers and ABC television. I enjoy my job. It's
a lot safer up there, and I don't get booed as much as I
did when I was catching. As a matter of fact, my career
might have been prolonged if Clete Boyer had hit one
less home run in 1967.

That year a Honda dealer in Atlanta had a promotion
going at the ball park. Any player who hit a homer or
pitched a shutout in the month of September received a
free Honda. Boyer hit one the last day of the season. The
next morning I dropped by his apartment to road-test it. I
was shoeless and shirtless when I roared off down the
street in front of Clete's place.

A pack of dogs, excited by the noise, began chasing
me. Feeling for the brake, my feet got tangled, I hit the
gas instead, jumped a curb and tipped over. I was lucky
to get away with a broken right arm and a pair of badly
slashed feet.

The cast was removed three weeks before I was to
report to camp the following spring. When a trainer tried
to "work out" the adhesions by yanking and twisting my
arm, he rebroke it. My arm was back in a cast when I got
to Florida, and the Braves put me on the roster as a
player-coach.

My luck continued pretty much in that vein. One day
the club went to Orlando to play the Minnesota Twins,
and I stayed behind because of my arm. Billy Martin was
the manager of the Twins then. Billy had been with the
Braves at the end of his career, and was still friendly with
Clete Boyer and Deron Johnson. He gave them a jug of
martinis to take back on the bus. I was to meet them that
night at the Cock 'n Bull restaurant in West Palm Beach.
I had been waiting maybe a half hour when they
appeared. They were loaded when they got off the bus.

The three of us were sitting at the bar, when the next thing I knew some drunk had jerked Boyer off his stool. I spun around, got to my feet and slugged him. He skidded through the dance floor area. The bartender jumped across the bar and yelled, "Bob, dammit, no more, that's all!"

I didn't want any more problems, but as I got up a friend of the first guy hit me across the head with a full beer bottle. Busted my head wide open. When I reached up and felt the blood I thought, "Oh, jeezus." I knew it wasn't beer. Not even light beer. Beer isn't red and sticky. The wound later took forty-eight stitches to close.

A terrific fight was breaking out all around me, like a scene from a "B" western. But at that point I had one goal in life: to get the hell away from that bar. I staggered out the nearest door and found myself looking at a dead-end alley, so I had to go back in and walk the length of the place to the front door. The cops were just pulling up to the curb as I fell into my car. Jim Britton, one of our pitchers, drove me to the hospital. I had my head sewn and paid the bill, $175. I went back to my hotel room, expecting to find Boyer. He wasn't there. I called the Cock 'n Bull and whoever answered said, "Yeah, he's still here. They're both here."

The doctor had wrapped my head in one of those white bandages piled up like a turban. I put on an old fishing hat and went back to the bar. Deron and Clete were sitting right where I had left them. They were so drunk they had never moved. Deron looked up and said, "Hot damn, look who's back. Uke's here. Give us another round."

I wasn't worried about Deron. His wife was in town and she could do the worrying. But Clete was rooming with me and it was past curfew and I had to get them out of there. I finally did. I dropped off Deron at his bungalow and half-carried Clete back to the room.

The next morning my head was killing me. I felt like I had the hangover they were saving for Judas, and no matter how hard I tried, I couldn't get Boyer out of bed. At ten I went to the ball park and told Luman Harris what had happened. He said, "Okay, go back to your room and if any of the writers call tell 'em you were in a car wreck."

I finally got Clete awake and he left for the park. At one o'clock he was back. Luman had found him asleep under the stands. After the game that day, I drove to the hospital to have my bandage changed. Now the news comes over the radio: *Three Atlanta players involved in a brawl.*

A week later the Braves released me. I guess they thought I had been a bad influence, but since I was so good at getting into trouble, they offered me a job in public relations, which is how I wound up making speeches and doing the game color on television.

I am able to look back on my career now with few illusions. The highest salary I ever drew, twenty-three thousand dollars, came after my best season . . . that's right, the one in which I played the fewest games. But I had my share of thrills. Probably the biggest was when I started my first game for the Braves, in my hometown of Milwaukee, in April 1962. My folks, my friends, my old schoolmates were there. And they were all cheering.

We were playing the Giants that day and Juan Marichal was pitching. I had his bubble gum card and that told me all I wanted to know about Marichal.

Before the game. Birdie Tebbetts, our manager, said he knew a lot of my relatives were in the park, but he didn't want me to be nervous or uptight. I assured him I was fine. I had been in the minors six years waiting to get here and I was ready to play.

As I walked toward the batting cage, he hollered after me: "Kid, you're doing good, except that up here in the big leagues most of us wear our athletic supporters on the inside of our uniforms."

I hit my only home run that year—the first of fourteen in my career—off Diomedes Olivo, a forty-two-year-old rookie relief pitcher for the Pittsburgh Pirates. When the ball landed in the seats, the fan who caught it threw it back. Years later, someone turned up a tape of that home run and put together a strip for a roast-and-toast, with a staff announcer giving it the H.V. Kaltenborn treatment:

"The great power hitters of days gone by recall their first home runs in the major leagues, their eyes filled with tears and their voices shaking with excitement, every detail of their first round-tripper as clear as if it had happened yesterday. It's the same for all the great ones . . . Steve Bilko, Harry Hannebrink, Clint Courtney, big Albie Pearson, Curt Blefary and Ed Bouchee.

"And so it is for Robert Uecker. He remembers that first looping line drive and so do all his fans. Recall with us now that thrilling day when Bob stepped to the plate still looking for Number One. Here's the play-by-play, as it happened, with Earl Gillespie at the microphone:

"'. . . oh and one, the pitch swung on and a drive [voice rising] INTO DEEP LEFT FIELD . . . GOING BACK TOWARD THE WALL . . . IT MAY BE . . . IT'S BACK AT THE WALL . . . HOME RUN FOR BOB UECKER!!! Well, Bob Uecker . . . quite a thrill . . .'"

Gillespie's description was followed by five minutes of the kind of laugh track you hear at a carnival fun house, interrupted by a wailing siren and Earl's voice repeating, over and over, "Well, Bob Uecker . . ."

Actually, a home run I remember even better than my first was a grand slam I delivered a few seasons later off Ron Herbel of the San Francisco Giants. After I connected, the manager, Herman Franks, came out of their dugout to remove the pitcher, and he was carrying Herbel's suitcase. For some reason, other teams took me lightly.

If you are really going to appreciate my career—and I am not sure it can be done—I guess we should start at the beginning. I was your average hot-shot athlete in high school, an all boys school in Milwaukee. My father wanted me to learn a trade. I did. By the end of my first semester I could hot-wire a car. Baseball and basketball were my games. As a freshman I was six feet one and weighed 130, and the other guys would wear my jockstrap as a wristband.

In class, my commitment to education was less than total. I had some growing up to do, and one day it occurred to me I might get there faster in the service. What helped me reach this decision was the fact that my father spent more time at school than I did. I was a total failure. I even flunked shop. I couldn't make a bread-board. In 1954, at nineteen, I enlisted in the army.

My baseball career began there, at Fort Leonard Wood, Missouri, where they had a sign inside the post that said: *IF YOU SCREW UP IN KOREA THIS IS WHERE THEY SEND YOU.* During orientation, an officer asked if any of us had played college or pro baseball. I raised my hand. He asked where I had played, and what position. I told him I had been a catcher at Marquette, which never had a baseball team. But I figured, correctly, what could they know about Marquette?

I had pitched in sandlot ball and the Braves had scouted me two years earlier, at seventeen. I had done some catching too, and I knew the base team was going to lose its starter, Bob Schmidt, in the spring. Before being drafted, Schmidt belonged to the San Francisco Giants. Later, at Fort Belvoir, I joined a team whose shortstop was Dick Groat, who would be my teammate at St. Louis.

A friend of my father's, Louie Zimmerman, talked the Braves into scouting me as a catcher. He was the editor of a German newspaper in Milwaukee, which shows you how casual the scouting system was back then. When I got out of the army I signed with Milwaukee for a three-thousand dollar bonus. The amount bothered my father at first. We were a poor family and, frankly, he didn't have that kind of cash. Finally, he scraped it up and got me to leave home again.

For the signing ceremony, the Braves' officials took us to one of the city's swankiest restaurants. My dad was so nervous he rolled down the window and the hamburgers fell off the tray.

My dad's name was Gus. He was a tool- and diemaker from Basel, Switzerland. He was also the best man I ever knew: stubborn, funny, impatient, generous and proud.

I remember reading a story about Ernie Banks, and how his father worked and sacrificed to give Ernie the chance to play ball. His father never saw the sunlight, leaving the house before dawn and getting home after dark. When Ernie signed his first contract with the Cubs he sent a three-word telegram to his father: "WE DID IT."

I relate to that story. My father got on my ass all the

time. He never said, in front of me, that he thought I could play, and at home, listening to the games on the radio, whenever I came to bat he would turn to my mother and say, "Ach, he'll probably strike out."

But without him I would never have gotten a shot. In the minors, when I was making $250 a month and the money ran out, he was right there. He was a great mechanic and a hard worker, who never let his family— his wife, a son, and two daughters—go without the basics, even in the meanest days of the Depression. He could always make three or four dollars a day working on cars.

When I got to the Braves to stay, in 1962, he was all fired up about it. Birdie Tebbetts was the manager then and they became drinking buddies. Birdie would tell me later how he would needle my old man, saying how horseshit I was, and Gus would argue with him. By the end of the season he was second-guessing Birdie.

Gus had a fearful circulation problem in his legs, a condition that caused him endless grief. He was a big man, in his sixties, when his legs were amputated.

He had kept his troubles to himself, as he usually did. The first indication I had came from my mother, who told me he had to sleep at night in a chair with his feet on a heating pad. They were always cold. My first day back, at the end of that season, I walked into his house and made him lift his trousers and show me his legs. They were black and blue from the toes to the knee.

Had he consulted a doctor, which he had never done in his life, his legs might have been saved. But he was proud and stubborn and he suffered on his own terms.

I practically dragged him to a doctor. The examination revealed that gangrene had already set in. He was in surgery the next day. Nylon tubes were inserted in both legs to replace the veins and increase the circulation of blood.

The operation seemed a success—for one full day. I spent the night at his bedside. The next morning he started clotting. Now the doctors had no choice but to amputate. They could not even wait for my mother to return to the hospital. I was the one who had to sign the papers. Later, I was the one who had to tell him.

I don't think my father's death, a few years later, saddened me any more than the sight of him being wheeled out of the operating room, his legs gone.

He was in the hospital for twenty weeks, and my old Milwaukee teammates helped him get through the bad times. I would walk into the room and Warren Spahn or Eddie Mathews or Johnny Logan or Lew Burdette would be visiting him. My father wasn't allowed to have liquor in the room, but they would sneak in a couple of bottles and after two or three hours we would all be blasted, including my old man. The nurses could never figure out why he was so cheerful.

I came home from St. Louis the next year and he had thrown away the artificial legs the doctors had fitted to him. He was more comfortable with smaller ones, and he had rockers attached so he could shuffle along and not fall. When he had them on he looked like Toulouse-Lautrec.

The first time I walked into the house and saw him on those short legs, I just cracked up. He didn't mind, so long as I didn't cry. I couldn't stop laughing. You could push him back and forth, like a rocking toy. He loved it. We were both whacko. We had exactly the same sense of humor.

For months he stayed close to home. He was embarrassed to go into his favorite gin mill on those little legs, and he couldn't use the restroom in his wheel chair. He had to carry a jar with him. I went by the house one day, threw a jacket on him, lifted him out of the wheel chair and drove him to the tavern, the Meadow Inn. His drinking and card-playing buddies were waiting for him. He had the time of his life.

I was in Atlanta in 1968, the season after my playing career had ended, when his heart gave out. Twice I flew to Milwaukee to be with him after major attacks. I was with him in intensive care when he had what the hospitals call a Code Four. I watched the doctors restart his heart with an electric shock and by pounding his chest. In the process, they cracked a couple of his ribs.

They literally brought him back to life. A few days later, he told me he was really hacked off. He said he felt himself going, everything was soft and mellow, and suddenly everyone was beating on him.

I made my mother promise that she would take him out of the hospital as soon as he could be moved. If he was going to die, I knew he would rather it happen at home. And so he did.

He went home with strict orders not to listen to any football or baseball games on the radio or TV. Of course, he paid no attention. Gus died two months after he left the hospital, during the 1968 World Series between the Tigers and one of my old teams, the Cardinals. I knew then, if I hadn't before, how important it was to me, and to both of us, that he had been able to see me play in the big leagues.

Sure, I had my critics, people who swore I would never make it. They never bothered me. I always thought I was bigger than baseball and I think my record proves it.

2. Down on the Farm

IN OUR SOCIETY, big league has become a synonym for "first class." A friend once told me of the time Judge Roy Hofheinz was trying to get a bill passed that would allow construction of his domed stadium in Houston. As part of a public relations blitz, he flew some sixty politicians and news people out west.

They stopped off in Los Angeles to stare at an enormous hole in the ground that would become Dodger Stadium, then flew on to San Francisco, where Candlestick Park was earing completion. Everywhere they went the propaganda machine kept rolling: this was big league; that was *not* big league; this was what you had to do if you wanted to go big league.

The junket ended in Las Vegas, with dinner and a show that featured one hundred topless, statuesque showgirls. Red-eyed and hung over, the party landed in Houston just after dawn, the early morning sun all but blinding the passengers. Amid the groans and stirrings, a man named Morris Frank, known for his twangy East

Texas wit, looked out the window of the plane and saw his wife among a small crowd gathered at the ramp.

"Wal," said Morris, stretching his arms, "it sure was great seein' all them big-league boobies, but it's back to the minors today."

One way or another, I spent some of the best years of my life in the minors. I feel sorry for any ballplayer who never had to work his way up through a farm system, who never lived on sliced meat sandwiches or dressed in clubhouses where your locker consisted of a nail driven into a board. It is like going through life without ever riding on a train.

I am going to ramble a bit now, which is the way I remember the minor leagues, as a slow, rambling, breezy time in my life. I loved it, the way people dressed and talked and thought, the way they cared and didn't mind showing it.

My dad drove me to the bus station and I reported to my first spring training camp at Waycross, Georgia, to an old air force base where the Braves' lower farm clubs trained. I had just received my discharge from the service, and here I was back in the barracks.

A player who has never gone through *that* kind of camp, where the prospects numbered in the hundreds, can never really appreciate spring training. They would pin a number on your back—you might be Number 317—and each morning a crowd would collect around the bulletin board in the camp office to see who had made the Greyhound squad that day. Meaning, adios.

The signs over the toilets warned, DON'T FLUSH WHILE SHOWER IS RUNNING. This was an invitation to every guy who walked in to flush the commode and scald whoever was in the shower. You would walk out of there with a red stripe down your back.

After curfew we'd string a wire across the barracks about knee high and wait for the drunken night watchman to make his rounds. The high point was hearing his body hit the floor. Days later, when the night watchman thought he had the knee wire figured out, we would string it neck high and almost garrote him.

Ah, memories. There were no fences in the outfield, and many a player chased a deep fly ball into the high grass, spotted a snake, and came out faster than he ever went in.

If you were lucky, you might wind up with the hand-me-down uniform of your favorite big-league player. A little tape here and there and the pants would look fairly decent.

Thus prepared, I joined my first professional team, Eau Claire, in the Northern League, in the late spring of 1956. I was twenty-one, just out of the service, making $250 a month and six dollars a day on the road for meal money—just enough to keep you from gnawing on the table leg in your favorite café.

I got off to a miserable start, even for me, and at mid-season was batting just .171 with seventeen runs driven in. So the Braves had me reassigned to Boise, Idaho, in the Pioneer League, and I went on to have the kind of summer people used to have in their dreams, when summers didn't cost much.

Boise was about thirty games out of first place when I got there in July, and the Braves had sent down a whole new team in an effort to pull the club out of last place. Boise was the quintessential minor-league town.

They had an old fart who, when all the new players came in, vowed not to shave until we were in first place. By the end of the season his beard was down to his knees. The fans had what they called a Hustle Fund. If you hit a homer you got five dollars, and they passed the hat in the stands. The winning pitcher got five. A triple was worth three bucks, a double was worth two and a single got you a dollar. If you hit a homer you could stop by Pierson's Café the next morning for a free breakfast.

With all those incentives going for us, we caught fire, came from thirty games out and won the pennant on the last day of the season.

At Eau Claire, I had gone something like oh for fifty before I picked up my first hit as a pro, a grand slam homer at Warsaw. But at Boise I was hot from the start. I batted .312 and drove in forty-one runs, with thirteen homers. Lots of free bacon and eggs.

A local VIP named A. J. Archibald owned a bus line that ran junkets—by bus—to Las Vegas. They were motor homes with a toilet and card tables. When one was available he loaded it with fresh fruit and let the ball club use it on road trips, some of which covered seven hundred miles. Hell, I didn't see how they could travel in a style any fancier in the big leagues.

Our manager was a low-keyed, soft-spoken Southerner named George McQuinn, who played first base on the only St. Louis Browns team ever to reach the World Series (in 1944). In 1947, he helped bat the Yankees to the pennant, playing on the same team with Joe DiMaggio, Phil Rizzuto, Tommy Henrich, King Kong Keller and a rookie named Yogi Berra.

McQuinn never talked about his big-league career, which was just as well. When you are that low in the minors, you can't relate to the New York Yankees. We didn't know about anything outside the Pioneer League, and that was how we liked it. What we related to were the signs McQuinn posted in the clubhouse, such as the one that read:

THROUGH THESE DOORS PASS THE HUSTLING BOISE
BRAVES.

He arrived when we did, at midseason, and had just
the right touch for a bunch of eager, know-nothing kids.
He was the same, win or lose. "Now you boys," he
would drawl before every game, "you got to get out
theah and do youah job."

Every night was an anecdote. Rufus (Big Train)
Johnson was one of the three blacks on the team. He was
on first base one night during a power failure—we had
them regularly—and when the lights came back on
Rufus was standing at third, as if nothing had happened.

Boise was the kind of place where the groundskeeper
lived at the ball park, in a cabin under the stands, with
his wife and kids. He was in charge of the fireworks
display. One night he was half in the bag when he started
lighting them. After the first few, about four hundred of
them went off at the same time, knocked down the left
field fence and burned up his quarters. It was beautiful.

The ball park held three to four thousand people and
was jammed every night. It was a neat, pretty park
surrounded by mountains. Years later, when I was with
the Braves, we came back to Boise to play an exhibition
game, and the other fellows asked me about the lights,
the infield, the power alleys. I told them the place was
great, wait until you see it, a miniature Dodger Stadium.

When I got off the bus and walked into the park, I
couldn't believe my eyes. There were only about ten
light poles, and it was so dark a cat burglar would have
felt right at home. The guys really got on me.

But what I remember best about my first year in the
Pioneer League was the ball park at Missoula, Montana.
I had heard stories about a trap door behind home plate
and I thought people were bullshitting me.

Missoula was a farm club of the Washington Senators, and the fans had a theme song, "Hurry Back, Timber Jacks." We walked into the park and the players were taking batting practice, future big-leaguers like Jim Kaat, Jay Ward, Chuck Witherspoon. I saw the trap door and I still couldn't believe it.

When the starting lineups were announced, the trap door flew open and out popped the players, led by their manager, Jack McKeown, while the organist played "Hurry Back, Timber Jacks." The fans loved it, just loved it. The trap door was flush with the ground, ten feet or so behind the catcher, and once inside, you walked down a stairway that led to the home team's clubhouse.

During the game, if you had to answer nature's call, you just grinned sheepishly and made a very public exit. In most parks you walk to the end of the dugout and through a tunnel, or around a corner. Here you had to walk behind the catcher and open the trap door. Everybody knew where you were going. It was like dropping your pants.

My minor-league career took me from Boise to Wichita, Evansville, back to Eau Claire, to Atlanta, back to Boise, Atlanta again, Jacksonville, Indianapolis and Louisville. I was in more hotel rooms than the Gideon Bible.

One of our stops in the Northern League was the Grand Hotel in Fargo, North Dakota, a transient hotel right next to the railroad tracks. The steam engines hissed and whistled and tooted all through the night. The lobby was a famous gathering place for drunk Indians.

On the kind of money we made entertainment was scarce, and we killed a lot of our idle time with water fights. We would start small, filling rubbers and dropping them out the window on people walking by. Then we would graduate to buckets, balancing them on top of a door, poised to spill on the first luckless soul who entered. By the end of the night, we were taking the fire hoses off the wall and facing each other in the hallway like gunfighters. With one spray you could knock a guy clear across a room.

It was a small world and at times a silly one. But twenty-five years ago, you didn't go into pro baseball thinking you had an automatic ticket to the big time. At least, you didn't say so out loud, not if you were a hustling Boise Brave, or even a Timber Jack.

We were like guys trying to break out of a prisoner-of-war camp, knowing that every so often a lucky bastard got through. Our goal was to move up to a higher league the next season. Each move was a step closer to the Taj Mahal.

But in those days a lot of fine players with great records never got out of the minors. The times had changed. The country had changed. The people had changed. But in 1956 baseball had just begun to change. The Braves were in Milwaukee, the A's were in Kansas City, the Dodgers and Giants were heading west. There were still just sixteen cities on the big-league map, and too many players for too few teams. An infielder in the Braves' system could bat .300 for ten years in Triple-A and never stick in the majors, with Mathews, Logan or Schoendienst ahead of him.

So the minors would become his career. He would marry a local girl, get a job in the off season, and enjoy the fact that he was recognized in the community, a small-bore celebrity.

I was fortunate in the minors to have managers who guided and encouraged me and moved me along to the next rung. They were always trying to convince someone in the Braves' office that I could play, even if I was not always convinced myself.

One was Bob Coleman, a legendary manager in the minors, who had won something like twenty pennants by the time I played for him at Evansville in the Three-I League. Bob was in his sixties then, a brawny, gruff, hard-bitten guy who had the look of an old sea captain. He owned a German shepherd named Silver, and he continued the line as each dog died, so now he was up to Silver Five.

Coleman had a habit of sitting naked after a game in a beach chair, with his balls dangling between the canvas webbing, and Silver Five curled up under the chair, snapping at flies. I don't mean to be crude, but players new to the team were endlessly fascinated by that sight.

That damned dog attacked me once. We were in spring training in Waycross, Georgia, and I was warming up a pitcher when the ball got away from me and rolled past the chair where Bob was sitting, in uniform, with Silver Five at his feet. I ran toward the ball and the dog leaped on me, got his teeth into my hand and wouldn't let go. He thought I was after the old man.

With the uniforms we wore then, he could have grabbed me anywhere but the hand and not broken skin. The uniforms were all hand-me-downs from other clubs, blousy things that made most of us look like we were suffering from elephantiasis.

That down-home atmosphere was what I missed when I finally got to the big leagues. You never saw a manager with his pet German shepherd dozing under his chair, and they didn't take you out to eat on Sunday after a road game, either. Bob Coleman did.

A manager in the minors was likely to be a father

figure. And, the way it worked out, you were likely to need one.

In the 1960s the minor leagues began to shrink, some said because of television, soaring costs and competition from other sports. Today the character of the farm system has changed. You used to get a mixture of young prospects, veterans playing out the string, and ex-big-leaguers hoping for the one good streak they needed to make it back.

Now the old-timers are virtually gone. The market is for kids only. And those who don't make the majors in two, three, or four years usually return to college, or move on to something else. No more will you find a fellow spending a dozen years in the minors, beating his way from town to town.

I am not sure there would be room for a Bob Uecker in the minor leagues today, much less the majors. My brand of horseplay probably would not be tolerated, unless more talent than mine went with it.

In my last year in Triple-A ball, I almost joked myself out of the league. At midseason the Braves sent down Stan Lopata, and he took over as the regular catcher. I went out to the bullpen and began to look around for new ways to amuse myself, and my friends.

Fireworks have always been one of my weaknesses. On the Fourth of July, I talked the fellow in charge of the fireworks display into giving me one of his launching tubes and thirty boomers, those heavy-duty jobs that go off like artillery shells.

I carried them out to the bullpen and stored them, with the idea of lighting one each time we hit a homer, as a celebration. They had a fuse a foot and a half long and I wasn't sure I had the courage to light one. But that same night Neil Chrisley homered, and I put a match to the fuse and everyone in the bullpen scattered. We were hiding under benches, behind bunkers, hands over ears.

The boomer rose out of the tube with a soft poof, like a bazooka's, and just as Chrisley reached second base the thing exploded—like a sonic boom. The crowd came unglued. In the bullpen, the boys cheered.

To my surprise, the general manager liked the reaction and told me to keep it up. I continued to set off a boomer after every home run for the next few weeks.

Then John McHale, the president of the Braves, flew into town to look over the club. When he left, I was told to forget about the fireworks. The people in the homes across from the ball park had been sending telegrams to Milwaukee, complaining that the boomers were going off as late as ten o'clock at night, damned near knocking them out of bed.

For a while I thought the Braves might hold it against me. But I guess they were impressed with my team spirit. The next year I was in Milwaukee, a big-leaguer, at last.

3. Planet of the Apes

BY THE TIME I went to my first spring training camp with the Braves, in 1961, there was one thing I knew. I could make people laugh. Most rookies approach their first training camp as though they were raising the flag on Iwo Jima. Not me.

Chuck Dressen was the manager that year. At the end of camp, he sent me back to the minors with the deathless words: "There is no room in baseball for a clown."

Even though I believe he was wrong, and I believed it then, I can see how Dressen might have felt that way.

Billy Martin opened the season with the Braves, and was traded after six games. Billy was at the very end of his stormy career, and still years away from his even stormier service as a manager, during which he would be fired by the Twins, the Tigers, the Rangers and the Yankees, twice. Billy would gain immortality as the last manager ever hired by Charles O. Finley, who sold the Oakland A's some weeks later, in 1980.

Johnny Logan was another kindred spirit in that camp. He would be traded the next year and out of the big leagues in two.

The three of us were on the scrubs. In the fifth inning of those spring training games, if the Braves were losing, Dressen would send in the reserves. We would shout and jump around and pound our gloves and, in general, act as though we were being sent in to save the game. We really pissed off Dressen.

He never forgave some of us for making fun of his cooking. He considered himself a gourmet cook, and frequently prepared a large vat of chili, his specialty, for the coaches, the writers, and his guests. He never offered any to the players.

For this and reasons less worthy, we would slyly drop cigarette butts, matches, and sand from the butt box into the chili when Dressen wasn't watching. Later, we would sit there and watch the VIPs eat that mess and laugh ourselves right out of the room.

I heard that the quality of Dressen's chili remained high the rest of the season, but the team didn't perform so well. He was fired with twenty-five games left and Birdie Tebbetts replaced him.

That year, 1961, would be the last full season I would spend in the minors. I batted .309 with fourteen homers at Louisville, and when I reported to the Braves the next spring I felt almost as though I belonged.

I would be hailed as the first Milwaukee native to play for the Braves. Later, I would be hailed as the first Milwaukee native to be traded by the Braves. Hometown boy makes good.

When I joined them the Braves were a fifth-place team going nowhere. Del Crandall was the starting catcher and a great one. I appeared in just thirty-three games and batted .250—just right, not high enough to raise their hopes or low enough to cut my pay. I woke up to a new world every day, thrilled to be in the big leagues, grateful to be around people I had heard and read about for years. But it was tough to be a young catcher working with a veteran pitching staff.

One day I went out to the mound to talk to Lew Burdette, after a couple of runners had reached base. When I got there, he said, "What the hell do you want?"

I said, "Nothing. I just came out to give you a break."

Lew said, "Don't be coming out here. I don't want you out here. They"—and he waved his gloved hand at the crowd—"think you're giving me advice. And the only thing you know about pitching is that you can't hit it."

My reaction was to go back behind the plate and tell the hitter what pitches were coming. I understood Lew's position.

Still, my stay with the Braves was not without a splash of reflected glory. I was on the receiving end of the game that made Warren Spahn the winningest left-handed pitcher of all time. Spahn was a joy to watch, a master craftsman. Some nights I would catch him without using signs. He didn't have the big breaking ball. Spahnie had a popping fast ball, screwball, and slider. If he wanted to pitch inside to a right-handed batter the pitch was always going to be a fast ball or slider. If he wanted to pitch away, it was going to be a fast ball or screwball.

The only sign I gave him was *in* or *out*. I'd just put up the mitt as a target. He would mouth the words: "Where do you want it?" And I'd mouth back: "In the web."

You can do that when you win and, in those days, Spahn nearly always won.

But overall the Braves had declined from their World

Series years, '57 and '58, and had become the one thing baseball fans can't accept. A mediocre team. Not good enough to compete, not bad enough to be lovable.

I would go on to sit on the bench for a lot of losing teams. Fans often asked me how the players were able to stay up, stay ready, when it was August and the sun was blazing and your team was out of the race?

I can only answer for myself. I would just go out and get likkered up. Same way under pressure. Just go to the bottle. The game is easy when you go out there and play it straight. But when you take half a jug of V.O. and toss it down, you make the game a challenge. I used to get a big kick out of someone coming up to me after a game and asking about a certain play, and I couldn't remember it.

In my day, which was before the age of the mega-bucks, these were the little things that held the players together. I do concede that the players are better behaved today. Chewing tobacco was more popular in my time. You would get dressed and walk onto the field in your clean, white, sanitary socks, with your shoes shined, and somebody would come up and drop a bad wad right on your ankle. Seemed like it was always just before the gum card people were going to take your picture. (Some habits are hard to outgrow. I admit it: I still chew. Even on airplanes.)

The funny thing is, people never believed me when I told them it didn't bother me if I didn't get to play. In the darkest, most insecure corner of my soul, it didn't. I always figured the more I played, the closer I was to going back to the minors.

For years, whatever reputation I had as a player was based entirely on my label as a "good defensive catcher who only needs a chance to play," and on my ability to hit . . . Sandy Koufax.

Koufax? *That* Sandy Koufax? Right. I hit him. I hit him hard. Neither one of us ever figured out why. But whenever Sandy is interviewed about the hitters who were tough on him, he always mentions my name. And he usually gets a laugh, even though he means it.

One night, with Koufax on the mound, the Dodgers gave me an intentional walk to load the bases and bring up the pitcher. Tom Gorman was the umpire and John Roseboro was catching. As I tossed the bat toward the dugout, I turned to the two of them and said, "Boy, if this ever gets out you guys are going to get a letter from the commissioner."

It was obvious I was not going to catch much in Milwaukee. Behind Crandall they had a fine young rookie coming up in Joe Torre. I would be gone from Milwaukee in 1964. (The Braves would be gone in 1966, bound for Atlanta.)

They did me what turned out to be a great kindness. The Braves traded me to a St. Louis team that was going to put on a terrific stretch kick and win the pennant in the National League. The season would be two-thirds gone before anyone knew the Cardinals were in the race—including the Cardinals.

My immediate role seemed to be to provide another character for the clubhouse act developed by Tim McCarver and Ray Sadecki. They had worked up a number of zany routines, inspired by the popular Jackie Gleason show, with Tim as Crazy Guggenheim and Sadecki as Joe the Bartender.

The movie *Planet of the Apes* would not be released until four years later, but in 1964 the two of them were ahead of their time. They went out and purchased gorilla masks. They wore them everywhere. On the plane, on the bus, in the clubhouse, sitting around naked in their hotel room. Believe me, many a maid went tearing out of their room, towels and bedsheets flying.

Some nights they would take a suit coat and trousers and concoct a dummy, stuffing it with sheets and pillows. Then they would arrange the clothing just so, put the mask on top and stick a cigar in his mouth and prop him up in one of those big, overstuffed chairs. Now, their room might be ten floors above mine, but they would carry that creation down the stairwell at four o'clock in the morning and knock on my door. I would get out of bed, stumble to the door, and there would be this ape, with a cigar in his mouth, sitting in a chair in the hall.

As a near legend among the fringe players of my time, I was a natural choice to be commissioner of the Batting Practice League, formed among the pitchers and reserves in St. Louis. We actually played a game every day. We chose up teams and had lineup cards. Even as the team was clawing the Phillies and Reds in the real pennant race, we were holding our own.

We used to get to the park early for the BPL. There was a lot of money involved. Ron Taylor was the captain of one team and Sadecki captained the other. As commissioner, I also had to pitch batting practice. One day, Ron Taylor's team hit out of turn. Sadecki let them bat and then, as the rules require, called it to my attention.

I walked off the mound to get Taylor's lineup card, and when he saw me coming he ate it. I mean, as I got within a few feet he yanked the card out of his pocket, stuffed it into his mouth, chewed gamely and then swallowed the pieces. It was better than a spy movie.

Afterward, Sadecki insisted we follow Taylor around

until he went to the toilet and passed the lineup card, so I could rule on whether his team had batted out of turn.

I drew the line at this indignity, but on the scrubs the craziness went on day in and day out. At the end of the year we awarded the trophies.

All in all, the '64 Cardinals were the perfect team for a player whose personality demanded expression. There was talent on the field, intrigue in the front office and madness in the clubhouse. We were curiously untouched by the pressures of a pennant race. We did not even know we were in one until September. This was the loosest, goosiest team ever to come from ten games behind to reach the World Series, a drive in which Robert George Uecker played his own, as shall be seen, crucial part.

PART II

Inside Baseball

In which he reveals that if an athlete works hard, stays in shape, never gives up, and hits .200, he can attract one of the funniest fan clubs anyone ever had.

"There were a great many people who thought that the Cards had made a mistake, trading two ballplayers for one Uecker. As the season wore on, Uecker proved that they were indeed correct . . ."

4. The Fan Club

THE STORY YOU are about to read is true. The names have not been changed to protect anybody, innocent or not, on the theory that if I'm willing to use mine so should they.

Some years ago the zaniest and most unlikely fan club in the annals of baseball was formed. The story behind it is the stuff of legend. How it came to be, the spirit and purpose of the club, the tenacity with which its hero was supported, would melt the heart of a Greek statue.

In 1964, a student at Drury College in Missouri, Mark Stillwell, and his brother, Paul, noticed that the St. Louis Cardinals had not won a game in which I had played from the start of the season until the second of July. This record struck them as worth celebrating, and they did so in what I thought was a commendable and logical way.

They organized The Bob Uecker Fan Club.

In four years the club attracted over five hundred members (names and addresses are on file with the club president, as well as the FBI and the CIA). Sweatshirts bearing my name and likeness were manufactured. An official matchbook was printed, a slogan adopted ("Bob Uecker is a Great American"). Attempts to plan an appreciation day had to be postponed, either because I kept getting traded or because the school cafeteria was not available.

It is hard to say what forces came together to start such a movement. I suppose it was a natural reaction to the pressures of the Vietnam War. Those were turbulent years.

Mark Stillwell was a clean-cut, otherwise normal college type, the sports editor of the Drury *Mirror*. We kept in touch during his undergraduate days, and later when he served in the navy. Eventually he returned to Drury as the school's director of sports information.

I don't think I ever met more than three or four club members at a time. Every so often one of them would show up at whatever ball park my team happened to be in, and if I played that day the news would soon be all over the campus. They would report back with all the excitement of a bird watcher sighting a gray-speckled spanarkel. "He went oh for three," they would say, breathlessly, or, "he chased a ball all the way to the backstop."

When Mickey Mantle retired, he began receiving scrapbooks kept by his fans throughout the country, more than fifty of them. Sometimes late at night he would take one out and thumb through it. "It gave me goose bumps," he said, "to know I had that kind of effect on people."

My first reaction to hearing that I had a fan club was to say nothing, and to lie low for about two weeks, until I could see if Ray Sadecki or Tim McCarver was behind it. There came a day when I received in the mail from Mark the scrapbook the club had maintained, in three or four volumes. Turning the pages, my entire career flashed before my eyes. It was a little like drowning.

The tone was set with the introduction, a little defensive, I thought, like a lawyer appealing to have a guilty verdict overturned. To quote Mark Stillwell, "This book is an attempt to present the case of Bob Uecker. Sometimes it is straightforward, sometimes it is biased against Bob Uecker and, mainly, it is biased in favor of Bob Uecker."

Now I like that approach. I am reminded of the vacuum cleaner salesman who knocks on a customer's door and says, "Let me give you the pros and cons of this product."

Mark goes on: "It was the kind of sudden impulse thing I couldn't explain, and this hurt my presentation. But my heart was soon fully in it and my enthusiasm won me a lot of support.

"This (scrapbook) tells it all. The pictures and words vividly record the course of the Bob Uecker Fan Club and the successes and failures of Bob Uecker. (It) is all collected here, and this is probably the greatest conglomeration of Bob Uecker data ever assembled anywhere."

The casual fan may feel that the kid was taking a lot for granted, not knowing what they might have had on file at, say, the British Museum. But when I first read that paragraph, I could envision the scrapbook being made into a television docu-drama, the highlights of my career in baseball: Bob Uecker getting on a plane to start a road trip; Bob Uecker sleeping on a plane; Bob Uecker getting off a plane.

The club caught on. Where all the members came from I never knew. I am not sure I wanted to know. I was told that several were under ten years of age. The oldest was ninety-two.

By the time the club was organized, I had spent nine years in organized ball—two of them in the majors—and had made fifteen moves to ten different cities.

As a big-leaguer, I had appeared in eighty-six games, with forty-one hits in 186 times at bats for an average of .220. I had scored sixteen runs and driven in fourteen, with five doubles and two homers—all in less than three seasons.

Jeez, no wonder I had my own fan club.

Mark Stillwell took special note of one part of my game: "There is a lot said about Bob Uecker's speed. Most everybody generally agrees that he is one of the slowest runners in the game. He had a race with Dick Groat in spring training to see who was the slowest on the team and Groat outran him. The fact also stands out that Uecker has stolen six bases in his career. All, however, before 1960, and all in the minor leagues. He swiped one base at Eau Claire in 1956 and two at Boise the same year. He got two more at Boise in 1958 and one at Jacksonville in 1959. And that's it."

This, I think, came under the heading of what the boys called "some of the good stuff" they had learned about my career.

Another item from early in the scrapbook: "Paul saw Uecker play in a minor league game at San Diego in July of 1963 against San Diego. Uecker played for Denver. He batted sixth and grounded out twice and walked as Denver lost, 3-0. His name had been left off the scoreboard and the box score in the San Diego paper the next day spelled his name 'Uekcer.'"

When the Braves traded me to the Cardinals only a few days before the start of the 1964 season, getting catcher Jim Coker and outfielder Gary Kolb in return, I was just another journeyman ballplayer. Although manager Johnny Keane announced that I had been obtained to back up Tim McCarver, and "make our catching solid," I did not instantly capture the hearts of the people of St. Louis. As the president of my own fan club would later observe: "There were a great many people who thought that the Cards made a great mistake, trading two ballplayers for one Uecker. As the season wore on, Uecker proved that they were indeed correct. He fielded like a slow, wounded turtle behind the plate. He ran like a batting cage with a flat tire, and he hit like he didn't know what the word meant. He cost the Cards some ballgames with poor throwing and hit into double plays or made outs at key spots. His batting average dwindled to the .200 mark. He became the butt of some jokes and his very presence in the lineup gave the Cards a defeatist attitude. He seemed to be a loser like the Cards hadn't had since the days of Dal Maxvill. He became the scapegoat. People began to blame things on Uecker. And Uecker deserved every bit of it."

At this point, you might conclude that the fans were not yet solidly behind me. No matter how poorly things were going for me, no one made excuses. They told it like it was with a bluntness that would have made Howard Cosell weep.

The diary of the 1964 season went on: "Johnny Keane constantly used pinch hitters for him and never played him unless McCarver was about to drop and it was the second game of a doubleheader and the team was on the road and the Cards were facing a lefthander.

"Uecker went from bad to worse to terrible. It seemed that the Cards just couldn't win with him in the lineup. Through the first three months of the season, the Cards lost every single game in which Uecker's name appeared

in the box score. No matter what he did, it never
failed . . . when he played, the Cards lost."

Some athletes can't handle compliments and are
embarrassed by praise. Thank the Lord I'm not one of
them. My patience paid off.

"On July 2, 1964, baseball history was made in
County Stadium in Milwaukee. The St. Louis Cardinals
won a game in which Bob Uecker played. Of course, he
didn't play the whole game. That would be expecting a
little too much. Uecker, whose true talent was probably
revealed when he won a cow-milking contest in Houston, has given Harry Caray what is probably another
good omen, and the Cardinal announcer values such
things.

"He caught three innings and the Cards maintained a
4-3 lead and finally won a game with him in the lineup.
He was rushed to a hospital for immediate observation.
Cardinal fans across the country postponed plans for the
biggest event of the year in St. Louis, Bob Uecker Night,
at which they intended to assassinate him.

"Uecker entered the game in the seventh. The Cards,
thanks to Julian Javier's second homer in two games and
tenth of the year, and a couple of pinch hits, had tied the
Braves, 3-3. The Braves brought in Hank Fischer to
pitch. Since Johnny Keane had unwisely batted for
McCarver, he had no other catcher. It is not unwise in
itself to bat for McCarver, but the thing is that when you
do you have to use Bob Uecker behind the plate. So,
when Fischer came in to pitch to Flood, who should
come riding in on the golf cart with him but Uecker, to
catch the seventh, eighth, and ninth. (The fans) shud-
dered. Another game lost, they figured. Flood walked
and Brock hit a sacrifice fly to center to give St. Louis a
4-3 lead.

"In the bottom of the seventh, Bob Humphreys walked the frst man he faced and sent him to second on a wild pitch. Same old Humphreys, we all thought. Then, Humphreys proceeded to retire the next nine men in a row to save Ray Sadecki's ninth victory of the season. He even struck out two men. When Uecker batted, of course, he was called out on strikes. Typical. The only reason the Cards won is that nobody, with the possible exception of Humphreys, knew that it was Uecker behind the plate."

The Uecker jinx had been broken. And a strange coincidence took place. The Cardinals caught fire. Cautiously, Keane tried me again. In a game at Pittsburgh I went hitless in five trips, but the Cards collected twenty hits and breezed, 12-5. The same week I caught again, and we rallied for eleven runs in the eighth innng to win, 15-7.

There was magic in the air. I refer to the scrapbook: "Four nights later, Uecker actually got a base hit. His batting average had dwindled to .173 and he boosted it to .179. On the twenty-fifth of July, he caught a full game. He came to the plate five times. He had three walks and two singles, scoring twice. He caught an excellent game and even got several closeup shots on national television when he *got hit in the neck by a foul tip*.

"He now had twelve hits in twenty games and his average was back around the .200 mark. He has four runs for the season and two runs batted in. Clearly, he intends to play a better brand of baseball for the rest of the season than he started with. . . . As Harry Caray said this afternoon, 'This is the catcher we traded for.'"

Blissfully unaware of the activity stirring on my behalf, I found myself blending into what had become, surprisingly, a pennant-contending team. At midsummer,

the rumors were buzzing around the league that Johnny
Keane was finished in St. Louis, to be replaced at the end
of the season by Leo Durocher.

But, suddenly, the Cardinals had begun to make a
charge at the leaders. On the last day of August, we beat
the Braves, 5-4, to pull within a couple of games of the
second-place Reds. The Phillies seemed uncatchable,
but as Yogi Berra once said, "It's never over until it's
over." My single in the last of the ninth drove in the
winning run to beat the Braves. We had rallied from four
runs down, and earlier I had hit my first homer of the
season off Denny Lemaster. The crowd went berserk. I
had the spirit. So did my fan club, which I still did not
know existed.

In Springfield, the kids at Drury College were taking
credit for turning around the pennant race. On the day
the Bob Uecker Fan Club was started, the Cardinals were
a game under .500 with forty-seven wns and forty-eight
losses. Since then we had won thirty and lost thirteen, a
.697 pace. No doubt about it. The formation of the club
had coincided with the revival of the Cardinals as a
factor in the pennant race. It was almost metaphysical.

Their "strange impulse" had undergone a change in
character. The club was still a put-on—hey, my kind of
game—but no longer a put-*down*.

I was soon to meet my two truest believers. On
September tenth, with the Reds in town, the Stillwell
brothers drove to St. Louis and arrived at Busch
Stadium, wearing their designer sweatshirts and armed
with their membership list and a carton of matchbooks.
Mark recorded the scene: "I watched Uecker for a while
as he sat in the dugout comparing hands with Ken Boyer,
and then he came out to play catch with his faithful
friend, Bob Skinner. There were several kids in the front

row of the box seats looking for autographs as Paul and I boldly walked down into an area which is no-man's-land for autograph hunters because of the nasty attitude of the ushers."

They had not been at the railing long when the printing on their sweatshirts caught my eye. I left Skinner and walked over to investigate, a little wary, my grin getting wider as I drew closer. Mark made the introductions and said, proudly, "I'll bet you didn't know you had a fan club with one hundred seventy-six members down in Springfield, did you?"

I laughed out loud. "No," I said, "I sure as hell didn't. You aren't the ones who have been booing me, are you?"

They assured me they were not. I signed a team picture and two scorecards, and Mark gave me a personalized Bob Uecker matchbook. I stuck it in my back pocket and went off to catch infield practice.

Mark continued his observations: "Happily, I went back to my seat to watch the Cards do battle with the Reds. Uecker caught the first game (of two) and reached base on an error in the second inning. Ken Boyer hit a towering two-run homer in the third to give the Cards the lead, and the first hit off Gibson was a line drive by Deron Johnson in the fourth into the left-field seats. Uecker grounded solidly into a double play in the fourth and bounced out in the seventh. He was on deck in the ninth when McCarver got the game-winning hit. The Cards won, 3-2.

"As I walked into the park I had been confronted by a teenager in civilian clothes talking to a scorecard vendor. I recognized him as Bob Baker, the Cardinal batboy. He said, pointing to my shirt, 'How many of youse are there?' I told him, one hundred seventy-six. 'Where are you from?' he asked. I told him Springfield. He asked if we were all boys. No, I replied, we do have some girls.

"All day people would look at my sweatshirt and either snicker, or come right out and laugh or make some smart comment or wisecrack. It was almost as if nobody ever heard of Bob Uecker and none of them ever appreciated him.

"However, it was late in the second game when I saw a sign above the Cardinals' bullpen in left field that read BOB UECKER ALL STAR. (There was another sign in front of the hot-dog stand in the left-field bleachers that said ED SPEZIO FAN CLUB.)

"Lou Brock homered in the first, McCarver homered in the seventh and Flood singled in Javier in the ninth with what was the winning run in a 3-2 victory that tied the Cards and Reds for second place.

"Later, we were walking up Sullivan Avenue and a young lady in a car saw my sweatshirt, leaned out the window and said, 'I agree.' I turned around, astonished, and yelled, 'Hey, a real Bob Uecker fan.'

"We decided to go to Stan Musial's restaurant to eat, but they told us we couldn't come in with that kind of attire. They were rather nasty about the whole thing, I thought. Maybe I should have had a McCarver sweatshirt on. We finally wound up eating at the old standby way out on Chippewa, at Chuck-a-Burger."

End of a perfect day.

The boys went back to the campus to push their membership drive with new vigor. I didn't *really* take it seriously, but, what the heck, in the weeks since the club was founded the Cardinals had swept from seventh place to second. Lay that secret handshake on me.

I am not the kind of player who lived by batting average alone. And I do feel that I made a contribution to the team's pennant charge, if only by helping to maintain the morale of the club. Actually, I won two or three games with clutch base hits, but there is no point in going into all the details. It gets to be too much like walking through a garden, admiring the roses, and saying over and over, "Here's another beauty."

Actually, I was getting my share of playing time. On September thirteenth, I was behind the plate when we became the first team since 1923 to score in every inning. We pounded the Cubs, 15-2, racking up eighteen hits—off six Chicago pitchers—and taking advantage of seven errors. Curt Simmons got the win, his fifteenth of the season. At Drury College, the club members said the game was a tribute to my greatness.

A moving team has a grace all its own. The Cardinals could do nothing wrong in September, winning twenty-one of twenty-nine games, and squeezing past the Reds and the Phillies in one of the wildest of all pennant races.

The Cardinals had approached the season with a huge question mark. Stan Musial, one of the game's legendary hitters, their spiritual leader—and left fielder—had retired. A spot in the lineup that had not required a second thought in twenty years was suddenly wide open.

Four players were tried there as the club limped through the season's early weeks. Just before the All-Star break, a trade with Chicago brought in Lou Brock, in return for pitcher Ernie Broglio. The deal was not a popular one in the locker room. Ernie had been a proven winner, and was one of the few players who never failed to laugh at our skits. Not much was known of Brock, a young outfielder with speed, a slight build and a newsboy's innocent face.

After a slow start, Lou began to run and hit. Left field ceased to be a problem. In another trade, Roger Craig arrived to help Barney Schultz in the bullpen, and Bob Gibson found his control and got hot.

Of course, there was another, less obvious factor. I suppose some people will feel that my quoting from the scrapbook, at this point, is merely a device I can hide behind to appear modest, to avoid saying things that sound self-serving. The best way to answer that charge is to quote from the scrapbook: "On July 26, 1964, the Bob Uecker Fan Club came into existence and was an immediate and lasting success. We of the club don't pretend to take complete credit for the events which occurred in the city of St. Louis and which culminated on the afternoon of October fourth when the St. Louis Cardinals became the National League champions. However, we do point to the record and will continue to point to it as long as skepticism to our cause appears.

"One quiet fact stands out. Prior to the time the Bob Uecker Fan Club was formed, the Cardinals were in seventh place. After that, they won forty-six and lost only twenty-one and rolled past team after team until they had moved into the National League throne room. They then defeated the New York Yankees to win the World Series.

"We don don't claim that *we* won the pennant. We don't claim that Bob Uecker won the pennant. And we don't claim that the Bob Uecker Fan Club won the pennant. We simply point to the record before and after the formation of the Bob Uecker Fan Club!"

Credit aside, I enjoyed the race as both a player and a spectator. In what has become one of the more celebrated collapses in all of baseball lore, the Phillies blew a lead of six and a half games with twelve games to play. "It was like watching someone drown," said Gene Mauch, the manager.

Gus Triandos, the big Greek catcher, called it "the year of the blue snow."

Meanwhile, the Reds were gallantly trying to win the pennant for their manager, Fred Hutchinson, who was dying of cancer, and who gave up the team to Dick Sisler in August. Sisler was called the "acting manager," a phrase with a reassuring temporary ring to it. But the Reds would never again jump to the orders of Fred Hutchinson. He knew it and they knew it. He died in November.

For the Cardinals, the finish was not without its bittersweet moments. The club at one point won eight in a row, five over the Pirates, to leap past the Phillies and Reds into first place.

The race went down to its final weekend, whereupon the Mets almost ruined it for us. The Mets. The lowly, comic-book Mets. They beat us in the first two games. They were like cockroaches. It wasn't what they ate or carried off, it was what they fell into and ruined. We still needed a win to clinch the pennant, and Gibson delivered on the final day.

So the Cardinals surprised not only the Phillies, the Reds, and the experts. They surprised the Cardinal ownership. Bing Devine, the team's general manager, and Johnny Keane's closest friend, had been fired in August, with the club trailing in third place. The papers were saying that the manager's job had been offered to Leo Durocher. Keane kept his silence.

Now here were the Cardinals, meeting the New York Yankees in the World Series. Mantle, Ford, Skowron and Howard. Naturally, the Series went the distance, and Bob Gibson beat the Yankees in the seventh game, on two days' rest, starting because, in the words of Johnny Keane, "I had a commitment to his heart."

As Jack Benny might have said, "W-e-l-l-l-l." Do you think the Cardinals's owners were red-faced when Keane's team turned around and won both the pennant and the World Series? Hastily, they broke off talks with Durocher. Keane was offered a new contract, with a respectable raise.

John was in the sweetly ironic position of being able to tell them to take their offer and stick it in a beer can. Which he did. In a startling postscript to the Series, the losing team fired its manager, Yogi Berra, and replaced him with the manager of the winning team, Johnny Keane. Sadly, he joined the Yankees in time to catch them on a downward slide, and was fired in 1966, proving again that in baseball, as in politics, there are no final victories.

According to my calculations, in my six years in the majors I did not play in 675 games, not counting All-Star games. A lot of the games I did not play in were big games, historic games—involving names like Stan Musial, Willie Mays, Roberto Clemente, Henry Aaron, Frank Robinson; two or three no-hitters, marathons that lasted eighteen or twenty innings, things like that.

Looking back over my entire career, I am proudest of the World Series I did not play in for the Cardinals in '64. Tim McCarver caught every inning of every game.

For the Series, McCarver batted .478, scored four runs, drove in five and even stole a base. In all sincerity, I doubt that I could have improved on his performance.

But in all modesty, I can say that I probably received as much publicity as any fellow could for not playing in a World Series. Before the first-game ceremonies in St. Louis, I was on the field shagging flies with the rest of the scrubs. All the players were using gloves except me.

I was wearing a tuba. That probably requires an explanation.

There were four Dixieland bands on the field that day to entertain the crowd before the game. When the band in the left-field corner took a break, I noticed a tuba sitting there, looking neglected.

So I whipped it on and started catching fly balls with it. I didn't catch them all. A few, possibly several, hit the rim. The Cardinals later received a bill from the tuba player, wanting to be reimbursed for the damages. I had to kick in for it.

The Series turned out well, and that was as close as I came to getting into it, so you would have to say the money was well spent.

5. The Best Defensive Catcher
in the League

MY LAURELS MAY be the only thing I never rested on in my career, and I know my fans felt the same way. By way of a preamble to the 1965 season, the fan club recorded this touching thought: "Last year our goal was to get one member for each point in Bob Uecker's batting average. A late spurt gave him a .198 average, leaving us slightly short . . ."

That spring of 1965, coming off the championship season, I found myself with the kind of opportunity second-stringers dream about and seldom get. Tim McCarver broke a finger toward the end of camp and was out of action opening day and longer. I figured to get a chance to catch every day.

Now being a second-stringer is just about the most awkward role in sports. You have to accept the fact that the only way you will see any substantial action is for the fellow ahead of you to get hurt. If it happens, you have to be ready, but you can't appear too eager or too pleased. I mean, you can't go up to Tim McCarver every day and ask, "How's the finger?"

Red Schoendienst had succeeded Johnny Keane as manager of the Cardinals, and every day I read in the papers how he wasn't worried by the thought of having to go with Uecker. "He'll get better with more work," said Red.

Of course, this went contrary to my own theory, which was that the less I played the more likely I was to stay in the big leagues. But I prepared myself to take the risk. At least once in your life, you have to gamble. I had a heckuva spring, hitting over .300 and even banging a couple of homers.

I was the starting catcher on opening day of 1965, with Bob Gibson on the mound, when the defending champion Cardinals met the Chicago Cubs at Wrigley Field. It was just another typical day in the life of Mr. Baseball, meaning that:

—The game was called on account of darkness at the end of eleven innings with the score tied, 10-10;

—The Cards scored five runs in the top of the first and Gibson, one of the great pitchers of his day, couldn't hold the lead;

—I tried to steal home in the fifth inning and was out at the plate . . . I thought the sign had been flashed for the suicide squeeze bunt, but apparently it hadn't. I was sorry about that;

—I drew a walk with the bases loaded in the first inning to drive in a run;

—In the sixth I crashed into the field boxes chasing a pop foul and badly bruised my left kneecap. There went my career as a temporary regular catcher. The Cards had to press into service Dave Ricketts, a utility man who had been signed two days before as an insurance move.

The omens were not good. My personal historian, Mark Stillwell, took note of the crisis: "The St. Louis Cardinals won the 1964 pennant with a furious stretch drive. Then they won the World Series. With the same team looking much improved, they were picked by many to win again in 1965. But they started badly, losing five of their first six games and eight of their first twelve. Clearly, action was called for as something had to be done to pick the team up. Something *big* was needed. The Bob Uecker Fan Club moved in and stemmed the tide."

Mark and three other members of the club, Joe Fisher, Mike McCloskey, and Mike Wright, arranged to be in St. Louis on Friday night, April 30, to watch a four-game, weekend series against the Pirates. I was not in the lineup as we won the first two games, both by scores of 3-2.

On Sunday, the boys got to the ball park early: "Uecker was standing out in front of the left field wall. Eventually he wandered in and went into the dugout. When the team came back out, he started playing catch with Boyer and Carl Warwick. McCloskey had a poster that had Uecker's picture on it and I yelled at Uecker and held it up for him to see. A broad grin crossed his face. Shortly he came over and I took some pictures of him. I asked him if he was going to catch one of the games and he said he was. After the dugout interview, I got the attention of Cardinal announcer Harry Caray. I handed him a clipping from the Drury *Mirror* (the student paper) and he started reading it eagerly with a smile on his face. He asked me if he could keep it. I was only too glad to oblige.

"Then the game started. Donn Clendenon and Willie Stargell homered off Gibson in the first to put the Pirates ahead, 2-0. Then, in the bottom of the first, it happened. At roughly 1:25 P.M., Harry Caray uttered those immortal words: 'Members of the Bob Uecker Fan Club are here today, hee hee, from Drury College.' Short, simple, and to the point.''

I didn't play in the first game as the Cards came back to win, 9-5. Mark continues: "Then came the big second game. Uecker's moment of glory . . . The Pirates had used sloppy Cardinal fielding and a general clobbering of Bob Purkey to get three runs and there were still men on first and second with two out in the third and Del Crandall at bat. He drilled a single to left and Jerry Lynch came charging around from second.

"Lou Brock fielded the ball in left and threw toward home. It wasn't a particularly strong or impressive throw at all. Uecker had to go several feet into foul territory away from the baseline to get the ball as Lynch barreled down the line toward home. At the last instant, Uecker grabbed the throw on one hop and lunged at Lynch. He stretched himself out horizontally and just managed to tag Lynch on the shins. Lynch bowled him over and Uecker quickly bounced up with the ball clenched tightly in his fist. The umpire raised his right arm high. The crowd roared. I was the loudest.

"In the lower third he got to bat. A wild cheer came up from our section after the play he had made to end the top of the third. Then he hit a long fly into right that had us all on our feet. Bill Virdon ran a long way and finally caught up with the ball on the warning track in front of the wall.

"Bob Veale was tough for the Pirates. As the bottom of the eighth rolled along, Veale was breezing, 4-1. He had given up just one hit (a homer by Ken Boyer) and

fanned nine. Then came his downfall. Bob Uecker
stepped to the plate.

"With grace and poise, Uecker took a ball in the dirt.
Crandall said something to the umpire as he picked up
the ball and through my field glasses I could see Uecker
grinning out of the side of his mouth. He carefully
watched the second pitch go high. We were pulling for
him now, vocally, and I think the people around us
sensed it as they kept turning around. The next pitch
came in and was again low. Ball three! One more and we
had a base runner. Veale wound up. He fired. It was
inside! Uecker trotted down to first base as the four of us
gave him a standing ovation. Veale had faltered. Just to
make things exciting, he threw over to first to try and get
Uecker. (Imagine Uecker trying to steal.)

"That brought up Phil Gagliano to bat for Barney
Schultz. The crowd was up and hungry for a rally. We
were up, too, yelling to Gagliano for a hit and warning
Uecker not to get picked off. Uecker is one of the slowest
men in the league. The danger of his scoring on a triple
by Gagliano was only slight.

"Gagliano amazed everybody as he lined a shot off
the right-field wall. Uecker took off for second base. The
ball bounded away from the right fielder as McCloskey
took a picture of Uecker lumbering along and we all
cheered wildly in an effort to give him more speed. The
ball bounced into the bullpen and the pitchers there
scattered. It rolled under the bench and the right fielder
chased it there and picked up the bench and looked for
the ball and then kicked it away and had to run after it
again.

"By this time Uecker had reached second base and
was getting a little tired and had to slow down from the
brisk pace he had been setting. The right fielder located

the ball, but tripped over the pitching rubber in the
bullpen and fell headlong out on the grass. The ball kept
rolling away. Uecker was digging for third, but was
obviously laboring. The right fielder picked up the ball
and fumbled it a couple of times and let loose a weak
throw that rolled into the second baseman, who also
fumbled it. Uecker started his slide. The second baseman
dropped the ball and picked it up and threw toward third
and it was another weak throw. The ball bounced in the
dust and caromed off the third baseman's forearm and
into the waiting arms of the pitcher who also bobbled it
before he picked it up and flipped it back to the third
baseman, who tried to put the tag on the sliding Uecker.
The play was close. He was safe!

"It was at this point that Joe Fisher remarked, 'He
looked like he was goin' up a forty-five-percent grade.'
By now we were all ecstatic that Uecker had started a
rally that might conceivably change the course of the
ballgame. Curt Flood came up and promptly singled to
left and in a blaze of speed, coming from a second wind,
Uecker roared home with his second run of the season to
make it 4-2. There was loud shouting in our box and
shaking of hands as our boy finally got off the base paths
and into the dugout. McCloskey grabbed my arm and
pointed to the scoreboard. 'That run up there belongs to
Uecker,' he shouted at me.

"Then Lou Brock singled and Gagliano came in to
make it 4-3. Groat bounced into a double play, but Flood
scored to tie it up. Boyer lined out to the shortstop to end
the eighth. We went wild, as the game was tied. And
Veale had been taken out.

"In the bottom of the ninth, Bill White led off against
Al McBean. All he had to do now was homer and the
Cards would win. He hit the second pitch into the right-

field pavilion for a 5-4 win. The Cards had won four straight from the Pirates and had reached the .500 mark for the season, and had climbed in three days from tenth in the National League to a tie for fourth.

"The boys had come through in the clutch. And Uecker was in the center of it all. As Joe remarked to me in the three-run rally in the eighth, 'He broke it open.' There was a woman in front of us who was enjoying our antics as much as she was the game. She turned around and looked at me and said, 'You're right! Uecker did it.' And then she turned to her husband and I heard her say, 'I never heard of Bob Uecker in my life until today.'"

I see that game, that rally, and that remark as a microcosm of my life. I guess it would be easy for some people to say that anyone's career could sound exciting if you described every pitch of it. On the other hand, perhaps not.

I am not trying to make a big deal of the fact that I drew a walk and scored the run that got us back into a rather meaningless game in May. Someone had to get us started. Nor do I care to say where that play ranks among all the most unforgettable plays of my career. That would be like trying to single out your favorite noodle at a spaghetti dinner. But out of that narrative, the line that appeals to me most is, *"Uecker started his slide."* The line has a kind of melancholy ring to it.

The season rocked along. McCarver and I were still nagged by injuries, but we struggled to stay in the lineup. A few days later, I hit my first home run of the season, but it went to waste. The Giants scored five runs in the top of the tenth inning to break a tie and beat us, 10-5. It was a weird inning, and I figured in it in a prominent way.

We had Ray Washburn on the mound. There were runners at first and third with one out when Ed Bailey, a backup catcher who was even slower then me, batted for the San Francisco pitcher. He swung at an 0-2 pitch and rapped a grounder toward Phil Gagliano at second base. The perfect double play mix: crisp ground ball, slow runner.

Phil charged the ball and juggled it. Then he picked it up, decided he had no chance to get two, and fired a strike to home.

The only problem was, I wasn't there. The ball almost hit the plate umpire in the gut. I had headed down the first-base line. If Gagliano fielded the ball cleanly, I needed to back up the relay to first. Meanwhile, the winning run scored and the Giants went on to get four more.

After the game, Bob Broeg, the veteran St. Louis baseball writer, bumped into Tom Sheehan, the round, red-faced Giants' scout who always reminded me of a house detective. Broeg told Sheehan that, man and boy, he had been watching the Cardinals for forty years and had never seen that play.

"No," boomed Sheehan, in his big, bass voice, "and man and boy, I'll bet you've never seen many catchers, either, whose last name begins with the letter *U*."

As the 1965 season unfolded, it developed that beneath the clown's mask, inside my bench-warmer's shell, beat the heart of a semi-regular and might-have-been .300 hitter. I darned near blew my image.

In May, Red Schoendienst decided to platoon me with Tim McCarver. I started twelve games. We won eight of them. That month the Cardinals made their best and last bid to move into first place, pulling to within a game and a half of the Dodgers.

My fan club began to suspect that they had created a monster. On May fifth I cracked my first homer of the season, against the Giants. Three nights later, I started rallies with a walk and a single, and kept the Phillies from scoring the winning run in the ninth by tagging out Alex Johnson on a close play at the plate. Over the radio network, Harry Caray exulted: "How Uecker ever held that ball I'll never know."

Like monks recording their daily prayers, my scribes committed every word to the club scrapbook.

May 16—"Uecker had a hit to raise his average forty points to .190. Jack Buck spoke for all of us when he said, 'Uecker has been really stinging the ball, but it just isn't falling in.'"

May 17—". . . threw out two runners attempting to steal, was the middle man on a double play and blocked the plate to keep the Phillies from scoring. Harry Caray called his arm 'phenomenal.'"

May 20—". . . had a hit and scored run as Bob Gibson won his eighth, 12-2."

May 21—". . . laced a single to center in the fourth, with a 2-2 count and the tying run on second, to drive in his third run of the year and raise his average to .214 (the highest it has been in some time). Two innings later he walked. It seems as if every time Uecker catches, he walks once. Never twice, but always once, except Thursday when he was hit by a pitch. He obviously has a good eye at the plate."

It is dangerous for an athlete to believe his own publicity, good or bad. I never believed mine, partly because I never read any until after I had retired. But for a fleeting moment there, in 1965, I was getting very good ink indeed.

In late May, we beat the Dodgers twice to cut their lead to one and a half games. I collected two hits off Claude Osteen and two—of course!—off Sandy Koufax, one a double that just missed being a homer.

I was only in the lineup against left-handers, which meant that I could look forward to a parade of people named Koufax, Bob Veale, Chris Short, Bo Belinsky, Dick Ellsworth, Al Jackson, Jim O'Toole and Claude Osteen. I had to adopt a new philosophy. I learned to dread one day at a time.

The win over Koufax turned out to be the high point of our season. I scored the winning run and lifted my average to .286, at the time the third highest on the club, behind Curt Flood and Lou Brock. We should have known right then that the Cardinals were in trouble.

Out last hurrah came in Los Angeles, on July 25, when we beat the Dodgers in ten innings, 3-2, before a crowd of fifty thousand. As luck would have it—I am trying to be humble about this—I had two hits off Koufax, one a homer. Poor Sandy. He was the greatest pitcher of his time, and whenever I stepped in to face him he didn't know whether to laugh or to cry.

After that we went right down the tubes. The Giants swept a three-game series from us at home, and by the first week in August we were just over .500 and out of the race. Typical of the way the season had gone, McCarver and I went on the injury list at the same time, just as we had in April. Once more Mike Shannon was yanked from the outfield to fill in as the emergency catcher. Tim had a spiked left thumb. I had a split right thumb. Between us we had a complete set.

Sometimes there is no way to explain why a championship team takes a pratfall. Some call it the Fat Cat syndrome. But the Cardinals had to fight too hard in 1964, won too late and by too little, to be complacent. True, we had changed managers, but Red was a clone of Johnny Keane: a good man, quiet, serious, diligent, with the same way of handling a team.

We had virtually the same lineup that had won the World Series. Yet at the point where we had begun our pennant drive the year before, our tank was empty. Injuries nagged us. Simmons and Sadecki won fifteen fewer games. Boyer, White, Flood, and Brock saw their averages drop between twenty and forty points. When the locusts come, they devour everything.

During this period I made an interesting discovery. These were all players with high standards, which they had set for themselves. When they failed to meet them, the fans and the management came down hard. I had no such problem.

I found myself a more frequent guest on Harry Caray's postgame radio show, reserved for The Star of the Game. I appeared in September after a win over the Mets, during which I picked a runner off second and singled off the shortstop's glove. The hit at first had been called an error.

Harry asked me if some players didn't worry a lot about whether balls were called hits or errors.

"Some players," I admitted, "will get on first base and reach down and pick up a handful of dirt and when nobody is looking, they'll glance up at the scoreboard."

Harry said, "What do you do when it's a close call?"

I said, "I reach down and pick up a handful of dirt and when nobody is looking, I glance up at the scoreboard."

"I guess you like to see them call it a hit."

"Well, I always like to count 'em as a hit myself," I

replied. "I count everything—hits, walks, fielder's choices, everything. If I hit the ball good, I count it."

Harry asked, "Well, by your own system, what are you hitting right now?"

"Six-forty-three," I said.

There was not a lot to laugh or cheer about by the time the Cardinals ended the season at home. We stood in front of the dugout while Lou Brock received a plaque at home plate for breaking the club record with sixty stolen bases. Without turning my head, I whispered to McCarver, "If I had been in the lineup every day that could be me out there."

I did, in fact, have my best season in the majors. I played in fifty-three games, batted 145 times, with thirty-three hits, seventeen runs, seven doubles, two homers and ten runs batted in—all career highs. I hit a hard .228.

I was the catcher when Roy McMillan, of the Mets, stepped in the batter's box to start his two thousandth game. When Sandy Koufax set the National League record for strikeouts in a season, 349, I was the hitter he fanned to tie the record.

Over the years we had a great personal rivalry, Koufax and I. Thank the Lord I didn't destroy the boy's confidence.

Although the Cardinals had tumbled to seventh place, I had performed reasonably well as a spot starter. No one would blame me for the decline. No one had said, "As Uecker goes, so go the Cards." I felt secure. I even thought I might get a small raise.

What I got was a trade to the Philadelphia Phillies, along with Dick Groat and Bill White. In return, the

Cardinals received pitcher Art Mahaffey, outfielder Alex Johnson and catcher Pat Corrales.

The news broke on October 27, 1965, on the heels of a trade that sent Ken Boyer to the Mets. The fan club felt betrayed and outraged. The kids stopped just short of asking the president to double the guard at Pearl Harbor.

Mark Stillwell took the news harder than I did: "To trade Bill White after the job he has done is in itself a crime against humanity. To trade Dick Groat might be partly understandable, much as the Boyer trade was. But to trade Uecker was the unkindest cut of all. This is an unpardonable sin. And, when you don't get anything for him in return, it's doubly bad.

"Myra Becker called me over in English and told me the Cards had traded Bob Uecker. I almost fainted. I called Dave Schulty down at the newspaper office and he confirmed the report. Never in my life had I been so sick about something. Joe Fisher almost keeled over when I told him. I can't in any way rationalize trading White, and I can't even stomach trading Uecker.

"The first thing I did was to write a story for the Drury Mirror, letting the world know that the Bob Uecker Fan Club will not desert its hero in his time of great need. Then I prepared to write a nasty letter to Bob Howsam, the general manager of the Cardinals, who perpetrated this great crime."

Howsam was not popular with the players, although I hasten to add that being popular with the players is not essential to being a general manager. At times, it isn't even desirable. But Howsam had replaced Bing Devine, who had spent his life with the St. Louis franchise and was widely admired for his fairness.

Howsam was no amateur. He had a long family history in sports, and had set minor-league attendance records in

Denver. He was a large, affable man, with a round face
and a high, soft voice. He sounded a little like Liberace.
He liked to dash off memos and post clippings on the
bulletin board in the clubhouse, and the players are
suspicious of anyone who makes them read things.

What Howsam had done was to follow an old and
honored custom. It is called cutting the payroll. Baseball
teams prefer to rebuild with younger players, especially
those with low overheads. Boyer, Groat and White drew
hefty salaries. I was thrown in, I think, just to confuse
people.

A pained and angry letter from Mark Stillwell poured
into the Cardinal offices the day after the trade:

Dear Mr. Howsam,

I've been a Cardinal fan for a long time and I
don't know when anything has happened that has
disappointed me and disgusted me so much as the
trade just completed with the Philadelphia Phillies.

In Bill White, the Cardinals had the best defensive first baseman in the National League, and also
one of the most dangerous power hitters around. In
Dick Groat they had a smart, steady ballplayer who
knew more about the game than most shortstops
ever learn. In Bob Uecker, they had the best
defensive catcher in the league and one of the
strongest throwing arms in baseball. These are three
men I would seriously doubt that the Cardinals
could afford to (lose) unless they obtained some
outstanding talent in return.

In Art Mahaffey, we've picked up a discontented
pitcher who won just two games. Pat Corrales has
good minor-league credentials, but not overly impressive. Alex Johnson may be the sleeper in the

deal, but he'll have to hit more than eight home runs to help the Cards.

If Red Schoendienst doesn't get an ulcer trying to decide what he has left when he gets to St. Petersburg next spring, I'll be surprised. But, while you're at the trading game, see if you can clear up some of this sadness by unloading part of this horde of pitchers that has piled up and come up with a bona fide power hitter.

> Yours truly,
> Mark Stillwell
> President
> Bob Uecker Fan Club

Nowhere, this side of politics, do people get madder, or choose up sides faster, than in baseball. A single trade can disrupt the pace of an entire city. People honk their horns. They are rude to each other in elevators. Children wet their beds.

We lost some of this emotional outpouring when the free-agent traffic began. When a player sells himself on the auction block, and his team gets little or nothing in return, the fans can't argue about which side got the better of the deal, or wonder how the front office could be so stupid. As a former player, I have mixed feelings about free agency. It is like coed housing in college. We are shocked and confused, and we ask why didn't it happen twenty years ago?

Howsam's answer to Mark was stock front-office stuff, soft-answer-turneth-away-wrath:

Dear Mr. Stillwell,
    Thank you for your letter of October 27 regarding the recent trade.

Naturally, it is never pleasant to trade ballplayers that have played such good baseball for the club and were so popular. But in order to try to keep our ball club strong and in contention, it is necessary to make changes.

When a trade is negotiated, it is the thinking of the entire Cardinal organization. Our manager is consulted, our scouts are consulted, because they are the ones who thoroughly check the records and actually watch the various players throughout the year; our minor-league department is consulted to find out what they know about the player or players involved. I could never be part of trading a player on the spur of the moment. A lot of research goes into the players we receive in a trade and also into a player before we trade him. We feel we have made trades which will be beneficial to the Cardinals.

I appreciate your interest, and thank you for taking the time to write to me. We hope you will have the opportunity to see many games in the new stadium next year.

> Kindest regards,
> Bob Howsam
> General Manager

In other words, they were not going to call off the trade. Uecker was going to Philadelphia, a town where, on Easter, they boo the little kids who don't find eggs.

6. Uecker's Last Hurrah

THE PHILLIES, like the Cardinals, were a team trying to regroup. No manager had survived more adversity than Gene Mauch. His first team had established a major-league record by losing twenty-three straight games in 1961. Near the end of the streak, they came off a road trip to find a large crowd waiting for them at the airport in Philadelphia. They figured, obviously, it was a lynch mob. A pitcher named Frank Sullivan called out, "leave the plane in single file. That way they can't get us with one burst."

But the fans came to welcome them home again, to cheer, to give them support. There is no way to know what makes a Phillies fan tick. They rallied behind Gene Mauch, and in time he gave them a contender, only to see the Phillies blow a ten-game lead in the nightmare season of 1964. The next year they were never a factor, and now Mauch had decided to retool the club.

I felt at home with the Phillies, when I reported to camp at Clearwater in March. The roster included such cashews as Richie Allen, who liked everything about a ball park except getting there; Bo Belinsky, the flamboyant left-hander who thought he had been Rudolph Valentino in a prior life, and John Boozer, a pitcher whose idea of fun was to eat bugs and worms and watch people gag. He did a better job in the clubhouse than D-Con. He would be talking to a writer and one of the players would hand him a live worm or a beetle. Some of the reactions were terrific.

Belinsky reported to camp two days late, explaining that he had been trapped by a snowstorm in Texas on the drive from California. Those Texas snowstorms can be murder.

In addition to the ex-Cardinal trio, Mauch had traded for Phil Linz, an infielder the Yankees had fired for playing the harmonica on the team bus after a loss, and Jackie Brandt, who once watched part of an All-Star Game while sitting in the dugout in the nude.

The Phillies had a terrific roster. I don't mean in talent, but in names, the kind that headline writers loved, like Wine and Boozer, and the kind that just had a certain ring, like Ferguson Jenkins, Cookie Rojas and Clay Dalrymple.

I had been brought in to back up Dalrymple, a seven-year vet and an underrated fellow, whose .213 average in 1965 was well below his form. Clay hit from the left side, which meant that once again I would have a chance to start against the left-handers. It was hard to tell if I had made any progress. I had been traded to my third team in three years. The Phillies issued me uniform Number 10. I had worn 9 in St. Louis and 8 in Milwaukee. Was this progress?

When the players talked about the best and the brightest managers, the name of Gene Mauch often came up. He was quick-tempered, but he did not give up on people easily. His career as a player had been similar to mine. He was a shortstop who always seemed to line up behind someone better, such as Phil Rizzuto, with the Yankees, or Pee Wee Reese, with the Dodgers.

Frustrated, still a kid, Mauch once confronted his manager, Casey Stengel, in the dining room of a hotel where the Yankees stayed. "Dammit, Casey," he blurted, "I've got to play."

Stengel looked up from his soup and nodded. "Go talk to Mr. Rizzuto," the old man said. "If it's okay with him, it's okay with me."

Mauch was the most intense manager I ever knew. He would sit on the bench with his arms folded and his eyes never stopped moving. He didn't miss a thing. They used to tell a story about when Mauch was playing for the Red Sox, and on the way to the airport the team bus got stuck under an overpass. The driver and the team got out to study the problem. Finally, Mauch said, "Let the air out of the tires and fill them up on the other side." And so they did.

I was in the lineup on opening day, 1966, caught Chris Short and drove in a run with a single as we beat the Reds and Joe Nuxhall, 3-1. Then a really uncharacteristic thing happened. I hit home runs on consecutive days at the end of April. In my first six games, I had produced four hits, half of them homers, and driven in six runs. A curious start, it was worth three stars and a full, hand-lettered page in the scrapbook:

TWO HOMERS
IN TWO
DAYS!

BIG UKE
IS STARTING TO
FIND THE RANGE

ONLY 505 CAREER
HOMERS BEHIND
MAYS & OTT!!

Ah, yes, the future stretched ahead as smooth and inviting as the Pennsylvania Turnpike. When I connected for my third homer on Memorial Day, against the Mets, Mark wrote a story for the school paper at Drury, and mailed a copy to Bob Howsam. The Cardinals were in the process of sending Mahaffey and Johnson to the minors. The trade was looking rather one-sided for the Phillies.

The story went like this: "Bob Howsam has finally, publicly, admitted in May that he was completely wrong in October. The story we got then was that we were trading White, Groat, and Uecker for Johnson, Corrales, and Mahaffey because we (the Cardinals) were fully committed to our youth movement.

"Well, it doesn't look too good for smiling Bob. How can you say you're in a youth movement and trade a thirty-one-year-old slugger like White and then keep a broken-down, thirty-seven-year-old pitcher named Curt Simmons, who only pitches against the Phillies and can't beat them?

"With his homer, double, and three runs batted in on Memorial Day, and his two singles two days later, Uecker raised his average to a lusty .266. With three homers . . . he seems likely to get a new career high in every hitting department, and last year had been his best. He's hitting better than either Bill White or Dick Groat, the men he was traded with, and that ought to make him the big man in the deal. The key man in the deal!

"Howsam, you're an idiot."

With aplomb, Howsam wrote back:

Dear Mr. Stillwell,

Thank you for sending along the article which appeared at Drury.

It's nice to know, too, that you have remained Cardinal fans.

We hope you and your Fan Club will have the opportunity to visit the new Busch Memorial Stadium and see the Cardinals play. I think you'll enjoy it.

> Kindest regards,
> Bob Howsam
> General Manager

The first time the teams met in 1966, the Phillies edged the Cards, 5-3. Bill White singled home our first two runs. I singled to open the winning rally and scored the tie-breaking run on a bases-loaded walk to Groat, who had two hits. It's true, hitting well is the best revenge.

On June 3, I slugged my fourth homer of the year, equaling the total for my entire big-league career. The blow was off an ex-teammate, Ray Sadecki, then pitching for the Giants. By the All-Star break I had raised my total to six, the same number as John Callison, a guy who was usually good for twenty-five to thirty a season.

I would have felt great, except that everybody around the Phillies kept wondering what was wrong with Callison. Four teams figured to stay in the pennant race most of the way, the Dodgers, Giants, Pirates, and the Phillies. We needed a big year from Callison. In fact, we needed a big year from everybody.

The point should be made right here that it can be harmful for a fellow who doesn't hit homers to suddenly start banging a few. It is like a guy who discovers girls late in life and thinks he can catch up all at once. And the next thing you know, you are in a jar at the Harvard Medical School.

But sooner or later you have to try. You see a Richie Allen twitch a muscle and the ball flies off the bat and lands five hundred feet away. And you think, is there any reason I can't do that? The next thing you know, your hands are down at the end of the bat and all your weight is on your heels.

In a way, those homers, hitting in the .270's, and getting four (4) votes for the All-Star Game may have been my undoing. Up to then my theories had stood the test of time, like milk of magnesia: 1) The more I played, the closer I was to getting shipped out, and 2) the better I performed, the more they expected.

If I had been content to just hit .200 every year, all singles, and throw out a runner now and then, I might have played as long as Gaylord Perry. Your body doesn't wear out very fast when you catch a game every four or five days.

On July 17, I tagged my seventh homer in what turned out to be a fifteen-inning win over the first-place Giants. On the Phillies, only Allen and Bill White had more, even though a total of twelve players had started more games.

I had no personal goals in mind, which was just as well because I did not hit another homer during the rest of the season.

We stayed in the race until September, then became the first of the four contenders to fade. Chris Short won twenty games and Jim Bunning finished with nineteen. A late-season slump by Bill White was costly, but he drove in 103 runs and popped twenty-two homers.

Seasons that end badly tend to blur, a series of pitches half-forgotten at the moment they are half-missed, in games that are half-played. But it was a thrill, that year, to watch Richie Allen, young and untamed, blossom into a superstar. He hit forty home runs and fought Hank Aaron for the title down to the final days. He drove in 110 runs and batted .317. And he was going to get stronger and better. He would in time overpower this game and, unfortunately, himself.

Allen was one of baseball's new talents, a prodigious long-ball hitter. He preferred horses and cars to the company of people, but he was seldom loud or rude. He asked only to be treated like a man. In view of what Richie accomplished, the request did not seem unreasonable.

Part of his problem was that no matter how much he accomplished, it was never enough to satisfy all of his critics. Some just didn't like him, his color, his style, his habits. Others simply felt that he didn't get the most out of his huge gifts. Many a time, on his way to the plate, Richie would tell us he was going to take two strikes and see if he could hit one pitch. He would do this against some of the best pitchers in the league. He drove Gene Mauch wild, but more often than not he came through. He was just that good.

Richie did not take direction well, he was careless about the time, and he liked to sip the cooking sherry. We would get in the back of the plane, glowing slightly, and sing harmony, all the old barbershop songs. We were a happy pair.

I was a witness to the events that led to Richie's famous car-pushing accident, which left him with a mangled hand. Someone had given him an old stock car. He had it at the ball park one day, and he invited Dick Groat, Bob Skinner and myself to ride back to the Presidential Apartments with him. On the way, he tried to show us how to speed shift a stock car, and going from first to second he jammed the gears into reverse. The gears locked. We pushed the jalopy over to the side of the road and that was where it stayed, until Richie had it towed to his apartment.

I don't know how long the car stayed there, but at last he decided to move it. He tried to push the car from the front and his hand slipped and went through the headlight. From then on his hand was like a claw, after the surgeons did what they could to repair the tendons. After that I called him "Crash" Allen. A lesser man would have been finished. Richie regained the use of his hand and played ten more stormy seasons.

My own season was a deceptive one, as my seasons sometimes were. In the final weeks my average shrank to .208. But I had almost as many runs batted in (thirty) as I did base hits (forty-three). I saw the most action of my career, catching seventy-six games and playing one inning at third base, although I no longer remember why. It probably had to do with whatever strategy Gene Mauch was using that night.

I figured I had done well enough to go another year, and that was as far as I ever planned. Big-league baseball players, as a group, fool no one but themselves. We are like Oskar in *The Tin Drum*, the little boy who would not grow up.

My fan club was growing older. It had somehow acquired 476 members, and the hard cord were now seniors preparing to graduate. We were bonded, in a curious kind of way. They were like having your own private gag, my Pookah, my Harvey the Rabbit made real. They redeemed my view of life; that the world belongs to those who know when to laugh at it. I am not sure what they got in return, other than a hero without the trimmings, a hero who could never let them down.

Well, almost.

At midseason, Mark had made the following entry in the scrapbook: "Since 1966 will probably be the last really active year of the Bob Uecker Fan Club, it seems significant that we should set a definite goal for ourselves. It would be altogether fitting and proper for the Phillies to get into the World Series and for Uecker to be the hero, but we have a much simpler goal.

"We want Uecker to either hit a triple or steal a base. He has never done either in his five-year career in the big leagues and we think it's high time for one or the other . . . We realize he isn't fast, but a determined man ought to be able to accomplish these things.

"He may not know how we feel about this. I ought to write and tell him."

Which he did. To no avail. Another year without a triple or a stolen base.

I continued to hear from the club. They had subscribed to the Philadelphia *Inquirer.* They had mailed a check to the Phillies for a yearbook and team pictures that as yet were undelivered, and they were thinking about setting fire to Connie Mack Stadium.

That winter I received a funny-serious letter from Mark:

Dear Bob,

The second volume of the Bob Uecker Story is all but complete and it looks like it's going to be every bit as good as the first. We had a lot of material to work with this year, largely because you came through with your best season. I only got to see one game, a Monday night affair at Pittsburgh late in August, but you delivered a key, run-scoring single.

The Cardinal fans discovered something this year. When you were traded for Corrales, we went from two catchers to one and your friend McCarver had a fine year but he had to play 150 games and that's a few too many. I think that is one trade that will go down in the books as a disaster for St. Louis. Now that Charlie Smith is gone, I'll see if we can't figure a way to get you back and let you play third base. . . .

I'll be graduating from Drury next May along with my number-one sidekick, so we won't have as much time for active fan-clubbing. The Navy has plans to send us somewhere for three years, but I'll get to St. Louis before July and catch some Phillie-Cardinal games. We're all hoping you'll turn in another fine year in 1967!

Sincerely,
Mark Stillwell
President
Bob Uecker Fan Club

The reference to Charlie Smith is worth noting now. The Cardinals traded Smith that winter to the Yankees in return for Roger Maris, who had chased Babe Ruth's ghost across the summer of 1961. It was an even trade, one for one. Does anyone remember Charlie Smith today, except as the answer to a trivia question? Funny game.

The problem with being a fringe player is that just about the time you get comfortable with a team, you're gone again. Wherever I had played, the scrubs banded together and developed our own esprit de corps. I don't think any of the teams ever suffered for it, although I am not sure all of my managers would agree. On the Phillies, we called ourselves The Avengers, and the group included Bobby Wine, Phil Linz and Jackie Brandt. Richie Allen was an honorary member. He was a great player, but he had the heart of a truant.

The career of another fellow, who was to become a special friend of mine, ended that year. Harvey Kuenn batted .296 for the Phillies and decided to call it a career. He was thirty-six, had played fifteen seasons and finished with a lifetime average of .303.

He had been a principal in one of the most publicized trades ever made. Harvey won the batting title at Detroit in 1959, and then was swapped for the man who had won the home run title, Rocky Colavito of Cleveland.

I admired Harvey as a fine agitator and one of the smartest hitters I had ever been around or caught behind. He stood in the deepest part of the batter's box and defied the pitcher to throw the ball on the outside corner of the plate. That was a pitch he could kill. He was an all-fields, line drive hitter, but if his team needed a run in the late innings to tie or win, he could take you downtown.

After our playing days, both of us came home to Milwaukee. Harvey joined the Brewers as a coach. I'm on the radio crew. And our friendship continues.

In February, three years ago, his right leg was

amputated because of a circulatory problem. By the end
of spring training, he was walking on an artificial limb.
By winter, he was playing golf every day. Sometimes a
fellow as big and active as Harvey Kuenn finds it hard to
accept such a blow. But those who knew him as a great
athlete found out he was much more. He wouldn't let life
slip one over the outside corner, either.

We were not far into the 1967 season when I knew my
days with the Phillies were numbered. I went to the plate
one night as a pinch hitter, and when I looked to the
third-base coach for a sign he turned his back on me.

The trade that sent me back to the Braves, my original
club, for another catcher, Gene Oliver, was announced on
June seventh. In truth, I felt a little guilty about leaving
Philadelphia. Richie Allen was brooding and threatening
not to play. I felt like a hostage who had been released
early.

The next morning, Rich said he wasn't going to the
ball park anymore. I called Donald Davidson, the
Braves' road secretary and an old friend, and told him I
couldn't report right away. He pleaded with me: "Uke,
dammit, you got to get your ass down here. Joe Torre is
hurt and you're the only catcher we have."

When I left, Allen was still boycotting the ball park.
Soon I heard from Charlie Meister, in the Phillies' front
office: "You have to talk to Richie. He hasn't suited up
since we made the trade." I called, reminded him that
the Braves would be flying into Philadelphia for a three-
game series that weekend, and convinced him to go back
to work.

Of course, it didn't take much to keep Richie away
from the ball park. He didn't like to practice. Always felt
it wasn't in his contract. He had signed up just for the
games.

I was fortunate to room with great, normal players like Eddie Mathews, and an occasional pure flake like Roger Craig.

Craig, my roomie in St. Louis, had one of the most uneven careers any pitcher ever had. He helped pitch the Dodgers to a pennant in 1959, and in two seasons with the Mets lost a total of forty-six games.

Influenced, perhaps, by his term with the Mets, Roger loved horror movies and sometimes imagined that he was in one. He had a problem with his neck for a while and wore a brace. I would open the closet door to put away my coat, and find him hanging on the inside of the door, his brace looped over the hook.

Those are the pictures you take out of baseball, more than the runs, hits, and errors. You remember the players and the people and the rhythm of the towns.

I honestly liked Philadelphia. The fans there were smart and mean and you could count on them. One of my biggest thrills in baseball was watching a guy fall out of the upper deck in Connie Mack Stadium. The crowd booed when he tried to get up.

On the other hand, I wasn't sure what to expect in Atlanta. The catching job would belong to Torre when he was well. But Paul Richards, the general manager, wanted to turn Phil Niekro into a starter, if he could find someone to catch his knuckleball.

The Braves had undergone many a change since I had last worn their uniform in 1963. For one thing, they were no longer in Milwaukee. Spahn, Burdette, Mathews and Crandall were gone.

When I walked into the Braves' clubhouse to rejoin the team I was given the white-carpet treatment. Literally. Joe Torre had laid out a path of white towels from the door to my new locker, above which were two handwritten signs. One, from Joe, had a heartfelt simplicity to it: THANK YOU VERY MUCH. GOD BLESS YOU.

The other said, LOTS OF LUCK. YOUR BUDDY, PHIL NIEKRO.

There was a third Brave eager to see me and renew an old acquaintance, Henry Aaron. Henry thought he had an old score to settle. The talk was just beginning to stir about his chances of breaking Ruth's career home-run record, and he accused me of taking one away from him in 1965.

Curt Simmons was on the mound that day for the Cardinals in St. Louis, Aaron had been frustrated by Simmons' assortment of slow curves. This time he ran up on the ball before the curve could break, and the pitch exploded off his bat, bouncing off the roof of the park in right field.

As Henry remembered it, I called the plate umpire's attention to the fact that he had stepped out of the batter's box. The umpire disallowed the homer and called him out.

The night I rejoined the Braves, Henry grinned and said, "If I miss Ruth's record by one homer, I'm going to be looking for you, Uecker."

I had to tell Henry the truth. It wasn't me. Tim McCarver was the catcher who took the homer away from him. But it was the sort of thing I would have been proud to do.

I was still a backup catcher, still the twenty-fourth or twenty-fifth man on the roster, still in the twilight of a mediocre career. But something was different this time. In a small way I had become necessary. All because of a maddening pitch that had carried Phil Niekro to the majors and now threatened to carry him right out.

It was a toss-up whether the batters hated to hit against Phil's knuckler as much as the catchers hated to catch it. He had played on teams in the minors where the catchers had simply refused. And he had lost more than one game when a third strike rolled back to the screen while the winning run crossed the plate.

I had caught Barney Schultz, in St. Louis, and Bob Tiefenauer, in Milwaukee, then the only other pitchers to rely almost exclusively on the knuckleball. I had one other thing going for me: my reputation as a defensive catcher. It occurred to me that when you don't hit much, teams tend to exaggerate your defensive skills.

I caught every game Niekro started the rest of the season, and I caught every day while Joe Torre recovered from his injury. In late June I had the biggest day at bat of my career, hitting my first grand-slam homer, off Ron Herbel of the Giants, and knocking in five runs.

Soon Niekro was giving me credit for keeping him in the big leagues. He was still doing it in 1981, fourteen years later. I don't know if this was the case, or a polite overstatement, but it was nice of Phil to say so. I am glad to claim him as the legacy of my big-league career. He won 150 games in those years, mostly for losing teams, and he is a fine legacy to have.

Niekro had a good slider and fastball, still has, but the knuckler was his strikeout pitch and he knew I wasn't afraid to call it with a runner at third. Every time he started I went through the same ritual before the game. I took four aspirin for the headache I knew I would have afterwards.

Once, after Phil had beaten the Pirates, 2-1, our trainer, Harvey Stone, looked up from rubbing his arm and told a reporter that Phil could probably pitch the next night.

Paul Richards overheard him. "No, he couldn't," Richards said, immediately.

"Why not?" asked the writer. "He needs more rest?"

"No," said Paul, "but Uecker does. Every time Niekro pitches, Uecker is the one who needs four days' rest."

Another problem with not having much talent is that it's hard to tell when you have begun to slip. But if I was on my way out of the big leagues, I was going more or less in style, and my fan club was going with me.

Baseball lore is filled with tearful stories of great players like Ruth and Mantle visiting hospitals and then slugging homers for a little sick kid. I made the same promise once, struck out three times and then found out the kid was an out-patient.

When it really counted, when it was not just a matter of drama but of justice, I am proud to say that I came through. When the Braves met the Cards in St. Louis on Sunday, July 23, Mark Stillwell showed up at Busch Stadium. Later, he described what happened: "There are in sports certain moments that come along perhaps only once in a lifetime. If you can take part in those special occurrences, you can treasure their memory always. If you miss them, you've missed them. The Home Run was such an occurrence.

"I was due to leave the twenty-fourth for Southern California to begin three years of active duty with the Navy. A Navy publication had recommended that the departing sailor should endeavor to spend his last hours at home with his loved ones. I did just that. I drove to St. Louis to see the Cardinals play a doubleheader with the Braves . . ."

I sat out the opener as the Braves lost, 3-1. In the nightcap, I started and struck out my first time out. Mark continues: "When he came up in the fourth with one out and nobody on, I snapped a picture of him taking a cut at the plate. A couple of pitches later Uecker got around on what was probably a hanging curve and hit a long fly ball down the line toward left field. It looked like just a routine fly ball and it hadn't sounded particularly solid but it kept carrying, and carrying, and finally fell deep into the loge reserved seats in left field for Uecker's third homer of the year.

"As Uecker started the home-run trot around the base paths, I realized what I had just witnessed. I set up a clamor like few around me could believe or understand. It dawned on me that I was the only guy yelling for Uecker in the entire crowd . . . I may well have been the only member of the Uecker Fan Club ever to see The Great One crack a home run."

In retrospect we know how he must have felt. I am told that some people never forget the first time they heard Heifitz play the violin, or Caruso sing an aria, or watched the sun set on Bo Derek's body. The homer had no bearing on the outcome of the game, which the Cards won, 8-3, to sweep the doubleheader. Of the thousands who were there, only two of us had any reason to care or remember it, and I am not so sure about myself.

So much for history. The Braves finished sixth and fired manager Billy Hitchcock. I played in eighty games, the most of my career, and hit .150, my lowest ever. I did lead the league in one category, and I could not have done it without Phil Niekro. I was charged with twenty-seven passed balls. The next-highest total was sixteen.

I kept intact my career record of never having stolen a base or legged out a triple. It was a letdown to the kids at Drury College, but I hoped they would overcome it in time.

And so the stage was set for the series of events I have described earlier: the accident on Clete Boyer's motorcycle, the barroom fight in Fort Lauderdale, my release as a player and coach, then signing with the Braves as a speaker and occasional broadcaster.

In 1971, Alan (Bud) Selig offered me a chance to return to Milwaukee as a full-time member of the radio crew. I jumped at it, completing a cycle as the first Milwaukee boy signed by the Braves, traded by the Braves, fired by the Braves, and hired by the Brewers.

As I think back on the zaniness of my years, I am grateful for the career I had. I mean, one good season and I might have blown my entire future in broadcasting. Today I speak frequently at banquets around the country, and the audiences often include youngsters. I always try to leave them with one sincere thought. If you can't play a sport . . . the hell with it.

As for the fan club, I never really felt that I deserved it. Of course, I have arthritis in one knee and I don't feel I deserve that, either.

And I am still in touch with Mark Stillwell, who was born to be a public relations man, and whose enthusiasm now serves the football Cardinals. After I had begun to appear as a repeat guest on the *Tonight Show*, I received a long and nostalgic letter from Mark. He closed by saying: "My brother asked me last week what the greatest satisfaction from the fan club had been. I told him it was being able to say that we had followed your career from the time you were a tuba player for the 1964 World Champions."

PART III

Outside Baseball

In which he looks at the world of radio and television; and a strike that could have hurt everyone except Bob Uecker, who can always go back into the service.

"He (Dave Winfield) also wanted a voice in team trades, more beef in the ground patties, and the right to change his name to Ronald McWinfield."

7. All My Tonights

WHEN ANYONE ASKS ME how to break into radio and television, I never know where to begin. Or where to end. I might tell them this truth: You have to be lucky. It isn't enough just to be crazy.

The only training I ever had was as an occasional guest on a postgame show. Of course, I also called the play-by-play of hundreds of games for the boys in the bullpen, broadcasting into a beer cup.

My career is a confirmation of one of the basic laws of success: Anything is obtainable if you don't need it.

There are advantages to not being a star athlete. When you retire no one feels cheated, and the adjustment to the Real World is more gentle, emotionally as well as financially. Some athletes need a decompression chamber when the time comes to take off the uniform. They suffer withdrawal pains when the cheering stops.

While it lasted, while the player was hot, the wine flowed and the dollies came waltzing through the green pastures and big offers and big deals became a part of his daily routine. Later the offers turned small and the deals disappeared.

The fringe player doesn't miss the cheers and his standard of living doesn't undergo a dramatic change. My highest salary in baseball was twenty-three thousand dollars. In a few years I would be earning more than that, from telling people what a failure I was.

I was perfectly content with my life in Atlanta in 1969, working in the speaker's bureau for the Braves and doing the color on their telecasts. Now and then I did a turn at the Playboy Club, managed by a friend of mine, John Barnes, who had once run the business end of Al Hirt's club in New Orleans.

That year Barnes talked Al into opening a saloon next to the Playboy Club, featuring the Dixieland sound and look, with jazz and red wall fabric.

Hirt flew in for the opening of the club and John asked me to ride out to the airport with him to meet the great trumpet player. Al got off the plane wearing a Cossack hat and a full-length fur coat and a dark beard. You got this overpowering impression of *fur*. If he had landed in the Himalayas, the natives would have set traps for him.

It was because of Al Hirt that I became a frequent guest on the *Tonight Show*, a debt I will describe later.

Even before we shook hands I knew we would hit it off. I began to rip him immediately about his size. Al is the best kind of friend to have, the kind you can't embarrass, and vice versa. And we have both tried.

Every November I try to spend three weeks in New Orleans, working with Al in his club on Bourbon Street. It has become a tradition. We drink, we jam, we fish. I have never found a more fulfilling way to spend my time. The part I enjoy most is not drowning.

Once, after an all-night jam session at the club, we

·drove to Shell Beach, Louisiana, a forty-minute drive from New Orleans, to the fishing camp where Al keeps a boat. He filled a cooler with sandwiches and beer and booze. The party included his clarinetist, Pee Wee, and his brother, Little Gerald, who is the same size as Al and looks just like him except that his beard is red.

Al and I climbed into one boat, a twenty-eight-foot whaler, and the others, Pee Wee, Gerald and a couple of fellows from the club, climbed into a larger one. We were still feeling frisky from the night before when we headed for the bayous, fifteen or twenty miles out. It was a damp, chilly morning and Al had on his Russian outfit, the hat and coat, with the collar turned up. The other boat took the lead and we followed, with Al at the controls.

We were going wide open through the canals, curving and hooking, kicking up a spray on either side of us. I was sitting forward in the whaler and saw the first boat make a wide turn. We didn't seem to be slowing and I suddenly realized Al was going to have to cut it pretty short if we were going to make the turn. So I looked over my shoulder to say something and I discovered that Al was fast asleep.

When I realized there was no hope of making the turn I began to scream at Al, my face reddening in the wind. The swamps were coming up fast. When I saw he wasn't going to wake up, much less throttle back, I stood up in the front of the boat. I am not sure why I did, unless it was to get a closer look at the disaster rushing to meet us. When we hit the bog I was like a missile going through the saw grass.

I landed face down, arms out, covered with muck and mud, and with only two thoughts on my mind:
ALLIGATORS AND SNAKES.

I struggled to my feet, rising out of the primeval goop, which was like quicksand, and turned to walk back to the boat. What I saw looked like a scene from *Boom Town*, with mud flying thirty feet in the air, as though we had brought in oil. The engines were still wide open. When I pulled myself back aboard, Al was no longer sitting in the same spot. He was on his hands and knees with his head stuck in the bait box. I yanked him up by the back of his coat. He was still asleep, live shrimp dangling from his beard like weird Christmas ornaments.

The group on the other boat had watched with horror as we went aground. They came alongside, their faces pale and anxious. That was their meal ticket sitting there, slumped over the bait box. Gerald said, "Christ, what happened?"

"Al was showing me a scene from 'Victory at Sea'," I said. "The son of a bitch fell asleep, going thirty miles an hour. We were wide open."

Finally, Al yawned and opened his eyes. When it became obvious he was unhurt, we all started laughing so hard nobody could speak. He looked at us suspiciously as he picked the shrimp out of his beard.

Another time I went out with Al and Pee Wee. On the way in, Al decided to sleep and he stretched out on the floor between a fishing chair and the side of the boat. We docked, took off the fishing gear and unloaded, then woke him up. He didn't move. "Hey, I'm stuck," he yelled. "I can't get out."

We thought he was joking. But he was wedged in. I don't know if the boat shrank or Al expanded, but it took us fifteen minutes of maneuvering to get him out of there. The longer it took the more nervous and ill-tempered he got. He had visions of becoming a permanent fixture, like the figurehead on a Viking sailing vessel. I had a great plan for getting him out of there quickly, but we couldn't find a harpoon.

Al Hirt has a heart bigger than a bass fiddle. When I married my wife, Judy, he made all the arrangements, picking the day, the church, the minister, and the music. He likes people, enjoys their successes, and is just as comfortable in the company of a Catholic priest as he is in that of a baseball player.

One of his closest friends in New Orleans was the fire and police chaplain, Father Pete Rogers. He would tell people, proudly: "Fodda Pete leads the world in talking guys down offa bridges. How many you talked down this year, Fodda? Seventeen?" Al would shake his head. "He's a great man. If I was the boss I'd make him pope."

Al was a child prodigy who could play the trumpet at six. At Jesuit High, in New Orleans, he was on the football team as a sophomore, changing uniforms at the half so he could march with the band. His father, a cop, made him quit football to concentrate on his music.

He owned a small piece of the New Orleans Saints in the early years. At the games he would walk through the stands and swing into "When the Saints Go Marching In." The noise of the crowd would explode, until opposing teams complained they could not hear the signals. Now Al only plays for the Super Bowl and other religious holidays.

And while it is true that in professional sports many owners can sing the blues, Al Hirt is the only one I know who ever made a living at it.

I knew the first time we met that he was my kind of degenerate. When Al opened the club in Atlanta, he invited me to take the stage during his breaks. I did a half hour of what I usually do. After the show, Al's agent,

Jerry Purcell, approached me. He asked me if I'd like to appear on the *Tonight Show*.

I thought to myself, "Yeah, sure, the *Tonight Show*. Me and ten million other characters."

Ten days later, I found myself walking through a curtain and taking a seat on a couch next to Johnny Carson. Purcell had called and told me to fly to New York. I went on that night, after meeting with Carson's talent coordinator, Craig Tennis.

That night, for one of the few times in my life, I was scared spitless. I was not a comic. Never thought of myself as one. I had performed in nightclubs and not been nervous, partly because I was always half boiled. I walked around backstage, trying to keep straight in my mind what I wanted to say. No one knew who the hell I was. I don't remember seeing any other faces. There were people there, but they didn't seem to have faces. That was how I knew I was nervous.

Whatever I said that night worked. The audience laughed. After the show I heard Carson turn to Ed McMahon and ask, "Is this guy really a baseball player?"

Three weeks after the first time, I was invited back. What happened next was not exactly the classic show biz story, with instant stardom and headlines in *Variety*. Nor did I rush out and hire an agent named Max.

But my career began to move. My speaking fees rose. ABC hired me to be a part of the original crew for *Monday Night Baseball*. I was signed to be a guest host on other national shows, such as *The Midnight Special*. For a guy who spent the better part of his life behind a mask, I suddenly had a face people knew.

Whatever the benefits of being on the *Tonight Show*, I accepted them without guilt or pressure. I have been a guest always for the fun of it—mine, if not theirs. I don't consider what I do to be show business. Or journalism. Or an art form. Or even a business. I don't consider it to be a lot of things. I broadcast sports, mostly baseball. My work is to these other things what recess is to school.

But I saw quickly that the exposure on the *Tonight Show* was terrific, the best stage ever created for anyone with a movie, TV series, song, or toy to sell. Of course, what makes it all work is Johnny Carson, his wit, discipline, and generosity.

If I were to rate Carson in baseball terms, I would say he can do it all: hit, hit with power, field, and throw. I don't know if he can run. It is hard to tell about a man you usually see sitting behind a desk.

I am not sure that even his most devoted fans really understand what Carson has achieved. There is simply no one else in the field to compare with him, with the freshness and endurance of the show he has done night after night, year after year. Though himself a master comic, he is probably the finest straight man alive. I found him generous when it counts most, when no one is watching. During a station break, sitting there, chatting idly, he would coach me a little: "You ought to be saying more about this," or "drop in another line about that."

As many amateurs do, I had a habit of protecting myself by warning him: "You've probably heard this one . . ." Johnny assured me, "Hey, I don't hear every joke in the world."

There is a kind of art to the way he puts you at ease, once you slip into the chair next to his. You can sense the empathy he has for a struggling comic or singer. He is a contained and private man, even with his staff, but not in a selfish way. I admire him for trying to keep his personal life separate from the show and his career.

I have a theory about Carson. I believe one reason he has survived so long, and so well, is that he has less ego than his critics think. He isn't always drawn to the center of the stage. He doesn't have to be "on" all the time.

Some performers feel obligated to crack jokes to a bunch of strangers riding in an elevator. I understand that feeling. Part of my disposition demands that people find me funny or amusing. If I were on a show, or at a banquet, and the laughs didn't come, I would drop my pants. Anything. I would get that laugh.

Carson would merely shrug, do a Jack Benny pause, and go on to the next one.

I never had the same determination about baseball, and maybe that was my undoing. No matter how badly I wanted to get a base hit, I knew the other guy was trying to stop me. And I might be overmatched. In front of an audience, no one can stop me but myself. The audience is on your side (usually).

I feel fortunate to have been on the *Tonight Show* when there occurred one or more Unforgettable Moments. I was a guest the night Burt Reynolds sat in for Johnny, and another guest was his ex-wife, Judy Carne, the actress and comedienne, who had emerged as a star of the new hit show, *Laugh-In*.

Burt took me aside backstage and confided, a bit nervously, that they had not seen each other since their divorce, three years or so earlier. "I don't know what the hell is going to happen," he said, "so if it gets a little tense or shaky feel free to jump in."

I came out first, then Judy, then Helen Gurley Brown, the editor of *Cosmopolitan*. It was the night Helen suggested that Burt pose for the centerfold in *Cosmo*. We all played around with that thought for a while, and Burt asked if I would do such a thing. I said, "Sure. As long as they'd let me wear a pair of shin-guards, I'd be all right."

Judy teasingly suggested that he could cover himself with his hand, and Burt immediately shouted, "You mean MY ARM, MY ARM."

The show was bright and funny. My own impression was that there still existed a warm affection between Burt and Judy. And, of course, he did pose for *Cosmopolitan*.

I was on another night with a guest named Foster Brooks, listed on the schedule as a professor from Harvard, or some such. We chatted backstage. I did my bit, and then Foster was introduced, and the moment he walked through the curtain I thought, "Oh, jeezus, the guy is plastered. Fifteen minutes ago he was sober, now he's just destroyed." I was embarrassed for him, until I realized, about the time the audience did, that he was doing his drunk act. He was hilarious. And later I learned he doesn't drink at all.

Don Rickles used to tape his television series, *CPO Sharkey*, in the studio next to the *Tonight Show*, and I would drop by to watch him work. I discovered early that I could play on his insecurity. It's true; like most comics, Don is sensitive and his feelings are easily bruised.

We developed a kind of ritual. He always asked me how I liked his show.

"Okay," I would say, forcing the word. "It was okay."

"No, dammit, how did you like it?"

"It was okay," I repeated, "but it wasn't you."

Now Rickles would give me that ear-to-ear grin, the one that makes him look like he should be sitting on a lily pad. "No, really, what did you think?"

"Hey, Don, if you want me to say it was great, if that's what you need to hear, yeah, it was great."

Then I would walk away and, over my shoulder, I'd whisper, "But it's not you."

Rickles is a fanatic about baseball and most other sports. He wasn't big enough to play sports in school, he says, "But I was always the kid who helped the gym teacher take the names of those who weren't practicing."

He can create a caricature, even his own, with words. "Actually," he says, "I would like to be a general manager and have the guys come and get them girls and sit and drink with them and tell them what bad years they had."

Once I offered to leave tickets for him any time the Brewers were in town to play the California Angels. His eyes lighted up. He said, "My kid really loves baseball. Do you think you could take him down to the clubhouse and show him around?"

I promised I would. Rickles was in Las Vegas when the next trip rolled around, but I called his house and talked to his son, a pre-teenager.

"This is Bob Uecker," I said.

"So what?" he said.

"I promised your dad I'd leave you tickets to the ballgame."

"Who cares?" he said.

The kid didn't go to the game. To this day I think Rickles put him up to it. Or else he is a Dodger fan.

The real pleasure, for me, of being on the *Tonight Show* was the chance it provided to meet and work with Burt Reynolds and Rickles, and other guest hosts such as David Brenner, David Letterman, Bob Newhart, Robert Klein, David Hartman and Joey Bishop—all these in addition to Johnny.

Not even Avis has gotten more mileage out of being Number 2 than Ed McMahon. The friendship of Ed and John, their loyalty, the fun they have, is part of what makes the *Tonight Show* an appealing place to be. Another key is the quality of the staff, starting with Freddie de Cordova, the producer; Jack Grant, the stage manager; Craig Tennis, Ginny Fosdick, Shirley Woods, and the fellows in the booth, Bob Ostberg and Bobby Quinn.

Many a night I have sat backstage for hours after a show with Tommy Newsom or Doc Severinsen, and the guys in the band, having a few pops and talking baseball.

There is no need to pinpoint which night it was that almost didn't end, causing me to nearly miss a baseball broadcast for the only time in my career. Nor will I mention which member of the staff was with me when I so nearly disgraced myself.

I didn't think I had a problem when I missed my flight at 10:00 P.M. I could still catch a breakfast flight in time to join the Brewers in New York for the game the next evening against the Yankees. And I would not have had a problem, except for a slight miscalculation. My plane was not leaving from the airport where my friend dropped me that morning, in a condition less than clear-headed.

The clerks at the airline counter were bemused, and offered me a place to lie down, when I tried to explain that the Brewers were in New York, I was in the wrong airport, and my partner, Merle Harmon, was off some-where televising a World Football League game. There was no one else to do the radio broadcast.

While my ticket was being changed, I placed a frantic phone call to Bob Sullivan, the team's equipment man, at the hotel in New York. I tried to sound calm, but after about thirty seconds of his saying, "I can't understand you, what was that?" I realized it wasn't working.

Finally, I said, "Look, Sully, get hold of Tom Ferguson and go up to the booth when the game starts." (Ferguson, now a vice-president and traveling secretary with the Brewers, had started out as a clubhouse boy with the Braves.) "Just open the show for me. Talk about anything. Talk about the difference in laundry prices in New York and what it costs to clean the uniforms. I'll get there as early as I can."

It looked as though baseball was about to record another first. An equipment man was going to open the radio broadcast of a game between the Yankees and the Brewers. Alas, I got the next flight out, grabbed a cab to the ball park, and collapsed in the booth five minutes before air time.

I don't think Sully or Fergie will ever forgive me for depriving them of his big chance.

8. The Boys in the Booth

MY TRAVELS LED ME one summer to what I thought would be a quiet night in Cincinnati, the kind of night you expect in Cincinnati. I should have known better.

It was the Sunday before a Monday night baseball game, to be televised over ABC. Sharing my table in the hotel dining room were Howard Cosell and Chet Forte, our director.

Cosell and Forte have known each other for years, ever since Chet was the nation's leading scorer in basketball his senior year at Columbia. Once, before a game, Chet agreed to be a guest on Howard's radio show. As they waited for a cue, the little guard asked, "What are we going to talk about, Howard?"

"Relax, kid," said Cosell. "Leave it to me. You'll do fine."

Whereupon Howard opened the interview, turned to his guest and said, "Chet, is it true that some of your teammates hate to pass to you because you shoot so much?"

As Rick said to Louie on the airstrip at Casablanca, it was the start of a great relationship. Chet knows Cosell so well that he is able to finish most of his meals, no matter how much Howard agitates the people around him. And Howard is one of the most artful agitators of this or any other time.

In the middle of dinner, two young ladies approached our table to confirm that the voice they were hearing really belonged to Howard Cosell. On a good night, Howard's voice can be heard in every corner of a restaurant, into the kitchen, and out the service door.

An incurable flirt, although a harmless one, Howard soon had a dialogue going with the one named Cindy, a blonde in her early twenties. When he learned that their boyfriends were at a table a few feet away, he raised his voice and said, "If those fellows continue to bother you, my dear, I am going to send Bob Uecker over there to break their legs."

Every few minutes, Howard would toss off a line of that general substance, and I began to get some hard looks from their table. I made a mental note of the fact that both were young and burly and they were drinking, not eating. Cindy was enjoying Cosell's attention, and I guessed that it was only a matter of time until her friend came over and hauled her away. You get a premonition about those things and you can almost put a watch to it.

Soon enough, this brute of a guy sidled up to the table and stood there looking puzzled. He put a hand lightly on the girl's shoulder, but before he could speak Howard warned him, "If you touch Cindy again I'll have Uecker tear your head off."

At that point, I leaned across the table, my chin almost touching the butter dish, and whispered: "Howie, I just want you to know something. This guy may drop me, but if I have time to get off one punch, you're going down with me."

As luck would have it, he was as curious about Cosell as she was. There was no menace in him, although you would not have been reassured if all you had heard was his name and avocation. His name was Tyrone Malone and he drag-raced SEMIS. He invited us out to the hotel parking lot in the morning for a demonstration.

When we arrived at the parking lot after breakfast, we rubbed our eyes in disbelief. He had three huge trailers painted red, white, and blue, with enough chrome on them to make the Hell's Angels weep. Probably cost a half million each. A tractor was attached to the back of one. Behind another was a truck, on the back of which was a frozen whale, with a catwalk leading up to it so people could get a close look.

In the mouth of the whale was a photograph, an eight-by-ten glossy of Gregory Peck, taken from a scene in the movie *Moby Dick*.

I have no idea how long that whale had been on the back of that truck. I did not ask. All I know is, that odor was the foulest I have ever smelled in my life, and I am a guy who has been in a baseball locker room after a doubleheader when the second game went eighteen innings.

Naturally, Tyrone Malone wanted to know if one of us would like to join him for a run in the parking lot, to get a feeling for this kind of drag racing. Naturally, Howard and Chet insisted they could not deny me this honor.

I took a pack of cigarettes and tucked them in my shirt sleeve and rolled up the sleeve the way I had seen drag racers do in the movies. Then I climbed into the cab of that monster next to Tyrone Malone, who is a six-footer, about 230, with brown hair and arms larger than most people's legs. He was leaning out the window, watching Cindy kick out the tire blocks, and telling me out the side of his mouth how he travels to fairs all over the country, drag racing his semis. I noticed Cosell and Forte moving back, smiling and flashing me the victory sign.

Tyrone dropped it in gear—he put it on the floor, as they say in CB talk—and announced: "I'm going to put the hammer down now."

I said, "Do whatever you want. I'm just along for the ride."

Tires smoking, he proceeded to run that baby through the parking lot, one hundred fifty yards long, and had the truck up to sixty miles an hour when he hit the brake. I was amazed that a diesel that size could burn rubber. After that run, he backed up and made another. I rattled around in that cab like a dice in a cup, the truck was vibrating so hard.

When I stumbled out of the cab, Chet and Howard said they were trying to remember the last time they laughed so hard. They thought and thought, but didn't come up with anything.

The first six years of my career with ABC—I started in 1975—went pretty much in this vein, by accident or design I can't say. In a sense I am their off-the-wall editor, the Walter Mitty of the staff, the fellow who will try anything once, or even twice, if once is not enough.

The baseball strike of 1981 afforded me a rare chance to report on the world lumberjack championships at Hayward, Wisconsin, held every July, in what would normally be the heart of the hardball season.

Lumberjacking is a hugely popular sport in Australia and New Zealand, and in our upper central and north-western states, where the timber industry is strong. They

have a circuit, a mystique, and a following all their own,
like rodeo.

On the first day of competition one fellow fell seventy
feet and broke both his legs. In the speed climb, their
tools are a telephone lineman's spike and a safety rope.
They pull themselves to the top of a one-hundred-foot
pole cut from a California redwood—the amateurs stop
at seventy feet—ring a bell and then descend. Some go
down so quickly they scrape the skin off their arms. The
man who fell lost his safety strap.

These are among the strongest, bravest, craziest
characters in the world. I watched them and wondered
how our best athletes would compete against them. That
is, if they could get in the same kind of shape, able to
saw through a thirty-inch log in twenty-four seconds,
using a chain saw powered by a motorcycle engine.

In another event, they put a thirty-inch log between
their legs, raise an axe sharpened like a straight razor,
and at the gun split the log with three or four swings.
One guy had the wrong angle on one swing and almost
took off his right calf.

On the third day, there was a break from the log rolling
and axe swinging and pole climbing, and the TV crew
and the contestants relaxed on a moonlight sail along the
Namagagon (an old Indian word meaning fielder's
choice). I joined the jacks for drinks and good talk.

You would not mistake any of them for adagio
dancers. They were huge men, most with beards, their
humor robust and earthy. I found that they needled and
insulted each other just as baseball players do, and I
jumped right in.

As the boat glided along, and the drinks went down
smooth, I asked a New Zealander named Jim Wass if

what I had heard was true: that a lumberjack was so tough he could shave himself with an axe.

He said, yeah, it was true.

I told him Americans were tough, too, and I vaguely remember making a speech about Paul Bunyan and his blue ox Babe. At one point I asked Wass if he thought he could shave me, if I was having an appendectomy. I am not sure what the appendectomy had to do with anything, or where I had in mind his shaving me, but he said, yeah, he could.

The next day I had forgotten the whole conversation. We had set up our cameras in front of the grandstand, which encircled a small lake. There was a pier nearby where the lumberjacks did their chopping. We had a clear view of the pit on the other side, where two hundred-foot pole rose against the sky, and two men climbed at a time.

Our producer, Ellie Riger, came up to me and asked if I was ready to go. I thought she was talking about an interview, and I looked around me, sort of absently, and asked, "Anyone special you want me to talk to?"

She said, "No, I want you to do the shaving thing."

I said, "The shaving thing?"

She nodded.

Just then Jim Wass strolled up, cradling a five-pound, single-bladed axe. The conversation of the night before started to come back to me. I heard myself say, "Oh, God, I was only kidding about the appendicitis."

But I was game. And I knew instinctively that the film would be something nice to stick in the show, the tough-but-oh-so-gentle shtick. People were moving around and rearranging cameras. Wass took out a pumice stone and started sharpening his axe.

I watched closely for a moment, then asked, "Is this thing going to do the job?"

He spit on his arm, wet it down and shaved a patch of hair. Then he looked up at me and said, "Don't worry about it."

I still did not feel quite the level of confidence I felt the stunt demanded. Every few minutes Wass would test the blade. The third time he cut himself and a small ribbon of blood ran across his arm.

I thought to myself, maybe this guy isn't as good as he says he is, or else we should have gone home earlier last night. Out loud I said, "Look, try that on my arm." So I wet my arm and the hair wouldn't come off. The blade would not shave my arm. I wondered about my face. I don't consider myself vain, but whether you are handsome or ugly, it is nice to have a face.

It was too late to back out. I touched the blade with my finger and it really did feel sharp as a razor. So I sat on a log, and while the cameras rolled and a few people shot still pictures, Jim got out a can of cream and I lathered up. He proceeded to shave me just like a barber, lifting my nose, tightening the skin under my neck.

As soon as he started I could tell he knew what he was doing. I looked down at the ground where the wood chips were and I didn't see any blood, and I didn't hear anybody cry out, "Oh, shit!" So I knew it was okay.

If I have a weakness, or even a talent, for ideas that are slightly off center, it wasn't something I developed for network television. It is an extension of what I have been doing all my life.

A few years ago, as a promotion, the Brewers decided to inflate a hot-air balloon before a game at County Stadium. Merle Harmon suggested that we could make history by doing a part of the broadcast from inside the gondola of the balloon. Specifically, my part of the broadcast.

The balloon, they assured me, would be tethered to a light tower and would not be allowed to rise above a couple hundred feet. We would not ascent at all if the winds were over twelve hundred feet because the stadium was in the landing pattern for the airport in Milwaukee, Mitchell Field.

On Saturday morning, the day of the game, the first thing I did was check the weather. It was windy as hell outside. I felt a surge of relief as I left for the park.

People were clutching their hats and women's skirts were flapping as I walked through the press gate. Hotdog wrappers and small objects whipped through the stands. The players were bending against the wind as I walked onto the field.

And in front of the fence in center field, the ground crew was trying to blow up the balloon. They had decided to at least do the pregame show from the gondola. The pilot, or captain, was directing the work, which had a certain mad urgency about it. The gondola was on its side, and things began to go badly as soon as they turned on the gas. The guy who was fluffing up the silk was burned by the flamethrower they use to heat the air, and needed first aid.

The captain told me, over the howl of the wind, that we would get her airborne, have the ground crewmen hold the lines, and let the balloon float around the park for a while. The crowd would love it, he assured me.

I climbed into the gondola with the unhappiest-looking radio engineer in captivity. We went on the air, and I tried to do the pregame show, and the wind kept tipping over the gondola. We were bouncing up and down like a golf ball on a driveway, and the guys on the ground crew were running around in all directions, eight or ten of them, trying to hang on to the ropes.

We would get up about fifteen feet, then bang down and tip over. I was hanging on to a safety bar with one hand, holding on to the microphone with the other, and my feet kept flying out from under me. The captain was yelling up at us, telling me to stop kicking the gas tanks, I was letting out the air.

We must have looked like those early slow-motion films of the rockets that kept falling off the launching pad. After twenty minutes of banging up and down, the gondola turned over and dumped us out, like kittens from a basket. The crowd never did figure out what we were supposed to be doing, but they loved every turbulent minute of it. When the engineer and I crawled off the field, they cheered.

As far as I know, that was the last time anyone attempted to broadcast a baseball game from a hot-air balloon.

Given the record of my own playing days, the bosses at ABC clearly decided that I was qualified to work on a show called *The Superstars*. I have done several, and my speciality has become the unusual, if not impossible, scene-set.

The first *Superstars* show I ever helped report, in 1976, I made my arrival by sea. Bob Goodrich and Roger Goodman, the director and producer of the show, had brought the crew to the Bahamas, where the water sparkles in the noonday sun and the sands are as fine as salt. They asked if I could suggest something funny for the opener. I said the first thing that popped into my head: "Why don't I put on a suit of clothes and swim in?"

Their eyes got big as saucers. Bob said, "Would you really do it?"

When I saw them next they were toting a box from a discount store in Freeport. It contained a double-breasted coat, slacks, shirt, and tie. Fully dressed, I waded about one hundred yards out into the water.

On the beach, Al Michaels, Don Drysdale and Reggie Jackson opened the show. Al mentioned the fact that Bob Uecker was supposed to be there but had not yet arrived. In the background, you could see me behind them, fighting my way through the surf.

I finally made it ashore and dragged myself onto the catamaran. The three of them all shouted, "Uke's here," and Drysdale looked me over and asked what happened.

Panting, I replied, "I had some extra time, so instead of flying to Freeport I took a boat. We were having a party and it got kind of loud and the captain told us to quiet down. We ignored him and started throwing bottles over the rail with notes. He came back a second time and told us either to get quiet or he'd put me overboard. I told him he didn't have the guts, and that was the last thing I remember."

We were back in Freeport in 1976, after the Olympics in Montreal. This time we did a scene-set—in the middle of the summer—with me decked out in a full winter ski outfit, trying to ski down the sand to Frank Gifford, Don Meredith and Reggie Jackson. I had supposedly taken a wrong turn on the cross-country trail in Montreal, and ended up on the beach at Freeport.

The joke worked fine, except for the fact that I had never skied before, the boots were a size eight and a half and I wear a ten, and we had to do three or four takes while the sweat poured out of me as though from a

THE MAN
WHO MADE
MEDIOCRITY
FAMOUS.

Left, looking for my contact lens.

Below, umpire and batter (Doug Rader) pay no attention as I faint after finally catching this knuckleball.

The young player is easy prey for seductive baseball groupies such as Phyllis Diller.

D. ELLIOTT

Big league athletes are subjected to the most malicious and unfounded rumors (Number 6 is Clete Boyer).

Left, Dick Bertell (Cubs) slides in. The worst part of being a catcher is always having your back to the camera.

Right, Tony Cloninger (Braves) slides in.

Above, Cardinals call time to review my performance.

Below, Being forcibly removed from the game
(by my own team).

Here I am trying to score from second on a three-base hit; out on a close play.

Celebration in Cardinal clubhouse after team announced I would not play in 1967 World Series; Carl Warwick pours.

BOB
UECKER
MILWAUKEE BRAVES   C

One of my first bubble gum cards.

I tricked the Topps people by posing lefthanded; no one noticed.

CARDS

CATCHER
BOB UECKER

With Del Crandall and Joe Torre in Milwaukee; too bad the other two never made it.

Once again the guys told me it was a night game; with Del Crandall, Henry Aaron, and Ed Mathews.

Joe Garagiola made the airwaves safe for ex-catchers.

Original Monday Night Baseball crew—Warner Wolf, Bob Prince and Bob Uecker became household words (the household was in Menomonee Falls, Wisconsin).

The cleanest shave I ever had; at World Lumberjack
Championships.

Yes, Johnny, I am . . .

Al Hirt and me filming a segment for the
Un-American Sportsman.

Al Hirt points me to the stage, I think.

A man for all seasons.

Diving for scuba in the Bahamas.

Portrait of a star.

garden hose. Of course, I didn't really ski. I just sort of shuffled along, with a pole in each hand, yodeling as I went.

Another time I was to do an opening with Gifford at the swimming pool, and Frank wasn't told what to expect. I put on every piece of equipment I could find that would be used in the *Superstars*: flippers, a snorkel mask, a pair of size nineteen tennis shoes over my neck, a bowling ball in one hand and a tennis racket under my arm. I came walking out and Frank looked up from his commentary just in time to see me talking through the snorkel. He got on a laughing jag and it took us six takes to get through the scene.

They are a good gang to work with, Keith Jackson, Michaels, Gifford, the entire SS army. I have a special respect for Chet Forte, a small, dark, snappy fellow who has won seven or eight Emmy awards. More important, his sense of humor is as warped as mine.

It was Forte who came up with the idea for the Gorilla Trick.

For years, on the football side of Monday night, Cosell had conducted a running gag with me as the target. Whenever a team appeared with a mascot, or a fan dressed in a chicken suit, or as an owl or a robot or a horse, anything weird, Howard would say, "Well . . . I . . . see . . . Bob Uecker . . . is . . . here . . . tonight."

Then Gifford and Meredith and Fran Tarkenton picked it up and began to act as Howard's spotter: "Hey, Howard, there's Uecker," pointing to someone dressed as a bumblebee or a duck.

In December of 1980, Chet called me from Miami, where he was to direct a game between the Dolphins and

New England. I was to fly down a few days later to film
another *Superstars* show. He asked if I could fly in early,
and be there in time for the game.

A car was waiting for me at the airport Monday
afternoon. I was taken by the freight elevator to my room
in the Sonesta Beach Hotel, and stayed there until the
broadcasting crew—Cosell, Gifford and Tarkenton—left
for the Orange Bowl.

At the stadium I went directly to the truck and waited
there with Forte and Bob Goodrich. We watched the
game on the monitor. At one point, Chet punched up a
picture of a guy in a Santa Claus suit. Gifford said,
"There's Bob Uecker."

Cosell added, "Yes, he's just back from the baseball
winter meetings."

A canary feather all but fluttered from Chet Forte's
smiling lips. "Now's the time," he said. I felt like an
agent about to be dropped behind enemy lines. They had
gone to a costume store and purchased a gorilla outfit. I
slipped into the suit, walked into the end zone and put on
the mask. A technician with a hand-held camera was
ready to cue me as soon as the boys mentioned my name.

He gave me the cue.

I took off the gorilla mask.

A sort of gargling noise came from Cosell's throat.

It was beautiful.

If Howard Cosell personally found the answer to
poverty, high interest rates, and bad officiating, there
would be those who criticized him. The truth is, Howard
is the kind of guy who will pull you out of a ditch. He
performs countless acts of kindness, large and small,
without getting (or wanting) credit for them.

On the Sunday before the baseball strike, Cosell flew

into Kansas City for the telecast on Monday night of the game between the Royals and the Yankees. That afternoon the Brewers were in town.

Howard caught a cab from the airport to the park, sat in the booth the entire game and kept up a running repartee with my partners and me. I compared him to Richard Arlen, the old, stylish actor who always wore a scarf.

Howard repaid the compliment by saying, "Personally, Uke, I don't understand what Bud Selig sees in you or why he keeps you on the air."

At the end of the game, as he left the booth, I said, "Nice to have seen you, Howie."

He said, "I wish I could say the same."

When Cosell was unable to appear at a roast and toast in my honor in Milwaukee, he sent instead a tape-recorded message. Imagine you can hear Howard's voice—it should not be difficult—as you read these words.

"People who have studied baseball in Milwaukee from its very beginning usually associate the sport with such names as Aaron and Mathews, Spahn and Burdette and Logan and Adcock and Bruton, and all the rest from the halcyon days of the Braves.

"And now those who are contemporary think of Caldwell and Hisle and that brilliant band of youngsters who are on the field for a young and promising and exciting team. You can throw in Bando's name, if you will, though he is hardly worthy of mention [note: Sal Bando was at the banquet] . . . but the point is, those of us on the inside of the so-called national pastime *know* that only two names ever really mattered in Milwaukee baseball . . . Osinski and Uecker. Osinski, of the spitball, and Uecker, of the knuckle head. Matter of fact, Bob, the more I've watched your career in broadcasting, the more it has made me realize the truth of what I have so often said, that there are only two professions in America where you can begin at the top. Prostitution and sportscasting.

"I don't know what your plans are for the rest of your life, but one thing is certain. You have got to find the right business. What you are doing now is purely and simply not for you, Uke. People in the broadcasting industry know it. And in your heart you know it, too. You've got to get out. *Now.* Test yourself, even as you did in baseball; when you knew you stank and couldn't play you accepted the fact, hung around for years . . . unsung . . . a third-stringer, copying down Joe Garagiola's old jokes, trying to get a dry, understated delivery that would, from time to time, get you on the Carson show and would produce lower ratings than anyone else in the history of that show.

"Now is the time to face reality, because you're still young enough to get out. If it means unemployment for a year, two years, whatever, fine! You can surmount adversity. Remember, adversity is what produces character. Now you've got to take a whole new look at your life; who you are, where you're at, what you are all about. And when you deduce all of that you will find that you are NOTHING. You are all about NOTHING.

"I'm glad they are roasting you tonight, Uke. It's the right way to go out."

I can hear those words, or read them, and immediately tell you three things: He did it without notes. He did it in one take. He got as close to the bone as you can get—as Don Rickles and Jack Carter and the great insult artists have always done—without causing actual pain. He is brilliant.

We were doing a baseball telecast in Minneapolis once and at one point Howard used the word "truculent." He looked at me and said, "Obviously, you don't know what I am talking about." I said, "Sure I do. If you had a truck and I borrowed it, that would be a truck-you-lent." Howard waited a beat and said, "Need I say more?"

I will let you in on a secret. For all of his blather about the "tired litany of the ex-jocks," and his belief that the networks are too quick and eager to take them on, Cosell respects those who work at the craft. And, although the self-put-down is part of my style, I do work at mine. I prepare. On the air, I care about being right. I had everything to learn about voice and delivery and the technical side of broadcasting, and I spent ten years learning them. I didn't try to wisecrack my way through it.

And like Cosell, I am not afraid to be controversial. I was among the first to take a stand when the question arose of whether to admit women reporters into the locker rooms. The issue was clouded with passionate speeches about freedom of the press, the First Amendment, and equal rights.

Not many people wanted to tangle with the true, bedrock issue, which is: If you were a lady, and found yourself in a clubhouse with twenty-five naked guys, would you look?

As a personal matter, I favor admitting women sportswriters and sportcasters to the locker rooms. I can't think of any place that figures to be more instantly improved by a few whiffs of cologne. But I do suspect that the ladies get distracted, even though they insist that they need to be there to write their stories. Sometimes, when you read their articles the next day, in the middle of a word you will notice a capital letter.

Sure, I can understand why some of the players are embarrassed by having women around while they (the players) are undressed. I know when I'm working in the broadcasting booth, and I'm nude, I don't want strangers coming in there, either.

The transition from player to announcer was hard for me in only one respect. There is a great temptation, for a former player, to be overly critical of the athletes now on the field. I just have to watch myself. It would not be fair for me to expect these fellows to do things the way I did them. Not fair at all.

And that is why my role on the Monday night telecasts is so clearly defined. The other guys can get all excited about the home runs and no-hitters and triple plays. I'm the one who gets excited when the catcher holds on to a third strike—or the warmup tosses. If the catcher drops a pop foul, I'm the one who explains how he did it. I'm the only one who knows his frame of mind.

I am at my best on passed balls. I'm like the expert at a golf tournament, or a coach at halftime. I am able to diagram the play for the viewers.

Now back to you, Howard.

9. One Strike and We're All Out

IT WAS LIKE a variation of the question that George Patton once posed to his troops, and kids of a later generation asked their fathers: "What did you do in the war, Daddy?"

Only this time the question was: "What did you do during the strike?"

I heard it all over America in the midsummer of 1981. The stadiums were still idle when Johnny Carson, on the *Tonight Show*, asked me how I had been spending my time.

I told him I had planned to go back into the army. I figured I still owed them a few weeks, having gone AWOL in 1956 after a disagreement with my first sergeant during hand-grenade training. He wanted me to use a lob throw, the way they do in the movies. I preferred a baseball throw, which is more accurate and gets better distance. We argued and I went over the hill. And never went back.

Unfortunately, when I contacted my nearest army

recruiting office I learned that I had leave time coming, so I had to continue with my broadcasting.

Carson nodded and asked, "What are you going to do when you leave here?"

I said, "Tomorrow I'll be at Craters of the Moon, Idaho. I'm going around the country promoting un-sportsmanlike conduct school for kids. This is for youngsters in peewee football, basically. If the referee throws a flag, we encourage the kid to blow his nose on it and hand it back. Or they can slip a little Crazy Glue on the tip of his whistle and watch him pull his lip off."

Johnny did a double-take. *"Craters of the Moon, Idaho?"* he repeated.

The funny thing is, he thought I had made it up. But there really is such a town, at the foot of a volcano, just outside of Boise. It was the scene of the last major eruption in the United States prior to Mount St. Helens. When I was in Class C ball, our bus trips used to take us right by there, and the players would try to remember whose face the terrain reminded us of.

If the loss of eight weeks out of the 1981 season proved anything, it proved that baseball is as strong and elastic as ever. A strike nobody wanted was followed by a split-season plan that nobody seemed to like, and it all worked fine.

That hole in the middle of the schedule meant that there would be no twenty-game winners, and no hitters who drove in one hundred runs. But the teams came back to four new pennant races, and isn't that why God created September?

Like many fans, I had a sinking feeling that the rest of the season was going to be wiped out. In which case, these things would have happened:

—The company in the East that packs Delaware River mud into cans, to be used to rub the gloss off new baseballs, would have gone out of business (for years we have begged them to diversify).

—The sportswriters would have fanned out across the country, interviewing the players at their new jobs in feed stores and filling stations. They would have found Pete Rose on a sandlot in Philadelphia, crouched behind first base, waiting for a game to break out.

—With the billions saved by fans not buying tickets, parking their cars, or eating hot dogs, popcorn, and peanuts, the nation's economy might have turned around. People would have invested in the stock market or remodeled their homes. The rest would have gone into certificates of deposit.

It is a good thing the strike ended, after all. The longer it went on, the more people argued about it on radio call-in shows, and the harder the media tried to explain the issue, and the madder and more confused everybody got.

Both sides claimed that money was not the issue. The owners said they needed to be compensated, off the twenty-five-man roster, for a player lost to free agency. They needed this, they said, to protect the "competitive balance." The players said they liked the system the way it was. They were fighting, they said, to protect a right they had "won in court."

The issue was money. Since 1976, player salaries had tripled, thanks to the seven-figure, multi-year contracts the owners were tossing at so many free agents.

The compromise that ended the strike after fifty playing dates were canceled boiled down to this: The most a team can lose for signing a free agent is the twenty-fifth man on its roster. The fans really didn't care who won or who lost. The reaction of the fans was: Shut up and deal.

When the walkout began, I asked myself what I would have done if there had been a reason for striking when I was still a player, making my twenty grand or less? And there were probably a lot more reasons than there are now.

The players have a point when they ask why they should make life easier for the owners, just because the owners lack the discipline to do it themselves. On the other hand, it is pointless when the players say, as they have said repeatedly, "The owners wouldn't be paying those big salaries if they couldn't afford them." What has affording it got to do with anything? That is why credit cards were invented.

Given a choice between winning and running up costs, the owners unfailingly will choose to win. The need to win tops anything else that life can offer. They already know how it feels to be rich.

It is hard at this point to work up any sympathy for the players or the owners. When a utility infielder, or a pitcher who wins fourteen games, can sell himself for five hundred thousand dollars a year, even the players giggle softly. They also take the logical position that it isn't their duty to stop it.

If someone reminds them that they could kill the fowl that lays the golden egg, they are likely to shrug and respond, "The fowl will find a way to survive."

So the players want to keep the *status quo,* which, in the words of an old country preacher, is Latin for "de mess we is in." They like their freedom, their salaries, their thirty-five dollars a day in meal money. You give the average housewife thirty-five dollars a day and she will feed five people and have her hair done with the change.

An ex-player, who played for modest wages and probably got what he deserved, risks coming off like a sourbelly if he doesn't stand with the troops. But some of what the players say is wearing thin.

I heard Dave Parker, of the Pirates, tell an interviewer: "This game is harder than people think. Some days, we're out at the ball park eight or nine hours." An image of a pipefitter smashing his beer can through his TV screen came to mind.

After Andy Messersmith signed with Atlanta for a multi-year contract valued at a million and three-quarter dollars, a TV reporter asked why the negotiations had dragged out for months. "Was it just a matter of money," he asked, "or was there a principle involved?"

"Well," said the pitcher, "it started out as a money thing, but then it became a principle thing."

There was a kind of wild poetry to Andy's words. For most athletes today, the principle is clear: Grab it while you can. A career in pro sports is short, unlike that of a brain surgeon, or even a judge, who gets to sit down a lot.

A popular parlor game today is to wonder what players of the stature of Babe Ruth, Ty Cobb, Joe DiMaggio, or Ted Williams would bring in the current market. Clearly, Ruth would not receive a contract. He would get a partnership. As his widow once noted, "In my husband's day .280 hitters were not regarded as stars. They sat on the bench." I could have sat on the bench in Ruth's day, as easily as I did in my own.

In 1981, Dave Winfield, a lifetime .280 hitter, signed a ten-year contract with the New York Yankees said to be worth fifteen million dollars, not including bonus clauses. Winfield won his free agency after the San Diego Padre refused to meet his price or his personal demands. It was rumored that Dave wanted a veto in the event Ray Kroc, the McDonald's hamburger tycoon, decided to move the club. He also wanted a voice in team trades, more beef in the ground patties, and the right to change his name to Ronald McWinfield.

Do you remember when sports was the nation's escape from the hustle and bustle of everyday commerce? Now the athletes no longer merely sign contracts, they cut deals. The owners grumble, but pay, and some of them, such as George Steinbrenner and Ted Turner, don't even grumble. The players, of course, are having orgasms. Big money, rather than big performance, has created today's breed of superstar. When a streak hitter like Reggie Jackson can get a candy bar named after him, you conclude that the word "superstar" has been devalued. Or even the word "candy bar." Of course, I'm not jealous. I had one named after me, too. The Zero bar.

As a close observer of trends, I have kept myself prepared in the event of another strike. Radio stations recreated old games and newspapers ran old box scores during the last one. The owners missed an opportunity by not keeping the parks open and showing old baseball movies, such as *The Babe Ruth Story,* or *Pride of the Yankees,* or *The Winning Team,* which starred Ronnie Reagan.

I will continue to keep open as many options as I can. I still have several business ventures, including the various Bob Uecker academies. One is my famous Passed Ball School for kids. We teach young catchers how to miss the ball. I got the idea from people asking me what was the best way to catch a knuckleball. I told them that what worked for me was to wait for the ball to stop rolling, then just pick it up.

Of course, we also have adult education classes, such as our School for Tall-Building Climbers. I got this idea after two fellows climbed the World Trade Center in New York. The work is exciting, although I must admit that up to now our graduates have enjoyed very little success. Two of them failed to climb the C.N. Tower Building in Toronto, seventeen hundred feet high. We prefer that they start off with something smaller, such as a one-story building, or a Winnebago.

The most important warning we give our students, when they go through spring training, is: Don't touch the ledges! We consider this to be of life-and-death importance. There might be pigeon droppings on those ledges. The first time you grab the ledge, and you feel the pigeon droppings, your natural instinct is to say, "Aaagghh," and let go. And that is that.

During an earlier baseball strike—there have been three since 1972—I went into a sport fishing investment with my friend Al Hirt, the jazz trumpetist. We set up the company in a first-class way, printing a four-color brochure that showed Al floating in a swamp near New Orleans, with me sitting on top of his stomach with my feet in the water, and holding a rod.

I decided to back out of the deal after I found out how Al wanted to fish. One day we got into a boat and I looked around and didn't see any rods or reels, just a tackle box. He said not to worry about it. Fifteen miles out into the lake he cut off the motor, opened the tackle box and took out a stick of dynamite. I was appalled, having always considered myself a pretty good sportsman.

Jumbo, as his friends call him, lit the fuse and pitched the stick into the water. With his first cast we got about two hundred fish. After two or three more I said, "Look, I've had enough of this." With that he picked up another stick, lit the fuse, handed it to me and asked if I wanted to fish.

It was my only throw but I guess we got another one hundred fifty, and most of them were already cleaned. But that was the end of my sport fishing venture.

I hope there will never be another strike in baseball. But if there is, I won't be hurt. I can always go back into the service.

PART IV

Short Subjects

*In which he examines the mystique of
spring training, managers, umpires, and
the underworld of Little League.*

"Baseball owes me a lot. If I had to go into the tank to
lose a game, I would do it. I was not one of those
guys you had to go back two and three times to ask a
favor. And this is what I tell kids. You have to make
up your mind sooner or later, do you want to be good,
or do you want to be a tanker?"

10. It Happens Every Spring

"WELCOME TO DIAMOND THREE, men. During your stay here you will be taught the art of fighting snakebite, how to survive for days without water, and how to extract water from the cactus plants behind second base. You will never see people out here. You will learn not to care when dirt gets in your bubble gum. And you will be given a chance to play baseball at its very worst. Welcome to Diamond Three, men."

Okay, so it won't make the world forget General George Patton's speech to the troops on the eve of D-Day. But this was my welcome each spring to the other scrubs, in my role as honorary captain of the irregulars, with the Braves, the Cardinals, and the Phillies.

Spring training was my favorite part of the baseball season. One year, with the Phillies, I took a call in the clubhouse. Hanging up the phone, I turned to the fellows around me and said, casually, "It was my wife. She wanted to know where I've been all winter."

They call it the Dreamer's Month. In March, on paper,

every team looks stronger than it did a year ago, and they are counting heavily on a player they got in a trade with a team that no longer wanted him.

It's the same every year. The rituals never vary. A pitcher may have nothing more on the ball than the autograph of the league president, but in March they all look like the reincarnation of Walter Johnson.

In short, spring training is a fantasy land, a place where rookies with rheumatism hit .400 and the ball *sounds* louder, whether it is off the bat or landing ka-pow in the catcher's glove. Reality doesn't sink in until mid-April is on the calendar.

Even the managers can sometimes suspend their critical judgment. In places like Bradenton and Orlando, West Palm Beach and Phoenix, they say to themselves, "Well, we all start even, and why shouldn't it be me this year?"

They also tell each other things like: "So help me, Max, this kid could be another DiMaggio. His name is Higgins or Hawkins, I'm not sure which, but he's sensational . . . gawd, if he could only hit."

Many people have the impression that players in the spring stay on a pretty tough schedule. The first two weeks are the worst. The pitchers and the catchers have it harder than anybody. They pitchers have to run, run, run. The catchers never get a break. You have to stick around until everyone is finished throwing. Or throwing up.

Anybody could do it.

Actually, the biggest setback the American players ever suffered was when the Japanese teams began making occasional visits to Florida. You get an idea of how well-conditioned the American baseball player is when you see a runner in June try for three bases. No sight is more pathetic, no effort sorrier, than the spectacle of a baseball player legging out a triple.

Sliding into the bag, he calls time for the ostensible purpose of dusting off his uniform. But he is so pooped, so exhausted, that you begin to think that his next move is to call in the paramedics.

By contrast, the Japanese go to something that resembles a Marine boot camp. They scale mountains, run obstacle courses and climb ropes.

At major-league training camps in the U.S., the players will touch their toes, run a little and then play golf, unless they prefer to go fishing. Fishing will give a man a hell of a workout, especially if he gets a bite every three hours.

A majority of the players manage to avoid the Spartan existence of camp life itself. They bring along their families, renting places on the sands of Vero Beach and St. Petersburg—or, if they are based on the desert, they occupy an oasis with pools at Scottsdale, Arizona.

The Japanese player, summoned for reville at six in the morning, will go for his bowl of rice under a thatched roof before he is asked to take a run up Mt. Fuji. This is an athlete lean and hard, and ready to leg out a triple.

For me, personally, the great thing about spring training was working on my tan. When the weather was bad I would just get liquored up and do a handstand and bring a flush to my face. Works almost as well.

It used to be, in the days before football and basketball were played twelve months a year, and golf and tennis players were not yet let in through the front door of the country club, that sports fans had little to do but wait for the start of spring training. There were always those first exciting clues that told us the season was just around the corner.

You would see a page-one photograph of a few early arrivals doing sit-ups or hopscotching their way through a broken field of old tires, or two guys throwing a medicine ball at each other's stomachs, a fairly decent target at that stage of training.

Of course, from my own experience I can tell you that those photographs were usually faked. In all probability, the ball wasn't even a medicine ball. More likely it was a rubber beach ball and a photographer borrowed it from a little kid at the going rate of twenty-five cents an hour.

No doubt the players tossed it around for a total of five minutes, at which point they noticed the sun was out and retired to the clubhouse for a beer.

All of which goes to the very heart of what spring training is all about. Traditionally, baseball players have never deliberately built a muscle in their lives. They have believed that either you had muscles or you didn't. March was a month to get the old timing and coordination down pat, and to prepare your *head*. Once you were in the right frame of mind to open the season, why, your body had no choice but to go along.

If nothing else, spring training is a rich and bottomless source of stories that reflect the romance and character of the sport. In a less frantic age, the teams traveled by train, and the players had time to talk about the sport and to agitate each other and concoct all kinds of wild schemes. They would do this traveling north out of Florida, with the countryside flashing by the window. The scenery, it should be noted, is not particularly absorbing, unless you happen to be attracted to cabbage palms and slash pines.

So the boys would sit around thinking up subjects to argue about, and this led naturally enough to a lot of enduring tales. One of them concerns the grizzled old catcher, Clint Courtney, known in the pits as Scrap Iron.

In his salad days, Courtney caught for the old Washington Senators, and one spring he promoted a footrace between Pedro Ramos, his battery mate, and Don Hoak of the Cincinnati Reds.

The teams were barnstorming through the South together, and the players entered into one of those club-car arguments about who was faster, Ramos or Hoak.

Ramos was then a skinny young pitcher who could fly, but nobody realized it because he did not know how to get off to a proper start. And, besides, he seldom got a base hit. Courtney baited the Cincinnati players by claiming that, "Anybody beats my man, he's got to put his feet down real regular."

So they decided to hold the race before a game in Chattanooga at one hundred yards. The guys on both clubs started making bets, and on the way north Courtney would stroll through the Reds' part of the train hustling bets that would be covered by the Washington players. Altogether, the pot was rumored to have reached seven thousand dollars.

The day before the race, Courtney received permission to go on ahead of the clubs to set up the racing course at the Chattanooga ball park. The players arrived in a state of great excitement, and everyone lined up along the way, most of them near the finish line.

At the starting point, Hoak crouched in the accepted American track stance, while Ramos was standing up with his arms dangling at his sides. As everyone expected, Hoak got off on top. He quickly opened a lead of about five yards, and then—as Courtney told it—here came Pedro Ramos.

He cut the margin down gradually, caught Hoak, then

won it pulling away. Ramos beat him by about ten yards, to the utter amazement of the Cincinnati players.

They paid off, and some of them probably do not know to this day that Clint Courtney's course measured *one hundred and twenty yards*.

The phrase "It happens every spring" wasn't invented to describe the craziness and mass optimism that grips baseball at that special time of the year, but it fits as snugly as a catcher's mask.

In the spring, even the writers are easily spoiled and tend to be temperamental. Chicago scribes are the treasurers of a classic story that dates back to when big-league teams moved like wrestlers from town to town, picking up expense money as they headed north to open the season.

The hero of this story is T-Bone Otto, a legendary Chicago scribe who was covering the White Sox on a tour across West Texas. The White Sox had played the Giants in a town called Alpine, and after finishing his account of the game, T-Bone Otto turned upstream in search of refreshments.

He looked all over town, a task that didn't consume a great deal of time, and found every eatery shut as tight as the lid on a jar of bees. When he returned to his hotel, grouchy and thirsty and hungry, he was informed that the White Sox had just purchased the contract of Willie Kamm, an infielder of some promise. He sat down at his typewriter and pounded out a story that began:

"ALPINE—In this lousy little Texas town, where a man can't get anything to eat after 9:00 P.M., the White Sox today acquired Willie Kamm."

Of course, a fellow doesn't have to be clairvoyant to

guarantee that certain things will happen every spring, such as:

—A manager who has no one else to play the position will announce, dramatically, that a certain rookie has the job until he loses it.

—The players who grumble the most about how hard they are working will sneak away after a game to play eighteen holes of golf.

—At least one player will be laid up with a serious sunburn.

—A guy who never hit over .220 in his life will say that this year he is going to wait for his pitch.

—No matter how homely the waitress in the motel coffee shop is, she will get a big play from the single players if she owns a car.

—Every manager will say at least once in every interview that, "You can always use another pitcher."

—An actor will put on a uniform and work out with the Dodgers.

—A player who was traded from a contender to a last-place team will be quoted as saying that he is glad to be with a team that wants him.

—The manager of a second-division club will predict that his team will be improved. (He will be fired in August by the general manager who put the team together.)

—George Steinbrenner will make headlines by criticizing his manager, another owner, one or more of his players, or all of these.

—Billy Martin will make headlines by getting into a fight, or by not getting into a fight.

—Yogi Berra will be credited with a funny remark that was originally uttered by a nightclub comedian.

—A sports columnist will warn that salaries have

gotten so out of line, the fans are being turned off, and the sport is in danger of dying. (A new attendance record will be set.)

—A star player will not report to camp, threatening to retire unless his contract is renegotiated. Both sides will wind up happy. The club will announce that it did not renegotiate the contract, which would have set a poor precedent, but merely extended the contract at a slightly higher figure. The player will have missed the first week or two of camp, the most boring part.

It was a matter of pride with some players never to report to camp on time. Mike Marshall, the great relief pitcher who had his finest years with the Dodgers and the Expos, was always working toward another degree in college, and usually showed up around St. Patrick's Day to chase the snakes out of Florida.

My old friend Richie Allen sometimes arrived on schedule, then quickly disappeared for several days to have his eyes checked, or to go visit a sick horse.

One of the masters of this art was the colorful Orestes (Minnie) Minoso, who held out not for financial gain, but because he loved his native Cuba and preferred to stay there as late as possible in the spring. Once, reporting five days late to the Cleveland camp, he was met by an irritated Hank Greenberg, then the general manager of the Indians.

"Suppose," Hank asked Minoso, "you were in my position?"

"You mean if I Greenberg and you Minnie?" asked Minoso.

"Exactly," said Greenberg.

Minoso smiled. "I pat you on back and I say, 'Minnie, you good boy, you fine fellow, you hustle all the time. All right if you take off four-five days.''

• • •

As a player, I always went to spring training in Florida, where the early weather was often so cool and so wet that the newspapers had to use pictures of last year's bathing beauties dipping their toes into the Atlantic.

There is always a basic conflict in the spring between management and the players. The management prefers an environment that is almost hermetically sealed, and goes to great lengths to keep the players away from the nearest beach, fearing that such a place offers too much in the way of temptations. The players complain that there are never enough temptations.

I can assure you that both complaints are justified.

One of the things I hated most about spring training was the long bus rides starting at 5:00 A.M. to play another team across the state. As they say, everything gets easier with practice except getting up in the morning. I would never recommend to anyone getting up before dawn to drive to a spring training game between say, the Braves and the Red Sox. Still, it might be worth doing once. You would remember it a long time, and that would save having to do it again.

But it really boils down to keeping things in perspective.

Once, we headed out of our camp at West Palm Beach to play a B game against the Twins at Orlando. We followed the coastal highway to the Astronaut trail, until our bus took us past the launching pad at what was then Cape Kennedy.

Poised like a great white bullet on the gantry was the rocket that would carry the crew of one of the Apollo flights toward the moon. The bus grew quiet. All of those aboard swung their eyes to the window and stared out through the early-morning mist, across the Banana River, at the huge ship visible through the wispy clouds like the first glimpse of the mountain Bali H'ai, in the movie *South Pacific*.

Finally, the silence was broken. From the back of the bus came the voice of one of the players. "Gee," he said, "it makes our B team game with the Twins seem almost insignificant."

11. The Fearless Leaders

Do you have trouble keeping track of which manager is with which team, and who was there before him? Of course you do. It is like trying to understand the price index on pork futures. It is even more confusing than keeping up with the ex-husbands of the wife of New York's Governor Carey. It makes your eyeballs burn.

In 1961, Phil Wrigley, the reclusive owner of the Chicago Cubs, decided to try a perfectly bold experiment. He decided not to have any manager at all. Instead, he appointed what he called a board of rotating coaches, six of them, each to take his turn at the helm of the team for a period of weeks.

The experiment ended in 1963, after it had become apparent that the Cubs played just as miserably without a manager as they did with one, and thus were deprived of someone to take most of the blame.

Charley Metro happened to be the coach-of-the-month during a game in 1962, when he was ejected for arguing with an umpire. At that moment, Joey Amalfitano, an infielder with Houston, jumped out of the visitors' dugout, pointed to the Chicago coaches sitting in a row, and shouted across the field: "Okay, each of you guys move up one seat!"

I played under six different managers in my six years in the big leagues: Birdie Tebbetts, Johnny Keane, Red Schoendienst, Gene Mauch, Bobby Bragan and Luman Harris. They were an interesting cross-section. Tebbetts was warm, outgoing, fatherly, quick with a funny line. Mauch was smart, hot-tempered, always trying to stay three innings ahead of the other guy. He surprised me one night, when I saw him quietly holding hands with his wife in a hotel lobby during spring training.

Keane was a gentle, proud man, who had spent his life in the minors, whose playing career was ended by a beanball, who managed farm clubs for twenty years and had one year of glory, when the Cardinals won the pennant for him in 1964.

Red Schoendienst had been a championship player in Milwaukee and St. Louis. He was no back-slapper, but he was businesslike and fair. Bragan had the look of a bartender in a Gay Nineties saloon; he smoked cigars, played the piano, liked a good laugh. Luman Harris had pitched for Connie Mack, was tough but not threatening.

All of them had one thing in common. All of them, sooner or later, would get fired.

You conclude that it takes a special kind of rainbow chaser to want to be a baseball manager. When Dave Bristol was hired in Atlanta, a reporter asked if he considered himself a fiery type of manager. "I guess so," he replied, "I've been fired three times." Later, he moved on to the Giants, and was fired a fourth time.

Do you know what the average tenure is among big-league managers? Two and a half years. Migrant fruit picking is more secure than that.

You begin to get the idea that the best way to get a manager's job is to be delivering bottled water to the team's office at the moment the last one is getting fired.

When Gil Hodges was named the manager of the Washington Senators, his old Dodger boss, Walter Alston, was asked for his reaction. "I'm happy for him," said Alston, "that is, if you think becoming a big-league manager is a good thing to have happen to you."

Hodges inherited a last-place team in Washington. One night, after another loss, Frank Slocum, a former newsman who had worked in the commissioner's office, stood in his doorway. "The Dodgers just released Gino Cimoli," said Slocum, mentioning a former Hodges teammate, and an outfielder of average talents.

Wearily, Hodges looked up from his desk. "Why are you telling me this?" he asked.

"I thought he might be able to help you," replied Slocum.

"Frank," said Hodges, "did it ever occur to you that if I thought Gino Cimoli could help this club, I'd quit right now?"

No one in America is second-guessed more often, or hears more unwanted advice, than the manager of a big-league baseball team. And that includes the President, plumbers, and producers of X-rated movies.

The fact is, one manager in twenty can influence a team emotionally. Technically, in terms of the moves that are open to him, a manager can win or lose—actually decide the outcome—of possibly eight to ten games a year, tops.

When a team finishes poorly, and elects to bring in a new field leader without making any serious roster changes, it is doing just one thing. It is grandstanding for the fans, saying to them: "Your good ownership is doing something, trying to bring you, our deserving fans, a winner."

Richie Allen used to say that the public is mistaken when it believes that managers are fired. "They aren't fired," said Richie, "they are only moved, like players. If you want to say that managers are fired, then I've been fired four times." That is a new but not unreasonable way to look at the practice of teams' hiring managers who have been fired elsewhere, usually more than once.

Considering the nature of the job, and the insecurity of it, you tend to ask yourself why any sane person would pursue this line of work. The answer is twofold. First, the job satisfies the power needs that exist in most of us. A manager controls twenty-five men, plus a staff. His words are recorded by press, radio, and television. His friendship and company are sought by important people, at least while he remains on the job.

What else could the average manager do that would pay as well and be as exciting? They will tell you that it beats operating a crane, driving a bread truck or selling jock-straps.

Yet the pressure of the job changes them as people. Even playful, fun-loving types like Bobby Bragan and Luman Harris became more serious and touchy and less approachable.

With a few exceptions, they turn into people you have trouble recognizing. Of course, Walter Alston stayed the same: quiet, aloof, steady as a rock. Casey Stengel was nutty and lovable when he won, more so when he lost. And nothing will ever change Billy Martin. He was a tough s.o.b. when he played and when he managed and he will still be on the day he dies. And I love him for it.

I was fond of Bobby Bragan and I still am. He had a great sense of humor. But he was more fun to be around when he was a coach than when the Braves hired him as their manager.

The first thing Bobby did when we returned to Milwaukee after spring training was go out to the bullpen and tear down a kind of recreation room the boys had created out there. We had taken wire clippers and cut out part of a snow fence and made an area for ourselves. We built a table, suspended it from under the stands, and arranged several boxes and crates so you could play cards and eat. The little guy who drove the scooter to the pitcher's mound was named George, and we would bribe him with a dozen baseballs and have a steady supply of hot dogs or bratwurst or whatever we wanted.

Bragan knew about the arrangement from his days as a bullpen coach with Houston. So he had everything ripped out and fired poor George. Bobby, Bobby. Where did we go wrong?

The year before, when Bragan was a coach, the hot-foot was just epidemic in baseball. Players would be sitting on the bench, watching the game, and you would crawl from one end of the dugout to the other, sticking matches in their shoes and lighting them, and then see those feet go up like someone running the keyboard on a piano.

Inevitably, the action got more complicated. Guys would smoke a cigarette down to about a half inch and stick it in your belt loop—even while you were on the field. I looked up one time and our second baseman was out in the field, beating out flames on his uniform.

The planning was elaborate, like spies preparing to blow up a factory. One trick was to chew a stick of gum, then press it against the side of the victim's shoe. You could just touch the cigarette but to the gum and it would hold. When the cigarette burned down far enough, it would go right through the leather, and the poor fellow couldn't get his shoe off fast enough.

Or someone would light your shoelaces. All of a sudden your shoes split right down the middle and the laces were gone. It was just one piece of nonsense after another.

One day the Houston team came into County Stadium, and Turk Farrell found me before the game. He said, "Uke, bring some lighter fluid out to the bullpen." I said, "Whaddya gonna do?" He said, "Just bring it. We're gonna torch Bragan."

I gave Farrell a can of fluid and he stashed it under the bench in the visitors' bullpen. When the game started Bragan sat down and kept his eyes on the field. I was leaning as far over the rail of our bullpen as I could. When I saw what Farrell was doing I couldn't believe it. He took the cap off the can and sprayed it up and down Bragan's shoes and pants legs. Then he took a match and threw it on him. Poof! Bragan did the damndest dance I have ever seen. Chief Nok-a-homa, the Indian who sat out in the teepee and did a few war whoops whenever the Braves homered, would have been proud.

Bragan was a product of the Branch Rickey system with the old Brooklyn Dodgers, and had come up through their farm clubs. He could really get on your case. He had a way of talking out of the side of his mouth, like Humphrey Bogart, and he could dust you off equally well with a sarcastic line or with your basic seaman's vocabulary.

One day, after the Braves had moved to Atlanta, the team was in a wretched slump, and Bobby and Del Crandall had gotten into a shouting match at the end of a road trip. So Bobby decided to call a clubhouse meeting to clear the air. He just started moving from locker to locker, and as he faced each player he would curl his lip and say, "Bleep you." And on to the next one.

Finally, he was a few feet away from Eddie Mathews, who seldom made trouble, but didn't suffer insults, real or imagined, lightly. When Bobby got to him, Eddie's fists were curled. Bragan paused, looked at his eyes, said nothing, and moved on to the next locker. No one ever accused Bragan of being stupid.

Each manager loses in his own way. Sometimes, in his own several ways. Some swear, some sulk, some suffer in silence. When Alvin Dark managed the Giants, he once picked up a clubhouse stool and threw it against a wall, unfortunately catching a finger in a hinge and ripping off the tip of it. When he showed up in a bandage the next day, the players started calling him "Lefty." Alvin also quoted the Bible a lot.

Silent, stern Walter Alston once stopped a bus and challenged his entire team to a fistfight.

After his New York Mets lost a doubleheader, one of the games in twenty-three innings, Casey Stengel took off his clothes, stood in the middle of the locker room, and leaped straight in the air. When heads swiveled in his direction, he shrugged and said, "I just wanted to see if I was still alive."

And when Fred Hutchinson was managing the Reds, teams that followed them into a town could always tell if the Reds had lost by the number of light bulbs and chairs that had been smashed in the visitors' clubhouse.

In my time, the manager who was most respected by the players was Hutchinson. The one we most liked to be around was Stengel, and the one we most liked to analyze was Gene Mauch.

Eddie Kasko was with the Cardinals in 1957 when Hutch was the manager there, and pushing the Braves for first place. "He sent up Del Ennis to pinch-hit one night in a tight spot," recalled Kasko, "and Ennis had that real big bat—the U-1 model. He swung at a two-and-oh pitch and popped it up.

"Coming back to the dugout, he was swinging that bat like a cane, walking along in that slow, shuffling sort of walk that he had. You could see that Hutch was seething, and he was trying hard to control himself.

"Just as Ennis stepped down into the dugout, he flung his bat toward the bat rack, and out of the corner of his eye Hutch saw it go by. He wheeled around and grabbed it and, man, you should have seen the players on the Cardinal bench scatter. Hutch took the bat and began beating it against those concrete steps.

"Then he threw it to the floor and began stomping on it, and you know what? The damned thing wouldn't break. Finally, Hutch picked it up and gently handed it back to Ennis. 'Here,' he said, 'keep it. It has good wood in it.' "

Fred Hutchinson was the hero of some of baseball's favorite essays on fury and indignation. In his time he wrecked more chairs than Duncan Phyfe built. He was seldom misunderstood. He was never patronizing, not to his players or to the batboy or to reporters, not necessarily in order of importance. He was a big bear of a man, restless, with curly hair and sad eyes. He was not a phrasemaker, but he had the knack of saying a lot in a small space.

In the winter before the pennant race of 1964—that great race between the Cards, the Reds, and the

Phillies—the story broke that Hutch was ill with cancer. It was in June that the word spread that he was dying. We heard it from the Cincinnati players. "He started to smoke again and to take an occasional drink," said one. "He knew he wasn't going to whip it and he figured, what the hell, he might as well do the things he enjoyed doing."

He turned the team over to Dick Sisler in August. He would still visit the ball park and his picture would be in the paper the next day. His friends winced at the photographs of the drawn, gaunt face.

He was in the clubhouse on the last day of the season, the day the Reds lost the pennant. Dick Sisler nodded in his direction and told reporters: "I'm only sorry we couldn't have won it for that gentleman there."

Hutchinson overheard him. "I'm only sorry," he said, "they couldn't have won it for themselves."

I never played under Casey Stengel, but I played against him, and I am reasonably sure we would have gotten along. I can still see Casey marching out to the mound with his hands jammed in his back pockets, or punching the air with a fist in the dugout, or sprawled on the bench like Cleopatra on a barge, regaling his writers.

It was a tossup whether Stengel's most memorable achievement was winning ten pennants with the Yankees, or finishing tenth three times with the Mets, and making them the greatest failure story in history.

He had one of those rubbery faces that make a fellow look as if he could swallow his nose. His legs were so lumpy it looked as though he were smuggling walnuts in his stockings. The week that Casey retired from the Mets, at seventy-four, *Look* magazine ran a picture of him stalking away from some umpires after arguing about a call. The umpires were all laughing.

In his heyday with the Mets, Casey came to Florida one spring with his hair dyed a strange, youthful shade of henna. It was a wild sight, that hair, above that wrinkled, cartoon face. The Mets players could hardly wait to tell you about it.

"Have you seen Casey?" they braced each visitor. "He looks like Dorian Gray's UNCLE."

He had his faults. He could be rough and impatient with young players, and cruel in his opinions. Of Jimmy Piersall, who had a history of odd behavior, he said: "He's great, but you gotta play him in a cage." Bobby Richardson was straight as an arrow, and Casey didn't know what to make of it: "He doesn't smoke, doesn't drink, doesn't run around with girls and doesn't stay out late, and he still can't hit .250."

But Stengel believed in the miracle of being young. "I'll tell you about youth," he said. "Look how big it is. They break a record every day."

I especially liked what he said when he turned eighty-one, and a reporter asked what his plans were. "To tell you the truth," he said, "what I'd like to become is an astronaut."

12. The Men in Blue

MANY YEARS AGO, when the world was young, an umpire named Jocko Conlan called a strike on Richie Ashburn, a career .300 hitter then with the Phillies.

"Where was that pitch?" Ashburn snarled, in the ballplayers' traditional retort to a call that went against them.

Conlan, who had the look of a leprechaun, did not answer, at least not directly. What he said was, "Okay, *you* umpire. *You* call the next pitch."

Ashburn, startled, never moved his bat as the next one popped into the catcher's mitt. Over his shoulder, he peeked at Jocko and said, tentatively, "Strike?"

Obligingly, Jocko threw up his right hand and called a strike. Then he marched out and dusted off home plate and finally poked a finger in Ashburn's chest. "Richie," he said, "you have just had the only chance a hitter has ever had in the history of baseball to bat and umpire at the same time. And you blew it."

Sports is not a perfect society, so the day is still distant when it will be run on an honor system in which the players call their own pitches. In fact, the 1979 baseball season, when the regular umpires went on strike, may be as close as we ever get.

Let's face it. Umpiring is not an easy or a happy way to make a living. In the abuse they suffer, and the pay they get for it, you see an imbalance that can only be explained by their need to stay close to a game they can't resist. They are like the fellow who cleans up after the elephants at the circus, and whose complaints are greeted with the suggestion that he quit. "What?" he replies, "and give up show business?"

The sad truth is that baseball has never shown a great deal of heart in its treatment of the veteran umpires. The minimum pay for that position is $17,500, rising to a top of around forty grand. Some players probably pay their tailor more than most big-league umpires make.

You picture an ump walking to the mound when Nolan Ryan or Tommy John or Phil Niekro is pitching, and they turn their backs and tell him to leave a message with their answering service.

Clearly, the umpires feel underpaid in a job that requires them to make judgments on performers earning up to a million dollars a year. Their expenses are high. They accept insults as a matter of course. Injuries are common. Crowds are seldom more amused than when an umpire gets hit by a foul tip on an important part of his body.

And the life they lead is so lonely, they are never in danger of running into Margaret Trudeau or Bianca Jagger. They do not mingle with the players, fly on the same plane, or sleep in the same hotels.

Meanwhile, ballplayers collect thirty-three dollars a day for meals alone, and most of them sleep until noon.

Insulting the umpire is a pastime as old as baseball itself. In organized baseball's first recorded game, in 1846, a New York player named Davis was fined six cents for cussing the ump.

It was Tom Gorman, among the best of my time, who spoke for all the men in blue when he said: "Nobody ever says anything nice about an umpire, unless it's when he dies and then somebody writes in the paper, 'he was a good umpire.' Oh, once in a while a player will tell you that you worked a good game behind the plate, but when that happens, it's always the winning pitcher who says it."

Yet the umpires have a special role in the structure of baseball. To many fans, their lasting image of the sport is the Norman Rockwell drawing of the four umpires huddled under an umbrella, one holding out his hand, testing for rain.

At one time the top names in umpiring was Paparella, Passarella, Donatelli, Dascoli, Guglielmi and Secory. All of which moved Walker Cooper, the hard-bitten Cardinal catcher of the 1940s, to a wry complaint. "Every guy that gets off the boat," said Cooper, "has an indicator in his hand."

Mostly they were frustrated players who never got beyond the low minors. Today they are more likely to be the products of umpiring schools, who paid their dues in the college, amateur and minor-league ranks.

My impression is that umpires today are regarded with more respect than in the past, and television is at least partly responsible. Instant replays have supported their decisions a dramatically high percentage of the time.

The good ones last twenty years or more, and it helps if they have a sense of humor, and a little discretion. "Sometimes," I once heard Tom Gorman say, "when a game gets close and tempers are short, you hear things from the dugout and you holler at 'em to shut up, and if they don't you walk over to the bench. Now, when you've committed yourself that far, you gotta chase somebody. You don't want to hurt the club so you pick maybe a guy who pitched the day before and isn't gonna be called on again that day.

"So one particular day in Ebbets Field I'm gettin' it pretty good from the Dodger bench, and I finally walk over there and somebody has to go. So I point in just a general direction and I say, 'Yer outta here, John Van Cuyk,' because he'd pitched yesterday, you see, and I'm doing them a favor.

"Chuck Dressen is managing in Brooklyn then and he says, 'Who you want out?' And I repeat, 'Van Cuyk.' and Chuck says, 'That's great, but you'll have to yell a little louder because I sent him back to the Texas League last night.'"

On another occasion, Gorman was umpiring a game involving Leo Durocher's New York Giants. It so happened that Tom called a close play at first base against the Giants, and Durocher stormed out of the dugout and demanded: "Why, Tom, why?"

To distract him, Gorman said the first thing that came into his mind, which was: "Your first baseman had the wrong foot on the bag."

Well, that stopped Leo, and he went back to the dugout, trying to decide for himself just exactly what went wrong in his argument with Gorman. Then it dawned on him, and he rushed back out to the field. "Look, Tom," he said, "you've been umpiring in the big leagues for five or six years now. You mean to tell me that nobody ever told you that it didn't make any difference which foot the first baseman has on the bag?"

As a class, umpires are tireless storytellers, and one of the best was Jocko Conlan, who was five-seven, left-handed, and as Irish as Finian's Rainbow. Jocko added a lot of rich pages to baseball's anthology of humor. Some of his National-League squabbles with Frank Frisch and Leo Durocher were like vaudeville acts. He threw them out of the games many times, but only for just cause.

Once, when Frisch was managing the Pirates against the Giants on a stifling day in the Polo Grounds, he called for time and walked down to home plate from the third-base coaching box. "Jocko," asked Frank, "put me out of the game."

"What for?" asked Conlan.

"Because," said Frisch, "I can't stand this heat and I can't stand those .225 hitters I got. Besides, my feet are killing me. I want to go home and sit by my petunias."

Conlan, honorable man that he was, refused.

The first time I ever met Jocko, he called a strike on me and I stepped out of the box, making small animal noises. "That was no strike," I moaned.

"The next one is," he said, mildly.

I don't remember whether it was or not, but I swung anyway. You didn't take chances with Jocko.

One of Jocko's fondest memories was of the day he outsmarted a bloodthirsty crowd at Ebbets Field. It so happened that Bobby Bragan, who later managed the Braves, was then a young catcher for the Dodgers, and he was on first base when Pete Reiser tried to stretch a double with two out against the Chicago Cubs.

Reiser was out on a close play at third, and since the slower Bragan had not yet crossed the plate Conlan ruled that the Dodger run didn't count. Durocher charged out of the Dodger dugout and kicked dirt on Jocko's pants. Jocko kicked back. Beer bottles began to fly.

"Get out to second base or you'll be killed," yelled Charlie Grimm, the manager of the Cubs, but Jocko stood his ground. Police finally quieted the crowd.

After the game, the police wanted to give Jocko an escort to the nearest subway, but he felt that such a move would only encourage more serious fan reaction. So, suddenly, a man stepped through the exit gate from Ebbets Field wearing a tan suit, straw hat, bow tie, and two-toned shoes. It was Conlan, who walked safely past a mob of three thousand fans, looking for a guy in a blue suit.

Jocko had a temper you could fry fish on. He was unorthodox in his approach to his profesion. No one could ever say of Jocko that he didn't want to become involved. If Charlie Dressen had listened to him in 1951, Bobby Thomson might never have hit that historic home run for the Giants. As Dressen motioned to his bullpen, Jocko shook his head. "You're bringing in what? Branca? A fast-ball pitcher?"

Years later, Dressen did listen to him. In Milwaukee, Charlie was about to remove pitcher Bob Hendley. Jocko wandered out to the mound. "Whaddya wanta make a change for?" he asked. "He's pitching good." The astonished Dressen listened, and maybe, just maybe, he remembered that fateful day at the Polo Grounds in 1951. Charlie changed his mind. Hendley stayed in the game and threw a shutout.

13. Big League, Little League

I AGREE WITH Yogi Berra, who once said that Little League baseball is a very good thing because it keeps the parents off the streets.

Sure, parents get in the way. That's why they're parents. But as a father of a former Little-Leaguer, I think there are a number of things you can do to help your youngster if he is not in the starting lineup. You can invite the kid who is playing in front of him over to your house the night before a game, and serve him a rotten meal. Or you can volunteer to drive the car pool that day, and just not bother to pick that boy up.

Listen, it is hard not to get involved when your child is out there, fulfilling your hopes and dreams. My youngest son was the one who took after me. I was proud of him. In their championship game one year he struck out three times. And in the final inning, with the bases loaded, he let a ground ball go right through his legs to let in the winning run.

It was a great feeling for me, and I know he felt the

same way, as we walked to our car together while the other parents threw eggs and garbage at us and broke in our windshield.

If you don't care to take the game quite so seriously, that attitude is all right, too. You have to remember what the country was like before we had Little Leagues. Berra, the great Yankee catcher, who later managed the Yankees and the Mets, recalled: "When I was a kid we didn't have no lighted stadiums. We didn't always have nine to a side. We'd play with four kids, two on a side, and sometimes if we had only three we made that do, too. One would pitch, one hit and one shag. We'd do it for hours."

Possibly the greatest tribute ever paid to Little League baseball came in September of 1964, in Houston, on a night when the Phillies were in the process of blowing a pennant. A baby-faced rookie named Joe Morgan had beaten the Phillies with a bloop single in the last of the ninth. By the time Gene Mauch, the manager of the Phillies, got to the locker room he found several of his players bellying up to the buffet table, stuffing their faces.

"WE GOT BEAT," screamed Mauch, "by a guy who looks LIKE A LITTLE-LEAGUER." So saying, and with a mighty sweep of his arm, Mauch cleared the table. Barbecued spareribs, cold cuts, watermelon slices, potato salad all went flying, spattering the street clothes hanging in the nearest lockers. "Boy," said one player, "the food sure goes fast around here."

Let me assure you, there is nothing wrong in being a Little-Leaguer or even looking like one. The endurance of the sport depends on the very young.

On his last visit to Yankee Stadium, his voice reduced to a hoarse whisper by the cancer that was killing him,

Babe Ruth urged the parents of the country, "Start him when he's young, teach him to play baseball when he's four years old." How Babe arrived at that age isn't clear, but no doubt he just considered three to be too immature.

When Ty Cobb, his own days numbered, took a final look around him at the game he loved, he, too, made a plea to young America: "Boys," he said, "strive to master the lost arts of a great game. Unless you dedicate yourself to that task now, as the old-timers die off one by one, they will have vanished forever."

Ruth and Cobb and the guardians of the game knew something the critics cannot understand: that there was never a game more ideally suited than baseball to the soaring spirit, the boundless energy of the eternal child. "With a bat and a ball and his imagination," Branch Rickey once said, "a boy is a complete team."

Today, of course, Rickey would have amended that statement to read, "a boy . . . or a girl . . ."

No one ever spoke more lyrically about the game than Rickey, the man who invented the farm system, discovered Dizzy Dean, brought Jackie Robinson across the color line and never took a drink in his life, even though he once managed the St. Louis Browns. Rickey understood kids and knew why they were important to baseball. He also knew why baseball was important to them. "Leisure is wonderful in creative hands," he said. "It accounts for great architecture, great paintings, and great music. Leisure, however, is a damnable thing in the hands of an adolescent."

Added Rickey: "Baseball is a romance that begins when a boy is very young; it brings a diamond into his vision where the bases are fixed and the outfield is endless."

My own four kids—Leann, Steve, Sue Ann and

Bobby—grew up around ball parks. Like all kids, they had their heroes. After every game they wanted to go home with a different player.

When I was a preteen, we made do with a lump of something that passed for a baseball, and maybe a broom handle for a bat. We could always get up a game and there was never a problem finding a vacant lot—Rickey's endless outfield. In the forties and early fifties, America was still rich in vacant lots, the diamonds of our boyhood dreams. The great urban problems, the crisis of the inner cities to come, would change all that.

Today it is far easier to find a mini-stadium than a vacant lot. Kids thrive on the scale-model big-league world around them: bleachers, scoreboards, press boxes, p.a. systems. They cultivate the mannerisms . . . the tap of the bat to knock dirt off rubber-cleated shoes, hitching the belt, rubbing rosin on their hands, spitting bubble-gum juice across the plate.

I have no interest in getting into the question of whether Little-League baseball does more good than harm, if there is such a question. I like what Doug Rader, who played third base for Houston and San Diego, once said about his boyhood in Northbrook, Illinois: "When I was a kid my dad, and a few of the other dads, maybe four or five of them, helped out with out neighborhood team. We had a little park across the road from a tavern. They'd dump all the equipment and say, 'Okay, you boys get together and choose up teams and play.' Then they'd go across the street and have a couple of beers and let us play. Every hour or so my dad would stick his head out the door and walk to the edge of the road and rub his hand across his shirt a few times—you know, flashing me the hit-and-run sign, or something. That's how we practiced. The kid who has the ability, the desire, if he plays it will surface. You can't force it."

Personally, I think Little League is valuable because it reminds us that the Parkers and the Winfields and the Reggie Jacksons are getting paid millions to play a game that small boys play for free. Which is one reason I find it hard to give kids advice, and so do most big-leaguers. The kids will learn soon enough that they have to find a style of their own.

For example, Pete Rose doesn't recommend his base-sliding technique, which is usually head-first, but he thinks it is a safer way to slide, on the theory that you are less likely to break your belly than your ankle or your leg. Also, you usually get your picture in the paper.

When someone asked Doug Rader what advice he would give a kid, he suggested that they eat bubble-gum cards. "Not the gum," he said, "but the cards. They have lots of good information on them."

Players are not always comfortable offering advice to youngsters, usually for reasons that are well-founded. Henry Aaron was asked once if he would like to teach the art of hitting to young players. "I'd like it very much," he replied, "but I wouldn't teach 'em to do it my way. I'd try to help a young player with his own style— not mine.

"I've got a hitch in my swing and I hit off the wrong foot. I've done it the wrong way my whole career."

Mike Marshall, who made his reputation as a relief pitcher who could work every day, urges kid pitchers not to experiment with trick pitches. What he won't do is tell them how HE did it. "On national television one season," he said, "I demonstrated how to throw a screwball. I specifically warned that no youngster under the age of fifteen should attempt to place his arm in this position because of possible injury.

"Immediately, I was deluged with letters from kids saying how they were working on their screwball and would I please tell them more." He wouldn't, and he didn't.

If there is one serious piece of advice I could give to kids, it would be this: *swing the bat*. Little League develops pitchers and discourages hitters. A ball is easier to throw than to hit at that age—at any age, actually. Nothing kills interest like failure. The kid who keeps striking out considers himself a failure, and he looks for something else to do.

Mike Marshall is right. A manager should not let his kid pitchers throw a screwball or a curve ball. Not only because of the risk to a young arm, but because such pitches take the fun out of the game for the kids who can't hit them.

I would tell a manager something else: No matter what the score, or the situation, let your hitters swing on a three-ball and no-strike count. Chances are he'll get a pitch he can handle, and if he does why shouldn't he swing? He's there to have fun. And a bat is no fun unless you swing it. Trust me.

In one respect, the Little Leagues achieved something that the big fellows never have: a really international World Series. An English writer, Brian Glanville, of London, once commented on this obvious American conceit: "It's very quaint. One team in the United States plays another team in the United States and is declared 'World' champion. We used to call the game 'rounders,' you know."

For years, the Little League World Series was regularly won by teams from Mexico, Taiwan, and Japan. There was a memorable scene in 1958, when a band of ragamuffins from Monterrey won the championship for the second year in a row.

The Mexican pitcher, a five-six beanpole named Hector Torres— who later made it to the majors as a shortstop—walked halfway to home plate as the final game came down to its last out. Mexico led, 10-1, over Kankakee, Illinois, with the bases empty and two away.

Torres doffed his cap and bowed low to his catcher, Carlos Trevino. *"Te dedico este bateador,"* he said. The hitter, not understanding Spanish, didn't know he had been insulted. Torres had said to his catcher: "I dedicate this batter to you."

It was a lovely gesture, and I am saddened to note that never in my entire career did a pitcher dedicate a hitter to me.

I owe a debt to Little-League baseball, and the debt should be acknowledged here and now. I was sitting by a pool with Merle Harmon in Anaheim, taking the rays, when Merle answered a call from Dennis Lewin, of ABC, in New York.

When Merle returned to his seat, he grinned and said ABC wanted me to fly to Williamsport, Pennsylvania, to telecast the Little League World Series with Keith Jackson.

I really didn't want to go. The Brewers had just arrived for a series against the Angels, and this was my first year (1973) of sharing the play-by-play with Harmon. I didn't feel in a position to be asking for favors. Also, working with a network, any network, was not one of my obsessions. I was not then, or now, a goal-oriented person.

Merle talked me into it. "You never know where it

might lead," he said. I flew across the country to Williamsport without even knowing what I would be paid—one thousand dollars, as it turned out. I did the Series with Keith and rejoined the Brewers.

A year later, ABC asked me to fly to New York to audition for the color spot on their Monday night baseball package, which would begin the next season. With Bob Prince, who was to do the play-by-play, I watched a silent videotape of a World Series game and recreated the action. They must have liked what they heard. I have been doing it ever since.

I guess that makes me another graduate of the Little Leagues.

PART V

Touching Some
Extra Bases

*In which he describes some of the great
players he admired, and some whose paths
he crossed, and some who were just his
kind of dustball. And a few stories straight
from the Hot Stove League.*

"The basic idea behind this book was to cover my
career and just talk about what a great guy I was. I
don't see how we can miss."

14. A Few of My Friends, and Then Some

WHEN A TEAM he was managing ended its season in winter ball, Doug Rader made a point of saying goodbye to one of his pitchers in the clubhouse. He told the fellow, a kind of nutcake, that he intended to request his services at Hawaii, where Rader would skipper San Diego's top farm club the next season.

The pitcher shook his head. "The way my arm feels right now," he said, frowning, "I don't even know if I'll be playing next season."

Rader jabbed him in the chest with a finger. "I don't care if you can throw or not," he said. "Every team needs a sick individual on it, and for me you're *it*."

Known in his playing days as the Red Rooster, Rader did not mean sick-sick, as in unhealthy. He meant goofy, off-the-wall, unpredictable, *weird*. It is a role Doug played on every team that employed him. As I did.

For the most part, Rader—the ex-Padre, ex-Astro, lifelong snowflake—was correct. But more and more today's teams are making an effort, a conscious one, I think, to get along without that kind of free spirit. The teams I see now, in my role as a broadcaster, can best be described as well-behaved, well-dressed young men building a base for that day when their arms or legs give out.

I can sum them up in two words: basically boring.

That remark is not a complaint, mind you, just a comparison. The teams of my day were less colorful than those of Babe Ruth's day, but the gap wasn't nearly as wide. We specialized in miscellaneous characters and that-was-burlesque humor. Hardly a flight took place that did not produce a scuffle, some tipsy barbershop harmony, or the occasional scream of a hostess darting up the aisle.

You never doubted the truth of the stories you heard, and an explanation was seldom required. No one ever explained what Turk Farrell was doing one night chasing Jim Owens through the halls of a Philadelphia hotel, both of them naked as newborn babes. They had been members of the famed Dalton Gang with the Phillies, later traded to Houston.

Farrell claimed that Owens had stabbed him with one of those desk pens you dip in an inkwell, and he had a blue dot on his bare hip to prove it.

In the 1960s, the cutting personal reference was as much a part of the game as hitting into a double play. A young catcher who had a low opinion of a veteran player's intellect didn't hesitate to let him know it: "Norm," he told him, "if it wasn't for baseball you'd be selling apples on a corner."

When a rookie infielder, a bonus baby, found himself in a terrible batting slump, an old hand advised him to switch to a lighter bat. The rookie said, yeah, with a lighter bat he could get around on the ball faster. The veteran said, "No, but it'll be easier to carry back to the dugout after you strike out."

I still hear that kind of affectionate cruelty in the bantering among the players of the 1980s. These players are smarter. I am not sure that they are better educated. And I would be reluctant to say that they love the game less than the players did when I broke in. But there is no doubt in my mind that they take themselves more seriously. Big money has that effect on people. It is like making out your will.

Today's players are more settled, more secure in their planning. Most of them have already picked out other careers. They have investments. They want to be seen and treated as responsible people. When the players board a plane, you see so many three-piece suits it looks like they have evacuated the offices of E. F. Hutton. You get the impression that management now picks a roster with the idea of getting the best possible team photograph.

When I was making around ten thousand dollars a year, you would begin to think about an off-season job in September. You thought in terms of unloading a beer truck.

Baseball has gone through such cycles before. The teams may go back to looking for players out of the Gashouse Gang, or the stick-it-in-his-ear school. Baseball people are great copycats. They will all try whatever wins for someone else. If one club finds a guy with hair all over his body and one eye in the middle of his forehead, and he eats glass and hits .400, soon you are going to see a lot of hairy, one-eyed glass-eaters around the league.

For now some of the fun is gone, and you don't have

to hunt long or far to understand why. When even the fringe players are knocking down a hundred grand a year, and more, you are not encouraged to cut up and take chances. In the past, it wasn't just the scrubs who horsed around, it was the stars, Mantle, Mays, Aaron, Spahn, who had the most laughs.

Of course, the conditions are not as favorable. You no longer have the wooden floors in the clubhouse, where you could nail a guy's shoes to the deck. Even the old bullpens are gone. Now they are all in the open, so the fans—and the manager—can see whatever is going on.

We used to run a closed society out there. Most of the people in the bullpen didn't care about starting. At least, we said we didn't. When a regular came down just to visit we chased him away. I mean, we protected our *turf*. It was like driving the snakes out of Ireland. Once, with the Phillies, Chris Short slipped down to the bullpen to hide from Gene Mauch before a game. He settled himself in a wheelbarrow and took a nap. While he slept, the rest of us tied him to the barrow, working like rodeo cowboys, using the ropes and chains the ground crew kept to drag the infield. When he woke up, and discovered he couldn't move, Chris yelled and cursed and carried on something fierce. We finally let him out fifteen minutes after the game had started.

A statement ought to be made about baseball humor. At its liveliest, it is crude and shameless and irreverent. It is army humor, with more sweat. For a few hours every day nothing exists outside the ball park. You are thrown together in this tight, remote, womanless (most of the time) world, and whether or not you like each other a bond is forged.

The team is everything. You are glad to belong, to be a

part of it, speeding along with it, or stumbling, as the case may be. Your body may be on a bus or a plane or in a hotel, but your mind is in the locker room, and the laughs grow out of this experience.

Two examples: In the early 1960s, a writer for *Sports Illustrated* heard that John Bateman, a catcher for the Houston Astros, was one of the funniest men in the big leagues. He followed the team for a week or two and kept asking for examples of Bateman's wit. The players assured him that the supply was endless, but nothing popped quickly to mind.

At last, one night behind the batting cage, an outfielder named Howie Goss approached the writer. "I've thought of a story that typifies Bateman's sense of humor," he said, "but I'm not sure you can use it."

"Don't worry about that," the man from *Sports Illustrated* said, whipping out his pad and pen. "I can fix the language."

Goss shrugged. "Well, one day X (the team's most popular player) was sitting on the crapper"—the writer's pen stopped in mid-stroke—"and Bateman called out, 'Hey, kid, did you weigh yourself before you got on there?'

"X said, no, why, and Bateman answered, 'In case you fall in, we want to know how much shit we have to fish out before we get to you.'"

The writer put his pad back in his hip pocket, gave a feeble laugh, and walked away.

A story out of Seattle a few years ago, when an expansion team was trying to survive there, captures some of the *esprit* of the bullpen. In the late innings of a losing game the bullpen was busy, as usual.

Ray Oyler, a reserve infielder, was warming up one of

the pitchers when he missed a sinker, and it caught him right on the cup. The pitch didn't bounce or tip his glove, it simply landed a direct hit. You hardly ever hear of that happening. The "twang" of ball striking metal echoed into the stands.

Oyler pitched forward, almost in slow motion, like a Tom-and-Jerry cartoon, and on all fours he started crawling toward the dugout, unable to cry out in pain or even make a sound. The players in the bullpen began to laugh, and the action came to a stop. He kept crawling. The laughter spread to the guys on the bench. Soon they were out of control. In the stands, the fans looked on, fascinated. Oyler reached the dugout, pulled himself onto a rail and threw up.

They were getting beat, and on the field people were running around the bases, and the Seattle players couldn't stop laughing. The manager, Joe Schultz, had to take off his glasses, wipe his eyes, and hide his head in the arm of his jacket.

The stadiums are bigger and fancier, the players higher paid and more secure, the fans less worshipful. But the baseball mentality hasn't changed in a hundred years.

Trust me. This is no mournful wail for a game that once was and will never be again. Memory can be a con man. Nostalgia should go back where it came from. The crackers in the ole cracker barrel were usually stale. Penny candy rotted your teeth just as fast when it didn't cost a quarter. Trains were dusty and bumpy and you were always getting a cinder in your eye.

As a product, baseball may be better than ever. I don't think so, but who knows? It is tempting to compare players, teams, and eras, and part of the fun is knowing that no one can prove us wrong. The arguments are forever. It is like judging pretty girls on a beach. The last one to walk by wins.

I am not sure when it dawned on me that the 1960s are the good old days to the young players of the 1980s. To this generation, Aaron, Allen, Mathews, Spahn, and Gibson, even Bo Belinsky, who lost more games than he won, are part of the mythology of the sport. I don't remember growing older. When did they?

It begins to sound like a singer or comic doing a Las Vegas lounge shtick when you say that, in the end, what lasts are the friendships you made. After you have blown the money and forgotten the batting averages and lost track of the wins and losses, the only thing that counts is the people.

Now I might not go quite that far. I knew some players whose friendship you would not have wished on J. R. Ewing, and who seemed to remember the exact count on every hit in their career. But I consider myself fortunate to have played on teams with men who, at what they did, were among the best, or the strangest, or the funniest who ever lived. I've touched on some of them earlier, but here they are again, a few of however many there were:

The Hammer

Henry Louis Aaron, as he is known in the *Baseball Register*, was the most underrated player of my time, and his. It may seem strange to make such a claim on behalf of the man who broke Babe Ruth's lifetime home run record, and went through the longest countdown the game has ever known.

But that's the point. Not until he collected his six hundredth homer in 1972, at the age of thirty-seven, did the press and fans catch on to what his opponents had always known: that Hank Aaron was one of a kind.

He had three things going against him: 1) He didn't play in New York or Los Angeles; 2) he was too predictable, meaning that most years he would get his forty homers, drive in a hundred runs and hit .320 . . . no surprises here; 3) he lacked showmanship. His cap didn't fly off when he caught a fly ball, and after a game you never saw him eat twenty hot dogs and wash them down with a six-pack of beer.

When Henry reached the majors in 1954, Ted Williams and Stan Musial were already legends. Willie Mays and Mickey Mantle were coming into their own. Aaron had been in the league eight or ten years—certainly it was after I had joined the Braves in 1962—before his name was mentioned with any of those. We would argue his case with out-of-town writers, and their eyes would glaze over.

I asked him once if he felt slighted. He said, "What difference does it make?"

I said, "You may not believe in beauty contests, but if you're in one you want the judges to vote you purty."

He shrugged.

I was a broadcaster with the Brewers, in 1976, when Aaron played out his string in Milwaukee, and hit the last of his 755 home runs. If you were to ask me what was the most remarkable thing about him, I would not single out any of the obvious points, his endurance, his power, his wrists. He had the quickest wrists I ever saw. Baseball scouts talked about Aaron's wrists the way male moviegoers of another time talked about Betty Grable's legs.

But none of it impressed me so much as how stable Henry has been. With the possible exception of Stan

Musial, it isn't likely that anyone played twenty years in the majors and changed less than Henry Aaron. For a fellow who came out of Southern poverty, who was one of the last players signed out of the Negro Leagues, and who met his share of prejudice on the way up, Henry seemed to have no rage in him.

One anecdote followed Aaron all through his career. The story revealed something about his nature. It also revealed how hard it was for the writers to come up with anecdotes about Henry.

During the 1957 World Series, the Yankee catcher, Yogi Berra, noticed that Aaron held the bat in a way contrary to the usual baseball practice. "Hey," said Berra, from his squat, "you got the bat facing the wrong way. Turn it around so you can see the trademark."

Henry continued to stare at the pitcher's mound. Out the side of his mouth, he said, "Didn't come up here to read. Came up here to hit."

Other players would marvel when they heard that Henry actually hit cross-handed when he signed with the Indianapolis Clowns. That is like playing a piano in handcuffs. In his first day in spring training, he began rifling base hits all over the park and the manager asked why he gripped the bat the way he did. Henry said it was the only way he knew.

Henry never confused chatter with conversation. He liked his privacy and his natural caution was sometimes taken for distrust.

Once he sat on a stool in front of his locker, an hour or so before game time, sorting two baskets filled with fan mail. His attention was diverted by a mild commotion at the clubhouse door.

"You can't come in here," an attendant was saying,

loudly, to a fellow who turned out to be Leroy Nieman, the sports artist.

"I just want to make a few sketches of Aaron," said Nieman, looking past the guard and catching the eye of Henry, who said nothing.

"We got a rule," said the attendant. "You can't come in here."

Nieman unzipped a leather case and began removing a sketchbook and other implements. "Okay," he said, agreeably, "then I'll just draw him right here, from the doorway." Twenty or thirty feet from his subject, he calmly sketched away.

Henry glanced up now and then as he disposed of the letters, flipping them into one basket or the other. Several minutes passed. Then the clubhouse man reappeared and motioned to the artist: "Hank says it's okay for you to come in."

Nieman pulled up a chair and without a word returned to his work. Aaron followed each stroke with interest. After a few minutes, he craned his neck to inspect the sketch. "You're not getting me," he said, with firmness. "You're not getting me."

"Take it easy," said Nieman. "You don't hit a homer every time up. I'm not finished."

More strokes. More color came alive on the sheet. "That's it," said Henry, his voice rising. "Now you got me. You got me."

When Nieman finished, Henry asked if he could have the sketch. "I don't give my work away," he was told.

Aaron looked startled. "People usually give me things like that," he said.

"I don't," said Nieman. "If you want mine you pay for it." He has a rack of black hair and a mustache that divides his face in half, and he is not intimidated by athletes. He grinned and added, "But I'll make a deal with you."

Nieman was in Atlanta to teach art classes to ghetto kids. He offered to trade the sketch if Aaron would pose for one of his classes. Henry agreed. You can guess how the kids reacted when their model turned out to be the home run king.

Henry did not talk much, even in the clubhouse, and what you learned about his early life came from stray remarks, spaced far apart. He was one of eight children, supported by a father who worked on the drydocks in Mobile. At eighteen, he joined the Indianapolis Clowns, where the meal money was two dollars a day. The players ate mostly out of grocery stores, on lunchmeat sandwiches.

He weighed 180 when he reached the big leagues, and he weighed the same when he retired. He was a small man as home run hitters go. He lacked the muscle or power of a Frank Robinson or a Frank Howard or a Willie Mays. He drove the ball with perfect wrists and perfect timing.

People used to say that the difference between Mays and Aaron was this: Willie attacked the game; Henry got it to cooperate. He was as smooth and effortless as a swan gliding along a lake.

Not many fans ever knew that the Giants could have had Mays and Aaron in the same outfield. Both the Giants and the Braves made bids after scouting him with the Clowns. Both wanted to start him in Class C, but the Braves offered him a Class A contract, worth two hundred dollars more a month. And for that difference, the Giants lost the man who would one day hit more home runs than Babe Ruth.

The Good-bye Kid

No player was more stubborn or more talented than Richie Allen, but he made up for it by being misunderstood.

Allen played for the Phillies, twice, the Cardinals, Dodgers, White Sox, and Oakland. Atlanta owned his contract at one time, but he never reported. He was described as a rebel, a militant, a truant, and a night walker. He was accused of having a drinking problem, an attitude problem and a keeping-track-of-time problem.

My kind of guy.

In truth, there was nothing wrong with Richie Allen's heart, or his instincts, but he felt a powerful resistance to having his mind made up for him. If he was pushed he tended to push back.

In baseball, this is the quickest way I know to be labeled a troublemaker. Once the label is attached it is hell to get off. Allen was the classic example of the guy who felt free only while he was playing the game. The rest of the time he wanted the world to go away. His clock started when the first pitch was thrown.

The Phillies signed Richie out of high school, at seventeen. He had the biceps of a heavyweight fighter and a thirty-inch waist and he could crush a baseball. He was just a kid, but so strong that people forgot to treat him like one—until he reached the majors. The wrong time and place.

I understood that part of him. We sat and talked and drank far into the night when we were teammates in Philadelphia, and he told me things I don't think he shared with many others.

His mother drove him to the airport, in Pittsburgh, when he caught the plane for his first trip to spring training. He was from the town of Wampum, in the same area of Pennsylvania that produced Joe Namath.

All the way to the airport, his mother gave Richie instructions on how to act. She had raised eight kids by doing day work and taking in laundry and sewing on the side. When you heard Richie talk about his mother, it was a hard image to square with all the headaches he had caused his managers.

"She kept telling me to remember my training at home," he said. "She told me to be sure and change my underwear every day. She told me to be careful what I ate. She also said she had packed a Bible and she handed me a slip of paper with instructions on what verses to read."

Richie had never been on a plane before. "I was scared stiff," he said. "The weather was rough. He knuckleballed all the way to Florida. Then when I got off in Clearwater I saw in the terminal that there were separate doors for white and colored. I had never seen this before and I was confused and frightened. If Bobby Del Greco (then a Philly player) hadn't come along and helped me, I probably would have gone back home."

He didn't join the team at its hotel in downtown Clearwater. He was taken to the home of a black woman and given a room. "After a while," he said, "they felt I might have been lonesome and they sent me company. It was Marcelino Lopez, a Cuban pitcher. We were great company for each other. He didn't speak English and I didn't speak Spanish."

In baseball, reputations are made or ruined in incidents that are small and sometimes silly. It isn't hard to pinpoint the exact moment that things started to go wrong for Allen. He was in his second season with the Phillies, and the team had landed at the airport in Los Angeles.

Frank Thomas, a veteran outfielder, large and a little klunky, flipped a quarter at Richie and said, "Hey, boy, take my bags!" He was only joking and meant no harm. But Allen was only twenty-two and not yet ready for that kind of humor.

That was the background for what happened a few days later at the batting cage in Philadelphia. Johnny Callison yelled across the cage to Thomas, calling him "Lurch," after a goonlike character on the television series *The Addams Family*. Thomas thought Allen had said it.

He yelled back, "There's no fence around me, Fifteen [Allen's number]. You may get a meal out of me, but I'll get a sandwich out of you."

Richie sprang at him. His punches came in a cluster, knocking Thomas down, and Frank responded by striking Richie on the shoulder with a bat. At that point the other players pulled them apart.

Later, in the clubhouse, Gene Mauch announced that anyone talking about the fight would be fined fifteen hundred dollars. Which explains why few of the details leaked out. Shortly, Thomas, whose gawky enthusiasm endeared him to the fans, was traded, and the boos began to swell for Richie Allen.

If ever a town had a love-hate relationship with a player, this was one in the making. They cheered his home runs and game-winning hits. But the boos deepened with each contract fight, each newspaper blast, each infraction.

The year after Richie injured his hand, with the papers and the fans thriving on the team's turmoil, Mauch moved to restore discipline. He ordered every player to be in his position on the field at 5:00 P.M., with no talking permitted. He had also appointed Allen as his captain.

Richie saw the move as an attempt to get him to accept responsibility. So he did. He went to Gene and told him that the players resented being treated like children. Recalls Richie: "He said that for every day I wasn't in position at five he would fine me a hundred and fifty dollars. It was a principle with me. I didn't show up— and I paid."

It became a team ritual, Allen arriving late or not at all for batting practice. The management was groping for an answer. The team knew it needed a happy, or at least an interested, Richie Allen to win. He was a threat to win the triple crown any year he was healthy. He was their big man. But only one man knew what went on inside his head, and Richie wasn't telling.

As a measure of his importance to the club, it is worth noting that on the night I was traded back to the Braves, in 1967, most of the concern in the clubhouse was for how Richie would react.

While I was driving in three runs with two doubles to give us a 9-8 win over the Cubs, in the second game of a doubleheader, the writers were being handed a press release. I was going to Atlanta for Gene Oliver.

As we trooped into the clubhouse, Gene Mauch motioned to a reporter, and said: "Tell those other guys not to tell anybody. Let them whoop it up a while before I call him in."

We stood around for ten minutes, shaking hands and snapping the tabs off cans of beer, before the word came that Mauch wanted to see me. In the *Daily News* the next afternoon, Bill Conlin wrote about Richie: "Allen was feeling desolate, even though he had just struck a homer that will become legend long after Connie Mack Stadium is torn down. Rich Allen is a man, but right then he felt like crying. You could see it in his eyes.

" 'I wish they were sending me instead,' he said softly. 'I wish they were sending us both. He was the best friend I've got on this club and now they're sending him away. That's the thing that bugs me about this game. You make a friend like him and then he's gone.' "

I know. Reading those words, you almost expect someone to lower his head and say, "Wherever he is, he'll be better off. He's at peace now."

Bo Geste

When I joined the Phillies in the spring of 1966, I knew Robert (Bo) Belinsky by reputation. *Everybody* knew Bo by reputation. You could not dislike him. He was a gassy guy, as Bo himself might put it, and probably did.

He was a man for all seasons: bon vivant, pool hustler, dog fancier, ladies' man and occasional left-handed pitcher.

It was often said of Belinsky, but never by Bo himself, that he had squandered his talent, had a great arm but not the discipline to use it and, finally, had thrown away his career for all the women he loved. Bo did not see things quite that way.

"I have never considered myself a great talent," I heard him say once. "I think I have gotten more publicity for doing less than any player who ever lived."

He may have been right. In his first five seasons in the majors, Bo won a total of twenty-five games and was traded three times. One way or another, he was seldom out of the headlines.

As a rookie with the Angels, he reported to Palm Springs a week late, called a press conference to explain that he had been delayed by a pool tournament, and then demanded a thousand-dollar raise.

That was for openers. In May he pitched a no-hitter against Baltimore and went on to win his first six games, all but standing baseball on its ear. There was not to be a flashier, more popular debut until Fernando Valenzuela came along in 1981.

Within a month Belinsky had bought a new Cadillac and acquired, more or less in order, a fiancée (Mamie Van Doren), a business agent, a lawyer and the readership of Walter Winchell. All on an annual salary of seven thousand dollars. He might have conquered the world.

"Instead," Bo said, "the no-hitter I pitched actually cost me money. I had to buy drinks for everyone. It was like making a hole-in-one."

In unrelated adventures, he once threw a blonde out of his car at five in the morning, slugged a sixty-four-year-old sportswriter, married a former Playmate of the Year, and adopted a stray, part-cocker spaniel named Alfie.

The dog became the mascot of the Houston club and was given its own sandbox in the clubhouse. The players accepted Alfie as easily as they accepted Bo, although Barry Latman, a pitcher, asked wearily, "How am I going to explain to my wife that I got a locker next to a dog?"

For a while they were inseparable. His teammates joked that you could always tell them apart because Alfie was the one who was serious about baseball.

If much of Bo's career was a con, it was a harmless con that did injury to no one but Bo. Wherever he went he may not have won a lot of games, but he was good for the club because he kept the manager and the writers busy.

Bo was street-smart. To engage him in conversation was like catching Bernard Baruch on his park bench or Snoopy on his doghouse. He is the author of such philosophical gems as: "Happiness is a first-class pad, good wheels, an understanding manager and a little action."

He had a fine eye for caricature. It was Bo who pointed out that Philadelphia fans "would boo a funeral." Hawaii "is where the goodies are." And when Houston threatened to ship him to its top farm club, he shrugged: "Oklahoma City is nice, if you bring enough Alka-Seltzer."

The few times I caught Bo, he still had the lively arm and enough stuff to win. What he didn't have was the frame of mind, the intensity you found in a Spahn, a Gibson, or a Koufax. He enjoyed the cheers, but didn't need them as a steady diet.

Whether Bo was overrated in the romance league, I can't say, but I saw him in action and can assure you that he did not believe his own publicity. "If I did everything they said I did," he confided, "I'd be in a jar at the Harvard Medical School."

In Los Angeles, Bo was often in the company of such beautiful women as Mamie, Ann-Margret and Tina Louise, when he was not in the company of Walter Winchell, the famed gossip columnist who had taken him under his wing.

That era is gone forever. The line between sports and the arts has been so blurred that the two sides are no longer so enthralled with each other. Babe Ruth once made the Broadway scene, and Hollywood swept up Bo, but it doesn't happen that way anymore.

Bo still had the telegram Winchell sent him, after he had been quoted on a road trip as saying that he knew his Hollywood friends would drop him if he stopped winning. Winchell printed the wire in his syndicated column and possibly sent copies to Mr. and Mrs. America and all the ships at sea:

"DEAR BO:

"YOU DON'T KNOW ME VERY WELL YET, KID. I'M THE GUY WHO PREFERS TO BE WITH LOSERS. I'M THE GUY WHO WROTE 'THERE IS NOTHING AS LONELY AS A LOSER'S DRESSING ROOM.' I WOULD LIKE IT VERY MUCH IF YOU NEVER WON ANOTHER GAME SO I COULD CONVINCE YOU OF THAT.

"A CHAMPION IS ONE WHO GETS UP FOR ONE MORE ROUND. IF THEY EVER KICK YOU OUT OF BASEBALL FOR BEING A BAD BOY YOU WILL FIND OUT THAT I PRACTICE WHAT I PREACH: TO WIT, A REAL FRIEND IS ONE WHO WALKS IN WHEN THE REST OF THE WORLD WALKS OUT. SIGNED. WALTER WINCHELL."

It was beautiful. It was also just about the last word Bo heard from Winchell as he began his descent to the minors, the Phillies, Houston, the minors, the Cardinals, the minors, the White Sox, and out of baseball.

I doubt that he left the game with any serious regrets. Baseball was never his passion, it just paid his motel bill.

If he made no other lasting contribution to the sport, Bo destroyed most of the universal theories about sex and baseball.

As Bo remembered it, managers were always telling him not to engage in indoor recreation on nights before he pitched. They recommended that he rest and save himself for after the game. But Belinsky had a problem. He had no interest after the game. Neither the spirit nor the flesh was willing.

Besides, he had rejected the night-before theory after his no-hitter with the Angels. He was still looking for the girl who had left his bed that morning. "This was some kind of good-luck girl," he recalled, his dark eyes glowing. "But she disappeared from the picture. I'd met her at a steak house. Here I was with an ordinary secretary, probably—no flashy gal in any way, but a very lean, beautiful gal. And this was how I trained for my no-hitter, and it came in."

Bo never found her, proof of which is that he never had another winning season.

Horseman, Pass This Way

I am reminded of Inspector Clouseau, the Peter Sellers character, who was always being ambushed by his valet, Kato.

In St. Louis, I had a roommate like Kato, except he was taller and balder and less Oriental-looking. For a guy who later went straight, and became a big-league manager, Roger Craig had as much deviltry in him as the worst of us. His sense of humor ran to Halloween pranks.

No matter where we were, or what we were doing, Roger had this compulsion to scare people. He would turn over trash cans as you walked down the street, or thump the side of the car as you drove. God forbid you should have to get up at three in the morning to use the toilet. When you eased out of the bathroom, he would be pressed against the wall, on the other side of the door, ready to let out a bloodcurdling scream. Or he might throw a wastebasket across the room.

Even when you knew it was coming, and braced yourself, the experience was still hard on the nerves. At such times I would ask myself if this was any kind of life for a grown person.

But it was easy to forgive Craig his occasional looniness. He was bright, he had guts, he could pitch and he had once lost twenty games for the New York Mets, sixteen of them in a row, and you were inclined to give him a little benefit of the doubt. I mean, he had suffered for his art.

Craig came over from the Mets in the middle of the 1964 season, pitched well out of the bullpen as the Cards drove to the pennant, and then won the fourth game of the World Series against the Yankees in relief.

Craig's looks were deceptive. He was tall and gangly, with a long, sad, gentle face. But he was physically tough, an outdoorsman, and good company if you didn't let him sneak up on you.

On our first road trip to Los Angeles, Roger invited me to stay at his home. He owned a riding stable nearby, and the next morning he insisted that we go horseback riding. Naturally, I had no proper clothes with me, so Roger loaned me a shirt and a pair of his Levi's. Craig is six-six. I'm six-one. When we walked up to the stables I must have looked like Emmett Kelly. I caught the stable hands exchanging looks. They were thinking, "Get a load of this Elwood."

Roger picked out one of his daughter's horses for me and we started down a trail, which was actually a flood-control ditch. We found ourselves at a parking lot on one of the main streets, and we tied the horses to some cars and walked into a restaurant to have lunch.

Craig sauntered inside like he was the sheriff of Dodge City. Everyone else was wearing suits and ties and we were in Levi's with horseshit on our shoes. I never did get my wingtips clean.

We ordered a sandwich and a couple beers, then headed home. On the way back, Roger began to tell me what a great trick horse he was riding, how he could get off and the horse was trained to follow him.

With that he said, "Watch this, Uke," and he swung his leg over the back of the horse and dropped to the ground. Thirty seconds later, the horse bolted away and headed for home, his hooves kicking up small clouds of dust as the distance between us widened.

Roger did a double take and said, "Jeezus, Uke, quick, get off your horse so I can go catch him."

I said, "Your ass. Go catch him yourself. If I get off this horse I know what will happen to me."

He walked alongside us for the next two miles, bitching every step of the way.

Little Big Man

I learned a long time ago never to get into a fight with a person who comes up to your waist. You never know where their punches will land, and God forbid they should bite.

No one has ever accused Donald Davidson of not fighting fair, not in a forty-five-year career that has made him one of the most distinctive figures in baseball. No one in the sport has a bigger heart, not a player or manager—need I include umpires and owners?—and that is a lot to say for someone who stands four feet, two inches high.

With his feisty nature, Donald stands out in a crowd, especially if the crowd is on its hands and knees. In such a case he would probably pass out his business card, which is one inch by two inches and resembles a large postage stamp.

It is safe to say that among National-League players, and among the fans of Milwaukee and Atlanta, no front-office type is as well known, or as popular, as Donald.

One afternoon he strolled through the streets of downtown Milwaukee with John Quinn, the general manager of the Braves. Every few feet a friend, or a fan, would stop Donald and greet him. Quinn looked on with growing amusement, then asked one stranger, "Tell me, how did you recognize Donald in his dark glasses?"

For forty years, Davidson gave his all to the Braves, first as a clubhouse boy, in the days when Lefty Grove was their star pitcher and the team traveled by train. Then he moved up to publicist, assistant to the president, and traveling secretary. His odyssey with the team took him from Boston to Milwaukee to Atlanta. He was their link to the past. Hall of Famers, managers, owners, entire cities had come and gone. But Donald went with the franchise, like the Indian head on the team uniform.

Then the unthinkable happened. In April of 1976, Donald was fired by Ted Turner, the team's new owner, who suffered what he himself later admitted was a colossal mental lapse. It was as if someone had bought the original thirteen American colonies and fired the American eagle.

As traveling secretary for the Braves, responsible for the team's housing, Donald always occupied a suite where he served as host to the press and other dignitaries. I guess what offended Ted was the fact that Donald could have slept in a bureau drawer, much less a suite.

But word of Donald's luxury reached Turner in a bad mood. The Braves were in a losing streak, as they often are. He decided that if standard rooms were good enough for the players, they ought to be good enough for Donald. Quite possibly, Turner didn't know that the Braves weren't paying for those suites. They are tossed in by hotels, grateful for the team's business.

Even if Atlanta had been paying, you had to wonder how Turner could hand out millions to players like Andy Messersmith and Claudell Washington, and try to reduce the living standards of a class act like Donald Davidson.

One word led to another, as they usually do, and the Braves and Donald parted company, after four decades. The next time Turner saw the little man, he had been hired for the same duties at more money by the Houston Astros, and the wrath of the public had alerted Ted to the size of his error.

"I guess I was wrong, Donald," he apologized. "Even my little boy gave me hell when he heard about it."

"It's okay," said Davidson. "You did me a favor."

The firing of a publicist, a traveling secretary, or even a general manager doesn't usually attract much attention. But Donald was different. Opinion was solidly against Turner, a famous yachtsman who has won the America's Cup and other great prizes.

But the general reaction was that Turner was probably accustomed to tight quarters. He might even sleep in a hammock. But he was in no position to compare himself with Davidson. How many Hall of Famers has ever dropped by his room for refreshments?

Had he ever been detained by Scotland Yard for looking at Buckingham Palace through binoculars from his hotel? When Donald did this in London, the British suspected that some alien ring working with an elf was trying to get information on the queen's movements.

All of which means that today Donald Davidson is smaller than life, if not more so. He is famous for his temper, his tireless spirit, and for winding up as the ironic victim of frequent jokes. One of the legends of baseball is the night he stepped into a hotel elevator with Warren Spahn and Lew Burdette.

He looked up from his key. "Punch twenty-six," said Donald, who couldn't reach that high.

Spahn exchanged cagey glances with Burdette. "We're only going to twenty-four," he said.

"Punch twenty-six, you s.o.b.," screamed Donald.

The two pitchers tumbled out of the elevator at the twenty-fourth floor, laughing, leaving Davidson to descend to the lobby. There he summoned the clerk and roared: "How many times have I told you never to give me a room above the third floor?"

In spirit and stature, if not in bloodline, Donald is related to Pearl Du Monville and Eddie Gaedel.

Created by the typewriter of James Thurber, Du Monville was a midget who became a part of baseball's library by pinch-hitting in a big-league game. The game took place in the pages of a short story entitled, "You Could Look It Up."

Thurber had a grand idea but no franchise. It was left to Bill Veeck to turn fiction into fact, for in 1953 Veeck sent Eddie Gaedel—thirty-six inches tall—to bat for the St. Louis Browns against the Detroit Tigers. Gaedel walked. The nation's sports pages the next day showed this wonderful picture of Bob Swift, the Detroit catcher, on his knees trying to provide a target for his pitcher.

Donald never swung a bat for the Braves, but it wasn't because he didn't want to strike a blow for his team. One way or another, he did.

One year, when the Braves were playing the Dodgers in a spring game at Sarasota, he was set up by the general manager of the Dodgers. Buzzy Bavasi told an elderly gatekeeper that a midget from the Ringling Brothers Circus would attempt to sneak into the park. "He'll get pretty nasty when you turn him down, and he'll make lots of threats," he cautioned. "But keep him out, and use force if necessary."

Then Bavasi hid in a passageway and watched as Donald appeared, loaded with record books and fact sheets and a brisk manner. In the argument that followed, the old fellow punched him in the nose.

The blow sent Donald sprawling. He picked up his sunglasses, gathered up his papers and then darted between the gatekeeper's legs and into the park. "You dirty bastard," he shouted over his shoulder.

When Birdie Tebbetts, then the vice-president of the Braves, and their former manager, heard that Donald had been slugged he went off to defend his honor. "Who did it?" Birdie demanded. "Nobody punches one of my men and gets away with it."

So Tebbetts was directed to the press gate. He looked at the gatekeeper, judged him to be around eighty years old, and turned around without a word.

When he encountered Donald, he said, "Thanks for getting hit by an old guy. You probably saved me from a beating."

This kind of craziness was common among clubs in

those years, and could go back and forth until the original complaint was forgotten.

Donald nursed his sore nose for several days, and his grudge for quite a bit longer. But that spring he got even with Bavasi. When the Dodgers showed up at Milwaukee's camp for a game, Buzzy walked up to the press entrance and identified himself.

"I'm sorry, sir," he was told, "but I have orders not to let you in without a pass from Mr. Davidson."

Of course, Donald needed no outside agitators as long as Spahn and Burdette were around. Once, after the players and officials had posed for a team picture, Spahn and Burdette threw him down and removed his trousers.

Donald bided his time. The next time Spahn went out to pitch, he strolled into the clubhouse, gathered up every garment he saw, including Spahn's socks, and tosed them into the shower, with the water running.

They say that when Spahn left the park that night, after he had dried his clothes as best he could, he looked like Ichabod Crane.

Clete Boyer and I once bought Donald a motor scooter, what kids call a mini-bike, for Christmas. We planned to deliver it on the appropriate day, but on Christmas Eve we sat around drinking in Clete's apartment and decided not to wait.

Our plan was to leave the scooter on his doorstep, ring the bell and hide in the bushes as he discovered his gift. Instead, we peeked into the house and saw Donald walking around. Clete checked the front door, found it unlocked and left it open. I drove the scooter right into the vestibule of the house.

His two dogs circled me, barking and snarling, followed by Donald, barking and snarling. Followed by several guests we didn't know he was entertaining. After a couple drinks, Donald settled down and we left.

The next morning, on his initial ride, he crashed the scooter into a mailbox and broke two ribs. The next time we saw Donald on the machine, it had training wheels. And that was how he kept it, when he rode around the field at spring training every year, wearing a motorcycle helmet Boyer and I had given him.

Donald is the object of endless one-liners. The players say his suits are made by Mattel. He isn't defensive about his size, the result of a siege of sleeping sickness when he was six.

He gets into situations that are not of his own making, but he grins and bears them. He was the unwitting cause, for example, of an engineering problem at Candlestick Park in San Francisco.

When the stadium was completed, it featured a fine, roomy, glass-enclosed press box. There was just one thing wrong with it. The work shelf was so high, and the seats so low, you couldn't see home plate. This loss tends to interfere with one's enjoyment of a baseball game, and the working press complained long and bitterly.

After many complaints and phone calls, a city architect came out to see what could be done to correct the problem. His visit coincided, unfortunately, with the arrival of the Braves for a series.

The architect walked in, discovered Donald Davidson sitting at a typewriter, perched on two pillows, and stormed out, convinced that the entire protest was a practical joke.

It was years before they ever raised the seats in the press box at Candlestick Park.

The Big D

In a tight spot, Don Drysdale looked at a batter digging in at the plate the way he would look at a snake crawling through the kitchen door.

Not many hitters dug in against him. He was an artist whose work I enjoyed watching. He is another one whose name is called when you talk about pitchers who were mean and tough.

I used to admire Drysdale's theory about the brushback or knockdown pitch—a part of every pitcher's basic weaponry. He would place the first one under your chin and put you on your pants. It was what Branch Rickey called a "purpose" pitch. It was meant to plant a thought, a fear. Then, when the hitter got up, dusted himself off and took his stance, the second pitch was the one that did the job.

There was a night when Drysdale was pitching for the Dodgers against the Phillies and Robin Roberts. As the night wore on, several Phillies were forced to dive into the nearest foxhole to avoid being hit by pitches. Not all of them dived in time. Gene Mauch took the target practice as a personal affront, and he ordered Roberts to retaliate when Drysdale came to bat. He wanted Drysdale to get plugged. Roberts declined. He was the kind of guy who wouldn't hurt a fly.

So Mauch looked for someone who would, and he turned to Turk Farrell, who lumbered out to the mound. His first pitch to Drysdale sailed three feet over his head. Mauch perched himelf on the top steps of the dugout, cupped his hands and yelled: "I said KNOCK HIM DOWN!"

This time the tall Dodger righthander went sprawling. As he dusted himself off, he was getting red around the ears. Don is a nice-looking guy, well groomed, and he doesn't like dirt any better than the next fellow.

So Drysdale teed off on the two-and-oh pitch and doubled to the wall. As he pulled up at second base, he yelled out to the mound: "There's your knockdown pitch, Farrell."

At that Turk turned and fired to second, trying to pick off the runner, it says here. The throw was hard and straight and caught Drysdale on the hip. "There's your two-base hit, Drysdale," he said.

As luck would have it, I heard the story from both parties over the years, and in all the important details there is no disagreement. Both, in fact, seemed rather fond of the episode, and its aftermath.

It came to pass that during the winter the Phillies traded Farrell to the Dodgers, of all teams, and the first thing he did in spring training was look up Drysdale and make his peace. Turk was six feet four and could hold his own in a bar fight. But Drysdale stood six-six and had a memory at least that long.

"Well, Don, old buddy," said the Turk, with a hearty grin, "we're teammates now. Whaddaya say? Let bygones be bygones."

"Okay," said Drysdale, shaking his hand. "And it's a good thing. I had your name in my book." He meant it, too. Drysdale pulled out a notebook, and turned to a page with a list of names on it, and there at the top was Farrell's.

There is no question in my mind that Drysdale's record of fifty-eight and two-thirds scoreless innings—six straight shutout games—was the darndest thing ever achieved by a guy who throws a ball. It is a record I doubt will ever be broken. Today it is a rarity for a pitcher to even finish six straight games, much less do it without allowing a run.

Drysdale was one of the people you would pay to watch pitch, and good enough at bat that the Dodgers sometimes used him as a pinch hitter. I liked his style even when we were on different teams, and I liked him more after we got to know each other through our work at ABC.

Don told me once that when I turned up in the Braves' lineup on a night in 1967, his manager, Walter Alston, asked him how he planned to pitch to me. He said, "Damned if I know, I've never seen him play." He was probably right. I had been in the league six years, and so seldom started against a righthander that I had never faced him.

That night I went three-for-four and walked once, one of my hits a bullet that went right between his legs. Don said he knew then that he was nearing the end of the line. He retired two seasons later.

A Dry Gibson

I caught a few great pitchers and batted against several others, although they may not have been as great as I sometimes made them appear.

But if I had to pick one pitcher, to start one game that my team simply dare not lose, Bob Gibson would be near the top of the list. If he was not in a class by himself, it did not take long to call the roll: Spahn, Koufax, Drysdale . . . take your choice. I would take him for the same reason Johnny Keane gave when he called on Gibson on two days' rest to pitch the seventh game of the 1967 World Series: "I had a commitment to his heart."

Gibson was one of the best athletes I ever saw. He had been a baseball and basketball star at Creighton, and he was another, like Aaron and Allen, whose story was familiar: up from poor. His father died three months before he was born. His mother worked in a laundry. He remembered the first home he ever lived in, a four-room shack on Omaha's north side, as the place where a rat bit him on the ear.

I don't think the man ever lived who hated to lose more than Bob Gibson. He was a quick learner who, if you gave him a week, could beat you at your own game.

However, the first time he ever let himself get talked into a celebrity golf tournament, he shot a score of 115. It was his own fault. He counted all his strokes.

In the privacy of the clubhouse, he was known as a practical joker, a fellow who would sing, strum a guitar or join in whatever was going on. But others saw him as a guy wound tight, cold to strangers and uneasy in crowds.

I used to study Gibby. He was one of those rare individuals who seemed to be driven best by anger. Different pitchers reacted in different ways. Before a big game, dry wit rolled off the tongue of a Whitey Ford. Sandy Koufax was quiet and unfailingly polite. A Ray Sadecki would go around looking for conversation, and a Denny McLain would be on the phone to his booking agent, lining up dates to play the accordion.

But Gibson did it his own way. He would be aloof, haughty, or snappish, building up a determination that was something to behold. Winning is important to every professional athlete. With Gibson the urge was overpowering. His makeup demanded it. He primed himself mentally for the big games, but if you asked him how, he could only shrug and say, "No special way. It's just in me."

On the field he was a lion, who twice came back from broken legs and in the final week of the 1964 pennant race started or relieved in four out of six games.

Unlike Allen, who liked people but whose actions confused them, or Aaron, who went about his job like a guy building a pyramid, Gibson had an electric presence, but was never comfortable with fame. He was abrupt with writers and uncertain with fans. When one asked for his autograph in a restaurant in Detroit, Bob said, sure, as soon as he finished his dinner. The guy tore up his sheet of paper and threw it on the table. Another time a little old lady grew angry and made a scene because Gibby wouldn't join her and her guests. And a small boy, in his eagerness to obtain the valuable Gibson signature, poked him in the eye with a pencil.

I heard him say often that he did not believe in hero worship and lacked the right disposition for either end of it. What he had was the perfect disposition for a righthanded pitcher.

In his middle years he developed a hard curve to go with his slider and fastball. But his money pitch was always the fast one, which sometimes rose and sometimes sank. You never knew which was coming.

I caught Gibson on a night when he struck out thirteen in Milwaukee, my home town, and he never had better stuff. It was a big moment for me, playing in front of my friends and relatives, handling one of the game's fastest pitchers.

With two out in one of the late innings, and two strikes on the hitter, he cut loose with a pitch that moved so sharply I didn't have time to raise my glove, and it smacked against my bare hand. It felt as if I had put my palm flat against a hot stove. I picked up the ball with my mitt, tagged the runner, walked away from the plate, walked into the dugout and up the runway toward the clubhouse, and then cut loose with a scream that would have Johnny Weissmuller sound like a sissy.

Gibson came looking for me. He knew what I was doing, that I didn't want to carry on in front of my hometown folks. He grinned, and nodded, and went back to the dugout. It hurt, but it was what we called in baseball a good hurt.

Leave Us Eddie Mattress

When Eddie Mattress was seventeen, it was a very good year (1949). He had all his hair and the kind of apple cheeks that old ladies and young girls like to pinch. He didn't own a car. He lived on the third floor of a boarding house four blocks from the ball park, and he walked it both ways.

What he did own was a batting average of .363 for his first summer in the baseball boondocks, down in North Carolina. The future beckoned clear and strong. Eddie would chase it to the Hall of Fame, and the most prolific home run career any third baseman ever knew. Wherever he went, glory and groceries followed him. The trail led to Atlanta and Milwaukee in the minors, and when he returned to those cities years later he brought the big leagues with him.

He is the only player I know who can make such a claim.

He was not yet twenty-one when he joined the Braves, still in Boston, an old and faded club trying to rebuild.

Among the rookies they brought in were Mathews, and a shortstop named Johnny Logan, and a young pitcher obtained from the Yankees, Lew Burdette.

That winter the team chartered a plane. They painted the sides with the name "The Rookie Rocket," piled aboard a dozen Boston writers and flew across the country to interview a dozen of their hottest prospects, the ones who would restore the Braves to greatness.

But not in Boston.

"The Rookie Rocket," Eddie would laugh about it years later, "never got off the ground. We finished last that season . . . way, way back. We were either very old or very young. We had graybeards like Earl Torgeson and Walker Cooper on the club. And kids like myself and Logan.

"We were so bad that we used to pray for rain. No kidding. The day the season ended, the manager, Cholly Grimm, let all the extra players go home early. On the bus after the game we had more writers than players.

"I hit a double in the top of the ninth to tie the game, and when I got back to the dugout everybody was mad as hell. They wanted to get home. We were playing the Dodgers, and they had already locked up the pennant, and the game didn't mean anything.

"After twelve innings the score was still tied, and the umpires called it on account of darkness. The sun was still out."

I always liked to hang around with Eddie, not only because he had a special corner in the history of the Braves. He was just a helluva guy and the biggest spender the club ever had. Nobody ever picked up a check around him. He bought drinks and dinner for everyone.

I roomed with Eddie on the road except when the team

was in Los Angeles, where he stayed with his mother. Then Bob Buhl and I moved into the suite the Braves provided for Mathews. There was always a refrigerator filled with beer.

After a game one night at Dodger Stadium, Buhl and I sat down and started popping beer tabs and telling baseball stories. The nostalgia was flowing nearly as fast as the beer, when I noted the room had a fireplace.

I said, "Why don't we start a fire and make it just like home?"

Buhl said, "Yeah, why not?" We had the air conditioner going and were feeling kind of laid back.

I threw a bunch of newspapers into the fireplace, and the cardboard from the six-packs we had already polished off. When the fire got going fairly well, I tossed in four bats that Mathews kept in the room for practice. He would swing them constantly. The bats didn't really burn that well because the fire wasn't hot enough, but for about ten minutes Buhl and I were in heaven. It was then that the sprinkler system went off. The floor we were on began to fill with smoke, and we discovered that it was a false fireplace. Shortly, the hotel manager appeared, accompanied by Donald Davidson, who took care of the problem, one way or another.

Mathews came back to the room the next morning. I had stacked his bats next to the fireplace, all blackened and smokey, but otherwise unharmed. Eddie went into a rage, but he gave up when Buhl and I couldn't stop laughing.

As a Milwaukee kid, I knew how large a role Mathews had played in what became known as The Milwaukee Story. The Braves drew two million fans in Wisconsin after they left Boston, and their success in Middle America inspired Walter O'Malley to move the Dodgers to Los Angeles, and Horace Stoneham's Giants tagged along to San Francisco, launching the expansion boom in all of professional sports.

In those years Mathews was the symbol of the Braves, the only survivor of the team that arrived from Boston, on its way to Atlanta.

On opening day of 1965, in what would be the team's last season in Milwaukee, a local group brought back most of the Braves who had played in County Stadium in 1953.

One by one the players were introduced, waving their caps and trotting out to their old positions, standing alongside the player who was the current keeper of it. When the ceremonies ended, only one player stood alone, at third base, the only player who had been a Brave in 1953 who was still with the club. And out in the bleachers a group of fans unfurled a banner that must have been sixty feet wide. It read: "ATLANTA YOU CAN HAVE THE REST . . . LEAVE US EDDIE MATTRESS, OUR HERO."

Mattress was as close as some of the old German burghers of Milwaukee could come to pronouncing his name. When he saw the banner Eddie swallowed hard, tipped his cap and looked down at his shoes as though he had never seen them before.

Of all the records he achieved in the years he spent in the home of the Braves, wherever that happened to be, Mathews cherished most the one he set with Henry Aaron: most home runs in a career by teammates (863). They broke a record previously held by a couple of fellows named Babe Ruth and Lou Gehrig.

"I'm not a crusader about race or creed," Eddie told the press, "but I think the fact that Hank is colored and

I'm white, and we set this record together, well, I think that is kind of significant."

A Long and Twisty Road

Satchel Paige was sixty-two years old, wore bifocals, and looked almost grandfatherly when the Atlanta Braves signed him as a pitcher-coach in 1968. It was an act of grace by the team's owner, Bill Bartholomay, to qualify the old fellow for his pension.

That was the only time our paths crossed, but every ballplayer was curious about the gangly patriarch who may have been the greatest pitcher who ever lived.

One day Dizzy Dean visited the ball park. Henry Aaron asked Dean if Paige could *really* throw, asking the question mainly for Satch's benefit, just to hear how Dean would react.

"Could he throw?" repeated Dizzy. "Is a pig pork? You bet he could throw. Listen. He was quick. Me and him would pitch in exhibitions and it sounded like firecrackers going off. Warming up it was like double-barreled shotguns. Boom-boom! That's all you'd hear. Cotton came out of the mitts. We'd saw the bats off . . . right at the top."

The Braves put Paige on their roster just long enough (158 days) to give him the time he needed for his pension. He never got into a game, although Lord knows he thought he could still pitch. He described his repertoire of pitches as the blooper, looper and drooper, the jump ball, hurry ball and nothing ball, and the ever-dangerous bat dodger. It disturbed him to see today's young pitchers use only their arms and not their heads. "They throw the two-strike pitch over the plate," he complained one day. "They don't waste it. Me, on a two-strike pitch, they get something from me a dog wouldn't want to hit."

Satchel spent his time that summer singing of the old days, spreading good will and jiving the troops. He was living at the Dinkler Plaza Hotel in Atlanta.

One day I got on the pay phone in the clubhouse, rang the switchboard upstairs and had them put me through to the house phone a few feet away. I asked for Satchel Paige. When he picked up the phone, I put on my best German accent and told him I was the manager of the hotel.

I said, "I vant you to get your schidt oudt of your room, ve got a chentz to rent your room."

Satchel said, "Hey, who the hell you say this is?"

I gave him a name, Hans Gruber.

He said, "Gruber, what the hell you tawkin' about? I pay my rent by the month and my rent is paid."

I said, "Look, I don't give a schidt vat you pay or who you tink you are. To me you just a wrinkled old man, and the Braves haf gone downhill effer zintz you came. So you get your schidt out of the room."

We were talking on the phone ten feet apart and the conversation ended with Satchel announcing that he was on his way to the hotel to kick my ass.

I let him hang up the phone, watched him go over to his locker and start taking his uniform off. He only dressed to pitch batting practice, so I let him get halfway undressed before I let him in on the gag. He didn't mind. Clubhouse humor, the endless pranks, delighted him.

The Phillies had Satchel in 1958 on their farm club at Miami with kids like Dick Farrell, Don Cardwell, Ed Bouchee and others destined for the majors. Farrell remembered how the younger cult tormented Satch by putting dead fish in his shoes and nailing his uniform to the ceiling. But Satch always had the last laugh.

"He would warm up by putting a silver chewing-gum wrapper on the plate and pitching for it," said Farrell. "In Columbus, Ohio, there was a knothole in the outfield fence. A hitter got five thousand dollars for a home run through it. Of course, nobody ever collected. Satch said he could hit the hole from twenty feet. The guys laughed. He missed it five times. Then the betting started and Satch hit it three times in a row."

No one knows what feats Paige might have performed in the twenty years he was barred from the majors because of the color of his skin. He was a star in both leagues, the black one and the white one. Dean and Bob Feller both called him the greatest pitcher they ever saw. In his prime, Satch slept on his suitcase in Southern towns, barnstorming for one hundred dollars a game. In 1934 he beat Dean four out of six on one tour, when Dean was a thirty-game winner in the big leagues and a World Series hero.

When Satchel gained his first fame in the Negro Leagues in 1926, Joe DiMaggio was eleven years old. By 1935 Satchel had become a legend, and DiMaggio was still a year away from his rookie season with the Yankees.

When Bill Veeck brought Satch to the majors at Cleveland in 1948, Joe was baseball's greatest star. In 1952, by then with the Browns and back with Veeck, Paige was voted the American League's best relief pitcher. DiMaggio had been retired for two seasons.

Veeck gave him his first, overdue break not only in the interest of justice. He wanted to reinforce a weak Cleveland bullpen, and the move won the pennant for the Indians. To some it smacked of a publicity stunt.

In the *Sporting News*, J. G. Taylor Spink editorialized: "Many well wishers of baseball fail to see eye to eye with the signing of Satchel Paige, the superannuated Negro pitcher. To bring in a pitching rookie of Paige's age is to demean the standards of baseball in the big circuits."

Years later, Satchel noted: "I demeaned the big circuits considerable that year. I won six and lost one."

In the office of the baseball commissioner, the birth date of Paige is listed as July 7, 1906. Chances are that not even Satch knows for certain his actual age. What he does say, with the purest of logic, is: "It must have been meant for me to be bawn when I was . . . or I wouldn't have been bawn. If there hadn't been a color line, I might have made more money and got into trouble with Sam. This way, the whole world got to see me pitch."

His every move was one of melancholy. He could Bogart a cigarette with the best of them, holding it between his thumb and index finger. His eyes were slow and sad, his face long and wrinkled. "We seen some sights, it and I," he once said, fondly, observing his face in a mirror.

It seems strange to me even now to realize that segregation was still practiced in the South when I went to my first big-league training camp, not that long ago, in 1961. The black players lived apart from the team in Florida. They were not housed in the same motels or served in the same cafés as the whites.

They stayed in rooming houses and ate their meals with families that boarded them. In Bradenton, they stayed at Mrs. Gibson's. She served the best fried chicken in town, and we made jokes about it: how they ate better than the white guys, home-cooked meals and no curfew or bed checks.

At least, we have a way of marking where we have been. And how far we have to go. It isn't generally known, but Jackie Robinson not only broke the color line, he got the blacks into the dining rooms. Even when all the players began sleeping in the same hotels—I mean in cities like St. Louis, not some pit stop in the South—it was still standard practice for the blacks to order room service, so as not to offend whites in the dining room.

One night in Cincinnati, Jackie Robinson decided to enter the dining room and ask for a table. The captain seated him, the waiter served him, and none of the diners, whatever their private feelings, walked out. As Satchel Paige said, "The past is a long and twisty road."

The Southpaw

It was Warren Spahn who changed the perception that all left-handed pitchers were a little crazy.

I'm not sure where or when the idea started, but the impression was still fairly general when Spahn came along to prove that a left-hander could act in a perfectly ordinary way, except for winning twenty games every year.

No doubt, the tradition dated back to pitchers like Rube Waddell, a legend in the 1920s, who once disappeared from a game—he was the pitcher—to follow a fire truck. He was sometimes discovered between innings under the stands, shooting marbles with a bunch of kids.

Lefty Gomez came along in the 1930s to add his own touch. Gomez could throw a lot faster than he ran, but hand or foot he liked a challenge. One day George Selkirk, his Yankee teammate, anoher happy soul, said he thought he could beat Gomez to the dugout, running in from right field. They bet five dollars on it.

With two out in the next inning, and two on, the batter drove a fly ball to deep center. Gomez watched it go, saw Joe DiMaggio lope after it and then glanced toward right. Here came Selkirk, racing like a sprinter. Gomez took off for the bench, and won by a stride, just as the ball settled into the glove of Joe DiMaggio, and manager Joe McCarthy looked on in bewilderment.

Then there was Warren Spahn. No one ever suggested that Spahn had an inch of craziness in him. But anyone who played on the same team would tell you he was obsessed.

The Braves joked about it for years after manager Chuck Dressen once complained, "All he thinks about is getting his twenty."

Yet Dressen knew as well as anybody what a good thing that was for a pitcher to think about, especially one who could go out and do it. When it came to winning, Warren was selfish, and not many people begrudged him. He just didn't make it very easy on a manager. He hated to lose. Hated to get rained out. Hated to miss a turn. And hated coming out of a game with such a passion that a manager got so he dreaded going to the mound to remove him. Many of them wouldn't, and instead sent their pitching coaches. In fact, that practice may have started with Spahn.

They would practically have to Indian-wrestle with him to get the ball.

I think part of what kept that flame burning inside Spahnie was the fact that he felt he had no time to lose. He was a late starter, and he never stopped catching up.

He was forty years old my rookie season. He had just won twenty games for the thirteenth time. The *Sporting News* had voted him Pitcher of the Year.

He had signed with the Braves in 1939, years before the big bonus era, and didn't collect a dime. He spent three years in the minors and three more in the army—he was the only major-leaguer to win a battlefield commission for bravery in action.

. He didn't spend a full year with the Braves until 1947, when he had the first of his twenty-game seasons (twenty-one and ten). The next year Spahn and Johnny Sain pitched the Braves to their first pennant in thirty-four years, inspiring the slogan, "Spahn and Sain and two days of rain."

I caught his record three-hundred twelfth win and he went on to add forty-one more before he retired, under protest, at the age of forty-five. His snapping fastball was gone, but he could still beat them with his off-speed pitches and his control and his head.

He was a joy to catch and a joy to watch, one of those rare people who strikes you up close just as he does from a distance. Not many ballplayers do.

Spahn moved in a peculiar sort of duck walk, his shoulders swinging from side to side, in the rambling way of a good high school athlete. His pitching form was perfect. From the side, he seemed to be turning over, automatically, like one of those old riverboat wheels, with no more strain on the arm itself than on the spoke of a wheel.

Spahnie considered himself immune to the attacks of time. When the Braves decided they needed to bring along younger pitchers, he signed on with the woeful New York Mets. He was listed as a coach, but he kept wanting to work with an old guy named Warren Spahn, rather than the bonus kids the Mets kept bringing in.

The first time he pitched against his old club in Milwaukee, the Braves scored seven runs off him in one inning, including a grand slam homer by Eddie Mathews. The fans gave Spahn a standing ovation and booed the Braves, who felt like booing themselves.

He was a grandpappy age for a pitcher, and his breaking pitches no longer dipped and wobbled like a tired moth. To Spahn it was a sad night only because he didn't win.

I have always thought that one remark typified him. The night he won his three-hundredth, he was asked what it meant, how badly he had wanted it.

He looked surprised anyone would ask. "I wanted this one," he said. "I wanted the last one, and I want the next one."

15. The All-Uke Team

I AM MORE FORTUNATE than most former big-leaguers, because I have no feelings of frustration, of promise unfulfilled. I think I got everything out of my talent I could.

To begin with, I lacked speed. I had to compensate with a few tricks. One was to knock my hat off as I ran down the first-base line, to make it appear that I was really moving.

I hated to lead off an inning, especially in a park that had Astroturf. I would hit a bouncing ball to third base and they'd whip the ball to second and then to first. It really made you look bad when they practiced their double plays with nobody on base.

The one ability I did have, and tried never to lose, was the ability to laugh at myself, or at the foibles of a game little kids play for free. After a long day, moving on to another town, the fellows usually needed some comic relief.

Once, with the Braves, we were coming in for a

landing. The time when many players tighten up is when the plane touches down, and there is this great whoosh before the brakes grab. I picked up the intercom mike in the back of the plane and announced, "This is your captain speaking. Please remain seated and keep your safety belts fastened until the plane HAS HIT THE SIDE OF THE TERMINAL BUILDING and come to a complete stop."

It was fun watching the blood leave their faces for a few seconds.

That was my way of bringing the guys together, of reminding them that man can't live by box score alone. I meant it one night, sort of, when I said on the *Tonight Show*: 'Winning and losing is nothing. Going out and prowling the streets after the game is what I liked. You'd get half in the bag and wake up the next morning with a bird in your room—that's what baseball is all about."

In that spirit, I have been persuaded to select my own All-Star team, an all-character team, composed of players whose contribution to the game went beyond winning or losing. To be eligible, their careers had to cross mine, meaning they had to have played at least one game in the National League in the years between 1961 and 1968. I gave special consideration to those whose service had a distinctive and human quality, and also to those I thought might be seriously offended by being left out. Herewith,

THE BOB UECKER ALL-STAR TEAM

FIRST BASE—*Marv Throneberry*, Mets. The competition was hotter here than at any other position, with the likes of Dick Stuart, Norm Larker and Gordy Coleman all in the running. A special honorable mention should go to Joe Pepitone, for his lasting contribution to the game. Pepitone is believed to be the first player to bring a hair blower into the locker room. Throneberry wins for a career that led not to the Hall of Fame, but to a Lite Beer commercial. He once was called out for failing to touch second base on a triple. When he complained, the umpires pointed out that he had missed first base, too.

SECOND BASE—*Rod Kanehl,* Mets. Led the league for three straight years in getting hit by pitches, and defined team spirit as being willing "to take one on the ass for the team." Once, as a pinch runner, he scored from second on a passed ball to give the Mets a 7-6 lead over the Phillies. Casey Stengel was so elated he told Hot Rod to stay in the game. When Kanehl asked which position, Casey said, "I don't care. Play any place you want to." Kanehl grabbed his glove and ran onto the field. He told Felix Mantilla to move from third to second, moved Elio Chacon from second to short, and put himself in at third. "That's the kind of ballplayers we want," Stengel said later. "Tell him to do something, and he does it."

SHORTSTOP—*Ruben Amaro,* Phillies. One of the slickest glove men ever to play the game, but I have included him for two reasons. Ruben hit even fewer homers (two) in his career than I did, and he is the only man I ever heard of who was drafted by both the American and Mexican armies. He deserves it.

THIRD BASE—*Doug Rader,* Astros. He was playing for Houston, in San Diego, the night that Padres owner Ray Kroc got on the p.a. system and apologized to the crowd for how lousy his team was. Rader rushed to the defense of the Padres, adding that Kroc "must have thought he was talking to a bunch of short-order cooks." The next week, Rader received angry letters from short-order cooks all over the country. The Padres turned the whole affair into a ticket promotion, letting in free anyone wearing a long white hat when the Astros returned to town. It all worked out swell in the off season, when Houston traded Rader to—you guessed it—San Diego.

OUTFIELD—*Roberto Clemente,* Pirates. One of the really complete players of his era, Roberto was also one of the great hypochondriacs. He suffered from insomnia, and claimed that sleeping pills kept him awake. The year he won his second batting title, he said he had gotten malaria from a mosquito, typhoid fever from a pig and food poisoning from a fish—all man's natural enemies. "I feel better when I am sick," he once said. Roberto was one beautiful wreck.

Frank Thomas, Pirates, Reds, Cubs, Mets, Phillies, Astros, Braves, etc. He played for eleven teams, three in one season. Known as the Big Donkey, partly because his bat had a kick in it (when it connected), and partly because he suffered from hoof-in-mouth disease. It seemed that every few months Thomas would be traded, always leaving with the same declaration: "It's nice to know that somebody wants you."

Frank Howard, Dodgers. It was a thrill to watch him play the outfield. Jim Murray wrote that at six-eight, Howard was the only player in baseball who clanked when he walked. Early in his career, you never knew if he would drive in more runs than he let in. He had one of the biggest swings in the game, and once took a mighty cut just as Maury Wills slid across the plate, trying to steal home. A gentle giant, Howard was more shaken than Wills. "Please, Maurice," he begged, "don't ever do that again."

PITCHERS—*Ken MacKenzie,* Mets, left-hander. The first Yale graduate I know of to pitch in the big leagues after World War II. Casey Stengel once brought him in from the bullpen to face the San Francisco Giants with the bases full. The next three hitters were Orlando Cepeda, Willie Mays and Willie McCovey. Stengel handed him the ball and said, "Pretend they are the Harvards." Another time, MacKenzie was sulking on the bench. "Do you realize," he said, "that I am the lowest-paid member of the Yale Class of '59?" Stengel reminded him, "Yes, but with the highest earned run average."

Honorable mention, *Masanori Murakami,* Giants, left-hander. There has to be a category for the only Japanese ever to pitch in the National League. Described as "sneaky fast," he compiled a 5-1 record in two seasons of relief, then returned to Japan, homesick for his native land. He spoke almost no English, but had a sense of humor. Or at least, the writers who covered the

Giants did. Asked to name his favorite American songs, Murakami replied, "Horro, Dorry," and "Up a Razy Liver."

Turk Farrell, Phillies, Dodgers, Astros, right-hander. Early in his career, as a member of the Phillies' famed Dalton Gang, he set a record for barro fights. A hard thrower, with a big follow-through, Turk later set a record for most times getting hit by batted balls on various parts of the body. A line drive by Henry Aaron once glanced off his forehead, but Farrell stayed in the game. He carried a gun in spring training one year in Arizona, and shot snakes as he walked from his hotel to the ball park. A Falstaffian figure, he beat his old club, the Phillies, in a game that went fourteen innings and ended shortly before 1:00 A.M., and boasted in the clubhouse: "Nobody beats Farrell after midnight."

Honorable mention, *Gaylord Perry,* many teams, right-hander. When he came to the big leagues, one scouting report said he was only a "marginal prospect" to stay in the majors. Twenty-two years later, he was gunning for his three hundredth win. Once, after Nellie Fox had singled in the winning run against him, Perry broke Nellie's bat at home plate. He confessed some of his other sins in a book called *Me and the Spitter,* but swore he had reformed and no longer threw the illegal pitch because he wanted to set a good example for the kids.

You may have noticed that my All-Star team has no catcher. There were several candidates for this honor. Some had talent, but their humor was just warped enough to keep them in contention, such as Tim

McCarver and Joe Torre. Others were not handicapped by their talent, such as John Bateman and Choo Choo Coleman.

In the end, I decided to leave the position vacant because I have been taught that it is in poor taste to give an award to yourself.

APPENDIX

The Record

UECKER, ROBERT GEORGE
B. Jan. 26, 1935, Milwaukee, Wisconsin
BR TR 6'1" 190 lbs

	G	AB	H	2b	3b	HR	R	RBI	SB	BA	BB	SO
1962 MIL N	33	64	16	2	0	1	5	8	0	.250	7	15
1963	13	16	4	2	0	0	3	0	0	.250	2	5
1964 STL N	40	106	21	1	0	1	8	6	0	.198	17	24
1965	53	145	33	7	0	2	17	10	0	.228	24	27
1966 PHI N	78	207	43	6	0	7	15	30	0	.208	22	36
1967 PHI N	18									.171		
" ATL N	62									.146		
tot 2 teams	80	193	29	4	0	3	17	20	0	.150	24	60
6 years	297	731	146	22	0	14	65	74	0	.200	96	167

Traded to St. Louis, April 1964, for Jim Coker and Gary Kolb.

Traded to Philadelphia, January 1966, with Dick Groat and Bill White, for Alex Johnson, Pat Corrales and Art Mahaffey.

Traded to Atlanta, July 1967, for Gene Oliver.

Bestselling Books
for Today's Reader

More Bestselling Books From Jove!

MS READ-a-thon— a simple way to start youngsters reading

Boys and girls between 6 and 14 can join the MS READ-a-thon and help find a cure for Multiple Sclerosis by reading books. And they get two rewards — the enjoyment of reading, and the great feeling that comes from helping others.

Parents and educators: For complete information call your local MS chapter. Or mail the coupon below.

Kids can help, too!

Cadfael was hurrying from the abbot's lodging towards the cloister when he saw Emma, and slowed his steps. In at the south door she went, and in after her, just as discreetly, he followed.

The girl slipped silently round into the nave, as though she would find herself a retired spot for prayer; but instead of turning aside, she continued her rapid silent passage towards the door that opened outside the convent walls.

Once outside, she turned towards the fairground and quickened her pace. Soon she came to a halt where a half-dozen booths were backed into the abbey wall. She was frowning doubtfully at the last of the booths. Cadfael recognized it. It was the booth of Euan of Shotwick, the glover, and Emma was at a loss, for the booth was fast-closed, every panel sealed, and business all around in full swing.

Cadfael drew nearer. Emma's young profile looked even more tender and vulnerable. She did not know what to do. She advanced a few steps, as though she would knock at the closed shutter, but then she wavered and drew back.

Why had she come here? Surely not to buy gloves . . .

SAINT PETER'S FAIR

Ellis Peters

The Fourth Chronicle of Brother Cadfael

FAWCETT CREST • NEW YORK

Library of Congress Catalog Card Number: 81-11020

ISBN: 0-449-21354-4

This edition published by arrangement with William Morrow and Company, Inc.

Manufactured in the United States of America

First Ballantine Books Edition: August 1984
Fourth Printing: September 1986

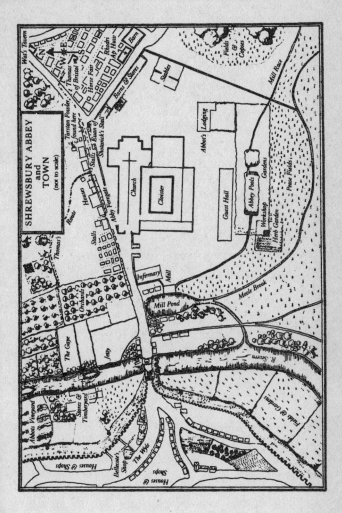

SHREWSBURY ABBEY
and
TOWN
(not to scale)

Wat's Tavern

E.

N.

of Bristol

St Thomas

Turstan Fowler,
found here

Rhodri
Ap Huw

Horse Fair

Barns & Stores

Barn

Stables

Abbot's Lodging

Abbey Foregate

Stalls

Stalls & Exam of
Shatnick's Stall

Houses

Route

Thomas's

Church

Cloister

Guest Hall

Abbot's

Abbey Ponds

Workshop
Herb Garden

Gardens

Pease Fields

Mill Race

Orchard

The Gaye

Jetty

Infirmary

Mill

Mill Pond

Meole Brook

R. Severn

Abbot's Vineyard

Stores &
Timberyard

Bellecote's
Shop

The Wyle

Houses &
Shops

Houses & Shops

Fields & Gardens

THE EVE OF
THE FAIR

ONE

IT BEGAN AT THE NORMAL DAILY CHAPTER IN THE BENEDICTINE monastery of Saint Peter and Saint Paul, of Shrewsbury, on the thirtieth day of July, in the year of Our Lord 1139. That day being the eve of the eve of Saint Peter ad Vincula, a festival of solemn and profitable importance to the house that bore his name, the routine business of the morning meeting had been devoted wholly to the measures necessary to its proper celebration, and lesser matters had to wait.

The house, given its full dedication, had two saints, but Saint Paul tended to be neglected, sometimes even omitted from official documents, or so abbreviated that he almost vanished. Time is money, and clerks find it tedious to inscribe the entire title, perhaps as many as twenty times in one charter. They had had to amend their ways, however, since Abbot Radulfus had taken over the rudder of this cloistral vessel, for he was a man who brooked no slipshod dealings, and would have all his crew as meticulous as himself.

Brother Cadfael had been out before Prime in his enclosed herb-garden, observing with approval the blooming of his oriental poppies, and assessing the time when the seed would be due for gathering. The summer season was at its height, and promising rich harvest, for the spring had been mild and moist after plenteous early snows, and June and July hot and sunny, with a few compensatory showers to keep the leafage fresh and the buds fruitful. The hay harvest was in, and lavish, the corn looked ripe for the sickle. As soon as the annual fair was over, the reaping would begin. Cadfael's fragrant domain, dewy from the dawn and already warming into drunken sweetness in the rising sun, filled his senses with the kind of pleasure on which an ascetic church sometimes

3

owns, finding something uneasily sinful in pure delight. There were times when young Brother Mark, who worked with him in this delectable field, felt that he ought to confess his joy among his sins, and meekly accept some appropriate penance. He was still very young, there were excuses to be found for him. Brother Cadfael had more sense, and no such scruples. The manifold gifts of God are there to be delighted in, to fall short of joy would be ingratitude.

Having put in two hours of work before Prime, and having no office in connection with the abbey fair, which was engaging all attention, Cadfael was nodding, as was his habit, behind his protective pillar in the dimmest corner of the chapter-house, perfectly ready to snap into wakefulness if some unexpected query should be aimed in his direction, and perfectly capable of answering coherently what he had only partially heard. He had been sixteen years a monk, by his own considered choice, which he had never regretted, after a very adventurous life which he had never regretted, either, and he was virtually out of reach of surprise. He was fifty-nine years old, with a world of experience stored away within him, and still as tough as a badger—according to Brother Mark almost as bandy-legged, into the bargain, but Brother Mark was a privileged being. Cadfael dozed as silently as a closed flower at night, and hardly ever snored; within the Benedictine rule, and in genial companionship with it, he had perfected a daily discipline of his own, that suited his needs admirably.

It is probable that he was fast asleep when the steward of the grange court, with appropriate apology, ventured into the chapter-house and stood waiting the abbot's permission to speak. He was certainly awake when the steward reported: 'My lord, here in the great court is the provost of the town, with a delegation from the Guild Merchant, asking leave to speak with you. They say the matter is important.'

Abbot Radulfus allowed his steely, level brows to rise a little, and indicated graciously that the fathers of the borough should be admitted at once. Relations between the town of Shrewsbury on one side of the river and the abbey on the other, if never exactly cordial—that was too much to expect, where their interests so often collided—were always correct, and their skirmishes conducted with wary courtesy. If the abbot scented battle, he gave no sign. But for all that, thought Cadfael, watching the shrewd, lean hatchet-face, he has a pretty accurate idea of what they're here for.

The worthies of the guild entered the chapter-house in a solid phalanx, no less than ten of them, from half the crafts in the town, and led by the provost. Master Geoffrey Corviser, named for his trade, was a big, portly, vigorous man not yet fifty, clean-shaven, brisk and dignified. He made some of the finest shoes and riding-boots in England, and was well aware of their excellence and his own worth. For this occasion he had put on his best, and even without the long gown that would have been purgatory in this summer weather, he made an impressive figure, as clearly he meant to do. Several of those grouped at his back were wellknown to Cadfael: Edric Flesher, chief of the butchers of Shrewsbury, Martin Bellecote, master-carpenter, Reginald of Aston, the silversmith—men of substance every one. Abbot Radulfus did not know them, not yet. He had been only half a year in office, sent from London to trim an easy-going provincial house into more zealous shape, and he had much to learn about the men of the borders, as he himself, being no man's fool, was well aware.

'You are welcome, gentlemen,' said the abbot mildly. 'Speak freely, you shall have attentive hearing.'

The ten made their reverences gravely, spread sturdy feet, and stood planted like a battle-square, all eyes alert, all judgments held in reserve. The abbot was concentrating courteous attention upon them with much the same effect. In his interludes of duty as shepherd, Cadfael had once watched two rams level just such looks before they clashed foreheads.

'My lord abbot,' said the provost, 'as you know, Saint Peter's Fair opens on the day after tomorrow, and lasts for three days. It's of the fair we come to speak. You know the conditions. For all that time all shops in the town must be shut, and nothing sold but ale and wine. And ale and wine are sold freely here at the fairground and the Foregate, too, so that no man can make his living in the town from that merchandise. For three days, the three busiest of the year, when we might do well out of tolls on carts and pack-horses and man-loads passing through the town to reach the fair, we

5

must levy no charges, neither murage nor pavage. All tolls belong only to the abbey. Goods coming up the Severn by boat tie up at your jetty, and pay their dues to you. We get nothing. And for this privilege you pay no more than thirty-eight shillings, and even that we must go to the trouble to distrain from the rents of your tenants in the town.'

'*No more* than thirty-eight shillings!' repeated Abbot Radulfus, and elevated the iron-grey brows a shade higher, but still with an urbane countenance and a gentle voice. 'The sum was appointed as fair. And not by us. The terms of the charter have been known to you many years, I believe.'

'They have, and often before now have been found burdensome enough, but bargains must be kept, and we have never complained. But bad years or good, the sum has never been raised. And it falls very hard on a town so pressed as we are now, to lose three days of trade, and the best tolls of the year. Last summer, as you must know, though you were not then among us, Shrewsbury was under siege above a month, and stormed at last with great damage to the town walls, and great neglect of the streets, and for all our efforts there's still great need of work on them, and it's costly labour, after all last summer's losses. Not the half of the dilapidations are yet put right, and in these troublous times, who knows when we may again be under attack? The very traffic of your fair will be passing through our streets and adding to the wear, while we get nothing to help make good the damage.'

'Come to the point, Master Provost,' said the abbot in the same tranquil tone. 'You are come to make some demand of us. Speak it out plainly.'

'Father Abbot, so I will! We think—and I speak for the whole guild merchant and borough gathering of Shrewsbury —that in such a year we have the best possible case for asking that the abbey should either pay a higher fee for the fair, or, better by far, set aside a proportion of the fair tolls on goods, whether by horse-load or cart or boat, to be handed over to the town, and spent on restoring the walls. You benefit by the protection the town affords you; you ought, we think, to bear a part with us in maintaining its defences. A tenth share of the profits would be welcomed, and we should thank you heartily for it. It is not a demand, with respect, it is

6

an appeal. But we believe the grant of a tenth would be nothing more than justice.'

Abbot Radulfus sat, very erect and lean and lofty, gravely considering the phalanx of stout burgesses before him. 'That is the view of you all?'

Edric Flesher spoke up bluntly: 'It is. And of all our townsmen, too. There are many who would voice the matter more forcibly than Master Corviser has done. But we trust in your fellow-feeling, and wait your answer.'

The faint stir that went round the chapter-house was like a great, cautious sigh. Most of the brothers looked on wide-eyed and anxious; the younger ones shifted and whispered, but very warily. Prior Robert Pennant, who had looked to be abbot by this time, and been sorely disappointed at having a stranger promoted over his head, maintained a silvery, ascetic calm, appeared to move his lips in prayer, and shot sidelong looks at his superior between narrowed ivory lids, wishing him irredeemable error while appearing to compassionate and bless. Old Brother Heribert, recently abbot of this house and now degraded to its ranks, dozed in a quiet corner, smiling gently, thankful to be at rest.

'We are considering, are we not,' said Radulfus at length, gently and without haste, "what you pose as a dispute between the rights of the town and the rights of this house. In such a balance, should the judgement rest with you, or with me? Surely not! Some disinterested judge is needed. But, gentlemen, I would remind you, there has been such a decision, now, within the past half-year, since the siege of which you complain. At the beginning of this year his Grace King Stephen confirmed to us our ancient charter, with all its grants in lands, rights and privileges, just as we held them aforetime. He confirmed also our right to this three-day fair on the feast of our patron Saint Peter, at the same fee we have paid before, and on the same conditions. Do you suppose he would have countenanced such a grant, if he had not held it to be just?'

'To say outright what I suppose,' said the provost warmly, 'I never supposed for a moment that the thought of justice entered into it. I make no murmur against what his Grace chose to do, but it's plain he held Shrewsbury to be a hostile town, and most like still does hold it so, because FitzAlan, who is fled to France now, garrisoned the castle and kept it over a month against him. But small say we of the town ever had in the matter, and little we could have done about it! The castle declared for the Empress Maud, and we must put up with the consequences, while FitzAlan's away, safe out of reach. My lord abbot, is that justice?'

'Are you making the claim that his Grace, by confirming the abbey in its rights, is taking revenge on the town?' asked the abbot with soft and perilous gentleness.

'I am saying that he never so much as gave the town a thought, or its injuries a look, or he might have made some concession.'

'Ah! Then should not this appeal of yours be addressed rather to the Lord Gilbert Prescote, who is the king's sheriff, and no doubt has his ear, rather than to us?'

'It has been so addressed, though not with regard to the fair. It is not for the sheriff to give away any part of what has been bestowed on the abbey. Only you, Father, can do that,' said Geoffrey Corviser briskly. It began to be apparent that the provost knew his way about among the pitfalls of words every bit as well as did the abbot.

'And what answer did you get from the sheriff?'

'He will do nothing for us until his own walls at the castle are made good. He promises us the loan of labour when work there is finished, but labour we could supply, it's money and materials we need, and it will be a year or more before he's ready to turn over even a handful of his men to our needs. In such a case, Father, do you wonder that we find the fair a burden?'

'Yet we have our needs, too, as urgent to us as yours to you,' said the abbot after a thoughtful moment of silence. 'And I would remind you, our lands and possessions here lie outside the town walls, even outside the loop of the river, two protections you enjoy that we do not share. Should we, then, be asked to pay tolls for what cannot apply to us?'

'Not all your possessions,' said the provost promptly. 'There are within the town some thirty or more messuages in your hold, and your tenants within them, and their children have to

8

wade in the kennels of broken streets as ours do, and their horses break legs where the paving is shattered, as ours do.'

'Our tenants enjoy fair treatment from us, and considerate rents, and for such matters we are responsible. But we cannot be held responsible for the town's dilapidations, as we can for those here on our own lands. No,' said the abbot, raising his voice peremptorily when the provost would have resumed his arguments, 'say no more! We have heard and understood your case, and we are not without sympathy. But Saint Peter's Fair is a sacred right granted to this house, on terms we did not draw up; it is a right that inheres not to me as a man, but to this house, and I in my passing tenure have no authority to change or mitigate those terms in the smallest degree. It would be an offence against the king's Grace, who has confirmed the charter, and an offence against those my successors, for it could be taken and cited as a precedent for future years. No, I will not set aside any part of the profits of the fair to your use, I will not increase the fee we pay you for it, I will not share in any proportion the tolls on goods and stalls. All belong here, and all must be gathered here, according to the charter.' He saw half a dozen mouths open to protest against so summary a dismissal, and rose in his place, very tall and straight, and chill of voice and eye. 'This chapter is concluded,' he said.

There were one or two among the delegation who would still have tried to insist, but Geoffrey Corviser had a better notion of his own and the town's dignity, and a shrewder idea of what might or might not impress that self-assured and austere man. He made the abbot a deep, abrupt reverence, turned on his heel, and strode out of the chapter-house, and his defeated company recovered their wits and marched as haughtily after him.

There were booths already going up in the great triangle of the horse-fair, and all along the Foregate from the bridge to the corner of the enclosure, where the road veered right towards Saint Giles, and the king's highway to London. There was a newly-erected wooden jetty downstream from the bridge, where the long riverside stretch of the main abbey gardens and orchards began, the rich lowland known as the

Gaye. By river, by road, afoot through the forests and over the border from Wales, traders of all kinds began to make their way to Shrewsbury. And into the great court of the abbey flocked all the gentry of the shire, and of neighbouring shires, too, lordlings, knights, yeomen, with their wives and daughters, to take up residence in the overflowing guest-halls for the three days of the annual fair. Subsistence goods they grew, or bred, or brewed, or wove, or span for themselves, the year round, but once a year they came to buy the luxury cloths, the fine wines, the rare preserved fruits, the gold and silver work, all the treasures that appeared on the feast of Saint Peter ad Vincula, and vanished three days later. To these great fairs came merchants even from Flanders and Germany, shippers with French wines, shearers with the wool-clip from Wales, and clothiers with the finished goods, gowns, jerkins, hose, town fashions come to the country. Not many of the vendors had yet arrived, most would appear next day, on the eve of the feast, and set up their booths during the long summer evening, ready to begin selling early on the morrow. But the buyers were arriving in purposeful numbers already, bent on securing good beds for their stay.

When Brother Cadfael came up from the Meole brook and his vegetable-fields for Vespers, after a hard and happy afternoon's work, the great court was seething with visitors, servants and grooms, and the traffic in and out of the stables flowed without cease. He stood for a few minutes to watch the pageant, and Brother Mark at his elbow glowed as he gazed, dazzled by the play of colours and shimmer of movement in the sunlight.

'Yes,' said Cadfael, viewing with philosophical detachment what Brother Mark contemplated with excitement and wonder, 'the world and his wife will be here, either to buy or sell.' And he eyed his young friend attentively, for the boy had seen little enough of the world before entering the order, being thrust through the gates willy-nilly at sixteen by a stingy uncle who grudged him his keep even in exchange for hard work, and he had only recently taken his final vows. 'Do you see anything there to tempt you back into the secular world?'

'No,' said Brother Mark, promptly and serenely. 'But I

may look and enjoy, just as I do in the garden when the poppies are in flower. It's no blame to men if they try to put into their own artifacts all the colours and shapes God put into his.'

There were certainly a few of God's more charming artifacts among the throng of visitors moving about the great court and the stable-yard, young women as bright and blooming as the poppies, and all the prettier for being in a high state of expectation, looking forward eagerly to their one great outing of the year. Some came riding their own ponies, some pillion behind husbands or grooms, there was even one horse-litter bringing an important dowager from the south of the shire.

'I never saw it so lively before,' said Mark, gazing with pleasure.

'You've not lived through a fair as yet. Last year the town was under siege all through July and into August, small hope of getting either buyers or sellers into Shrewsbury for any such business. I had my doubts even about this year, but it seems trade's well on the move again, and our gentlefolk are hungrier than ever for what they missed a year ago. It will be a profitable fair, I fancy!'

'Then could we not have spared a tithe to help put the town in order?' demanded Mark.

'You have a way, child, of asking the most awkward questions. I can read very well what was in the provost's mind, since he spoke it out in full. But I'm by no means so sure I know what was in the abbot's, nor that he uttered the half of it. A hard man to read!'

Mark had stopped listening. His eyes were on a rider who had just entered at the gatehouse, and was walking his horse delicately through the moving throng towards the stables. Three retainers on rough-coated ponies followed at his heels, one of them with a cross-bow slung at his saddle. In these perilous times, even here in regions summarily pacified so short a time ago, no gentleman would undertake a longer journey without provision for his own defence, and an arbalest reaches further than a sword. This young man both wore a sword and looked as if he could use it, but he had also brought an archer with him for security.

11

It was the master who held Mark's eyes. He was perhaps a year or two short of thirty, past the uncertainties of first youth—if, indeed, he had ever suffered them—and at his resplendent best. Handsomely appointed, elegantly mounted on a glistening dark bay, he rode with the negligent ease of one accustomed to horses almost from birth.. In the summer heat he had shed his short riding-cotte, and had it slung over his lap, and rode with his shirt open over a spare, muscular chest, hung with a cross on a golden chain. The body thus displayed to view in simple linen shirt and dark hose was long and lissome and proud of its comeliness, and the head that crowned it was bared to the light, a smiling, animated face nicely fashioned about large, commanding dark eyes, and haloed in a cropped cap of dark gold hair, that would have curled had it been allowed to grow a little longer. He came and passed, and Mark's eyes followed him, at once tranquil and wistful, quite without any shade of envy.

'It must be a pleasant thing,' he said thoughtfully, 'to be so made as to give pleasure to those who behold you. Do you suppose he realises his blessings?'

Mark was rather small himself, from undernourishment from childhood, and plain of face, with spiky, straw-coloured hair round his tonsure. Not that he ever viewed himself much in the glass, or realised that he had a pair of great grey eyes of such immaculate clarity that common beauty faltered before them. Nor was Cadfael going to remind him of any such assets.

'As the world usually goes,' he said cheerfully, 'he probably has a mind that looks no further ahead or behind than the length of his own fine eyelashes. But I grant you he's a pleasure to look at. Yet the mind lasts longer. Be glad you have one that will wear well. Come on, now, all this will keep till after supper.'

The word diverted Brother Mark's thoughts very agreeably. He had been hungry all his life until he entered this house, and still he preserved the habit of hunger, so that food, no less than beauty, was unflawed pleasure. He went willingly at Cadfael's side towards Vespers, and the supper that would follow. It was Cadfael who suddenly halted, hailed by name

12

in a high, delighted voice that plucked his head about towards the summons gladly.

A lady, a slender, young, graceful lady with a heavy sheaf of gold hair and a bright oval face, and eyes like irises in twilight, purple and clear. Her body, as Brother Mark saw in his first startled glance, though scarcely swollen as yet, and proudly carried, was girdled high, and rounded below the girdle. There was a life there within. He was not so innocent that he did not know the signs. He should have lowered his eyes, and willed to do so, and could not; she shone so that it was like all the pictures of the Visiting Virgin that he had ever seen. And this vision held out both hands to Brother Cadfael, and called him by his name. Brother Mark, though unwillingly, bent his head and went on his way alone.

'Girl,' said Brother Cadfael heartily, clasping the proffered hands with delight, 'you bloom like a rose! And he never told me!'

'He has not seen you since the winter,' she said, dimpling and flushing, 'and we did not know then. It was no more than a dream, then. And *I* have not seen you since we were wed.'

'And you are happy? And he?'

'Oh, Cadfael, can you ask it!' There had been no need, the radiance Brother Mark had recognised was dazzling Cadfael no less. 'Hugh is here, but he must go to the sheriff first. He'll certainly be asking for you before Compline. I have come to buy a cradle, a beautiful carved cradle for our son. And a Welsh coverlet, in beautiful warm wool, or perhaps a sheepskin. And fine spun wools, to weave his gowns.'

'And you keep well? The child gives you no distress?'

'Distress?' she said, wide-eyed and smiling. 'I have not had a moment's sickness, only joy. Oh, Brother Cadfael,' she said, breaking into laughter, 'how does it come that a brother of this house can ask such wise questions? Have you not somewhere a son of your own? I could believe it! You know far too much about us women!'

'As I suppose,' said Cadfael cautiously, 'I was born of one, like the rest of us. Even abbots and archbishops come into the world the same way.'

'But I'm keeping you,' she said, remorseful. 'It's time for Vespers, and I'm coming, too. I have so many thanks to pour

13

out, there's never enough time. Say a prayer for our child!'
She pressed him by both hands, and floated away through the
press towards the guest-hall. Born Aline Siward, now Aline
Beringar, wife to the deputy sheriff of Shropshire, Hugh
Beringar of Maesbury, near Oswestry. A year married, and
Cadfael had been close friend to that marriage, and felt
himself enlarged and fulfilled by its happiness. He went on
towards the church in high content with the evening, his own
mood, and the prospects for the coming days.

When he emerged from the refectory after supper, into an
evening still all rose and amber light, the court was as animated as at noon, and new arrivals still entering at the
gatehouse. In the cloister Hugh Beringar sat sprawled at ease,
waiting for him; a lightweight, limber, dark young man, lean
of feature and quizzical of eyebrow. A formidable face,
impossible to read unless a man knew the language. Happily,
Cadfael did, and read with confidence.

'If you have not lost your cunning,' said the young man,
lazily rising, 'or met your overmatch in this new abbot of
yours, you can surely find a sound excuse for missing
Collations—and a drop of good wine to share with a friend.'

'Better than an excuse,' said Cadfael readily, 'I have an
acknowledged reason. They're having trouble in the grange
court with scour among the calves, and want a brewing of my
cure in a hurry. And I daresay I can find you a draught of
something better than small ale. We can sit outside the
workshop, such a warm evening. But are you not a neglectful
husband,' he reproved, as they fell companionably into step
on their way into the gardens, 'to abandon your lady for an
old drinking crony?'

'My lady,' said Hugh ruefully, 'has altogether abandoned
me! A breeding girl has only to show her nose in the guest-
hall, and she's instantly swept away by a swarm of older
dames, all cooing like doves, and loading her with advice on
everything from diet to midwives' magic. Aline is holding
conference with all of them, hearing details of all their
confinements, and taking note of all their recommendations.
And since I can neither spin, nor weave, nor sew, I'm
banished.' He sounded remarkably complacent about it, and
being well aware of it himself, laughed aloud. 'But she told

14

me she had seen you, and you needed no telling. How do you think she is looking?'

'Radiant!' said Cadfael. 'In full bloom, and prettier than ever.'

In the herb-garden, shaded along one side by its high hedge from the declining sun, the heavy fragrances of the day hung like a spell. They settled on a bench under the eaves of Cadfael's workshop, with a jug of wine between them.

'But I must start my draught brewing,' said Cadfael. 'You may talk to me while I do it, I shall hear you within, and I'll be with you as soon as I have it stirring. What's the news from the great world? Is King Stephen secure on his throne now, do you think?'

Beringar considered that in silence for a few moments, listening contentedly to the soft sounds of Cadfael's movements within the hut. 'With all the west still holding out for the empress, however warily, I doubt it. Nothing is moving now, but it's an ominous stillness. You know that Earl Robert of Gloucester is in Normandy with the empress?'

'So we'd heard. It's not to be wondered at, he is her half-brother, and fond of her, so they say, and not an envious man.'

'A good man,' agreed Hugh, doing an opponent generous justice, 'one of the few on either side not grasping for what he himself can get. The west, however quiet now, will do what Robert says. I can't believe he'll hold off for ever. And even out of the west, he has kinsmen and influence. The word runs that he and Maud, from their refuge in France, are working away quietly to enlist powerful allies, wherever they see a hope. If that's true, this civil war is by no means over. Promised enough support, there'll be a bid for the lady's cause, soon or late.'

'Robert has daughters married about the land,' said Cadfael thoughtfully, 'and all of them to men of might. One of them to the earl of Chester, I recall. If a few of that measure declared for the empress, you might well have a war on your hands to some purpose.'

Beringar drew a long face, and then shrugged off the thought. Earl Ranulf of Chester was certainly one of the most powerful men in the kingdom, virtually king himself of an

15

immense palatine where his writ ran, and no other. But for that very reason he was less likely to feel the need to declare for either side in the contention for the throne. Himself supreme, and unlikely ever to be threatened in his own possessions by either Maud or Stephen, he could afford to sit back and watch his own borders, not merely with a view to preserving them intact, rather to extending them. A land at odds with itself offers opportunities, as well as threats.

'Ranulf will need a lot of persuading, kinsman or no. He's very well as he is, and if he does move it will be because he sees profit and power in it for himself, and the empress will come a poor second. He's not the man to risk anything for any cause but his own.'

Cadfael came out from the hut to sit beside him, drawing grateful breath in the evening coolness, for he had his small brazier burning within, beneath his simmering brew. 'That's better! Now fill me a cup, Hugh, I'm more than ready for it.' And after a long and satisfying draught he said thoughtfully: 'There were some fears this disturbed state of things could ruin the fair even this year, but it seems trade keeps on the move while barons skulk in their castles. The prospects are excellent, after all.'

'For the abbey, perhaps,' agreed Hugh. 'The town is less happy about the outlook, from all we heard as we passed through. This new abbot of yours has set the burgesses properly by the ears.'

'Ah, you've heard about that?' Cadfael recounted the course of the argument, in case his friend had caught but one side of it. 'They have a case for seeking relief, no question. But so has he for refusing it, and he's standing firm on his rights. No way round it in law, he's taking no more than is granted to him. And no less!' he added, and sighed.

'Feelings are running high in the town,' warned Beringar seriously. 'I would not be sure you may not have trouble yet. I doubt if the provost made any too much of their need. The word in the town is that this may be law, but it is not justice. But what's the word with you? How are you faring in the new dispensation?'

'You'll hear murmurs even within our walls,' admitted Cadfael, 'if you keep your ears open. But for my part, I have no complaint. He's a hard man, but fair, and at least as hard on himself as on others. We've been spoiled and easy with Heribert, and the new curb pulled us up pretty sharply, but that's the sum of it. I have much confidence in the man. He'll chasten where he sees fault, but he'll stand by his own against any power where they are threatened blameless. He's a man I'd be glad to have beside me in any battle.'

'But his loyalty's limited to his own?' said Beringar slyly, and cocked a slender black brow.

'We live in a contentious world,' said Brother Cadfael, who had lived more than half his life in the thick of the battles. 'Who says peace would be good for us? I don't know the man well enough yet to know what's in his mind. I have not found him limited, but his vows are to his vocation and this house. Give him room and time, Hugh, and we shall see what follows. Time was when I was in two minds, or more, about *you!*' His voice marvelled and smiled at the thought. 'Not very long, however! I shall soon get the measure of Radulfus, too. Hand me the jug, lad, and then I must go and stir this brew for the calves. How long have we yet to Compline?'

TWO

ON THE THIRTY-FIRST OF JULY THE VENDORS CAME FLOODING IN, BY road and by river. From noon onward the horse-fair was marked out in lots for stalls and booths, and the abbey stewards were standing by to guide pedlars and merchants to their places, and levy the tolls due on the amount of merchandise they brought. A halfpenny for a modest man-load, a penny for a horse-load, from twopence to fourpence for a cart-load, depending on the size and capacity, and higher fees in proportion for the goods unloaded from the river barges that tied up at the temporary landing-stage along the Gaye. The entire length of the Foregate hummed and sparkled with movement and colour and chatter, the abbey barn and stable outside the wall was full, children and dogs ran among the booths and between the wheels of the carts, excited and shrill.

The discipline of the day's devotions within the walls was not relaxed, but between offices a certain air of holiday gaiety had entered with the guests, and novices and pupils were allowed to wander and gaze without penalty. Abbot Radulfus held himself aloof, as was due to his dignity, and left the superintendence of the occasion and the collection of tolls to his lay stewards, but for all that he knew everything that was going on, and had measures in mind to deal with any emergency. As soon as the arrival of the first Flemish merchant was reported to him, together with the news that the man had little French, he dispatched Brother Matthew, who had lived for some years in Flanders in his earlier days, and could speak fluent Flemish, to deal with any problems that might arise. If the fine-cloth merchants were coming, there was good reason to afford them every facility, for they were profitable visitors. It was a mark of the significance of the Shrewsbury fair that they should undertake so long a journey from the East Anglian ports where they put in, and find it worth their while to hire carts or horses for the overland pilgrimage.

The Welsh, of course, would certainly be present in some numbers, but for the most part they would be the local people who had a foot on either side the border, and knew enough English to need no interpreters. It came as a surprise to Brother Cadfael to be intercepted once again as he left the refectory after supper, this time by the steward of the grange court, preoccupied and breathless with business, and told that he was needed at the jetty, to take care of one who spoke nothing but Welsh, and a man of consequence, indeed of self-importance, who would not be fobbed off with the suspect aid of a local Welshman who might well be in competition with him on the morrow.

'Prior Robert gives you leave, for as long as you're needed. It's a fellow by the name of Rhodri ap Huw, from Mold. He's

18

brought a great load up the Dee, and ported it over to Vrnwy and Severn, which must have cost him plenty.'

'What manner of goods?' asked Cadfael, as they made for the gatehouse together. His interest was immediate and hearty. Nothing could have suited him better than a sound excuse to be out among the noise and bustle along the Foregate.

'What looks like a very fine wool-clip, mainly. And also honey and mead. And I thought I saw some bundles of hides —maybe from Ireland, if he trades out of the Dee. And there's the man himself.'

Rhodri ap Huw stood solid as a rock on the wooden planking of the jetty beside his moored barge, and let the tides of human activity flow round him. The river ran green and still, at a good level for high summer; even boats of deeper draught than usual had made the passage without mishap, and were unloading and unbaling on all sides. The Welshman watched, measuring other men's bales with shrewd, narrowed dark eyes, and pricing what he saw. He looked about fifty years old, and so assured and experienced that it seemed strange he had never picked up English. Not a tall man, but square-built and powerful, fierce Welsh bones is-landed in a thick growth of thorny black hair and beard. His dress, though plain and workmanlike, was of excellent material and well-fitted. He saw the steward hurrying towards him, evidently having carried out his wishes to the letter, and large, white teeth gleamed contentedly from the thicket of the black beard.

'Here am I, Master Rhodri,' said Cadfael cheerfully, 'to keep you company in your own tongue. And my name is Cadfael, at your service for all your present needs.'

'And very welcome, Brother Cadfael,' said Rhodri ap Huw heartily. 'I hope you'll pardon my fetching you away from your devotions . . .'

'I'll do better. I'll thank you! A pity to have to miss all this bustle, I can do with a glimpse of the world now and again.'

Sharp, twinkling eyes surveyed him from head to toe in one swift glance. 'You'll be from the north yourself, I fancy. Mold is where I come from.'

'Close by Trefriw I was born.'

'A Gwynedd man. But one who's been a sight further

19

through the world than Trefriw, by the look of you, brother. As I have. Well, here are my two fellows, ready to unload and porter for me before I send on part of my cargo downriver to Bridgnorth, where I have a sale for mead. Shall we have the goods ashore first?'

The steward bade them choose a stand at whatever point Master Rhodri thought fit when he had viewed the ground, and left them to supervise the unloading. Rhodri's two nimble little Welsh boatmen went to work briskly, hefting the heavy bales of hides and the wool-sacks with expert ease, and piling them on the jetty, and Rhodri and Cadfael addressed themselves pleasurably to watching the lively scene around them; as many of the townsfolk and the abbey guests were also doing. On a fine summer evening it was the best of entertainments to lean over the parapet of the bridge, or stroll along the green path to the Gaye, and stare at an annual commotion which was one of the year's highlights. If some of the townspeople looked on with dour faces, and muttered to one another in sullen undertones, that was no great wonder, either. Yesterday's confrontation had been reported throughout the town, they knew they had been turned away empty-handed.

'A thing worth noting,' said Rhodri, spreading his thick legs on the springy boards, 'how both halves of England can meet in commerce, while they fall out in every other field. Show a man where there's money to be made, and he'll be there. If barons and kings had the same good sense, a country could be at peace, and handsomely the gainer by it.'

'Yet I fancy,' said Cadfael dryly, 'that there'll be some hot contention here even between traders, before the three days are up. More ways than one of cutting throats.'

'Well, every wise man keeps a weapon about him, whatever suits his skill, that's only good sense, too. But we live together, we live together, better than princes manage it. Though I grant you,' he said weightily, 'princes make good use of these occasions, for that matter. No place like one of your greater fairs for exchanging news and views without being noticed, or laying plots and stratagems, or meeting someone you'd liefer not be seen meeting. Nowhere so solitary as in the middle of a market-place!'

'In a divided land,' said Cadfael thoughtfully, 'you may very well be right.'

'For instance—look to your left a ways, but don't turn. You see the meagre fellow in the fine clothes, the smooth-shaven one with the mincing walk? Come to watch who's arriving by water! You may be sure if *he's* here at all, he's come early, and has his stall already up and stocked, to be free to view the rest of us. That's Euan of Shotwick, the glover, and an important man about Earl Ranulf's court at Chester, I can tell you.'

'For his skill at his trade?' asked Cadfael dryly, observing the lean, fastidious, high-nosed figure with interest.

'That and other fields, brother. Euan of Shotwick is one of the sharpest of all Earl Ranulf's intelligencers, and much relied on, and if he's setting up a booth here as far as Shrewsbury, it may well be for more purposes than trade. And then on the other side, look, that great barge standing ready to come alongside—downstream of us. See the cut of her? Bristol-built, for a thousand marks! Straight out of the west country, and the city the king failed to take last year, and has let well alone ever since.'

Above the softly-flowing surface of Severn, its green sil-vered now with slanting evening sunlight, the barge sidled along the grassy shore towards the end of the jetty. She loomed impressively opulent and graceful, cunningly built to draw hardly more water than boats half her capacity, and yet steer well and ride steadily. She had a single mast, and what seemed to be a neat, closed cabin aft, and three crewmen were poling her inshore with easy, light touches, and waiting to moor her alongside as soon as there was room. Twenty pence, as like as not, thought Cadfael, before she gets her load ashore and cleared!

'Made to carry wine, and carry it steady,' said Rhodri ap Huw, narrowing his sharply-calculating eyes on the boat. 'Some of the best wines of France come into Bristol, they should have a ready sale as far north as this. I should know that rig!'

A considerable number of the onlookers, whether they recognised her port and rig or not, were curious enough to come down from the bridge and the highroad to see the Bristol boat come in. She was remarkable enough among her fellow-craft to draw all eyes. Cadfael caught sight of a number of known faces craning among the crowd: Edric Flesher's wife Petronilla, Aline Beringar's maid Constance leaning over the bridge, one of the abbey stewards forgetting his duties to stare; and suddenly sunlight on a head of dark gold hair, cropped short, and a young man came running lightly down from the highway, to halt on the grass slope above the jetty, and watch admiringly as the Bristol boat slid alongside, ready to be made fast. The lordling whose assured beauty had aroused Mark's wistful admiration was evidently just as inquisitive as the raggedest barefoot urchin from the Foregate.

The two Welshmen had completed their unloading by this time, and were waiting for orders, and Rhodri ap Huw was not the man to let his interest in other men's business interfere with his own.

'They'll be a fair while unloading,' he said briskly. 'Shall we go and choose a good place for my stall, while the field's open?'

Cadfael led the way along the Foregate, where several booths had already been set up. 'You'll prefer a site on the horse-fair itself, I fancy, where all the roads meet.'

'Ah, my customers will find me, wherever I am,' said Rhodri smugly; but for all that, he kept a shrewd eye on all the possibilities, and took his time about selecting his place, even when they had walked the length of the Foregate and come to the great open triangle of the horse-fair. The abbey servants had set up a number of more elaborate booths, that could be closed and locked, and supply living shelter for their holders, and these were let out for rents. Other traders brought their own serviceable trestles and light roofs, while the small country vendors would come in early each morning and display their wares on the dry ground, or on a woven brychan, filling all the spaces between. For Rhodri nothing was good enough but the best. He fixed upon a stout booth near the abbey barn and stable, where all customers coming in for the day could stable their beasts, and in the act could not fail to notice the goods on the neighbouring stalls.

'This will serve very well. One of my lads will sleep the nights here.' The elder of the two had followed them, balancing the first load easily in a sling over his shoulders, while the other remained to guard the merchandise stacked on the jetty. Now he began to stow what he had brought, while Rhodri and Cadfael set off back to the river to dispatch his fellow after him. On the way they intercepted one of the stewards, notified him of the site chosen, and came to terms for the rental. Brother Cadfael's immediate duty was done, but he was as interested in the growing bustle along the road and by the Severn as any other man who saw the like but once a year, and there was time to spare yet before Compline. It was good, too, to be speaking Welsh, there was seldom need within the walls.

They reached the point where the track turned aside from the highway to go down to the waterside, and looked down upon a lively scene. The Bristol boat was moored, and her three crewmen beginning to hoist casks of wine on to the jetty, while a big, portly, red-faced elderly gentleman in a long gown of fashionable cut, his capuchon twisted up into an elaborate hat, swung wide sleeves as he pointed and beckoned, giving orders at large. A fleshy but powerful face, round and choleric, with bristly brows like furze, and bluish jowls. He moved with surprising agility and speed, and plainly he considered himself a man of importance, and expected others to recognise him as such on sight.

'I thought it might well be!' said Rhodri ap Huw, pleased with his own acuteness and knowledge of widespread affairs. 'Thomas of Bristol, they call him, one of the biggest importers of wine into the port there, and deals in a small way in fancy wares from the east, sweetmeats and spices and candies. The Venetians bring them in from Cyprus and Syria. Costly and profitable! The ladies will pay high for something their neighbours have not! What did I say? Money will bring men together. Whether they hold for Stephen or the empress, they'll come and rub shoulders at your fair, brother.'

'By the look of him,' said Cadfael, 'a man of consequence in the city of Bristol.'

'So he is, and I'd have said in very good odour with Robert of Gloucester, but business is business, and it would take more than the simple fear of venturing into enemy territory to keep him at home, when there's good money to be made.'

They had turned to begin the descent to the riverside when

23

they were aware of a growing murmur of excitement among the people watching from the bridge, and of heads turning to look towards the town gates on the other side of the river. The evening light, slanting from the west, cast deep shadows under one parapet and half across the bridge, but above floated a faint, moving cloud of fine dust, glittering in the sunset rays, and advancing towards the abbey shore. A tight knot of young men came into sight, shearing through the strolling onlookers at a smart pace, like a determined little army on the march. All the rest were idling the time pleasurably away on a fine evening, these were bound somewhere, in resolution and haste, the haste, perhaps, all the more aggressive lest the resolution be lost. There might have been as many as five and twenty of them, all male and all young. Some of them Cadfael knew. Martin Bellecote's boy Edwy was there, and Edric Flesher's journeyman, and scions of half a dozen respected trades within the town; and at their head strode the provost's own son, young Philip Corviser, jutting a belligerent chin and swinging clenched hands to the rhythm of his long-striding walk. They looked very grave and very dour, and people gazed at them in wonder and speculation, and drew in at a more cautious pace after their passing, to watch what would happen.

'If this is not the face of battle,' said Rhodri ap Huw alertly, viewing the grim young faces while they were still safely distant, 'I have never seen it. I did hear that your house has a difference of opinion with the town. I'll away and see all those goods of mine safely stacked away under lock and key, before the trumpets blow.' And he tucked up his sleeves and was off down the path to the jetty as nimbly as a squirrel, and hoisting his precious jars of honey out of harm's way, leaving Cadfael still thoughtfully gazing by the roadside. The merchant's instincts, he thought, were sound enough. The elders of the town had made their plea and been sent away empty-handed. To judge by their faces, the younger and hotter-headed worthies of the town of Shrewsbury had resolved upon stronger measures. A rapid survey reassured him that they were unarmed, as far as he could see not even a staff among them. But the face, no question, was the face of battle, and the trumpets were about to blow.

THREE

THE ADVANCING PHALANX REACHED THE END OF THE BRIDGE, AND checked for no more than a moment, while their leader cast calculating glances forward along the Foregate, now populous with smaller stalls, and down at the jetty, and gave some brisk order. Then he, with perhaps ten of his stalwarts on his heels, turned and plunged down the path to the river, while the rest marched vehemently ahead. The interested townspeople, equally mutely and promptly, split into partisan groups, and pursued both contingents. Not one of them would willingly miss what was to come. Cadfael, more soberly, eyed the passing ranks, and was confirmed in believing that they came with the most austere intentions; there was not a bludgeon among them, and he doubted if any of them ever carried knives. Nothing about them was warlike, except their faces. Besides, he knew most of them, there was no wilful harm in any. All the same, he turned down the path after them, not quite easy in his mind. The Corviser sprig was known for a wild one, clever, bursting with hot and suspect ideas, locked in combat with his elders half his time, and occasionally liable to drink rather more than at this stage he could carry. Though this evening he had certainly not been drinking; he had far more urgent matters on his mind.

Brother Cadfael sighed, descending the path to the waterside half-reluctantly. The earnest young are so dangerously given to venturing beyond the point where experience turns back. And the sharper they are, the more likely to come by wounds.

He was not at all surprised to find that Rhodri ap Huw, that most experienced of travellers, had vanished from the jetty, together with his second porter and all his goods. Rhodri

25

himself would not be far, once he had seen all his merchandise well on its way to being locked in the booth on the horse-fair. He would want to watch all that passed, and make his own dispositions accordingly, but he would be out of sight, and somewhere where he could make his departure freely whenever he deemed it wise. But there were half a dozen boats of various sizes busy unloading, dominated by Thomas of Bristol's noble barge. Its owner heard the sudden surge of urgent feet on the downhill track, and turned to level an imperious glance that way, before returning to his business of supervising the landing of his goods. The array of casks and bales on the boards was impressive. The young men surging down to the river could not fail to make an accurate estimate of the powers they faced.

'Gentlemen . . . !' Philip Corviser hailed them all loudly, coming to a halt with feet spread, confronting Thomas of Bristol. He had a good, ringing voice; it carried, and lesser dealers dropped what they were doing to listen. 'Gentlemen, I beg a hearing, as you are citizens all, of whatever town, as I am of Shrewsbury, and as you care for your own town as I do for mine! You are here paying rents and tolls to the abbey, while the abbey denies any aid to the town. And we have greater need than ever the abbey has, of some part of what you bring.'

He drew breath hard, having spent his first wind. He was a gangling lad, not yet quite in command of his long limbs, being barely twenty and only just at the end of his growing. Spruce in his dress, but down at the heel, Cadfael noticed— proof of the old saying that the shoemaker's son is always the one who goes barefoot! He had a thick thatch of reddish dark hair, and a decent, homely face now pale with passion under his summer tan. A good, deft workman, they said, when he could be stopped from flying off after some angry cause or other. Certainly he had a cause now, bless the lad, he was pouring out to these hard-headed business men all the arguments his father had used to the abbot at chapter, in dead earnest, and—heaven teach him better sense!—even with hopes of convincing them!

'If the abbey turns a cold eye on the town's troubles, should you side with them? We are here to tell you our side of the story, and appeal to you as men who also have to bear the burdens of your own boroughs, and may well have seen at home what war and siege can do to your own walls and pavings. Is it unreasonable that we should ask for a share in the profits of the fair? The abbey came by no damage last year, as the town did. If they will not bear their part for the common good, we address ourselves to you, who have no such protection from the hardships of the world, and will have fellow-feeling with those who share the like burdens.'

They were beginning to lose interest in him, to shrug, and turn back to their unloading. He raised his voice sharply in appeal.

'All we ask is that you will hold back a tithe of the dues you pay to the abbey, and pay them instead to the town for murage and pavage. If all hold together, what can the abbey stewards do against you? There need be no cost to you above what you would be paying in any event, and we should have something nearer to justice. What do you say? Will you help us?'

They would not! The growl of indifference and derision hardly needed words. What, set up a challenge to what was laid down by charter, when they had nothing to gain by it? Why should they take the risk? They turned to their work, shrugging him off. The young men grouped at his back set up among themselves a counter murmur, still controlled but growing angry. And Thomas of Bristol, massive and contemptuous, waved a fist in their spokesman's face, and said impatiently: 'Stand out of the way, boy, you are hindering your betters! Pay a tithe to the town indeed! Are not the abbey rights set down according to law? And can you, dare you tell me they do not pay the fee demanded of them by charter? If you have a complaint that they are failing to keep the law, take it to the sheriff, where it belongs, but don't come here with your nonsense. Now be off, and let honest men get on with their work.'

The young man took fire. 'The men of Shrewsbury are as honest as you, sir, though something less boastful about it. We take honesty for granted here! And it is not nonsense that our town goes with broken walls and broken streets, while

27

abbey and Foregate have escaped all such damage. No, but listen . . .'

The merchant turned a broad, hunched back, with disdainful effect, and stalked away to pick up the staff he had laid against his piled barrels, and motion his men to continue their labours. Philip started indignantly after him, for the act was stingingly deliberate, as though a gnat, a mere persistent nuisance, had been brushed aside.

'Master merchant,' he called hotly, 'one word more!' And he laid an arresting hand to Thomas's fine, draped sleeve.

They were two choleric people, and it might have come to it even at the best, sooner or later, but Cadfael's impression was that Thomas had been genuinely startled by the grasp at his arm, and believed he was about to be attacked. Whatever the cause, he swung round and struck out blindly with the staff he held. The boy flung up his arm, but too late thoroughly to protect his head. The blow fell heavily on his forearm and temple, and laid him flat on the planking of the jetty, with blood oozing from a cut above his ear.

That was the end of all peaceful and dignified protest, and the declaration of war. Many things happened on the instant. Philip had fallen without a cry, and lay half-stunned, but someone had certainly cried out, a small, protesting shriek, instantly swallowed up in the roar of anger from the young men of the town. Two of them rushed to their fallen leader, but the rest, bellowing for vengeance, lunged to confront the equally roused traders, and closed with them merrily. In a moment the goods newly disembarked were being hoisted and flung into the river, and one of the raiders soon followed them, with a bigger splash. Fortunately those who lived all their lives by Severn usually learned to swim even before they learned to walk, and the youngster was in no danger of drowning. By the time he had hauled himself out and returned to the fray, there was a fully-fledged riot in progress all along the riverside.

Several of the cooler-headed citizens had moved in, though cautiously, to try to separate the combatants, and talk a little sense into the furious young; and one or two, not cautious enough, had come in for blows meant for the foe, the common fate of those who try to make peace where no one is inclined for it.

Cadfael among the rest had rushed down to the jetty, intent on preventing what might well be a second and fatal blow, to judge by the merchant's congested countenance and brandished staff. But someone else was before him. A girl had clambered frantically up out of the tiny cabin of the barge, kilted her skirts and leaped ashore, in time to cling with all her weight to the quivering arm, and plead in agitated tones:

'Uncle, don't, please don't! He did no violence! You've hurt him badly!'

Philip Corviser's brown eyes, all this time open but unseeing, blinked furiously at the sound of so unexpected a voice. He heaved himself shakily to his knees, remembered his injury and his grievance, and gathered his sprawled limbs and faculties to surge to his feet and do battle. Not that his efforts would have been very effective; his legs gave under him as he tried to rise, and he gripped his head between steadying hands as though it might fall off if he shook it. But it was the sight of the girl that stopped him short. There she stood, clinging to the merchant's arm and pleading angelically into his ear, in tones that could have cooled a dragon, her eyes all the time dilated and anxious and pitying on Philip. And calling the old demon 'uncle'! Philip's revenge was put clean out of his reach in an instant, but he scarcely felt a pang at the deprivation, to judge by the transformation that came over his bruised and furious face. Swaying on one knee, still dazed, he stared at the girl as pilgrims might stare at miraculous visions, or lost wanderers at the Pole star.

She was well worth looking at, a young thing of about eighteen or nineteen years, bare-armed and bare-headed, with two great braids of blue-black hair swinging to her waist, and framed between them a round, childish face all roses and snow, lit by two long-lashed dark blue eyes, at this moment huge with alarm and concern. No wonder the mere sound of her voice could tame her formidable uncle, as surely as the sight of her had checked and held at gaze the two young men who had rushed to salvage and avenge their leader, and who now stood abashed, gaping and harmless.

It was at that moment that the fight on the jetty, which had become a melee hopelessly tangled, reeled their way, thudding along the planks, knocked over the stack of small barrels, and sent them rolling thunderously in all directions. Cadfael grasped young Corviser under the arms, hoisted him to his feet and hauled him out of harm's way, thrusting him bodily into the arms of his friends for safe-keeping, since he was still in a daze. A rolling cask swept Thomas's feet from under him, and the girl, flung aside in his fall, swayed perilously on the edge of the jetty.

An agile figure darted past Cadfael with a flash of gold hair, leaped another rolling cask as nimbly as a deer, and plucked her back to safety in a long arm. The almost insolent grace and assurance was as familiar as the yellow hair. Cadfael contented himself with helping Thomas to his feet, and drawing him aside out of danger, and was not particularly surprised, when that was done, to see that the long arm was still gallantly clasped round the girl's waist. Nor was she in any hurry to extricate herself. Indeed, she was gazing at the smiling, comely, reassuring face of her rescuer wide-eyed, much as Philip Corviser had gazed at her.

'There, you're quite safe! But let me help you back aboard, you'd do best to stay there a while, your uncle, too. I advise it, sir,' he said earnestly. 'No one will offer you further offence. With this lady beside you, no one could be so ungallant,' he said, his eyes wide in candid admiration. The cream of the girl's fair skin turned all to rose.

Thomas of Bristol dusted himself down with slightly shaky hands, for he was a big man, and had fallen heavily. 'I thank you, sir, warmly, for your help. You, too, brother. But my wines—my goods—'

'Leave them to us, sir. What can be salvaged, shall be. You stay safe aboard, and wait. This cannot continue, the law will be out after these turbulent young fools any moment. Half of them are off along the Foregate, overturning stalls and hounding the abbey stewards. Before long they'll be in the town gaol with sore heads, wishing they'd had better sense than pick a fight with the abbot of a Benedictine house.'

His eye was on Cadfael, who was busy righting and retrieving the fugitive casks, and still within earshot. He felt himself being drawn companionably into this masterful young man's planning, perhaps as reassurance and guarantee of respectability. The eyes were slightly mischievous, though the face retained its decent gravity. The nearest Benedictine was being gently teased as representative of his order.

'My name,' said the rescuer blithely, 'is Ivo Corbière, of the manor of Stanton Cobbold in this shire, though the main part of my honour lies in Cheshire. If you'll allow me, I'm happy to offer my help . . .' He had taken his arm from about the girl's waist by then, decorously if reluctantly, but his gaze continued to embrace and flatter her; she was well aware of it, and it did not displease her. 'There!' cried Corbière triumphantly, as a shrill whistle resounded from a youth hanging over the parapet of the bridge above them. 'Now watch them dive to cover! Their look-out sees the sheriff's men turning out to quell the riot.'

His judgment was accurate enough. Half a dozen heads snapped up sharply at the sound, noted the urgently waving arm, and half a dozen dishevelled youths extricated themselves hastily from the fight, dropped whatever they were holding, and made off at speed in several directions, some along the Gaye, towards the coverts by the riverside, some up the slope into the tangle of narrow lanes behind the Foregate, one under the arch of the bridge, to emerge on the upstream side with no worse harm than wet feet. In a few moments the sharp clatter of hooves drummed over the bridge, and half a dozen of the sheriff's men came trotting down to the jetty, while the rest of the company swept on towards the horse-fair.

'As good as over!' said Ivo Corbière gaily 'Brother, will you lend an oar? I fancy you know this river better than I, and there's many a man's hard-won living afloat out there, and much of it may yet be saved.'

He asked no leave; he had selected already the smallest and most manageable boat that swung beside the jetty, and he was across the boards and down into it almost before the sheriff's men had driven their mounts in among the still-locked combatants, and begun to pluck the known natives out by the hair. Brother Cadfael followed. With Compline but ten minutes away, by his mental clock, he should have made his escape and left the salvage to this confident and commanding young man, but he had been sent out here to aid a client of the abbey fair, and could he not argue that he was still about the very same business? He was in the borrowed boat, an oar in his hand and his eye upon the nearest cask bobbing on the bright sunset waters, before he had found an answer; which was answer enough.

The noise receded soon. Everyone left here was busily hooking bales and bundles out of the river, pursuing some downstream to coves where they had lodged, abandoning one or two small items too sodden and too vulnerable to be saved, writing off minor losses, thankfully calculating profits still to be made after fees and rentals and tolls were paid. The damage was not so great, after all, it could be carried. Along the Foregate stalls were being righted, goods laid out afresh. Doubtful if the pandemonium had ever reached the horse-fair, where the great merchants unrolled their bales. In the stony confines of the castle and the town gaol, no doubt, some dozen or so youngsters of the town were nursing their bruises and grudges, and wondering how their noble and dignified protest had disintegrated into such a shambles. As for Philip Corviser, nobody knew where he had fetched up, once he shook off the devotees who had helped him away from the jetty in a daze. The brief venture was over, the cost not too great. Not even the sheriff, Gilbert Prestcote, was going to bear down too hard on those well-meaning but ill-advised young men of Shrewsbury.

'Gentlemen,' said Thomas of Bristol, eased and expansive, 'I cannot thank you enough for such generous help. No, the casks will have taken no hurt. Those who buy my wines should and do store them properly a good while before tapping, their condition will not be impaired. The sugar confections, thanks be, were not yet unloaded. No, I have suffered no real hurt. And my child here is much in your debt. Come, my dear, don't hide there within, make your respects to such good friends! Let me present my niece Emma, my sister's daughter, Emma Vernold, heiress to her father, who was a master-mason in our city, and also to me, for I have no other kin. Emma, my dear, you may pour the wine!'

The girl had made good use of the interval. She came forth now with her braids of hair coiled in a gilded net on her neck, and a fine tunic of embroidered linen over her plain gown. Not, thought Cadfael, for my benefit! It was high time for him to take his leave and return to his proper duties. He had missed Compline in favour of retrieving goods from the waters, and he would have to put in an hour or so in his workshop yet before he could seek his bed. No one would be early to bed on this night, however. Thomas of Bristol was not the man to leave the supervision of his booth and the disposition of his goods to others, however trustworthy his three servants might be; he would soon be off to the horse-fair to see everything safely stowed to his own satisfaction, ready for the morrow. And if he thought fit to leave those two handsome young people together here until his return, that was his affair. Mention of the manor of Stanton Cobbold, and as the least part of Corbière's honour, at that, had made its impression. There had been no real need for that careful mention of Mistress Emma's prospective wealth; but dutiful uncles and guardians must be ever on the alert for good matches for their girls, and this young man was already taken with her face before ever he heard of her fortune. Small wonder, she was a beautiful child by any standards.

Brother Cadfael excused himself from lingering, wished the company goodnight, and walked back at leisure to the gatehouse. The Foregate stretched busy and populous, but at peace. Order had been restored, and Saint Peter's Fair could open on the morrow without further disruption.

FOUR

HUGH BERINGAR CAME BACK FROM A FINAL PATROL ALONG THE Foregate well past ten o'clock, an hour when all dutiful brothers should have been fast asleep in the dortoir. He was by no means surprised to find that Cadfael was not. They met in the great court, as Cadfael came back from closing his workshop in the herb-garden. It was still a clear twilight, and the west had a brilliant afterglow.

'I hear you've been in the thick of it,' said Hugh, stretching and yawning. 'Did ever I know you when you were not? Mad young fools, what did they hope to do, that their elders could not! And then to run wild as they did, and ruin their case even with those who had sympathy for them! Now their sires will have fines to pay, and the town lose more for the night's work than ever it stood to gain. Cadfael, I take no joy in heaving decent, silly lads into prison, I have a foul taste in my mouth from it. Come into the gatehouse for a while, and share a cup with me. You may as well stay awake until Matins now.'

'Aline will be waiting for you,' objected Cadfael.

'Aline, bless her good sense, will be fast asleep, for I'm bound to the castle yet to report on this disturbance. I doubt I shall be there over the night. Come and tell me how all this went wrong, for they tell me it began down at the jetty, where you were.'

Cadfael went with him willingly. They sat together in the anteroom of the gatehouse, and the porter, used to such nocturnal activities when the deputy sheriff of the shire was lodged within, brought them wine, made tolerant enquiry of progress, and left them to their colloquy.

'How many have you taken up?' asked Cadfael, when he had given an account of what had happened by the river.

'Seventeen. And it should have been eighteen,' owned Hugh grimly, 'if I had not hauled Bellecote's boy Edwy aside without witnesses, put the fear of God into him, and sent him home with a flea in his ear. Not sixteen yet! But sharp enough to know very well what he was about, the imp! I should not have done it.'

'His father was one of yesterday's delegates,' said Cadfael, 'and he's a loyal child, as well as a bold one. I'm glad you let him away home. And young Corviser?'

'No, we've not laid hand on him, though a dozen witnesses say he was the ringleader, and captained the whole enterprise. But he has to go home some time, and he'll not get in at the gate a free man. Not a hope of it!'

'He came lecturing like a doctor,' said Cadfael seriously, 'and never a threatening move. It was when he was struck down that the wild lads took the bit between their teeth and laid about them. I saw it! The man who struck him lashed out in alarm, I grant you, but without cause.'

'I take your word for that, and I'll stand by it. But he led the attack, and he'll end with the rest, as he should, seeing he loosed this on us all. They'll be bailed by their fathers, the lot of them,' said Hugh wearily, and passed long fingers over tired eyelids. 'Do I seem to you, Cadfael, to be turning horribly into a crown official? That I should not like!'

'No,' said Cadfael judicially, 'you're not too far gone. Still a glint in the eye and a quirk in the mind. You'll do yet!'

'Gracious in you! And you say this Bristol merchant struck the silly wretch down without provocation?'

'He imagined provocation. The boy laid a detaining hand on his arm from behind, meaning no ill, but the man took fright. He had a staff in his hand, he turned on him and hit out. Felled him like an ox! I doubt if he had the strength to knock the trestle from under a stall, after that. For all I know, he may be fallen out of his senses, somewhere, unless his friends have kept their hands on him.'

Hugh looked at him across the trestle on which their own elbows were spread, and smiled. 'If ever I want for an advocate, I'll come running to you. Well, I do know the lad, he has a well-hung tongue, and lets it wag far too freely, and he has a hot temper and a warm heart, and lets the pair of them run away with his own sense—if you claim he has any!'

The lay porter put his bald brown crown and round red face into the room. 'My lord, there's a lady here at the gate has a trouble on her mind, and asks a word. One Mistress Emma Vernold, niece to the merchant Thomas of Bristol. Will you have her come in?'

They looked at each other across the board with raised brows and startled eyes. 'The same man?' said Beringar, marvelling.

'The same man, surely! And the same girl! But the uproar was all over. What can she be wanting here at this hour, and what's her uncle about, letting her venture loose into the night?'

'We'd best be finding out,' said Hugh, resigned. 'Let the lady come in, if I'm the man she wants.'

'She asked first for a guest here, Ivo Corbière, but I know he's still out viewing the preparations along the Foregate. And when I mentioned that you were here, she begged a word with you. Glad to find the law here and awake, seemingly.'

'Ask her to step in, then. And Cadfael, stay, if you'll be so good, she's had speech with you already, she may be glad of a known face.'

Emma Vernold came in hurriedly yet hesitantly, unsure of herself in this unfamiliar place, and made a hasty reverence. 'My lord, I pray your pardon for troubling you so late . . .' She saw Brother Cadfael, and half-smiled, relieved but distracted. 'I am Emma Vernold, I came with my uncle, Thomas of Bristol, we have our own living-space on his barge by the bridge. And this is my uncle's man Gregory.' It was the youngest of the three who attended her, a gawky, lean but powerful fellow of about twenty.

Beringar took her by the hand and put her into a seat by the table. 'I'm here to serve you, as best I can. What's your trouble?'

'Sir, my uncle went to see to the stocking of his booth at the horse-fair, it was not long after the good brother here left us. You'll have heard all that happened, below there? My uncle went to join his other two men, who were busy there before him, and left only Gregory with me. But that's nearly two hours ago, and he has not come back.'

'He will have brought a great deal of merchandise with him,' suggested Hugh reasonably. 'It takes time to arrange things to the best vantage, and I imagine your uncle will have things done well.'

'Oh, yes, indeed he will. But it isn't just that he is so long. The two men with him were his journeyman, Roger Dod, and the porter Warin, and Warin sleeps in the booth to mind the goods. Roger came back to the barge an hour ago, and was surprised not to find my uncle back, for he said he left the booth well before him. We thought perhaps he had met some acquaintance on the way, and stopped to exchange the news with him, so we waited some while, but still he did not come. And now I have been back to the booth with Gregory, to see

36

if by some chance he had turned back there for something, something forgotten, perhaps. But he has not, and Warin says, as Roger does, that my uncle left first, intending to come straight home to me, it being so late. He never liked—he does not like,' she amended, paling, 'for me to be alone with the men, without his company.' Her eyes were steady and clear, but her lip quivered, and there was the faint suggestion of disquiet even in the unflinching firmness of her regard.

She knows she is fair, Cadfael thought, and she's right to take account of it. It may even be that one of them—Roger Dod, the most privileged of the three, perhaps?—has a fancy for her, and she knows that, too, and has no fancy for him, and whether justly or not, is uneasy about being close to him without her guardian by.

'And you are sure he has not made his way home by some other way,' asked Hugh, 'while you've been seeking him at his booth?'

'We went back. Roger waited there, for that very case, but no, he has not come. I asked those still working in the Foregate if they had seen such a man, but I could get no news. And then I thought that perhaps—' She turned in appeal to Cadfael. 'The young gentleman who was so kind, this evening—he is staying here in the guest-hall, so he told us. I wondered if perhaps my uncle had met him again on his way home, and lingered . . . And he, at least, knows his looks, and could tell me if he has seen him. But he is not yet back, they tell me.'

'He left the jetty earlier than your uncle, then?' asked Cadfael. The young man had looked very well settled to spend a pleasant hour or two in the lady's company, but perhaps her formidable uncle had ways of conveying, even to lords of respectable honours, that his niece was to be approached only when he was present to watch over her.

Emma flushed, but without averting her eyes; eyes which were seen to be thoughtful, resolute and intelligent, for all her milk-and-roses baby-face. 'Very soon after you, brother. He was at all points correct and kind. I thought to come and ask for him, as someone on whom I could rely.'

'I'll ask the porter to keep a watch for him,' offered Cadfael, 'and have him step in here when he returns. Even

37

the horse-fair should be on its way to bed by now, and he'll be needing his own sleep if he's to hunt the best bargains tomorrow, which is what I take it he's here for. What do you say, Hugh?'

'A good thought,' said Hugh. 'Do it, and we'll make provision to look for Master Thomas, though I trust all's well with him, for all this delay. The eve of a fair,' he said, smiling reassurance at the girl, 'and there are contacts to be made, customers already looking over the ground . . . A man can forget about his sleep with his mind on business.'

Brother Cadfael heard her sigh: 'Oh, yes!' with genuine hope and gratitude, as he went to bid the porter intercept Ivo Corbière when he came in. His errand could hardly have been better timed, for the man himself appeared in the gateway. The main gate was already closed, only the wicket stood open, and the dip of the gold head stepping through caught the light from the torch overhead, and burned like a minor sun. Bare-headed, with his cotte slung on one shoulder in the warm last night of July, Ivo Corbière strolled towards his bed almost rebelliously, with a reserve of energy still unspent. The snowy linen shirt glowed in the lambent dark with a ghostly whiteness. He was whistling a street tune, more likely Parisian than out of London, by the cadence of it. He had certainly drunk reasonably deep, but not beyond his measure, nor even up to it. He was alert at a word.

'What, you, brother? Out of bed before Matins?' Amiable though his soft laughter was, he checked it quickly, sensing something demanding gravity of him. 'You were looking for me? Something worse fell out? Good God, the old man never killed the fool boy, did he?'

'Nothing so dire,' said Cadfael. 'But there's one within here at the gatehouse came looking for you, with a question. You've been about the Foregate and the fairground all this time?'

'The whole round,' said Ivo, his attention sharpening. 'I have a new and draughty manor to furnish in Cheshire. I'm looking for woollens and Flemish tapestries. Why?'

'Have you seen, in your wanderings, Master Thomas of Bristol? At any time since you left his barge earlier this evening?'

'I have not,' said Ivo, wondering, and peered closely in the strange, soft light of midsummer, an hour short of midnight.

'What is this? The man made it clear—he has practice, which is no marvel!—that his girl is to be seen only in his presence and with his sanction, and small blame to him, for she's gold, with or without his gold. I respected him for it, and I left. Why? What follows?'

'Come and see,' said Cadfael simply, and led the way within.

The young man blinked in the sudden light, and opened his eyes wide upon Emma. It was a question which of them showed the more distracted. The girl rose, reaching eager hands and then half-withdrawing them. The man sprang forward solicitously to welcome the clasp.

'Mistress Vernold! At this hour? Should you. . . .' He had a grasp of the company and the urgency by then. 'What has happened?' he asked, and looked at Beringar.

Briskly, Beringar told him. Cadfael was not greatly surprised to see that Corbière was relieved rather than dismayed. Here was a young, inexperienced girl, growing nervous all too easily when she was left alone an hour or so too long, while no doubt her uncle, very travelled and experienced indeed, and well able to take care of himself, was in no sort of trouble at all, but merely engaged in a little social indulgence with a colleague, or busy assessing the goods and worldly state of some of his rivals.

'Nothing ill will have happened to him,' said Corbière cheerfully, smiling reassurance at Emma, who remained, for all that, grave and anxious of eye. And she was no fool, Cadfael reflected, watching, and knew her uncle better than anyone else here could claim to know him. 'You'll see, he'll come home in his own good time, and be astonished to find you so troubled for him.'

She wanted to believe it, but her eyes said she could not be sure. 'I hoped he might have met you again,' she said, 'or that at least you might have seen him.'

'I wish it were so,' he said. 'It would have been my pleasure to set your mind at rest. But I have not seen him.'

'I think,' said Beringar, 'this lies now with me. I have still half a dozen men here within the walls, we'll make a search for Master Thomas. In the meantime, the hour is late, and you should not be wandering in the night. It will be best if your man here returns to the barge, while you, madam, if you consent, can very well join my wife, here in the guest-hall. Her maid Constance will make room for you, and find you whatever you need over the night.' There was no knowing whether he had noted her uneasiness about returning to the barge, just as acutely as Cadfael had, or was simply placing her in the nearest safe charge, and the best; but she brightened so eagerly, and thanked him so fervently, that there was no mistaking the relief she felt.

'Come, then,' he said gently, 'I'll see you safely into Constance's care, and then you may leave the searching to us.'

'And I,' said Corbière, shrugging enthusiastically into the sleeves of his cotte, 'will bear a hand with you in the hunt, if you'll have me.'

They combed the whole length of the Foregate, Beringar with his six men-at-arms, Ivo Corbière, as energetic and wide-awake as at noon, and Brother Cadfael, who had no legitimate reason to go with them at all, beyond the pricking of his thumbs, and the manifest absurdity of going to his bed at such an hour, when he would in any case have to rise again at midnight for Matins. If that was excuse enough for sharing a drink with Beringar, it was excuse enough for taking part in the hunt for Thomas of Bristol. For truly, thought Cadfael, shaking his head over the drastic events of the evening, I shall not be easy until I see that meaty blue-jowled face again, and hear that loud, self-confident voice. Corbière might shrug off the merchant's non-return as a mere trivial departure from custom, such as every man makes now and again, and on any other day Cadfael would have agreed with him; but too much had happened since noon today, too many people had been trapped into outrageous and uncharacteristic actions, too many passions had been let loose, for this to be an ordinary day. It was even possible that someone had stepped so far aside from his usual self as to commit deliberate violence by stealth in the night, to avenge what had been done openly and impulsively in the day. Though God forbid!

They had begun by making certain that there was still no word or sign at the jetty. No, Thomas had neither appeared nor sent word, and Roger Dod's forays among the other traders along the riverside, as far as he dared go from the property he guarded, had elicited no news of his master.

He was a burly, well-set-up young man of about thirty, this Roger Dod, and very personable, if he had not been so curt and withdrawn in manner. No doubt he was anxious, too. He answered Hugh's questions in the fewest possible words, and gnawed an uncertain lip at hearing that his master's niece was now lodged in the abbey guest-hall. He would have come with them to help in their search, but he was responsible for his master's belongings, and would have to be answerable for their safety when his master returned. He stayed with the barge, and sent the mute and sleepily resentful Gregory to lead them straight to the booth Master Thomas had rented. Beringar's sergeant, with three men, was left behind to work his way gradually along the Foregate after them, questioning every waking stallholder as he went, while the rest followed the porter to the fairground. The great open space was by this time half-asleep, but still winking with occasional torches and braziers, and murmuring with subdued voices. For these three days in the year it was transformed into a tight little town, busy and populous, to vanish again on the fourth day.

Thomas had chosen a large booth almost in the centre of the triangular ground. His goods were neatly stacked within, and his watchman was awake and prowling the ground uneasily, to welcome the arrival of authority with relief. Warin was a leathery, middle-aged man, who had clearly been in his present service many years, and was probably completely trusted within his limits, but had not the ability ever to rise to the position Roger Dod now held.

'No, my lord,' he said anxiously, 'never a word since, and I've been on watch every moment. He set off for his barge a good quarter of an hour before Roger left. We had everything stowed to his liking, he was well content. And he'd had a fall not so long before—you'd know of that?—and was glad enough, I'd say, to be off home to his bed. For after all, he's none so young, no more than I am, and he carries more weight.'

'And he set off from here, which way?'

'Why, straight to the highroad, close by here. I suppose he'd keep along the Foregate.'

Behind Cadfael's shoulder a familiar voice, rich and full and merrily knowing, said in Welsh: 'Well, well, brother, out so late? And keeping the law company! What would the deputy sheriff of the shire want with Thomas of Bristol's watchman at this hour? Are they on the scent of all Gloucester's familiars, after all? And I claimed commerce was above the anarchy!' Narrowed eyes twinkled at Cadfael in the light of the dispersed torches and the far-distant stars in a perfect midsummer sky. Rhodri ap Huw was chuckling softly and fatly at his own teasing wit and menacing sharpness of apprehension.

'You keep a friendly eye out for your neighbours?' said Cadfael, innocently approving. 'I see you brought off all your own goods without scathe.'

'I have a nose for trouble, and the good sense to step out of its way,' said Rhodri ap Huw smugly. 'What's come to Thomas of Bristol? He was not so quick on the scent, it seems. He could have loosed his moorings and poled out into the river till the flurry was over, and been as safe as in the west country.'

'Did you see him struck down?' asked Cadfael deceitfully; but Rhodri was not to be caught.

'I saw him strike down the other young fool,' he said, and grinned. 'Why, did he come to grief after I left? And which of them is it you're looking for, Thomas or the lad?' And he stared with marked interest to see the sheriff's men probing at the backs of stalls, and under the trestles, and followed inquisitively on their heels as they worked their way back along the highroad. Evidently nothing of moment was to be allowed to happen at this fair without Rhodri ap Huw being present at it, or very quickly and minutely informed of it. And why not make use of his perspicacity?

'Thomas's niece is in a taking because he has not come back to his barge. That might mean anything or nothing, but now it's gone on so long, his men are getting uneasy, too. Did you see him leave his booth?'

'I did. It might be as much as two hours ago. And his

42

journeyman some little while after him. A fair size of a man, to be lost between here and the river. And no word of him anywhere since then?'

'Not that we've found, or likely to find, without questioning every trader and every idler in all this array. And the wiser half of them getting their sleep in ready for the morning.'

They had reached the Foregate and turned towards the town, and still Rhodri strode companionably beside Cadfael, and had taken to peering into the dark spaces between stalls just as the sheriff's men were doing. Lights and braziers were fewer here, and the stalls more modest, and the quiet of the night closed in drowsily. On their left, under the abbey wall, a few compact but secure booths were arrayed. The first of them, though completely closed in and barred for the night, showed through a chink the light of a candle within. Rhodri dug a weighty elbow into Cadfael's ribs.

'Euan of Shotwick! No one is ever going to get at *him* from the rear, he likes a corner backed into two walls if he can get it. Travels alone with a pack-pony, and wears a weapon, and can use it, too. A solitary soul because he trusts nobody. His own porter—luckily his wares weigh light for their value—and his own watchman.'

Ivo Corbière had loitered to go aside between the stalls, some of which in this stretch were still unoccupied, waiting for the local traders who would come with the dawn. The consequent darkness slowed their search, and the young man, not at all averse to spending the night without sleep, and probably encouraged by the memory of Emma's bright eyes, was tireless and thorough. Even Cadfael and Rhodri ap Huw were some yards ahead of him when they heard him cry after them, high and urgently:

'Good God, what's here? Beringar, come back here!'

The tone was enough to bring them running. Corbière had left the highway, probing between stacked trestles and leaning canvas awnings into darkness, but when they peered close there was lambent light enough from the stars for accustomed eyes to see what he had seen. From beneath a light wooden frame and stretched canvas jutted two booted feet, motionless, toes pointed skywards. For a moment they all stared in silence, dumbstruck, for truth to tell, not one of them had believed that the merchant could have come to any harm, as they all agreed afterwards. Then Beringar took hold of the frame and hoisted it away from the trestles against which it leaned, and dim and large in the darkness they saw a man's long shape, from the knees up rolled in a cloak that hid the face. There was no movement, and no noticeable sound.

The sergeant leaned in with the one torch they had brought with them, and Beringar reached a hand to the folds of the cloak, and began to draw them back from the shrouded head and shoulders. The movement of the cloth released a powerful wave of an odour that made him halt and draw suspicious breath. It also disturbed the body, which emitted an enormous snore, and a further gust of spirituous breath.

'Dead drunk and helpless,' said Beringar, relieved. 'And not, I fancy, the man we're looking for. The state he's in, this fellow must have been here some hours already, and if he comes round in time to crawl away before dawn it will be a miracle. Let's have a look at him.' He was less gingerly now in dragging the cloak away, but the drunken man let himself be hauled about and dragged forth by the feet with only a few disturbed grunts, and subsided into stertorous sleep again as soon as he was released. The torch shone its yellow, resinous light upon a shock-head of coarse auburn hair, a pair of wide shoulders in a leather jerkin, and a face that might have been sharp, lively and even comely when he was awake and sober, but now looked bloated and idiotic, with open, slobbering mouth and reddened eyes.

Corbière took one close look at him, and let out a gasp and an oath. '*Fowler!* Devil take the sot! Is this how he obeys me? By God, I'll make him sweat for it!' And he filled a fist with the thick brown hair and shook the fellow furiously, but got no more out of him than a louder snort, the partial opening of one glazed eye, and a wordless mumble that subsided again as soon as he was dropped, disgustedly and ungently, back into the turf.

'This drunken rogue is mine . . . my falconer and archer, Turstan Fowler,' said Ivo bitterly, and kicked the sleeper in the ribs, but not savagely. What was the use? The man would not be conscious for hours yet, and what he suffered afterwards would pay him all his dues. 'I've a mind to put him to

44

cool in the river! I never gave him leave to quit the abbey precinct, and by the look of him he's been out and drinking—Good God, the reek of it, what raw spirit can it be?—since ever I turned my back.'

'One thing's certain,' said Hugh, amused, 'he's in no case to walk back to his bed. Since he's yours, what will you have done with him? I would not advise leaving him here. If he has anything of value on him, even his hose, he might be without it by morning. There'll be scavengers abroad in the dark hours—no fair escapes them.'

Ivo stood back and stared down disgustedly at the oblivious culprit. 'If you'll lend me two of your men, and let us borrow a board here, we'll haul him back and toss him into one of the abbey's punishment cells, to sleep off his swinishness on the stones, and serve him right. If we leave him there unfed all the morrow, it may frighten him into better sense. Next time, I'll have his hide!'

They hoisted the sleeper on to a board, where he sprawled aggravatingly into ease again, and snored his way along the Foregate so blissfully that his bearers were tempted to tip him off at intervals, by way of recompensing themselves for their own labour. Cadfael, Beringar and the remainder of the party were left looking after them somewhat ruefully, their own errand still unfulfilled.

'Well, well!' said Rhodri ap Huw softly into Cadfael's ear, 'Euan of Shotwick is taking a modest interest in the evening's happenings, after all!'

Cadfael turned to look, and in the shuttered booth tucked under the wall a hatch had certainly opened, and against the pale light of a candle a head leaned out in sharp outline, staring towards where they stood. He recognised the high-bridged, haughty nose, the deceptively meagre slant of the lean shoulders, before the hatch was drawn silently to again, and the glover vanished.

They worked their way doggedly, yard by yard, all the way back to the riverside, where Roger Dod was waiting in a fume of anxiety, but they found no trace of Thomas of Bristol.

*   *   *

A late boat coming up the Severn from Buildwas next day, and tying up at the bridge about nine in the morning, delayed its unloading of a cargo of pottery to ask first that a message be sent to the sheriff, for they had other cargo aboard, taken up out of a cove near Atcham, which would be very much the sheriff's business. Gilbert Prestcote, busy with other matters, sent from the castle his own sergeant, with orders to report first to Hugh Beringar at the abbey.

The particular cargo the potter had to deliver lay rolled in a length of coarse sail-cloth in the bottom of the boat, and oozed water in a dark stain over the boards. The boatman unfolded the covering, and displayed to Beringar's view the body of a heavily-built man of some fifty to fifty-five years, fleshy, with thinning, grizzled hair and bristly, bluish jowls, his pouchy features sagging doughily in death. Master Thomas of Bristol, stripped of his elaborate capuchon, his handsome gown, his rings and his dignity, as naked as the day he was born.

'We saw his whiteness bobbing under the bank,' said the potter, looking down upon his salvaged man, 'and poled in to pick him up, the poor soul. I can show you the place, this side of the shallows and the island at Atcham. We thought best to bring him here, as we would a drowned man. But this one,' he said very soberly, 'did not drown.'

No, Thomas of Bristol had not drowned. That was already evident from the very fact that he had been stripped of everything he had on, and hardly by his own hands or will. But also, even more certainly, from the incredibly narrow wound under his left shoulder-blade, washed white and closed by the river, where a very fine, slender dagger had transfixed him and penetrated to his heart.

THE FIRST
DAY OF THE FAIR

ONE

THE FIRST DAY OF SAINT PETER'S FAIR WAS IN FULL SWING, AND THE merry, purposeful hum of voices bargaining, gossiping and crying wares came over the wall into the great court, and in at the gatehouse, like the summer music of a huge hive of bees on a sunny day. The sound pursued Hugh Beringar back to the apartment in the guest-hall, where his wife and Emma Vernold were very pleasurably comparing the virtues of various wools, and the maid Constance, who was an expert spinstress, was fingering the samples critically and giving her advice.

On this domestic scene, which had brought back the fresh colour to Emma's cheeks and the animation to her voice, Hugh's sombre face cast an instant cloud. There was no time for breaking news circuitously, nor did he think that this girl would thank him for going roundabout.

'Mistress Vernold, my news is ill, and I grieve for it. God knows I had not expected this. Your uncle is found. A boat coming up early this morning from Buildwas picked up his body from the river.'

The colour ebbed from her face. She stood with frightened, helpless eyes gazing blindly before her. The prop of her life had suddenly been plucked away, and for a moment it seemed that all balance was lost to her, and she might indeed fall for want of him. But by the time she had drawn breath deep, and shaped soundlessly: 'Dead!' it was clear that she was firm on her own feet again, and in no danger of falling. Her eyes, once the momentary panic and dizziness passed, looked straight at Hugh and made no appeal.

'Drowned?' she said. 'But he swam well, he was raised by the river. And if he drank at all, it was sparingly. I do not

49

believe he could fall into Severn and drown. Not of himself!' she said, and her large eyes dilated.

'Sit down,' said Hugh gently, 'for we must talk a little, and then I shall leave you with Aline, for of course you must remain here in our care for this while. No, he did not drown. Nor did he come by his death of himself. Master Thomas was stabbed from behind, stripped, and put into the river after death.'

'You mean,' she said, in a voice low and laboured, but quite steady, 'he was waylaid and killed by mere sneak-thieves, for what he had on him? For his rings and his gown and his shoes?'

'It is what leaps to the mind. There are no roads in England now that can be called safe, and no great fair that has not its probable underworld of hangers-on, who will kill for a few pence.'

'My uncle was not a timid man. He has fought off more than one attack in his time, and he never avoided a journey for fear in his life. After all these years,' she said, her voice aching with protest, 'why should he fall victim now to such scum? And yet what else can it be?'

'There are some people recalling,' said Hugh, 'that there was an ugly incident on the jetty last evening, and violence was done to a number of the merchants who were unloading goods and setting up stalls for the fair. It's common knowledge there was bad blood between town and traders, of whom Master Thomas was perhaps the most influential. He was involved bitterly with the young man who led the raid. An attack made in revenge, by night, perhaps in a drunken rage, might end mortally, whether it was meant or no.'

'Then he would have been left where he lay,' said Emma sharply. 'His attacker would think only of getting clean away unseen. Those angry people were not thieves, only townsmen with a grievance. A grievance might turn them into murderers, but I do not think it would turn them into thieves.'

Hugh was beginning to feel considerable respect for this girl, as Aline, by her detached silence and her attentive face, had already learned to do. 'I won't say but I agree with you there,' he admitted. 'But it might well occur to a young man turned murderer almost by mishap, to dress his crime as the common sneak killing for robbery. It opens so wide a field. Twenty young men bitterly aggrieved and hot against your uncle for his scorn of them could be lost among a thousand unknown, and the most unlikely suspects among them, at that, if this passes as chance murder for gain.'

Even in the bleak newness of her bereavement, this thought troubled her. She bit a hesitant lip. 'You think it may have been one of those young men? Or more of them together? That they burned with their grudge until they followed him in the dark, and took this way?'

'It's being both thought and said,' owned Hugh, 'by many people who witnessed what happened by the river.'

'But the sheriff's men,' she pointed out, frowning, 'surely took up many of those young men long before my uncle went to the fairground. If they were already in prison, they could not have harmed him.'

'True of most of them. But the one who led them was not taken until the small hours of the morning, when he came reeling back to the town gate, where he was awaited. He is in a cell in the castle now, like his fellows, but he was still at liberty long after Master Thomas failed to come back to you, and he is under strong suspicion of this death. The whole pack of them will come before the sheriff this afternoon. The rest, I fancy, will be let out on their fathers' bail, to answer the charges later. But for Philip Corviser, I greatly doubt it. He will need to have better answers than he was able to give when they took him.'

'This afternoon!' echoed Emma. 'Then I should also attend. I was a witness when this turmoil began. The sheriff should hear my testimony, too, especially if my uncle's death is in question. There were others—Master Corbière, and the brother of the abbey, the one you know well . . .'

'They will be attending, and others besides. Certainly your witness would be valuable, but to ask it of you at such a time . . .'

'I would rather!' she said firmly. 'I want my uncle's murderer caught, if indeed he was murdered, but I pray no innocent man may be too hurriedly blamed. I don't know—I would not have thought he looked like a murderer . . . I should like to tell what I do know, it is my duty.'

Beringar cast a brief glance at his wife for enlightenment and Aline gave him a smile and the faintest of nods.

'If you are resolved on that,' he said, reassured, 'I will ask Brother Cadfael to escort you. And for the rest, you need have no anxieties about your own situation. It will be necessary for you to stay here until this matter is looked into, but naturally you will remain here in Aline's company, and you shall have every possible help in whatever dispositions you need to make.'

'I should like,' said Emma, 'to take my uncle's body back by the barge to Bristol for burial.' She had not considered, until then, that there would be no protector for her on the boat this time, only Roger Dod, whose mute but watchful and jealous devotion was more than she could bear, Warin who would take care to notice nothing that might cause him trouble, and poor Gregory, who was strong and able of body but very dull of wit. She drew in breath sharply, and bit an uncertain lip, and the shadow came back to her eyes. 'At least, to send him back . . . His man of law there will take care of his affairs and mine.'

'I have spoken to the prior. Abbot Radulfus sanctions the use of an abbey chapel, your uncle's body can lie there when he is brought from the castle, and all due preparations will be made for his decent coffining. Ask for anything you want, it shall be at your disposal. I must summon your journeyman to attend at the castle this afternoon, too. How would you wish him to deal, concerning the fair? I will give him whatever instructions you care to send.'

She nodded understanding, visibly bracing herself again towards a world of shrewd daily business which had not ceased with the ending of a life. 'Be so kind as to tell him,' she said, 'to continue trading for the three days of the fair, as though his master still presided. My uncle would scorn to go aside from his regular ways for any danger or loss, and so will I in his name.' And suddenly, as freely and as simply as a small child, she burst into tears at last.

When Hugh was gone about his business, and Constance had withdrawn at Aline's nod, the two women sat quietly until Emma had ceased to weep, which she did as suddenly as she had begun. She wept, as some women have the gift of doing, without in the least defacing her own prettiness and without caring whether she did or no. Most lose the faculty, after the end of childhood. She dried her eyes, and looked up straightly at Aline, who was looking back at her just as steadily, with a serenity which offered comfort without pressing it.

'You must think,' said Emma, 'that I had no deep affection for my uncle. And indeed I don't know myself that you would be wrong. And yet I did love him, it has not been only loyalty and gratitude, though those came easier. He was a hard man, people said, hard to satisfy, and hard in his business dealings. But he was not hard to me. Only hard to come near. It was not his fault, or mine.'

'I think,' said Aline mildly, since she was being invited closer, 'you loved him as much as he would let you. As he *could* let you. Some men have not the gift.'

'Yes. But I would have liked to love him more. I would have done anything to please him. Even now I want to do everything as he would have wished. We shall keep the booth open as long as the fair lasts, and try to do it as well as he would have done. All that he had in hand, I want to see done thoroughly.' Her voice was resolute, almost eager. Master Thomas would certainly have approved the set of her chin and the spark in her eye. 'Aline, shall I not be a trouble to you by staying here? I—my uncle's men—there's one who likes me too well. . . .'

'So I had thought,' said Aline. 'You're most welcome here, and we'll not part with you until you can be sent back safely to Bristol, and your home. Not that I can find it altogether blameworthy in the young man to like you, for that matter,' she added, smiling.

'No, but I cannot like *him* well enough. Besides, my uncle would never have allowed me to be there on the barge without him. And now I have duties,' said Emma, rearing her head determinedly and staring the uncertain future defiantly in the face. 'I must see to the ordering of a fine coffin for him, for the journey home. There will be a master-carpenter, somewhere in the town?'

'There is. To the right, halfway up the Wyle, Master

53

Martin Bellecote. A good man, and a good craftsman. His lad was among these terrible rioters, as I hear,' said Aline, and dimpled indulgently at the thought, 'but so were half the promising youth of the town. I'll come in with you to Martin's shop.'

'No,' said Emma firmly. 'It will all be tedious and long at the sheriff's court, and you should not tire yourself. And besides, you have to buy your fine wools, before the best are taken. And Brother Cadfael—was that the name?—will show me where to find the shop. He will surely know.'

'There's very little to be known about this precinct and the town of Shrewsbury,' agreed Aline with conviction, 'that Brother Cadfael does not know.'

Cadfael received the abbot's dispensation to attend the hearing at the castle, and to escort the abbey's bereaved guest, without question. A civic duty could not be evaded, whether by secular or monastic. Radulfus had already shown himself both an austere but just disciplinarian and a shrewd and strong-minded business man. He owed his preferment to the abbacy as much to the king as to the papal legate, and valued and feared for the order of the realm at least as keenly as for the state of his own cure. Consequently he had a use for those few among the brothers who shared his wide experience of matters outside the cloister.

'This death,' he said, closeted with Cadfael alone after Beringar's departure, 'casts a shadow upon our house and our fair. Such a burden cannot be shifted to other shoulders. I require of you a full account of what passes at this hearing. It was of me that the elders of the town asked a relief I could not grant. On me rests the load of resentment that drove those younger men to foolish measures. They lacked patience and thought, and they were to blame, but that does not absolve me. If the man's death has arisen out of my act, even though I could not act otherwise, I must know it, for I have to answer for it, as surely as the man who struck him down.'

'I shall bring you all that I myself see and hear, Father Abbot,' said Cadfael.

'I require also all that you think, brother You saw part of what happened yesterday between the dead man and the living youth. Is it possible that it could have brought about such a death as this? Stabbed in the back? It is not commonly the method of anger.'

'Not commonly.' Cadfael had seen many deaths in the open anger of battle, but he knew also of rages that had bred and festered into killings by stealth, with the anger as hot as ever, but turned sour by brooding. 'Yet it is possible. But there are other possibilities. It may indeed be what it first seems, a mere crude slaughter for the clothes on the body and the rings on the fingers, opportune plunder in the night, when no one chanced to be by. Such things happen, where men are gathered together and there is money changing hands.'

'It is true,' said Radulfus, coldly and sadly. 'The ancient evil is always with us.'

'Also, the man is of great importance in his trade and his region, and he may have enemies. Hate, envy, rivalry, are as powerful motives even as gain. And at a great fair such as ours, enemies may be brought together, far from the towns where their quarrels are known, and their acts might be guessed at too accurately. Murder is easier and more tempting, away from home.'

'Again, true,' said the abbot. 'Is there more?'

'There is. There is the matter of the girl, niece and heiress to the dead man. She is of great beauty,' said Cadfael plainly, asserting his right to recognise and celebrate even the beauty of women, though their enjoyment he had now voluntarily forsworn, 'and there are three men in her uncle's service, shut on board a river barge with her. Only one of them old enough, it may be, to value his peace more. One, I think, God's simpleton, but not therefore blind, or delivered from the flesh. And one whole, able, every way a man, and enslaved to her. And this one it was who followed his master from the booth on the fairground, some say a quarter of an hour after him, some say a little more. God forbid I should therefore point a finger at an honest man. But we speak of possibilities. And will speak of them no more until, or unless, they become more than possibilities.'

'That is my mind, also,' said Abbot Radulfus, stirring and almost smiling. He looked at Cadfael steadily and long. 'Go and bear witness, brother, as you are charged, and bring me word again. In your report I shall set my trust.'

Emma had on, perforce, the same gown and bliaut she had worn the evening before, the gown dark blue like her eyes, but the tunic embroidered in many colours upon bleached linen. The only concession she could make to mourning was to bind up her great wealth of hair, and cover it from sight within a borrowed wimple. Nevertheless, she made a noble, mourning figure. In the severe white frame her rounded, youthful face gained in concentrated force and meaning what it lost in pure grace. She had a look of single-minded gravity, like a lance in rest. Brother Cadfael could not yet see clearly where the lance was aimed.

When she caught sight of him approaching, she looked at him with pleased recognition, as the man behind the lance might have looked round at the fixed, partisan faces of his friends before the bout, but never shifted the focus of her soul's intent, which reached out where he could not follow.

'Brother Cadfael—have I your name right? It's Welsh, is it not? You were kind, yesterday. Lady Beringar says you will show me where to find the master-carpenter. I have to order my uncle's coffin, to take him back to Bristol.' She was quite composed, yet still as simple and direct as a child. 'Have we time, before we must go to the castle?'

'It's on the way,' said Cadfael comfortably. 'You need only tell Martin Bellecote, whatever you ask of him he'll see done properly.'

'Everyone is being very kind,' she said punctiliously, like a well-brought-up little girl giving due thanks. 'Where is my uncle's body now? I should care for it myself, it is my duty.'

'That you cannot yet,' said Cadfael. 'The sheriff has him at the castle, he must needs see the body for himself, and have the physician also view it. You need be put to no distress on that account, the abbot has given orders. Your uncle will be brought with all reverence to lie in the church here, and the brothers will make him decent for burial. I think he might well wish, could he tell you so now, that you should leave all to us. His care for you would reach so far, and your obedience could not well deny him.'

56

Cadfael had seen the dead man, and felt strongly that she should not have the same experience. Nor was it for her sake entirely that he willed so. The man she had respected and admired in his monumental dignity, living, had the right to be preserved for her no less decorously in death.

He had found the one argument that could deflect her absolute determination to take charge of all, and escape nothing. She thought about it seriously as they passed out at the gatehouse side by side, and he knew by her face the moment when she accepted it.

'But he did believe that I ought to take my full part, even in his business. He wished me to travel with him, and learn the trade as he knew it. This is the third such journey I have made with him.' That reminded her that it must also be the last. 'At least,' she said hesitantly, 'I may give money to have Masses said for him, here where he died? He was a very devout man, I think he would like that.'

Well, her reserves of money might now be far longer than her reserves of peace of mind were likely to be; she could afford to buy herself a little consolation, and prayers are never wasted.

'That you may surely do.'

'He died unshriven,' she said, with sudden angry grief against the murderer who had deprived him of confession and absolution.

'Through no fault of his own. So do many. So have saints, martyred without warning. God knows the record without needing word or gesture. It's for the soul racing death that the want of shriving is pain. The soul gone beyond knows that pain for needless vanity. Penitence is in the heart, not in the words spoken.'

They were out on the highroad then, turning left towards the reflected sparkle that was the river between its green, lush banks, and the stone bridge over it, that led through the drawbridge turret to the town gate. Emma had raised her head, and was looking at Brother Cadfael along her shoulder, with faint colour tinting her creamy cheeks, and a sparkle like a shimmer of light from the river in her eyes. He had not seen her smile until this moment, and even now it was a very wan smile, but none the less beautiful.

'He was a good man, you know, Brother Cadfael,' she said earnestly. 'He was not easy upon fools, or bad workmen, or people who cheated, but he was a good man. Good to me! And he kept his bargains, and he was loyal to his lord . . .' She had taken fire, for all the softness of her voice and the simplicity of her plea for him; it was almost as though she had been about to say 'loyal to his lord to the death!' She had that high, heroic look about her, to be taken very seriously, even on that child's face.

'All which,' said Cadfael cheerfully, 'God knows, and needs not to be told. And never forget you've a life to live, and he'd want you to do him justice by doing yourself justice.'

'Oh, yes!' said Emma, glowing, and for the first time laid her hand confidingly on his sleeve. 'That's what I want! That's what I have most in mind!'

TWO

AT MARTIN BELLECOTE'S SHOP, OFF THE CURVE OF THE RISING street called the Wyle, which led to the centre of the town, she knew exactly what she wanted for her dead, and ordered it clearly; more, she knew how to value a matching clarity and forthrightness in the master-carpenter, and yet had time to be pleasantly distracted by the invasion of his younger children, who liked the look of her and came boldly to chatter and stare. As for the delinquent Edwy, sent home overnight after his tongue-lashing from Hugh Beringar, the youngster worked demurely with a plane in a corner of the shop, and was not too subdued to cast inquisitive glances of bright hazel eyes at the lady, and one impudent wink at Brother Cadfael when Emma was not noticing.

On the way through the town, up the steep street to the

High Cross, and down the gentler slope beyond to the ramp which led up to the castle gateway, she fell into a thoughtful silence, putting in order her recollections. The shadow of the gate falling upon her serious face and cutting off the sunlight caused her eyes to dilate in awe; but the casual traffic of the watch here was no longer reminiscent of siege and battle, but easy and brisk, and the townspeople went in and out freely with their requests and complaints. The sheriff was a strong-minded, taciturn, able knight past fifty, and old in experience of both war and office, and while he could be heavy-handed in crushing disorder, he was trusted to be fair in day to day matters. If he had not given the goodmen of the town much help in making good the dilapidations due to the siege, neither had he permitted them to be misused or heavily taxed to restore the damage to the castle. In the great court one tower was still caged in timber scaffolding, one wall shored up with wooden buttresses. Emma gazed, great-eyed.

There were others going the same way with them, anxious fathers here to bail their sons, two of the abbey stewards who had been assaulted in the affray, witnesses from the bridge and the jetty, all being ushered through to the inner ward, and a chill, stony hall hung with smoky tapestries. Cadfael found Emma a seat on a bench against the wall, where she sat looking about her with anxious eyes but lively interest.

'Look, there's Master Corbière!'

He was just entering the hall, and for the moment had no attention to spare for anyone but the hunched figure that slouched before him; blear-eyed but in his full wits today, going softly in awe of his irate lord, Turstan Fowler made his powerful form as small and unobtrusive as possible, and mustered patience until the storm should blow over. And what had he to do here, Cadfael wondered. He had not been on the jetty, and by the state in which he had been found near midnight, his memories of yesterday should in any case be vague indeed. Yet he must have something to say to the purpose, or Corbière would not have brought him here. By his mood last night, he had meant to leave him locked up all day, to teach him better sense.

'Is this the sheriff?' whispered Emma.

Gilbert Prestcote had entered, with a couple of lawmen at

59

his elbows to advise him on the legalities. This was no trial, but it rested with him whether the rioters would go home on their own and their sires' bond to appear at the assize, or be held in prison in the meantime. The sheriff was a tall, spare man, erect and vigorous, with a short black beard trimmed to a point, and a sharp and daunting eye. He took his seat without ceremony, and a sergeant handed him the list of names of those in custody. He raised his eyebrows ominously at the number of them.

'All these were taken in riot?' He spread the roll on his table and frowned down at it. 'Very well! There is also the graver matter of the death of Master Thomas of Bristol. At what hour was the last word we have of Master Thomas alive and well?'

'According to his journeyman and his watchman, he left his booth on the horse-fair, intending to return to his barge, more than an hour past the Compline bell. That is the last word we have. His man Roger Dod is here to testify that the hour was rather more than a quarter past nine of the evening, and the watchman bears that out.'

'Late enough,' said the sheriff, pondering. 'The fighting was over by then, and Foregate and fairground quiet. Hugh, prick me off here all those who were then already in custody. Whatever their guilt for damages to goods and gear, they cannot have had any hand in this murder.'

Hugh leaned to his shoulder, and ran a rapid hand down the roster. 'It was a sharp encounter, but short. We had it in hand very quickly, they never reached the end of the Foregate. This man was picked up last, it might be as late as ten, but in an ale-house and very drunk, and the ale-wife vouches for his having been there above an hour. A respectable witness, she was glad to get rid of him. But he's clear of the killing. This one crept back to the bridge a little later, and owned to having been one among the rabble, but we let him home, for he's very lame, and there are witnesses to all his moves since before nine. He's here to answer for his part in the muster, as he promised. I think you may safely write him clear of any other blame.'

'It leaves but one,' said Prestcote, and looked up sharply into Beringar's face.

'It does,' said Hugh, and committed himself to nothing further.

'Very well! Have in all the rest, but keep him aside. Let us hold these two matters apart, and deal with the lesser first.'

Into the space roped off along one side the hall, the sheriff's officers herded their prisoners, a long file of sullenly sheepish young men, bruised, dishevelled and sorry for themselves now, but still nursing the embers of a genuine resentment. There were some torn coats among them, and a purple eye or two, and the lingering signs of bloody noses and battered crowns, and a night on the stones of indifferently swept cells had done their best clothes, donned for dignified battle as knights case themselves in ceremonial armour, no good at all. There would be indignant mothers scolding bitterly as they scrubbed and mended, or here and there a young wife doing the nagging on behalf of all women. The offenders stood in line doggedly, set their jaws, and braced themselves to endure whatever might follow.

Prestcote was thorough. Plainly he was preoccupied with the more serious evil, and little disposed to fulminate over-much about this civic discord, which in the end had done comparatively little harm. So though he called every culprit separately, and had him answer for his own part in the affray, he got through them rapidly and reasonably. Most of them freely owned that they had taken part, maintained that the intention had been entirely lawful and peaceable, and the disintegration later had been unintentional and none of their making. Several bore witness that they had been with Philip Corviser on the jetty, and told how he had been assaulted, thus letting loose the riot that followed. Only one here and there sought to prove that he had never so much as overset one trestle under a stall, nor even been on the abbey side of Severn that evening. And those few were already committed deep on the evidence of law-abiding citizens.

Agitated fathers, vengeful rather than doting, came forward to claim each dejected hero, pledged attendance at the assize, and offered surety for the pledge. The lame lad was lectured perfunctorily, and dismissed without penalty. Two who had been particularly voluble in asserting that they were elsewhere at the time, and unjustly accused, were returned to their prison for a day or two, to reconsider the nature of truth.

'Very well!' said Prestcote, dusting his hands irritably. 'Clear the hall, but for those who have evidence to give concerning Master Thomas of Bristol. And bring in Philip Corviser.'

The line of young men had vanished, hustled out and shepherded away by loyal but exasperated families. At home they would have to sit and nurse sore heads and sore hearts while fathers hectored and dames wept, pouring out on them all the fear and worry they had suffered on their behalf. Emma looked after the last of them with round, sympathetic eyes, as he was haled away by the ear by a diminutive mother half his size, and shrill as a jay. Poor lad, he needed no other punishment, he was drowning in mortification already.

She turned about, and there where his fellows had been, but monstrously alone in the middle of that stony wall, was Philip Corviser.

He gripped the rope with both hands, and stood rigidly erect, neck as stiff as a lance, though for the rest he looked as if his flesh might melt and droop off the bone, he was so haggard. His extreme pallor, which Cadfael knew for what raw wine can do the beginner, the day after his indulgence, Emma almost certainly took for the fruit of dire injury and great anguish of mind. She paled in reflection, staring piteously, though he was nothing to her, except that she had seen him struck down, and been afraid he might not rise again.

For all his efforts, he was a sorry figure. His best cotte was torn and soiled, and worse, speckled with drops of blood under his left ear, and vomit about the skirts. He mustered his gangling limbs gallantly but somewhat uncertainly, and his harmless, sunburned face, unshaven now and ashen under its tan, blushed to an unbecoming and unexpected purple when he caught sight of his father, waiting with laboured patience among the onlookers. He did not look that way again, but kept his bruised brown eyes fixed upon the sheriff.

He answered to his name in a voice too loud, from nervous defiance, and agreed to the time and place of his arrest. Yes, he had been very drunk, and hazy about his movements, and even about the circumstances of his arrest, but yes, he would try to answer truthfully to what was charged against him.

There were several witnesses to testify that Philip had been the originator and leader of the whole enterprise which had ended so ignominiously. He had been in the forefront when the angry young men crossed the bridge, he had given the signal that sent some of the party ahead along the Foregate, while he led a handful down to the riverside, and entered into loud argument with the merchants unloading goods there. Thus far all accounts tallied, but from then on they varied widely. Some had the youths beginning at once to toss merchandise into the river, and were certain that Philip had been in the thick of the battle. One or two of aggrieved merchants alleged with righteous indignation that he had assaulted Master Thomas, and so begun the whole turmoil.

Since they would all have their say, Hugh Beringar had held back his preferred witnesses until last.

'My lord, as to the scene by the river, we have here the niece of Master Thomas, and two men who intervened, and afterwards helped to rescue much of what had been cast into the river: Ivo Corbière of Stanton Cobbold, and Brother Cadfael of the abbey, who was assisting a Welsh-speaking trader. There were no others so close to the affair. Will you hear Mistress Vernold?'

Philip had not realised until that moment that she was present. The mention of her caused him to look round wildly, and the sight of her stepping shyly forward to stand before the sheriff's table brought out a deep and painful blush, that welled out of the young man's torn collar and mounted in a great wave to his red-brown hair. He averted his eyes from her, wishing, thought Cadfael, for the floor to open and swallow him up. It would not have mattered so much looking a piteous object to others, but before her he was furious and ashamed. Not even the thought of his father's mortification could have sunk his spirits so low. Emma, after one rapid glance, sympathetic enough, had also turned her eyes away. She looked only at the sheriff, who returned her straight gaze with concern and compunction.

'Was it needful to put Mistress Vernold to this distress, at such a time? Madam, you could well have been spared an appearance here, the lord Corbière and the good brother would have been witness enough.'

'I wished to come,' said Emma, her voice small but steady. 'Indeed I was not pressed, it was my own decision.'

'Very well, if that is your wish. You have heard these varying versions of what happened. There seems little dispute until these disturbers of the peace came down to the jetty. Let me hear from you what followed.'

'It is true that young man was the leader. I think he addressed himself to my uncle because he seemed the most important merchant then present, but he spoke high to be heard by all the rest. I cannot say that he uttered any threats, he only stated that the town had a grievance, and the abbey was not paying enough for the privilege of the fair, and asked that we, who come to do business here, should acknowledge the rights of the town, and pay a tithe of our rents and tolls to the town instead of all to the abbey. Naturally my uncle would not listen, but stood firm on the letter of the charter, and ordered the young men out of his way. And when he— the prisoner here—would still be arguing, my uncle turned his back and shrugged him off. Then the young man laid a hand on his arm, wanting to detain him still, and my uncle, who had his staff in his hand, turned and struck out at him. Thinking, I suppose, that he intended him offence or injury.'

'And did he not?' The sheriff's voice indicated mild surprise.

She cast one brief glance at the prisoner, and one in quest of reassurance at Brother Cadfael, and thought for a moment. 'No, I think not. He was beginning to be angry, but he had not said any ill word, or made any threatening movement. And my uncle, of course in alarm, hit hard. It felled him, and he lay in a daze.' This time she did turn and look earnestly at Philip, and found him staring at her wide-eyed. 'You see he is marked. His left temple.' Dried blood had matted the thick brown hair.

'And did he then attempt retaliation?' asked Prestcote.

'How could he?' she said simply. 'He was more than half stunned, he could not rise without help. And then all the others began to fight, and to throw things into the river. And Brother Cadfael came and helped him to his feet and delivered him to his friends, and they took him away. I am sure he could not have walked unaided. I think he did not know what he was doing, or how he came to such a state.'

'Not then, perhaps,' said Prescote reasonably. 'But later in the evening, somewhat recovered, and as he has himself admitted, very drunk, he may well have brooded on a revenge.'

'I can say nothing as to that. My uncle would have struck him again, and might have done him desperate hurt if I had not stopped him. That is not his nature,' she said firmly, 'it was most unlike him, but he was in a rage, and confused. Brother Cadfael will confirm what I say.'

'At all points,' said Brother Cadfael. 'It is a perfectly balanced and just account.'

'My lord Corbière?'

'I have nothing to add,' said Ivo, 'to what Mistress Vernold has so admirably told you. I saw the prisoner helped away by his fellows, and what became of him after that I have no knowledge. But here is a man of mine, Turstan Fowler, who says he did see him later in the evening, drinking in an ale-house at the corner of the horse-fair. I must say,' added Ivo with resigned disgust, 'that his own recollection of the night's events ought to be as hazy as the prisoner's, for we took him up dead drunk past eleven, and by the look of him he had been in the same state some time then. I had him put into a cell in the abbey overnight. But he claims his head is clear now, and he knows what he saw and heard. I thought it best he should speak here for himself.'

The archer edged forward sullenly, peering up under thick frowning brows, as though his head still rang.

'Well, what is it you claim to know, fellow?' asked Prescote, eyeing him narrowly.

'My lord, I had no call to be out of the precinct at all, last night, my lord Corbière had given me orders to stay within. But I knew he would spend the evening looking the ground over, so I ventured. I got my skinful at Wat's tavern, by the north corner of the horse-fair. And this fellow was there, drinking fit to beat me, and I'm an old toper, and can carry it most times. The place was full, there must be others can tell you the same. He was nursing his sore head, and breathing fire against the man that gave it him. He swore he'd be up with him before the night was out. And that's all the meat of it, my lord.'

'At what hour was this?' asked Prestcote.

'Well, my lord, I was still firm on my feet then, and clear in my mind, and that I certainly was not later in the evening. It must have been somewhere halfway between eight and nine. I should have borne my drink well enough if I had not gone from ale to wine, and then to a fierce spirit, and that last was what laid me low, or I'd have been back within the wall before my lord came home, and escaped a night on the stones.'

'It was well earned,' said Prestcote dryly. 'So you took yourself off to sleep off your load—when?'

'Why, about nine, I suppose, my lord, and was fathoms deep soon after. Troth, I can't recall where, though I remember the inn. They can tell you where I was found who found me.'

At this point it dawned abruptly upon Brother Cadfael that by pure chance this whole interrogation, since Philip had been brought in, had been conducted without once mentioning the fact that Master Thomas at this moment lay dead in the castle chapel. Certainly the sheriff had addressed Emma in tones of sympathy and consideration appropriate to her newly-orphaned state, and her uncle's absence might in itself be suggestive, though in view of the importance of his business at the fair, and the fact that Emma had once, at least, referred to him in the present tense, a person completely ignorant of his death would hardly have drawn any conclusion from these hints, unless he had all his wits about him. And Philip had been all night in a prison cell, and haled out only to face this hearing, and moreover, was still sick and dulled with his drinking, his broken head and his sore heart, and in no case to pick up every inference of what he heard. No one had deliberately laid a trap for him, but for all that, the trap was there, and it might be illuminating to spring it.

'So these threats you heard against Master Thomas,' said Prestcote, 'can have been uttered only within an hour, probably less, of the time when the merchant left his booth to return alone to his barge. The last report we have of him.'

That was drawing nearer to the spring, but not near enough.

Philip's face was still drawn, resigned and bewildered, as though they had been talking Welsh over his head. Brother Cadfael struck the prop clean away; it was high time.

'The last report we have of him *alive*,' he said clearly.

The word might have been a knife going in, the slender kind that is hardly felt for a moment, and then hales after it the pain and the injury. Philip's head came up with a jerk, his mouth fell open, his bruised eyes rounded in horrified comprehension.

'But it must be remembered,' continued Cadfael quickly, 'that we do not know the hour at which he died. A body taken from the water may have entered it at any time during the night, after *all* the prisoners were in hold, and all honest men in bed.'

It was done. He had hoped it would settle the issue of guilt and innocence, at least to his satisfaction, but now he still could not be quite sure the boy had not known the truth already. How if he had only held his peace and listened to the ambiguous voices, and been in doubt whether Master Thomas's corpse had yet been found? On the face of it, if he had had any hand in that death, he was a better player than any of the travelling entertainers who would be plying their trade among the crowds this evening. His pallor, from underdone dough, had frozen into marble, he tried to speak and swallowed half-formed words, he drew huge breaths into him, and straightened his back, and turned great, shocked eyes upon the sheriff. On the face of it—but every face can dissemble if the need is great enough.

'My lord,' pleaded Philip urgently, when he had his voice again, 'is this truth? Master Thomas of Bristol is dead?'

'Known or unknown to you,' said Prestcote dryly, '—and I hazard no judgment—it is truth. The merchant is dead. Our main purpose here now is to examine how he died.'

'Taken from the water, the monk said. Did he drown?'

'That, if you know, you may tell us.'

Abruptly the prisoner turned his back upon the sheriff, took another deep breath into him, and looked directly at Emma, and from then on barely took his eyes from her, even when Prestcote addressed him. The only judgment he cared about was hers.

'Lady, I swear to you I never did your uncle harm, never saw him again after they hauled me away from the jetty. What befell him I do not know, and God knows I'm sorry for your loss. I would not for the world have touched him, even if we had met and quarrelled afresh, knowing he was your kinsman.'

'Yet you were heard threatening harm to him,' said the sheriff.

'It may be so. I cannot drink, I was a fool ever to try that cure. I recall nothing of what I said, I make no doubt it was folly, and unworthy. I was sore and bitter. What I set out to do was honest enough, and yet it fell apart. All went to waste. But if I talked violence, I did none. I never saw the man again. When I turned sick from the wine I left the tavern and went down to the riverside, away from the boats, and lay down there until I made shift to drag myself back to the town. I admit to the trouble that arose out of my acts, and all that has been said against me, all but this. As God sees me, I never did your uncle any injury. Speak, and say you believe me!'

Emma gazed at him with parted lips and dismayed eyes, unable to say yes or no to him. How could she know what was true and what was lies?

'Let her be,' said the sheriff sharply. 'It is with us you have to deal. This matter must be probed deeper than has been possible yet. Nothing is proven, but you stand in very grave suspicion, and it is for me to determine what is to be done with you.'

'My lord,' ventured the provost, who had kept his mouth tightly shut until now, against great temptation, 'I am prepared to stand surety for my son to whatever price you may set, and I guarantee he shall be at your disposal at the assize, and at whatever time between when you may need to question him. My honour has never been in doubt, and my son, whatever else, has been known as a man of his word, and if he gives his bond here he will keep it, even without my enforcement. I beg your lordship will release him home to my bail.'

'On no terms,' said Prestcote decidedly. 'The matter is too grave. He stays under lock and key.'

'My lord, if you so order, under lock and key he shall be, but let it be in my house. His mother—'

'No! Say no more, you must know it is impossible. He stays here in custody.'

'There is nothing against him in the matter of this death,' offered Corbière generously, 'as yet, that is, except my rogue's witness of his threats. And thieves do haunt such gatherings as the great fairs, and if they can cut a man out from his fellows, will kill him for the clothes on his back. And surely the fact that the body was stripped accords better with just such a foul chance crime for gain? Vengeance has nothing to feed on in a bundle of clothing. The act is all.'

'True,' agreed Prestcote. 'But supposing a man had killed in anger, perhaps simply gone too far in an assault meant only to injure, he might be wise enough to strip his victim, to make it appear the work of common robbers, and turn attention away from himself. There is much work to be done yet in this case, but meantime Corviser must remain in hold. I should be failing in my duty if I turned him loose, even to your care, master provost.' And the sheriff ordered, with a motion of his hand: 'Take him away!'

Philip was slow to move, until the butt of a lance prodded him none too gently in the side. Even then he kept his chin on his shoulder for some paces, and his eyes desperately fixed upon Emma's distressed and doubting face. 'I did not touch him,' he said, plucked forcibly away towards the door through which his guards had brought him. 'I pray you, believe me!' Then he was gone, and the hearing was over.

Out in the great court they paused to draw grateful breath, released from the shadowy oppression of the hall. Roger Dod hovered, with hungry eyes upon Emma.

'Mistress, shall I attend you back to the barge? Or will you have me go straight back to the booth? I had Gregory go there to help Warin, while I had to be absent, but trade was brisking up nicely, they'll be hard pushed by now. If that's what you want? To work the fair as he'd have worked it?'

'That is what I want,' she said firmly. 'To do all as he would have done. You go straight back to the horse-fair,

Roger. I shall be staying with Lady Beringar at the abbey for this while, and Brother Cadfael will escort me.'

The journeyman louted, and left them, without a backward glance. But the very rear view of him, sturdy, stiff and aware, brought back to mind the intensity of his dark face and burning, embittered eyes. Emma watched him go, and heaved a helpless sigh.

'I am sure he is a good man, I know he is a good servant, and has stood loyally by my uncle many years. So he would by me, after his fashion. And I do respect him, I must! I think I could like him, if only he would not want me to love him!'

'It's no new problem,' said Cadfael sympathetically. 'The lightning strikes where it will. One flames, and the other remains cold. Distance is the only cure.'

'So I think,' said Emma fervently. 'Brother Cadfael, I must go to the barge, to bring away some more clothes and things I need. Will you go with me?'

He understood at once that this was an opportune time. Both Warin and Gregory were coping with customers at the booth, and Roger was on his way to join them. The barge would be riding innocently beside the jetty, and no man aboard to trouble her peace. Only a monk of the abbey, who did not trouble it at all. 'Whatever you wish,' he said. 'I have leave to assist you in all your needs.'

He had rather expected that Ivo Corbière would come to join her once they were out of the hall, but he did not. It was in Cadfael's mind that she had expected it, too. But perhaps the young man had decided that it was hardly worthwhile making a threesome with the desired lady and a monastic attendant, who clearly had his mandate, and would not consent to be dislodged. Cadfael could sympathise with that view, and admire his discretion and patience. There were two days of the fair left yet, and the great court of the abbey was not so great but guests could meet a dozen times a day. By chance or by rendezvous!

Emma was very silent on the way back through the town. She had nothing to say until they emerged from the shadow of the gate into full sunlight again, above the glittering bow of the river. Then she said suddenly: 'It was good of Ivo to speak so reasonably for the young man.' And on the instant, as Cadfael flashed a glance to glimpse whatever lay behind the words, she flushed almost as deeply as the unlucky lad Philip had blushed on beholding her a witness to his shame.

'It was very sound sense,' said Cadfael, amiably blind. 'Suspicion there may be, but proof there's none, not yet. And you set him a pace in generosity he could not but admire.'

The flush did not deepen, but it was already bright as a rose. On her ivory, silken face, so young and unused, it was touching and becoming.

'Oh, no,' she said, 'I only told simply truth. I could do no other.' Which again was simple truth, for nothing in her life thus far had corrupted her valiant purity. Cadfael had begun to feel a strong fondness for this orphan girl who shouldered her load without timidity or complaint, and still had an open heart for the burdens of others. 'I was sorry for his father,' she said. 'So decent and respected a man, to be denied so. And he spoke of his wife . . . she will be out of her wits with worry.'

They were over the bridge, they turned down the green path, trodden almost bare at this busy, hot time, that led to the riverside and the long gardens and orchards of the Gaye. Master Thomas's deserted barge nestled into the green bank at the far end of the jetty, close-moored. One or two porters laboured along the boards with fresh stocks from the boats, shouldered them, and tramped away up the path to replenish busy stalls. The riverside lay sunlit, radiantly green and blue, and almost silent, but for the summer sounds of bees drunkenly busy among the late summer flowers in the grass. Almost deserted, but for a solitary fisherman in a small boat close under the shadow of the bridge; a comfortable, squarely-built fisherman stripped to shirt and hose, and bristling thornily with black curls and black bush of beard. Rhodri ap Huw clearly trusted his servant to deal profitably with his English customers, or else he had already sold out all the stock he had brought with him. He looked somnolent, happy, almost eternal, trailing his bait along the current under the archway, with an occasional flick of a wrist to correct the drift. Though most likely the sharp eyes under the sleepy eyelids were missing nothing that went on about him. He had the gift, it seemed, of being everywhere, but everywhere disinterested and benevolent.

'I will be quick,' said Emma, with a foot on the side of the barge. 'Last night Constance lent me all that I needed, but I must not continue a beggar. Will you step aboard, brother? You are welcome! I'm sorry to be so poor a hostess.' Her lips quivered. He knew the instant when her mind returned to her uncle, lying naked and dead in the castle, a man she had revered and relied on, and perhaps felt to be eternal in his solidity and self-confidence. 'He would have wished me to offer you wine, the wine you refused last night.'

'For want of time only,' said Cadfael placidly, and hopped nimbly over on to the barge's low deck. 'You go get what you need, child, I'll wait for you.'

The space aboard was well organised, the cabin aft rode low, but the full width of the hull, and though Emma had to stoop her neat head to enter, stepping down to the lower level within, she and her uncle would have had room within for sleeping. Little to spare, yet enough, where no alien or suspect thing might come. But taut, indeed, when she was short of her natural protector, with three other men closely present on deck outside. And one of them deeply, hopelessly, in love. Uncles may not notice such glances as his, where their own underlings are concerned.

She was back, springing suddenly to view in the low doorway. Her eyes had again that look of shock and alarm, but now contained and schooled. Her voice was level and low as she said: 'Someone has been here! Someone strange! Someone has handled everything we left here on board, pawed through my linen and my uncle's, too, turned every board or cover. I do not dream, Brother Cadfael! It is true! Our boat has been ransacked while it was left empty. Come and see!'

It was without guile that he asked her instantly, 'has anything been taken?'

Still possessed by her discovery, and unguardedly honest, Emma said: 'No!'

THREE

EVERYTHING IN THE BOAT, AND CERTAINLY EVERYTHING IN THE
small cabin, seemed to Cadfael to be in immaculate order, but
he did not therefore doubt her judgement. A girl making her
third journey in this fashion, and growing accustomed to
making the best use of the cramped space, would know
exactly how she had everything folded and stowed, and the
mere disturbance of a fold, the crumpling of a corner in the
neat low chest under her bench-bed would be enough to alert
her, and betray the intervention of another hand. But the very
attempt at perfect restoration was surprising. It argued that the
interloper had had ample time at his disposal, while all the
crew were absent. Yet she had said confidently that nothing
had been stolen.

'You are sure? You've had little time to examine everything here. Best look round thoroughly and make sure, before
we report this to Hugh Beringar.'

'Must I do that?' she asked, a little startled, even, he
thought, a little dismayed. 'If there's no harm? They are
burdened enough with other matters.'

'But do you not see, child, that this comes too aptly on the
other? Your uncle killed, and now his barge ransacked. . . .'

'Why, there can surely be no connection,' she said quickly.
'This is the work of some common thief.'

'A common thief who took nothing?' said Cadfael. 'Where
there are any number of things worth the taking!'

'Perhaps he was interrupted . . .' But her voice wavered
into silence, she could not even convince herself.

'Does it look so to you? I think he must have been through
all your belongings at leisure, to leave them so neat for you.

73

And removed himself only when he was satisfied.' But of what? That what he wanted was not there?

Emma gnawed a dubious lip, and looked about her thoughtfully. 'Well, if we must report it . . . You're right, I spoke too soon, perhaps I should go through everything. No use telling him but half a tale.'

She settled down methodically to take out every item of clothing and equipment from both chests, laying them out on the beds, even unfolding those which showed, to her eyes at least, the most obvious signs of handling, and refolding them to her own satisfaction. At the end of it she sat back on her heels and looked up at Cadfael, thoughtfully frowning.

'Yes, there have been some things taken, but so cunningly. Small things that would never have been missed until we got home. There's a girdle of mine missing, one with a gold clasp. And a silver chain. And a pair of gloves with gold embroidery. If my thumbs had not pricked when I came in here, I should not have missed them, for I shouldn't have wanted to wear any of them. What could I want with gloves in August? I bought them all in Gloucester, on the way up the river.'

'And of your uncle's belongings?'

'I think there is nothing missing. If some moneys were left here, certainly none are here now, but his strong-box is at the booth. He never carried valuables on such journeys as this, except the rings he always wore. I should not have had such rich trifles here myself, if I had not but newly bought them.'

'So it seems,' said Cadfael, 'whoever took the opportunity of stepping aboard boldy, to see what he could pick up, had the wit to take only trifles he could slip in his sleeve or his pouch. That makes good sense. However naturally it was done, he'd be likely to cause some curiosity if he stepped ashore with his arms full of your uncle's gowns and shirts.'

'And we must trouble Hugh Beringar and the sheriff over so trivial a loss?' wondered Emma, jutting a doubtful lip. 'It seems a pity, when he has so many graver matters on his mind. And you see this is only an ordinary, vulgar filching, because the boat was left empty a while. Small creatures of prey have an eye to such chances.'

'Yes, we must,' said Cadfael firmly. 'Let the law be the

judge whether this has anything to do with your uncle's death or no. That's not for us to say. You find what you need to take with you, and we'll go together and see him, if he's to be found at this hour.'

Emma put together a fresh gown and tunic, stockings and shift and other such mysteries as girls need, with a composure which Cadfael found at once admirable and baffling. The immediate discovery of the invasion of her possessions had startled and disturbed her, but she had come to terms with it very quickly and calmly, and appeared perfectly indifferent to the loss of her finery. He was just considering how odd it was that she should be so anxious to disconnect this incident from her uncle's death, when she herself, in perverse and unthinking innocence, restored the link.

'Well, at any rate,' said Emma, gathering her bundle together neatly in the skirt of the gown, and rising nimbly from her knees, 'no one can dare say that the provost's son was to blame for this. He's safe in a cell in the castle, and the sheriff himself can be his witness this time.'

Hugh Beringar had shrugged off his duties to enjoy at least the evening meal with his wife. Mercifully the first day of the fair had passed so far without further incident, no disorders, no quarrels, no accusations of cheating or overcharging, no throat-cutting or price-cutting, as though the uproar of the previous evening, and its deadly result, had chastened and subdued even the regular offenders. Trade was thriving, rents and tolls bringing in a high revenue for the abbey, and sales seemed set to continue peacefully well into the night.

'And I have bought some spun wool,' said Aline, delighted with her day's shopping, 'and some very fine woollen cloth, so soft—feel it! And Constance chose two beautiful fleeces from Cadfael's Welsh merchant, she wants to card and spin them herself for the baby. And I changed my mind about a cradle, for I saw nothing in the fair to match what Martin Bellecote can do. I shall go to him.'

'The girl is not back yet?' said Hugh, mildly surprised. 'She left the castle well before me.'

'She'll have gone to bring some things from the barge. She had nothing with her last night, you know. And she was going to Bellecote's shop, too, to bespeak the coffin for her uncle.'

'That she'd done on the way,' said Hugh, 'for Martin came to the castle about the business before I left. They'll be bringing the body down to the chapel here before dark.' He added appreciatively: 'A fair-minded lass, our Emma, as well as a stout-hearted one. She would not have that fool boy of Corviser's turned into the attacker, even for her uncle's sake. A straight tale as ever was. He opened civilly, was brusquely received, made the mistake of laying hand on the old man, and was felled like a poled ox.'

'And what does he himself say?' Aline looked up intently from the bolt of soft stuff she was lovingly stroking.

'That he never laid eyes on Master Thomas again, and knows no more about his death than you or I. But there's that falconer of Corbière's says he was breathing fire and smoke against the old man in Wat's tavern well into the evening. Who knows! The mildest lamb of the flock—but that's not his reputation!—may be driven to clash foreheads when roused, but the knife in the back, somehow—that I doubt. He had no knife on him when he was taken up at the gate. We shall have to ask all his companions if they saw such a thing about him.'

'Here is Emma,' said Aline, looking beyond him to the doorway.

The girl came in briskly with her bundle, Brother Cadfael at her shoulder. 'I'm sorry to have been so long,' said Emma, 'but we had reason. Something untoward has happened—oh, it is not so grave, no great harm, but Brother Cadfael says we must tell you.'

Cadfael forbore from urging, stood back in silence, and let her tell it in her own way, and a very flat way it was, as though she had no great interest in her reported loss. But for all that, she described the bits of finery word for word as she had described them to him, and went into greater detail of their ornaments. 'I did not wish to bother you with such trumpery thefts. How can I care about a lost girdle and gloves, when I have lost so much more? But Brother Cadfael insisted, so I have told you.'

'Brother Cadfael was right,' said Hugh sharply. 'Would it surprise you, child, to know that we have had not one complaint of mispractice or stealing or any evil all this day, touching any other tradesman at the fair? Yet one threat follows another where your uncle's business is concerned. Can that truly be by chance? Is there not someone here who has no interest in any other, but all too much in him?'

'I knew you would think so,' she said, sighing helplessly. 'But it was only by chance that our barge was left quite unmanned all this afternoon, by reason of Roger being needed with the rest of us at the castle. I doubt if there was another boat there unwatched. And common thieves have a sharp eye out for such details. They take what they can get.'

It was a shrewd point, and clearly she was not the girl to lose sight of any argument that could serve her turn. Cadfael held his peace. There would be a time to discuss the matter with Hugh Beringar, but it was not now. The questions that needed answers would not be asked of Emma; where would be the use? She had been born with all her wits about her, and through force of circumstances she was learning with every moment. But why was she so anxious to have this search of her possessions shrugged aside as trivial, and having no bearing on Master Thomas's murder? And why had she stated boldly, in the first shock of discovery, indeed without time to view the field in any detail, that nothing had been taken? As though, disdaining the invasion, she had good reason to know that it had been ineffective?

And yet, thought Cadfael, studying the rounded, resolute face, and the clear eyes she raised to Hugh's searching stare, I would swear this is a good, honest girl, no way cheat or liar.

'You'll not be needing me,' he said, 'Emma can tell you all. It's almost time for Vespers, and I have still to go and speak with the abbot. There'll be time later, Hugh, after supper.'

Abbot Radulfus was a good listener. Not once did he interrupt with comment or question, as Brother Cadfael recounted for him all that had passed at the sheriff's hearing, and the unexpected discovery at the barge afterwards. At the end of it he sat for a brief while in silence still, pondering what he had heard.

'So we now have one unlawful act of which the man charged cannot possibly be guilty, whatever may be the truth concerning the other. What do you think, does this tend to weaken the suspicion against him, even on the charge of murder?'

'It weakens it,' said Cadfael, 'but it cannot clear him. It may well be true, as Mistress Vernold believes, that the two things are no way linked, the filching from the barge a mere snatch at what was available, for want of a watchman to guard it. Yet two such assaults upon the same man's life and goods looks like methodical purpose, and not mere chance.'

'And the girl is now a guest within our halls,' said Radulfus, 'and her safety our responsibility. Two attacks upon one man's life and goods, you said. How if there should be more? If a subtle enemy is pursuing some private purpose, it may not end with this afternoon's violation, as we have seen it did not end with the merchant's death. The girl is in the care of the deputy sheriff, and could not be in better hands. But like them, she is a guest under our roof. I do not want the brothers of our community distracted from their devotions and duties, or the harmony of our services shaken. I would not have these matters spoken of but between you and me, and of course as is needful to aid the law. But you, Brother Cadfael, have already been drawn in, you know the whole state of the case. Will you have an eye to what follows, and keep watch on our guests? I place the interests of the abbey in your hands. Do not neglect your devotional duties unless you must, but I give you leave to go in and out freely, and absent yourself from offices if there is need. When the fair ends, our halls will empty, our tenant merchants depart. It will be out of our hands then to protect the just or prevent the harm that threatens from the unjust. But while they are here, let us do what we can.'

'I will undertake what you wish, Father Abbot,' said Cadfael, 'to the best I may.'

He went to Vespers with a burdened heart and a vexed mind, but for all that, he was glad of the Abbot's charge. It was, in any case, impossible to give up worrying at so tangled a knot, once it had presented itself to his notice, even apart from the natural concern he felt for the girl, and there was no denying that the Benedictine round, dutifully observed, did limit a man's mobility for a large part of the day.

Meantime, he drove the affairs of Emma Vernold from his thoughts with a struggle that should have earned him credit in heaven, and surrendered himself as best he could to the proper observance of Vespers. And after supper he repaired to the cloister, and was not surprised to find Hugh Beringar there waiting for him. They sat down together in a corner where the evening breeze coiled about them very softly and gratefully, and the view into the garth was all emerald turf and pale grey stone, and azure sky melting into green, through a fretwork of briars blowsy with late, drunken-sweet roses.

'There's news in your face,' said Cadfael, eyeing his friend warily. 'As though we have not had enough for one day!'

'And what will you make of it?' wondered Hugh. 'Not an hour ago a lad fishing in Severn hooked a weight of sodden cloth out of the water. All but broke his line, so he let it back in, but was curious enough to play it to shore until he could take it up safely. A fine, full woollen gown, made for a big man, and one with money to spend, too.' He met Cadfael's bright, alerted eyes, rather matching certainties than questioning. 'Yes, what else? We did not trouble Emma with it—who would have the heart! She's drawing Aline a pattern for an embroidered hem for an infant's robe, one she got from France. They have their heads together like sisters. No, we fetched Roger Dod to swear to it. It's Master Thomas's gown, no question. We're poling down the banks now after hose and shirt. To any wandering thief that gown was worth a month's hunting.'

'So no such leech would have thrown it away,' said Cadfael. 'Never!'

'There were also rings taken from his fingers. But rings, I suppose, might be too good to discard, even to prove that this was a murder for hate, not for gain. Rings would sink, even if hurled into the Severn. So why hurl them?'

'As usual,' said Hugh, elevating thin black brows, 'you're ahead of me rather than abreast. On the face of it, this was a killing for private malice. So while we examine it, Ivo Corbière very sensibly points out that a murderer so minded would not have stayed to strip the body and put it into the river, but left it lying, and made off as fast as he could. Vengeance, he says rightly, has nothing to feed on in a bundle of clothing. The act is all! And that moved my sheriff to remark that the same thought might well have occurred to the murderer, and caused him to strip his victim naked for that very reason, a hoodwink for the law. Now we drag out of the river the dead man's gown. And where does that leave you and me, my friend?'

'In two minds, or more,' said Cadfael ruefully. 'If the gown never had been found, the notion of common robbery would have held its ground and told in young Corviser's favour. Is it possible that what was said in the sheriff's court put that thought into someone's mind for the first time, and drove him to discard the gown where it was likely to be found? There's one person it would suit very well to have the case against your prisoner strengthened, and that's the murderer himself. Supposing yon fool boy is not the murderer, naturally.'

'True, half a case can come to look almost whole by the addition of one more witness. But what a fool your man would be, to toss the gown away for proof the killing was not for robbery, thus turning suspicion back upon Philip Corviser, and then creep aboard the barge and steal, when Philip Corviser is in a cell in the castle, and manifestly out of the reckoning.'

'Ah, but he never supposed the theft would be discovered until the barge was back in Bristol, or well on the way. I tell you, Hugh, *I* could see no trace of an alien hand anywhere among those stores on deck or the chattels in the cabin, and Emma herself said she would not have missed the lost things until reaching home again. They were bought on this journey, she had no intention of wearing them. Nothing obvious was stolen, she had almost reached the bottom of her chest before she found out these few bits of finery were gone. But for her sharp eye for her own neat housekeeping, she would not have known the boat had been visited.'

'Yet robbery points to two separate villains and two separate crimes,' pointed out Hugh with a wry smile, 'as Emma insists on believing. If hate was the force behind the man's death, why stoop to pilfer from him afterwards? But do *you* believe the two things are utterly separate? I think not!'

'Strange chances do jostle one another sometimes in this world. Don't put it clean out of mind, it may still be true. But I cannot choose but believe that it's the same hand behind both happenings. And the same purpose and it was neither theft nor hatred, nor the death would have ended it.'

'But Cadfael, in heaven's name, what purpose that demanded a man's death could get satisfaction afterwards from stealing a pair of gloves, a girdle and a chain?'

Brother Cadfael shook his head helplessly, and had no answer to that, or none that he was yet prepared to give.

'My head spins, Hugh. But I have a black suspicion it may not be over yet. Abbot Radulfus has given me his commission to have an eye to the matter, for the abbey's sake, and permission to go in and out as I see fit for the purpose. It's at the back of his mind that if there's some malignant plot in hand against the Bristol merchant, his niece may not be altogether safe, either. If Aline can keep her at her side, so much the better. But I'll be keeping a watchful eye on her, too.' He rose, yawning. 'Now I must be off to Compline. If I'm to scamp my duties tomorrow, let me at least end today well.'

'Pray for a quiet night,' said Hugh, rising with him, 'for we've not the men to mount patrols through the dark hours. I'll take one more turn along the Foregate with my sergeant, as far as the horse-fair, and then I'm for my bed. I saw little enough of it last night!'

The night of the first of August, the opening day of Saint Peter's Fair, was warm, clear, and quiet enough. Traders along the Foregate kept their stalls open well into the dark hours, the weather being so inviting that plenty of customers were still abroad to chaffer and bargain. The sheriff's officers withdrew into the town, and even the abbey servants, left to keep the peace if it were threatened, had little work to do. It was past midnight when the last lamps and torches were quenched, and the night's silence descended upon the horse-fair.

Master Thomas's barge rocked very softly to the motion of the river. Master Thomas himself lay in a chapel of the abbey, decently shrouded, and in his workshop in the town

Martin Bellecote the master-carpenter worked late upon the fine, lead-lined coffin Emma had ordered from him. And in a narrow and dusty cell in the castle, Philip Corviser tossed and turned and nursed his bruises on a thin mattress of straw, and could not sleep for fretting over the memory of Emma's doubting, pitying face.

THE SECOND
DAY OF THE FAIR

ONE

THE SECOND DAY OF THE FAIR DAWNED BRILLIANTLY, A GOLDEN SUN climbing, faint mist hanging like a floating veil over the river. Roger Dod rose with the dawn, shook Gregory awake, rolled up his brychan, washed in the river, and made a quick meal of bread and small ale before setting off along the Foregate to his master's booth. All along the highroad traders were clambering out of their cloaks, yawning and stretching, and setting out their goods ready for the day's business. Roger exchanged greetings with several of them as he passed. Where so many were gathered at close quarters, even a dour and silent man could not help picking up acquaintance with a few of his fellows.

The first glimpse of Master Thomas's booth, between the busy stirrings of its neighbours, brought a scowl to Roger's brow and a muttered oath to his tongue, for the wooden walls were still fast closed. Every hatch still sealed, and the sun already climbing! Warin must be fast asleep, inside there. Roger hammered on the front boards, which should by this hour have been lowered trimly on to their trestles, and set out with goods for sale. He got no response from within.

'Warin!' he bellowed. 'Devil take you, get up and let me in!'

No reply, except that several of the neighbours had turned curiously to listen and watch, abandoning their own activities to attend to this unexpected clamour.

'Warin!' bawled Roger, and thumped again vigorously. 'You idle swine, what's come to you?'

'I did wonder,' said the cloth-merchant nextdoor, pausing with a bolt of flannel in his arms. 'There's been no sign of him. A sound sleeper, your watchman!'

'Hold hard!' The armourer from the other side leaned excitedly over Roger's shoulder, and fingered the edge of the wooden door. 'Splinters, see?' Beside the latch the boards showed a few pale threads, hardly enough to be seen, and at the thrust of his hand the door gave upon a sliver of darkness. 'No need to hammer, the way in is open. A knife has been used on this!' said the armourer, and there fell a momentary silence.

'Pray God that's all it's been used on!' said Roger in an appalled whisper, and thrust the door wide. He had a dozen of them at his back by then; even the Welshman Rhodri ap Huw had come rolling massively between the stalls to join them, sharp black eyes twinkling out of the thicket of his hair and beard, though what he made of the affair, seeing he spoke no English, no one stopped to consider.

From the darkness within welled the warm scent of timber, wine and sweetmeats, and a faint, strange sound like the breathy grunting of a dumb man. Roger was propelled forward into the dimness by the eager helpers crowding at his back, all agape with curiosity. The stacked bales and small casks of wine took shape gradually, after the brief blindness of entering this dark place from sunlight. Everything stood orderly and handy, just as it had been left overnight, and of Warin there was no sign, until Rhodri ap Huw, ever practical, unbolted the front hatch and let it down, and the brightness of the morning came flooding in.

Stretched along the foot of the same front wall, where Rhodri must almost have set foot on him, Warin lay rolled in his own cloak and tied at elbows, knees and ankles with cords, so tightly that he could barely wriggle enough to make the folds of cloth rustle. There was a sack drawn over his head, and a length of linen dragged the coarse fibres into his mouth and was secured behind his neck. He was doing his best to answer to his name, and at least his limited jerkings and muted grunts made it plain that he was alive.

Roger uttered a wordless yell of alarm and indignation, and fell on his knees, plucking first at the linen band that held the sack fast. The coarse cloth was wet before with spittle, and the mouth within must be clogged and stung with ropey fibres, but at least the poor wretch could breathe, his strangled grunts were trying to form words long before the linen parted, and let him spit out his gag. Still beneath his sack, his hoarse croak demanded aggrievedly: 'Where were you so long, and me half-killed?'

A couple of pairs of willing hands were at work on the other bonds by that time, all the more zealously now they had heard him speak, and indeed complain, in such reassuringly robust tones. Warin emerged gradually from his swaddlings, unrolled unceremoniously out of the cloak so that he ended face-down on the ground, and still incoherently voluble. He righted himself indignantly, but so spryly that it was plain he had no broken bones, no painful injuries, and had not even suffered overmuch from the cramps of his bonds. He looked up from under his wild grey thatch of hair, half defensive and half accusing, glaring round the circle of his rescuers as though they had been responsible for his hours of discomfort.

'Late's better than never!' he said sourly, and hawked, and spat out fibres of sacking. 'What took you so long? Is everybody deaf? I've been kicking here half the night!'

Half a dozen hands reached pleasurably to hoist him to his feet and sit him down gently on a cask of wine. Roger stood off and let them indulge their curiosity, scowling blackly at his colleague meantime. There was no damage done, not a scratch on the old fool! the first threat, and he had crumpled into a pliable rag.

'For God's sake, what happened to you? You had the booth sealed. How could any man break in here, and you not know? There are other merchants sleep here with their wares, you had only to call.'

'Not all,' said the cloth-merchant fairly. 'I myself lie at a tavern, so do many. If your man was sound asleep, as he well might be with all closed for the night. . . .'

'It was long past midnight,' said Warin, scrubbing aggrievedly at his chafed ankles. 'I know because I heard the little bell for Matins, over the wall, before I slept. Not a sound after, until I awoke as that hood came over my head. They rammed the stuff into my mouth. I never saw face or form, they rolled me up like a bale of wool, and left me tied.'

'And you never raised a cry!' said Roger bitterly. 'How many were they? One or more?'

Warin was disconcerted, and wavered, swaying either way. 'I think two. I'm not sure. . . .'

'You were hooded, but you could hear. Did they talk together?'

'Yes, now I recall there was some whispering. Not that I could catch any words. Yes, they were two. There was moving about of casks and bales here, that I know . . .'

'For how long? They durst not hurry, and have things fall and rouse the fairground,' said the armourer reasonably. 'How long did they stay?'

Warin was vague, and indeed to a man blindfolded and tied by night, time might stretch out like unravelled thread. 'An hour, it might be.'

'Time enough to find whatever was of most value here,' said the armourer, and looked at Roger Dod, with a shrug of broad shoulders. 'You'd better look about you, lad, and see what's missing. No need to trouble for anything so weighty as casks of wine, they'd have needed a cart for those and a cart in the small hours would surely have roused someone. The small and precious is what they came for.'

But Roger had already turned his back on his rescued fellow, and was burrowing frantically among the bales and boxes stacked along the wall. 'My master's strong-box! I built it in behind here, out of sight. . . . Thank God I took the most of yesterday's gains back to the barge with me last night, and have them safe under lock and key, but for all that, there was a good sum left in it. And all his accounts, and parchments . . .'

He was thrusting boxes and bags of spices aside in his haste, scenting the air, pushing out of his way wooden caskets of sugar confections from the east, come by way of Venice and Gascony, and worth high prices in any market. 'Here, against the wall. . . .'

His hands sank helplessly, he stood staring in dismay. He had bared the boards of the booth; goods stood piled on either side, and between them, nothing. Master Thomas's strong-box was gone.

Brother Cadfael had taken advantage of the early hours to put in an hour or two of work with Brother Mark in the herb-gardens, while he had no reason to anticipate any threat to Emma, for she was surely still asleep in the guest-hall with Constance, and out of reach of harm. The morning was clear and sunny, the mist just lifting from the river, shot through with oblique gold, and Mark sang cheerfully about his weeding, and listened attentively and serenely as Cadfael instructed him in all the particulars of the day's work.

'For I may have to leave all things in your hands. And so I can, safely enough, I know, if I should chance to be called away.'

'I'm well taught,' said Brother Mark, with his grave smile, behind which the small spark of mischief was visible only to Cadfael, who had first discovered and nurtured it. 'I know what to stir and what to let well alone in the workshop.'

'I wish I could be as sure of my part outside it,' said Cadfael ruefully. 'There are brews among us that need just as sure a touch, boy, and where to stir and where to let be is puzzling me more than a little. I'm walking a knife-edge, with disastrous falls on either side. I know my herbs. They have fixed properties, and follow sacred rules. Human creatures do not so. And I cannot even wish they did. I would not have one scruple of their complexity done away, it would be lamentable loss.'

It was time to go to Prime. Brother Mark stooped to rinse his hands in the butt of water they kept warming through the day, to be tempered for the herbs at the evening watering. 'It was being with you made me know that I want to be a priest,' he said, speaking his mind as openly as always in Cadfael's company.

'I had never the urge for it,' said Cadfael absently, his mind on other matters.

'I know. That was the one thing wanting. Shall we go?'

They were coming out from Prime, and the lay servants already mustering for their early Mass, when Roger Dod came trudging in at the gatehouse, out of breath, and with trouble plain to be read in his face.

'What, again something new?' sighed Cadfael, and set off to intercept him before he reached the guest-hall. Suddenly aware of this square, sturdy figure bearing down on him with obvious purpose, Roger checked, and turned an anxious face. His frown cleared a little when he recognised the same monk who had accompanied the deputy sheriff in the vain search for Master Thomas, on the eve of Saint Peter. 'Oh, it's you, brother, that's well! Is Hugh Beringar within? I must speak to him. We're beset! Yesterday the barge, and now the booth, and God knows what's yet to come, and what will become of us before ever we get away from this deadly place. My master's books gone—money and box and all! What will Mistress Emma think? I'd rather have had my own head broke, if need be, than fail her so!'

'What's this talk of broken heads?' asked Cadfael, alarmed. 'Whose? Are you telling me there've been thieves ransacking your booth now?'

'In the night! And the strong-box gone, and Warin tied up hand and foot with a throatful of sacking, and nobody heard sound while they did it. We found him not half an hour ago . . .'

'Come!' said Cadfael, grasping him by the sleeve and setting off for the guest-hall at a furious pace. 'We'll find Hugh Beringar. Tell your tale once, and save breath!'

In Aline's apartments the women were only just out of bed, and Hugh was sitting over an early meal in shirt and hose, shoeless, when Cadfael rapped at the door, and cautiously put his head in.

'Your pardon, Hugh, but there's news. May we come in?'

Hugh took one look at him, recognised the end of his ease, and bade them in resignedly.

'Here's one has a tale to tell,' said Cadfael. 'He's new come from the horse-fair.'

At sight of Roger, Emma came to her feet in astonishment and alarm, the soft, bemused bloom of sleep gone from her eyes, and the morning flush from her cheeks. Her black hair, not yet braided, swung in a glossy curtain about her shoulders, and her loose undergown was ungirdled, her feet bare. 'Roger, what is it? What has happened now?'

'More theft and roguery, mistress, and God knows I can see no reason why all the rascals in the shire should pick on us for prey.' Roger heaved in deep breath, and launched headlong into his complaint. 'This morning I go to the stall as

90

usual, and find it all closed, and not a sound or a word from within for all my shouting and knocking, and then come some of the neighbours, wondering, and one sees that the inside bar has been hoisted with a knife—and a marvellous thin knife it must have been. And we go in and find Warin rolled up like baggage in his own cloak, and fast tied, and his mouth stuffed with sacking—a bag over his head, fit to choke him. . . .'

'Oh, no!' breathed Emma in a horrified whisper, and pressed a fist hard against trembling lips. 'Oh, poor Warin! He's not . . . oh, not dead?'

Roger gave vent to a snort of contempt. 'Not he! Alive and fit as a flea, barring being stiff from the cords. How he could sleep so sound as not to hear the fumbling with the latch, nor even notice when the door was opened, there's no guessing. But if he did hear, he took good care not to give the robbers any trouble. You know Warin's no hero. He says he was only shook awake when the sack went over his head, and never saw face nor form, though he thinks there were two of them, for there was some whispering. But as like as not he heard them come, but chose not to, for fear they'd slip the knife in his ribs.'

Emma's colour had warmed into rose again. She drew a deep breath of thankfulness. 'But he's safe? He's taken no harm at all?' She caught Aline's sympathetic eye, and laughed shakily with relief. 'I *know* he is not brave. I'm *glad* he is not! Nor very clever nor very industrious, either, but I've known him since I was a little girl, he used to make toys for me, and willow whistles. Thank God he is not harmed!'

'Not a graze! I wish,' said Roger, his eyes burning jealously upon her childish morning beauty, not yet adorned and needing no adornment, 'I wish to God I'd stayed there to be watchman myself, they'd not have broken in there unscathed, and found everything handed over on a platter.'

'But then you might have been killed, Roger. I'm glad you were *not* there, you'd surely have put up a fight and come to harm. What, against two, and you unarmed? Oh, no, I want no man hurt to protect my possessions.'

'What followed?' asked Hugh shortly, stamping his feet into his shoes and reaching for his coat. 'You've left him there to mind the stall? Is he fit?'

'As you or me, my lord. I'll send him to you to tell his own tale when I get back.'

'No need, I'm coming with you to view the place and the damage. Finish your tale. They'll scarcely have left empty-handed. What's gone with them?'

Roger turned devoted, humble, apologetic eyes upon Emma. 'Sorrow the day, mistress, my master's strong-box is gone with them!'

Brother Cadfael was watching Emma's face just as intently as was her hopeless admirer, and it seemed to him that in the pleasure of knowing that her old servant had survived unharmed, she was proof against all other blows. The loss of the strong-box she received with unshaken serenity. In these surroundings, safe from any too pressing manifestation of his passion, she was even moved to comfort Roger. A kindhearted girl, who did not like to see any of her own people out of sorts with his competence and his self-respect.

'You must not feel it so sharply,' she said warmly. 'How could you have prevented? There is no fault attaches to you.'

'I took most of the money back to the barge with me last night,' pleaded Roger earnestly. 'It's safe locked away, there's been no more tampering there. But Master Thomas's account books, and some parchments of value, and charters . . .'

'Then there will be copies,' said Emma firmly. 'And what is more, if they took the box, supposing it to be full of money, they'll keep what money was left there, and most likely discard the box and the parchments, for what use can they make of those? We may get most of it back, you will see.'

Not merely a kind girl, but a girl of sense and fortitude, who bore up nobly under her losses. Cadfael looked at Hugh, and found Hugh looking at him, just as woodenly, but with one lively eyebrow signalling slightly sceptical admiration.

'Nothing is lost,' said Emma firmly, 'of any value to compare with a life. Since Warin is safe, I cannot be sad.'

'Nevertheless,' said Hugh with deliberation, 'it might be well if one abbey sergeant stood guard on your booth until the fair is over. For it does seem that all the misfortunes that should by rights be shared among all the abbey's clients are falling solely upon you. Shall I ask Prior Robert to see to it?'

She looked down, wary and thoughtful, for a moment, and then lifted deep blue eyes wide and clear as the sky, and a degree more innocent than if they had but newly opened on the world. 'It's kind of you,' she said, 'but surely everything has now been done to us. I don't think it will be necessary to set a guard upon us now.'

Hugh came to Cadfael's workshop after the midday meal, leaving Emma in Aline's charge, helped himself to a horn of wine from Cadfael's private store, and settled down on the bench under the eaves, on the shady side. The fragrance of the herbs lay like a sleepy load on the air within the pleached hedges, and set him yawning against his will and his mood, which was for serious discussion. They were well away from the outer world here, the busy hum of the marketplace drifted to them only distantly and pleasantly, like the working music of Brother Bernard's bees. And Brother Mark, weeding the herb-beds with delicate, loving hands, habit kilted to his knees, was no hindrance at all to their solitude.

'A separate creature,' said Brother Cadfael, eyeing him with detached affection. 'My priest, my proxy. I had to find some way of evading the fate that closed on me. There goes my sacrificial lamb, the best of the flock.'

'Some day he will take *your* confession,' said Hugh, watching Mark pluck out weeds as gently as though he pitied them, 'and you'll be a lost man, for he'll know every evasion.' He sipped wine, drew it about his mouth thoughtfully, swallowed it and sat savouring the after-taste for a moment. 'This fellow Warin had little to add,' he said then. 'What do you say now? This *cannot* be chance.'

'No,' agreed Cadfael, propping the door of his workshop wide to let in the air, and coming to sit beside his friend, 'it cannot be chance. The man is killed, stripped, his barge searched, his booth searched. Not a soul besides, at this fair where there are several as wealthy, has suffered any attack or any loss. No, there is nothing done at hazard here.'

'What, then? Expound! The girl claimed there were things stolen from the barge. Now something positive, a strong-box, the single portable thing in the booth that might confidently be supposed to hold valuables, is demonstrably stolen from this last assault. If these are not simple thefts, what are they? Tell me!'

'Stages in a quest,' said Cadfael. 'It seems to me there's a hunt afoot for something. I do not know what, but some quite single, small thing, and precious, which was, or was thought to be, in the possession of Master Thomas. On the night he came here he was murdered, and his body stripped. The first search. And it was fruitless, for the next day his barge was visited and ransacked. The second search.'

'Not altogether fruitless this time,' said Beringar dryly, 'for we know on the best authority, do we not, that whoever paid that visit left the richer by three things, a silver chain, a girdle with a gold clasp, and a pair of embroidered gloves.'

'Hmmm!' Cadfael twitched his brown nose doubtfully between finger and thumb, and eyed the young man sidewise.

'Oh, come!' said Hugh indulgently, and flashed his sudden smile. 'I may not stumble on these subtleties as quickly as you, but since knowing you I've had to keep my wits about me. The lady has a bold mind and an excellent memory, and I have no hope in the world of getting her to make a mistake in one detail of the embroidery on those lost gloves, but for all that, I doubt if they ever existed.'

'You might,' Cadfael suggested, though without much hope, 'try asking her outright what it is she's hiding.'

'I did!' owned Hugh, ruefully grinning. 'She opened great, hurt eyes at me, and could not understand me! She knows nothing, she's hiding nothing, she has nothing to tell more than she's already told, and every word of that is truth. But for all that, and however angelically, the girl's lying. What was it stuck in your craw, and brought you up against the same shock before ever it dawned upon me?'

'I should be sorry,' said Cadfael slowly, 'if anything I have done or said made you think any evil of the girl, for I think none.'

'Neither do I, you need not fear it. But I do think she may be meddling in something she would do better to let well alone, and I would rather, as you would, as Abbot Radulfus would, that no harm should come to her under our care. Or ever, for that matter. I like her well.'

'When we went together to the barge,' said Cadfael, 'and

she took no more than a minute within to cry out that someone had been there, pawing through all their belongings, I never doubted she was telling truth. Women know how they leave things, it needs only a wrong fold to betray an alien hand, and certainly it shocked and startled her, that was no feigning. Nor was it the next moment, when I asked if anything had been taken, and without pause for thought, she said: "No!" An absolute no, I would say even triumphant. I thought little of it then, but urged her to look thoroughly and make sure. When I said she must report the matter, she thought again, and took pains to discover that indeed a few things had been stolen. I think she regretted that ever she had cried out in the first place, but if the law must know of it, she would ensure that it was accepted as a trivial theft by some common pickpurse. Truth is what she told unguardedly, with that scornful "no" of hers. Afterwards she made to undo the effect by lying, and for one not by nature a liar she did it well. But for all that, I think, like you, those pretty things of hers never existed, or never were aboard the barge.'

'Still remains the question,' said Hugh, considering, 'of why she was so sure in the first place that nothing had been taken.'

'Because,' said Cadfael simply, 'she knew what the thief must have come looking for, and she knew he had not found it, because she knew it was not there to be found. The second search was also vain. Whatever it may be, it was not on Master Thomas's person, which was clearly the most likely place, nor was it on his barge.'

'Hence this third search! So now divine for me, Cadfael, whether this third attempt has succeeded or no. The merchant's strong-box is vanished—again a logical place to keep something so precious. Will this be the end of it?'

Cadfael shook his head emphatically. 'This attempt has fared no better than the others,' he said positively. 'You may take that as certain.'

'How can you be so sure of it?' demanded Hugh curiously.

'You saw all that I saw. She does not care a farthing for the loss of the strong-box! As soon as she knew that the man Warin was unhurt, she took everything else calmly enough. Whatever it is the unknown is seeking, she knew it was not in the barge, and she knew it was not in the booth. And I can think of only one reason why she should know so well where it is *not*, and that is that she knows equally well where it *is*.'

'Then the next possibility the enemy will be considering,' said Hugh with conviction, 'is where *she* is—on her person or in some hiding-place only she knows of. Well, we'll keep a vigilant eye on Emma, between us. No,' said Hugh reflectively, 'I cannot imagine any evil of her, but neither can I imagine how she can be tangled in something grim enough to bring about murder, violence and theft, nor why, if she knows herself to be in danger and in need of help, she won't speak out and ask for it. Aline has tried her best to get her to confide, and the girl remains all sweetness and gratitude, but lets no word drop of any burden she may be carrying. And you know Aline, she draws out confidences without ever asking a probing question, and whoever can resist her is beyond the reach of the rest of us . . .'

'I'm glad to see you so fond a husband,' said Cadfael approvingly.

'So you should be, it was you tossed the girl into my arms in the first place. You'd best be worrying now about what manner of father I shall make! And you might put in a prayer for me on the issue, some time when you're on your knees. No, truly, Cadfael . . . I wonder about this girl. Aline likes her, and that's recommendation enough. And she seems to like Aline—no, more than like! Yet she never lets down her veils. When she seems most to cherish my most cherishable lady, she is also most careful not to let slip one unguarded word about her own situation.'

Brother Cadfael saw no paradox there. 'So she would be, Hugh,' he said gravely. 'If she feels herself to be in danger, the last thing she will do is to draw in beside her someone she values and likes. By every means in her power—and I think she is a clever and resourceful girl—she will stand off her friends from any share in what she is about.'

Beringar considered that long and sombrely, nursing his empty horn. 'Well, all we can do is hedge her about thick enough to stand off, likewise, whatever move may be made against her.'

It had not occurred to him, it was only now insinuating

itself into Cadfael's thoughts, that the next decisive move might come from Emma herself, rather than being made against her. A piece of this mystery, apparently the vital piece, she had in her hands; if any use was to be made of it, it might well be at her decree.

Hugh set aside his drinking-horn and rose, brushing the summer dust from his cotte. 'Meantime, the sheriff is left with a murder on his hands, and I tell you, Cadfael, that affair now looks less than ever like a drunken revenge by an aggrieved youth of the town—though to tell truth, it never did look too convincing, even if we could not discard it out of hand.'

'Surely there's good ground now for letting the provost bail his lad out and take him home?' said Cadfael, encouraged. 'Of all the young men around this town, Philip must be the clearest from any suspicion of this last outrage, or the raid on the barge, either. The gaoler who turns the key on him can witness where *he's* been all this while, and swear he never left it.'

'I'm off to the castle now,' said Hugh. 'I can't vouch for the sheriff, but I'll certainly speak a word in his ear, and in the provost's, too. It's well worth making the approach.'

He looked down, flashing out of his preoccupation with a sudden mischievous smile, combed the fingers of one hand through the hedge of bushy greying hair that rimmed Cadfael's sunburned tonsure, leaving it bristling like thornbushes, snapped a finger painfully against the nut-brown dome between, and took his departure with his usual light stride and insouciant bearing, which the unwary mistook for the mark of a frivolous man. Such small indulgences he was more likely to permit himself, strictly with friends, when he was engaged on something more than usually grave.

Cadfael watched him go, absently smoothing down the warlike crest Hugh had erected. He supposed he had better be stirring, too, and hand over charge here to Brother Mark until evening. It would not do to take his eyes off Emma for any length of time, and Aline, to please a solicitous husband, consented to doze for an hour or two in the afternoon, for the sake of the child. Grandchildren by proxy, Cadfael reflected, might be a rare and pleasurable recompense for a celibate prime. As for old age, he had not yet begun to think about it; no doubt it had its own alleviations.

TWO

'FOR ALL I SAID,' EMMA MUSED ALOUD, PUTTING FINE STITCHES into a linen band for an infant's cap, in the lofty midday light in the window of Aline's bedchamber, 'I do grieve for those gloves of mine. Such fine leather, supple and black, and a wealth of gold in the embroidery. I never bought such expensive ones before.' She reached the end of her seam, and snipped off the thread neatly. 'They say there's a very good glover has a stall in the fair,' she said, smoothing her work. 'I thought I might take a look at his wares, and see if he has anything as fine as those I've lost. They tell me he's wellknown in Chester, and the countess buys from him. I think perhaps I'll walk along the Foregate this afternoon, and see what he has. What with all these upsets, I've hardly seen anything of the fair.'

'A good idea,' said Aline. 'Such a fine day, we should not be spending it here withindoors. I'll come with you.'

'Oh, no, you should not,' protested Emma solicitously. 'You have not had your sleep this afternoon. No need to keep me company that short way. I should be distressed if you tired yourself on my account.'

'Oh, folly!' said Aline cheerfully. 'I am so healthy I shall burst if I have too little to do. It's Constance and Hugh who want to make an invalid of me, just because I'm in a woman's best and happiest estate. And Hugh is gone to the sheriff, and Constance is visiting with a cousin of hers in the Wyle, so who's to fret? I'll slip on my shoes, and we'll go. I should like to buy a box of those sugared fruits your uncle brought from the east. We'll do that, too.'

It seemed that Emma had, after all, lost her taste for the expedition. She sat stroking the embroidered band she had just finished, and eyed the shape of linen cut for the crown. 'I don't know—I should finish this, perhaps. After tomorrow there may be no chance, and I should be sorry to leave it for someone else to finish. As for the candied fruits, I'll ask Roger to bring you a box, when he comes again this evening to tell me how the day has gone. Tomorrow it will be here.'

'That's kind,' said Aline, slipping on her shoes none the less, 'but he could hardly try on a pair of gloves for you, or choose with your eye. So let's go and see for ourselves. It won't take long.'

Emma sat hesitating, but whether in a genuine endeavour to make up her mind, or in search of a way of extricating herself from an unsatisfactory situation, Aline could not be sure. 'Oh, no, I should not! How can I give my mind to such vanity, at a time like this! I'm ashamed that I ever thought of it. My uncle dead, and here am I yearning after trumpery bits of finery. No, I won't be so shallow. Let me at least go on with my work for the child, instead of thinking only of my own adornment.' And she picked up the cut linen. Aline noted that the hand holding it trembled a little, and wondered whether to persist. Plainly the girl wanted to go forth for some purpose of her own, but would not go unless it could be alone. And alone, said Aline firmly to herself, she certainly shall not go, if I can prevent.

'Well,' she said doubtfully, 'if you're determined to be so penitential, I won't play the devil and tempt you. And I'm the gainer, your sewing is so fine, I could never match it. Who taught you so well?' She slipped off her soft leather shoes, and sat down again. Something, at least, she had learned, better to let well alone now. Emma welcomed the change of subject eagerly. Of her childhood she would talk freely.

'My mother was a famous embroidress. She began to teach me as soon as I could manage a needle, but she died when I was only eight, and Uncle Thomas took me in. We had a housekeeper, a Flemish lady who had married a Bristol seaman, and been widowed when his ship was lost, and she taught me everything she knew, though I could never equal her work. She used to make altar cloths and vestments for the church, such beautiful things . . .'

So a plain pair of good black gloves, thought Aline, would have done well enough for you at any time, since you could have adorned them to your own fancy. And those who can do such things exquisitely, seldom prefer the work of others.

It was not difficult to keep Emma talking, but for all that, Aline could not help wondering what was going through the girl's mind, and how soon, and how cunningly, she would make the next bid to slip away solitary about her mysterious business. But as it fell out, she need not have troubled, for late in the afternoon came a lay brother from the gatehouse, to announce that Martin Bellecote had brought down Master Thomas's coffin, and desired permission to proceed with his business. Emma rose instantly, laying down her sewing, her face pale and intent. If there was one thing certain, it was that no other matter, however urgent, would take her away from the church until her uncle was decently coffined and sealed down for his journey home, and prayers said for his repose, as later she would attend the first Mass for him. Whatever he had been to others, he had been uncle and father and friend to his orphaned kinswoman, and no reverence, no tribute, would be omitted from his obsequies.

'I will come myself,' said Emma. 'I must say my farewell to him.' She had not yet seen him, dead, but the brothers, long expert in the gentle arts that reconcile life to death, would have made sure that she would be able to remember him without distress.

'Shall I come with you?' offered Aline.

'You are very good, but I would rather go alone.'

Aline followed as far as the great court, and watched the little procession cross to the cloister, Emma walking beside the handcart on which Martin and his son wheeled the coffin. When they had lifted the heavy box and carried it in by the south door of the church, with Emma following, Aline stood for some minutes looking about her. At this hour most of the guests and many of the lay servants were out at the fair, only the brothers went about their business as usual. Through the wide gate of the distant stable-yard she could see Ivo

100

Corbière's young groom rubbing down a pony, and the archer Turstan Fowler sitting on a mounting-block, whistling as he burnished a saddle. Sober and recovered from his debauch, he was a well-set-up and comely fellow, with the open face of one who has not a care in the world. Evidently he was long since forgiven, and back in favour.

Brother Cadfael, coming from the gardens, saw her still gazing pensively towards the church. She smiled at sight of him.

'Martin has brought the coffin. They are within there, she'll think of nothing else now. But, Cadfael, she intends to give us all the slip when she can. She has tried. She would see, she said, if the glover at the fair has something to take the place of the ones she lost. But when I said I would go with her, no, that would not do, she gave up the idea.'

'Gloves!' murmured Brother Cadfael, scrubbing thoughtfully at his chin. 'Strange, when you think of it, that it should be gloves she has on her mind, in the middle of summer.'

Aline was in no position to follow that thought, she took it at its surface meaning. 'Why strange? We know there were some stolen from her, and here we are at one of the few fairs where rare goods are to be bought, it follows naturally enough. But of course the glover is only a handy excuse.'

Cadfael said no more then, but he went away very thoughtfully towards the cloister. The strange thing was not that a girl should want to replace, while chance offered, a lost piece of finery. It was rather that when she was suddenly confronted by the need to pass off as simple robbery a raid she knew to be something very different, one of the articles she claimed to have lost should be a thing so inappropriate to the season that she felt obliged to account for it by saying she had newly bought it in Gloucester on the journey. Why gloves, unless she had gloves running in her mind already for another reason? Gloves? Or glovers?

In the transept chapel Martin Bellecote and his young son set up the heavy coffin on a draped trestle, and reverently laid the body of Master Thomas of Bristol within it. Emma stood looking down at her uncle's dead face for a long time, without tears or words. It would not be painful, she found, to remember him thus, dignified and remote in death, the bones of his cheeks and brow and jaw more strongly outlined than in life, his florid flesh contracted and paled into waxen austerity. Now at the last moment she wanted to give him something to take with him into his grave, and realised that in the buffeting of these two days she had not been able to think clearly enough to be ready for the parting. Not the fact of death, but the absolute need of some ceremonial tenderness, separate from the public rites, suddenly seemed to her overwhelmingly important.

'Shall I cover him?' asked Martin Bellecote gently.

Even so soft a sound startled her. She looked round almost wonderingly. The man, large, comely and calm, waited her orders without impatience. The boy, grave and silent, watched her with huge hazel eyes. From her four years superiority over him she pondered whether so young a creature should be doing this office, and then she understood that those eyes were preoccupied rather with her living self than with the dead, and the vigorous, flowing sap in him reached up towards light and life as to the sun, and recognised shadow only by virtue of its neighbouring brightness. That was right and good.

'No, wait just a moment,' she said. 'I'll come back!'

She went quickly out into the sunlight, and looked about her for the path that led into the gardens. The green lines of a hedge and the crowns of trees within drew her, she came into a walk where flowers had been planted. The brothers were great gardeners, and valued food crops for good reason, but they had time also for roses. She chose the one bush that bore a bloom like no other, pale yellow petals shading into rose at the tips, and plucked one flower only. Not the buds, not even the one perfect globe, but a wide-open bloom just beyond its prime but still unflawed. She took it back, hurrying, into the church with her. He was not young, not even at his zenith, but settling into his autumn, and this was the rose for him.

Brother Cadfael had watched her go, he watched her come again, and followed her into the chapel, but held aloof in the shadows. She brought her single flower and laid it in the coffin, beside the dead man's heart.

'Cover him now,' she said, and stood well back to let them

102

work in peace. When it was done, she thanked them, and they withdrew and left her there, as clearly was her wish. So, just as silently, did Brother Cadfael.

Emma remained kneeling on the stones of the transept, unaware of discomfort, a great while, her eyes wide open all that time upon the closed coffin, on its draped stand before the altar. To lie thus in the church of a great abbey, to have a special Mass sung for him, and then to be taken home in a grand coffin for burial with still further rites, surely that was glory, and he would have liked it. All was to be done as he would have liked. All! He would be pleased with her.

She knew her duty; she said prayers for him, a great many prayers, because the form was blessedly laid down, and her mind could range while her lips formed the proper words. She would do what he had wanted done, what he had half-confided to her, as he had to no other. She would see his task completed, and he would rest, pleased with her. And then . . . she had hardly looked beyond, but there was a great, summer-scented breeze blowing through her spirit, telling her she was young and fair, and wealthy into the bargain, and that boys like the coffin-maker's young son looked upon her with interest and pleasure. Other young men, too, of less green years . . .

She rose from her knees at last, shook out her crumpled skirts, and walked briskly out of the chapel into the nave of the church, and rounding the clustered stone pillars at the corner of the crossing, came face to face with Ivo Corbière.

He had been waiting, silent and motionless, in his shadowy corner, refraining even from setting foot in the chapel until her vigil was over, and the resolution with which she had suddenly ended it flung her almost into his arms. She uttered a startled gasp, and he put out reassuring hands to steady her, and was in no haste to let go. In this dim place his gold head showed darkened to bronze, and his face, stooped over her solicitously, was so gilded by the summer that it had almost the same fine-metal burnishing.

'Did I alarm you? I'm sorry! I didn't want to disturb you. They told me at the gatehouse that the master-carpenter had come and gone, and you were here. I hoped if I waited patiently I might be able to talk with you. If I have not pressed my attentions on you until now,' he said earnestly, 'it is not because I haven't thought of you. Constantly!'

Her eyes were raised to his face with a fascinated admiration she would never have indulged in full light, and she quite forgot to make any move to withdraw herself from his hold. His hands slid down her forearms, but halted at her hands, and the touch, by mutual consent, became a clasp.

'Almost two days since I've spoken with you!' he said. 'It's an age, and I've grudged it, but you were well-friended, and I had no right . . . But now that I have you, let me keep you for an hour! Come out and walk in the gardens. I doubt if you've even seen them yet.'

They went out together into the sunlight, through the cloister garth and out into the bustle and traffic of the great court. It was almost time for Vespers, the quietest hours of the afternoon now spent, the brothers gathering gradually from their dispersed labours, guests returning from the fairground and the riverside. It was a gratifying thing to walk through this populous place on the arm of a nobleman, lord of a modest honour scattered through Cheshire and Shropshire. For the daughter of craftsmen and merchants, a very gratifying thing! They sat down on a stone bench in the flower-garden, on the sunny side of the pleached hedge, with the heady fragrance of Brother Cadfael's herbarium wafted to them in drunken eddies on a soft breeze.

'You will have troublesome dispositions to make,' said Corbière seriously. 'If there is anything I can arrange for you, let me know of it. It will be my pleasure to serve you. You are taking him back to Bristol for burial?'

'It's what he would have wished. There will be a Mass for him in the morning, and then we shall carry him back to his barge for the journey home. The brothers have been kindness itself to me.'

'And you? Will you also return with the barge?'

She hesitated, but why not confide in him? He was considerate and kind, and quick to understand. 'No, it would be—unwise. While my uncle lived it was very well, but without him it would not do. There is one of our men—I must say no evil of him, for he has done none, but . . . He is too fond. Better we should not travel together. But neither do I want to offer him insult, by letting him know he is not quite trusted. I've told him that I must remain here a few days, that I may be needed if the sheriff has more questions to ask, or more is found out about my uncle's death.'

'But then,' said Ivo with warm concern, 'what of your own journey home? How will you manage?'

'I shall stay with Lady Beringar until we can find some safe party riding south, with women among them. Hugh Beringar will advise me. I have money, and I can pay my way. I shall manage.'

He looked at her long and earnestly, until his gravity melted into a smile. 'Between all your well-wishers, you will certainly reach your home without mishap. I'll be giving my mind to it, among the rest. But now let's forget, for my sake, that there must be a departure, and make the most of the hours while you are still here.' He rose, and took her by the hand to draw her up with him. 'Forget Vespers, forget we're guests of an abbey, forget the fair and the business of the fair, and all that such things may demand of you in future. Think only that it's summer, and a glorious evening, and you're young, and have friends . . . Come down with me past the fish-ponds, as far as the brook. That is all abbey land, I wouldn't take you beyond.'

She went with him gratefully, his hand cool and vital in hers. By the brook below the abbey fields it was cool and fresh and bright, full of scintillating light along the water, and birds dabbling and singing, and in the pleasure of the moment she almost forgot all that lay upon her, so sacred and so burdensome. Ivo was reverent and gentle, and did not press her too close, but when she said regretfully that it was time for her to go back, for fear Aline might be anxious about her, he went with her all the way, her hand still firmly retained in his, and presented himself punctiliously before Aline, so that Emma's present guardian might study, accept and approve him. As indeed she did.

It was charmingly and delicately done. He made himself excellent company for as long as was becoming on a first visit, invited and deferred to all Aline's graceful questions, and withdrew well before he had even drawn near the end of his welcome.

'So that's the young man who was so helpful and gallant when the riot began,' said Aline, when he was gone. 'Do you know, Emma, I do believe you have a serious admirer there.' A wooer gained, she thought, might come as a blessed counter-interest to a guardian lost. 'He comes of good blood and family,' said the Aline Siward who had brought two manors to her husband in her own right, but saw no difference between her guest and herself, and innocently ignored the equally proud and honourable standards of those born to craft and commerce instead of land. 'The Corbières are distant kin of Earl Ranulf of Chester himself. And he does seem a most estimable young man.'

'But not of my kind,' said Emma, as shrewd and wary as she sounded regretful. 'I am a stone-mason's daughter, and niece to a merchant. No landed lord is likely to become a suitor for someone like me.'

'But it's not someone *like* you in question,' said Aline reasonably. 'It is *you!*'

Brother Cadfael looked about him, late in the evening after Compline, saw all things in cautious balance, Emma securely settled in the guest-hall, Beringar already home. He went thankfully to bed with his brothers, for once at the proper time, and slept blissfully until the bell rang to wake him for Matins. Down the night stairs and into the church the brothers filed in the midnight silence, to begin the new day's worship. In the faint light of the altar candles they took their places, and the third day of Saint Peter's Fair had begun. The third and last.

Cadfael always rose for Matins and Lauds not sleepy and unwilling, but a degree more awake than at any other time, as though his senses quickened to the sense of separateness of the community gathered here, to a degree impossible by daylight. The dimness of the light, the solidity of the enclosing shadows, the muted voices, the absence of lay worshippers, all contributed to his sense of being enfolded in a sealed haven, where all those who shared in it were his own flesh and blood and spirit, responsible for him as he for them, even some for whom, in the active and arduous day, he could feel no love, and pretended none. The burden of his vows became also his privilege, and the night's first worship was the fuel of the next day's energy.

So the shadows had sharp edges for him, the shapes of pillar and capital and arch clamoured like vibrant notes of music, both vision and hearing observed with heightened sensitivity, details had a quivering insistence. Brother Mark's profile against the candle-light was piercingly clear. A note sung off-key by a sleepy elder stung like a bee. And the single pale speck lying under the trestle that supported Master Thomas's coffin was like a hole in reality, something that could not be there. Yet it persisted. It was at the beginning of Lauds that it first caught his eye, and after that he could not get free of it. Wherever he looked, however he fastened upon the altar, he could still see it out of the corner of his eye.

When Lauds ended, and the silent procession began to file back towards the night stairs and the dortoir, Cadfael stepped aside, stooped, and picked up the mote that had been troubling him. It was a single petal from a rose, its colour indistinguishable by this light, but pale, deepening round the tip. He knew at once what it was, and with this midnight clarity in him he knew how it had come there.

Fortunate, indeed, that he had seen Emma bring her chosen rose and lay it in the coffin. If he had not, this petal would have told him nothing. Since he had, it told him all. With hieratic care and ceremony, after the manner of the young when moved, she had brought her offering cupped in both hands, and not one leaf, not one grain of yellow pollen from its open heart, had fallen to the floor.

Whoever was hunting so persistently for something believed to be in Master Thomas's possession, after searching his person, his barge and his booth, had not stopped short of the sacrilege of searching his coffin. Between Compline and Matins it had been opened and closed again; and a single petal from the wilting rose within had shaken loose and been wafted unnoticed over the side, to bear witness to the blasphemy.

THE THIRD
DAY OF THE FAIR

ONE

EMMA AROSE WITH THE DAWN, STOLE OUT OF THE WIDE BED SHE shared with Constance, and dressed herself very quietly and cautiously, but even so the sense of movement, rather than any sound, disturbed the maid's sleep, and caused her to open eyes at once alert and intelligent.

Emma laid a finger to her lips, and cast a meaning glance towards the door beyond which Hugh and Aline were still sleeping. 'Hush! she whispered. 'I'm only going to church for Prime. I don't want to wake anyone else.'

Constance shrugged against her pillow, raised her brows a little, and nodded. Today there would be the Mass for the dead uncle, and then the transference of his coffin to the barge that would take him home. Not surprising if the girl was disposed to turn this day into a penitential exercise, for the repose of her uncle's soul and the merit of her own. 'You won't go out alone, will you?'

'I'm going straight to the church,' promised Emma earnestly.

Constance nodded again, and her eyelids began to close. She was asleep before Emma had drawn the door to very softly, and slipped away towards the great court.

Brother Cadfael rose for Prime like the rest, but left his cell before his companions, and went to take counsel with the only authority in whom he could repose his latest discovery. Such a violation was the province of the abbot, and only he had the right to hear of it first.

With the door of the abbot's austere cell closed upon them, they were notably at ease together, two men who knew their own minds and spoke clearly what they had to say. The rose petal, a little shrunken and weary, but with its yellow and

111

pink still silken-bright, lay in the abbot's palm like a golden tear.

'You are sure this cannot have fallen when our daughter brought it as an offering? It was a gentle gift,' said Radulfus.

'Not one grain of dust fell. She carried it like a vessel of wine, in both hands. I saw every move. I have not yet seen the coffin by daylight, but I doubt not it has been dealt with competently, and looks as it looked when the master-carpenter firmed it down. Nevertheless, it has been opened and closed again.'

'I take your word,' said the abbot simply. 'This is vile.'

'It is,' said Cadfael, and waited.

'And you cannot put name to the man who would do this thing?'

'Not yet.'

'Nor say if he has gained by it? As God forbid!'

'No, Father! But God will forbid.'

'Give your might to it,' said Radulfus, and brooded for a while in silence. Then he said: 'We have a duty to the law. Do what is best there, for I hear you have the deputy sheriff's ear. As for the affront to the church, to our house, to our dead son and his heiress, I am left to read between rubrics. There will be a Mass this morning for the dead man. The holy rite will cleanse all foulness from his passing and his coffin. As for the child, let her be at peace, for so she may, her dead is in the hand of God, there has no violence been done to his soul.'

Brother Cadfael said, with hearty gratitude: 'She will rest the better if she knows nothing. She is a good girl, her grief should have every consolation.'

'See to it, brother, as you may. It is almost time for Prime.'

Cadfael was hurrying from the abbot's lodging towards the cloister when he saw Emma turn in there ahead of him, and slowed his steps to be unnoticed himself while he watched what she would do. On this of all days Emma was entitled to every opportunity of prayer and meditation, but she also had a very private secular preoccupation of her own, and which of these needs she was serving by this early-rising zeal there was no telling.

In at the south door went Emma, and in after her, just as discreetly, went brother Cadfael. The monks were already in their stalls, and concentrating all upon the altar. The girl slipped silently round into the nave, as though she would find herself a retired spot there in privacy; but instead of turning aside, she continued her rapid, silent passage towards the west door, the parish door that opened on to the Foregate, outside the convent walls. Except during times of stress, such as the siege of Shrewsbury the previous year, it was never closed.

In at one door and out at another, and she was free, for a little while, to go where she would, and could return by the same way, an innocent coming back from church.

Brother Cadfael's sandals padded soundlessly over the tiled floor after her, keeping well back in case she should look round, though here within he was reasonably sure she would not. The great parish door was unlatched, she had only to draw it open a little way, her slenderness slipped through easily, and since this was facing due west, no betraying radiance flooded in. Cadfael gave her a moment to turn right or left outside the door, though surely it would be to the right, towards the fairground. What should she have to do in the direction of the river and the town?

She was well in sight when he slid through the doorway and round the corner of the west front, and looked along the Foregate. She did not hurry now, but curbed her pace to that of the early buyers who were sauntering along the highroad, halting at stalls already busy, handling goods, arguing over prices. The last day of the fair was commonly the busiest. There were bargains to be snapped up at the close, and lowered prices. There was bustle everywhere, even at this hour, but the pace of the ambulant shoppers was leisurely. Emma matched hers to it, as though she belonged among them, but for all that, she was making her way somewhere with a purpose. Cadfael followed at a respectful distance.

Only once did she speak to anyone, and then she chose the holder of one of the larger stalls, and it seemed that she was asking him for directions, for he turned and pointed ahead along the street, and towards the abbey wall. She thanked him, and went on in the direction he had indicated, and now she quickened her pace. Small doubt that she had known all along to whom she was bound; apparently she had not known precisely where to find him. Now she knew. By this time all the chief merchants gathered here knew where to find one another.

Emma had come to a halt, almost at the end of the Foregate, where a half-dozen booths were backed into the abbey wall. It seemed that she had arrived at her destination, yet now stood hesitant, gazing a little helplessly, as if what she confronted surprised and baffled her. Cadfael drew nearer. She was frowning doubtfully at the last of the booths, backed into a corner between buttress and wall. Cadfael recognised it; a lean, suspicious face had peered out from that hatch as the sheriff's officers had hoisted Turstan Fowler on to a board and borne him away to an abbey cell on the eve of the fair. The booth of Euan of Shotwick. Here they came again, those imagined gloves, so feelingly described, so soon stolen!

And Emma was at a loss, for the booth was fast-closed, every panel sealed, and business all around in full swing. She turned to the nearest neighbour, clearly questioning, and the man looked, and shrugged, and shook his head. What did he know? There had been no sign of life there since last night, perhaps the glover had sold out and departed.

Cadfael drew nearer. Beneath the austere white wimple, so sharp a change from the frame of blue-black hair, Emma's young profile looked even more tender and vulnerable. She did not know what to do. She advanced a few steps and raised a hand, as though she would knock at the closed shutter, but then she wavered and drew back. From across the street a brawny butcher left his stall, patted her amiably on the shoulder, and did the knocking for her lustily, then stood to listen. But there was no move from within.

A large hand clapped Cadfael weightily on the back, and the cavernous voice of Rhodri ap Huw boomed in his ear in Welsh: 'What's this, then? Master Euan not open for trade? That I should see the day! I never knew him to miss a sale before, or any other thing to his advantage.'

'The stall's deserted,' said Cadfael. 'The man may have left for home.'

'Not he! He was there past midnight, for I took a turn

along here to breathe the cool before going to my inn, and there was a light burning inside there then.' No gleam from within now, though the slanting sunlight might well pale it into invisibility. But no, that was not so, either. The chinks between shutter and frame were utterly dark.

It was all too like what Roger Dod had found at another booth, only one day past. But there the booth had been barred from within, and the bar hoisted clear with a dagger. Here there was a lock, to be mastered from within or without, and certainly no visible key.

'This I do not like,' said Rhodri ap Huw, and strode forward to try the door, and finding it, as was expected, locked, to peer squint-eyed through the large keyhole. 'No key within,' he said shortly over his shoulder, and peered still. 'Not a movement in there.' He had Cadfael hard on his heels by then, and three or four others closing in. 'Give me room!'

Rhodri clenched the fingers of both hands in the edge of the door, set a broad foot against the timber wall, and hauled mightily, square shoulders gathered in one great heave. Wood splintered about the lock, small flinders flying like motes of dust, and the door burst open. Rhodri swayed and recovered in recoil, and was first through the opening, but Cadfael was after him fast enough to ensure that the Welshman touched nothing within. They craned into the gloom together, cheek by jowl.

The glover's stall was in chaos, shelves swept clear, goods scattered like grain over the floor. On a straw palliasse along the rear wall his cloak lay sprawled, and on an iron stand beside, a quenched candle sagged in folds of tallow. It took them a few seconds to accustom their eyes to the dimness and see clearly. Tangled in his spilled stock of belts, baldrics, gloves, purses and saddle-bags, Euan of Shotwick lay on his back, knees drawn up, a coarse sacking bag drawn half-over his lean face and greying head. Beneath the hem of the hood his thin-lipped mouth grinned open in a painful rictus, large white teeth staring, and the angle at which his head lay had the horrible suggestion of a broken wooden puppet.

Cadfael turned and flung up the shutter of the booth, letting in the morning light. He stooped to touch the contorted neck and hollow cheek. 'Cold,' said Rhodri, behind him, not attempting to verify his judgment, which for all that was accurate enough. Euan's flesh was chilling. 'He's dead,' said Rhodri flatly.

'Some hours,' said Cadfael.

In the stress of the moment he had forgotten Emma, but the shriek she gave caused him to swing round in haste and dismay. She had crept in fearfully to peer over the shoulders of the neighbours, and stood staring with eyes wide with horror, both small fists crushed against her mouth. 'Oh, no!' she said in a whisper. 'Not dead! Not he, too. . . .'

Cadfael took her in his arms, and thrust her bodily before him out of the booth, elbowing the gaping onlookers out of his way. 'Go back! You mustn't stay here. Go back before you're missed, and leave this to me.' He wondered if she even heard his rapid murmur into her ear; she was shaking and white as milk, her blue eyes fixed and huge with shock. He looked about him urgently for someone to whom he could safely confide her, for he doubted if she should be left to return alone, and yet he did not care to leave this scene until Beringar should be here to take charge, or one of the sheriff's sergeants at least. The sudden alarmed shout of recognition that came from the rear of the gathering crowd was a most welcome sound.

'Emma! Emma!' Ivo Corbière came cleaving an unceremonious way through the press, like a sudden vehement wind in a cornfield, bludgeoning the standing stems out of its path. She turned at the call, and a spark of returning life sprang up in her eyes. Thankfully Cadfael thrust her into the young man's arms, which reached eagerly and anxiously to receive her.

'For God's sake, what has happened to her? What . . .' His glance flashed from her stunned visage to Cadfael's, and beyond, to the open door with its splintered panel. Over her head his lips framed silently for Cadfael: 'Not again? Another?'

'Take her back,' said Cadfael shortly. 'Take care of her. And tell Hugh Beringar to come. We have sheriff's business here within.'

*   *   *

All the way back along the Foregate, Corbière kept a supporting arm about her, and curbed his long stride to hers, and all the way he poured soothing, caressing words into her ear, while she, until they had almost reached the west door of the church, said nothing at all, simply walked docilely beside him, distantly aware of the lulling sound and the comforting touch. Then suddenly she said: 'He's dead. I saw him, I know.'

'A bare glimpse you had,' said Ivo consolingly. 'It may not be so.'

'No,' said Emma, 'I know the man is dead. How could it happen? Why?'

'There are always such acts, somewhere, robberies, violence and evil. It is sad, but it is not new.' His fingers pressed her hand warmly. 'It is no fault of yours, and alas, there is nothing you or I can do about it. I wish I could make you forget it. In time you will forget.'

'No,' she said. 'I shall never forget this.'

She had meant to return by the church, as she had left, but now it no longer mattered. As far as he or any other was concerned, she had simply set out early to buy some gloves, or at least to view what the glover had to offer. She went in with Ivo by the gatehouse. By the time he had brought her tenderly on his arm to the guest-hall she had regained her composure. There was a little colour in her face again, and her voice was alive, even if its tone indicated that life was painful.

'I'm recovered now, Ivo,' she said. 'You need not trouble for me further. I will tell Hugh Beringar that he is needed.'

'Brother Cadfael entrusted you to me,' said Ivo with gentle and confident authority, 'and you did not reject me. I shall fulfil my errand exactly. As I hope,' he said, smiling, 'I may perform any other missions you may care to entrust to me hereafter.'

Hugh Beringar came with four of the sheriff's men, dispersed the crowd that hung expectantly round the booth of Euan of Shotwick, and listened to the accounts rendered by the neighbouring stall-holders, by the butcher from over the road, and by Rhodri ap Huw, for whom Cadfael interpreted sentence by sentence. In no haste to go, for as he said, his best lad was back with the boat from Bridgnorth and competent to take charge of what stock he still had to sell, the Welshman nonetheless showed no unbecoming desire to linger, once his witness was taken. Imperturbable and all-beholding, he ambled away at the first indication that the law had done with him. Others, more persistent, hung about the booth in a silent, watchful circle, but were kept well away from earshot. Beringar drew the door to. The opened hatches gave light enough.

'Can I take the man's account for fair and true?' asked Hugh, casting a glance after Rhodri's retreating back. There was no backward glance from the Welshman, his assurance was absolute.

'To the letter, for all that happened here from the time I came on the scene. He's an excellent observer, there's little he misses of what concerns him, or may concern him, and what does not. He does business, too, his trade here is no pretext. But it may be only half his business that we see.'

There were only the two of them within there now, two living and the dead man. They stood one either side of him, drawn back to avoid disturbing either his body or the litter of leatherwork scattered about and over him.

'He says there was a light showing through the chinks here past midnight,' said Beringar. 'The light is quenched now, not burned out. And if he locked his door after closing the booth for the night . . .'

'As he would,' said Cadfael. 'Rhodri's account of him rings true. A man complete in himself, trusting no one, able to take care of himself, until now. He would have locked his door.'

'Then he also unlocked it, to let in his murderer. The lock never was forced until now, as you saw. Why should a wary man unlock his door to anyone in the small hours?'

'Because he was expecting someone,' said Cadfael, 'though not the someone who came. Because, it may be, he had been expecting someone all these three days, and was relieved when the expected message came at last.'

'So relieved that he ceased to be cautious? Given your Welshman's estimate of him, I should doubt it.'

118

'So should I,' agreed Cadfael, 'unless there was a private word he was waiting for, and it was known and given. A name, perhaps. For you see, Hugh, I think he was already well aware that the one he had expected to deliver the message was never going to tap at his door by night, or stop in the Foregate by day to pass the time with him.'

'You mean,' said Hugh, 'Thomas of Bristol, who is dead.'

'Who else? How many strange chances can come together, all against what is likely, or even possible? A merchant is killed, his barge searched, his booth searched, then, dear God, his coffin! I have not yet had time, Hugh, to tell you of that.' He told it now. He had the rose-petal in the breast of his habit, wrapped in a scrap of linen; it still spoke as eloquently as before. 'You may trust my eyes, I know it did not fall earlier, I know it has been in the coffin with him. Now that same man's niece makes occasion to come by stealth to this glover's stall, only to find the glover dead like her uncle. It is a long list of assaults upon all things connected with Thomas of Bristol. Now, since this unknown treasure was not found even in his coffin, for safe-conduct back to Bristol in default of delivery, the next point of search has been here—where Master Thomas should have delivered it.'

'They would need to have foreknowledge of that.'

'Or good reason to guess aright.'

'By your witness,' said Hugh, pondering, 'the coffin was opened and closed between Compline and Matins. Before midnight. When would you say, Cadfael—your experience is longer than mine—when would you say this man died?'

'In the small hours. By the second hour after midnight, I judge, he was dead. After the coffin, it seems, they were forced to the conclusion that somehow, for all they had a watch on Master Thomas from his arrival, and disposed of him before ever the fair started, yet somehow he, or someone else on his behalf, must have slipped through their net, and delivered the precious charge. This poor soul certainly opened his door last night to someone he believed had business with him. The mention of a privileged name . . . a password . . . He let in his murderer, but what he had expected was the thing promised.'

119

'Then even now,' said Hugh sharply, 'with two murders on their souls, they have not what they wanted. He thought they were bringing it. They trusted to find it here. And neither of them had it. Both were deceived.' He brooded with a brown fist clamping his jaw, and his black brows down-drawn in unaccustomed solemnity. 'And Emma came here . . . by stealth.'

'She did. Not every man,' said Cadfael, 'has your view of women, or mine. Most of your kind, most of mine, would never dream of looking in a woman's direction to find anything of importance in hand. Especially a mere child, barely grown. Not until every other road was closed, and they were forced to notice a woman there in the thick of the matter. Who just might be what they sought.'

'And who has now betrayed herself,' said Hugh grimly. 'Well, at least she reached the guest-hall safely, thanks to Corbière. I have left her with Aline, very shaken, for all her strength of will, and she will not stir a step this day unguarded. That I can promise. Between us I think we can take care of Emma. Now let's see if this poor wretch has anything to tell us that we don't yet know.'

He stooped and drew back the coarse sack that covered half the glover's narrow face, from eyebrow on one side to jaw on the other. A broken bruise in the greying hair above the left temple indicated a right-handed blow as soon as the door was opened to his visitor, meant to stun him, probably, until he could be muffled in the sack and gagged like Warin. Here it was a case of gaining entry and confronting a wide-awake man, not a timid sleeper.

'Much the same manner as the other one,' said Cadfael, 'and I doubt if they ever meant to kill. But he was not so easily put out of the reckoning. He put up a fight. And his neck is broken. By the look of it, one made round behind him to secure this blindfold, and in the struggle he gave them, tried all too hard to haul him backwards by it. He was wiry and agile, but his bones were aging, and too brittle to sustain it. I don't think it was intended. We should have found him neatly bound and still alive, like Warin, if he had not fought them. Once they knew he was dead, they made their search in haste, and left all as it fell.'

Beringar brushed aside the light tangle of girdles and straps and gloves that littered the floor and lay over the body. Euan's right arm was covered from the elbow down by the skirts of his own gown, kicked out of the way of the searchers in their hunt. When the folds were drawn down Hugh let out a sharp whistle of surprise, for in the dead man's hand was a long poniard, the naked blade grooved, and ornamented with gilding near the hilt. At his belt, half-hidden now under his right hip, the scabbard lay empty.

'A man of his hands! And see, he's marked one of them for us!' There was blood on the point of the blade, and drawn up by the grooving for some three fingers' breadth in two thin crimson lines, now drying to black.

'Rhodri ap Huw said of him,' Cadfael remembered, 'that he was a solitary soul who trusted nobody—his own porter and his own watchman. He said he wore a weapon, and knew how to use it.' He went on his knees beside the body, and cleared away the debris that still lay about it, eyeing and handling from head to foot. 'You'll have him away to the castle, I suppose, or the abbey, and look him over more carefully, but I do believe the only blood he's lost is this smear on his brow. This on the dagger is not his.'

'If only we could as easily say whose it is!' said Hugh dryly, sitting on his heels with the nimbleness of the young on the other side of the body. Brother Cadfael eased creaky elderly knees on the hard boards, and briefly envied him. The young man lifted the stiffening arm, and tested the grip of the clenched fingers. 'He holds fast!' It took him some effort to loosen the convulsive grasp enough to slip the hilt of the dagger free. In the slanting light from the open hatch something gleamed briefly, waving at the tip of the blade, and again vanished, as motes of dust come and go in gold in bright sunlight. There was also what seemed at first to be a thin encrustation of blood fringing the steel on one edge. Cadfael exclaimed, leaning to point. 'A yellow hair—There it shows again!' The flashing gleam curled and twisted as Hugh turned the dagger in his hand.

'Not a hair, a fine, yellowish thread. Thread of flax, not bleached. This grooving has ripped out a shred of cloth, and the blood has stuck it fast. See!'

A mere wisp of brown material it was, a fringe along the groove that had held it. Narrow as a blade of grass, but when Cadfael carefully took hold of a thread at the end and drew it out straight, it stretched to the length of his hand. The colour, though fouled by dried blood, showed plain at one edge, a light russet-brown; and at the end of the sliver floated gaily the long, fine flax thread, scalloped like a curly hair.

'A sliced tear a hand long,' said Cadfael, 'and ending at a hem, for surely this thread sewed the edging, and the dagger ripped out a length of the stitching.' He narrowed his eyes, and considered, imagining Euan facing the door as he opened it, the instant blow that failed to tame him, and then his rapid drawing of his poniard and striking with it. Almost brow to brow and breast to breast, a man good with his right hand, and his attacker's heart an open target.

'He struck for the heart,' said Cadfael with conviction. 'So would I, or so would I have done once. The other man, surely, slipped round behind him and spoiled the stroke, but that is where he aimed. Someone, somewhere, has a torn cotte. It might be in the left breast, or it might be in the sleeve. The man's arms would be raised, reaching to grapple him. I should say the left sleeve, ripping from the hem halfway to the elbow. The sewing thread was caught first, and pulled out a length of stitches.'

Hugh considered that respectfully, and found no fault with it. 'Much of a scratch, would you guess? He did not drip blood to the doorway. It could not have been enough to need much stanching.'

'The sleeve would hold it. Likely only a graze, but a long graze. It will be there to be seen.'

'If we knew where to look!' Hugh gave a short bark of laughter at the thought of sending sergeants about this teeming marketplace to ask every man to roll up his left sleeve and show his arm. 'A simple matter! Still, no reason why you and I, and all the men I can spare and trust, should not be keeping our eyes open all the rest of this day for a torn sleeve—or a newly cobbled one.'

He rose, and turned to beckon his nearest man from the open hatch. 'Well, we'll have him away from here, and do what we can. A word with your Rhodri ap Huw wouldn't come amiss, and I fancy you might get more out of him in his own tongue than ever I should at second hand. If he knows this man so well, prick him on to talk, and bring me what you learn.'

'That I'll do,' said Cadfael, clambering stiffly from his knees.

'I must go first to the castle, and report what we've found. One thing I'll make certain of this time,' said Hugh. 'The sheriff was in no mood to listen too carefully last night, but after this he'll have to turn young Corviser loose on his father's warranty, like the rest of them. It would take a more pig-headed man than Prestcote to believe the lad had any part in the first death, seeing the trail of offences that have followed while he was in prison. He shall eat his dinner at home today.'

Rhodri was not merely willing to spend an hour pouring the fruits of his wisdom and experience into Brother Cadfael's ear, he was hovering with that very thing in mind as soon as the corpse of Euan of Shotwick had been carried away, and the booth closed, with one of the sheriff's men on guard. Though ever-present, he had the gift of being unobtrusive until he chose to obtrude, and then could appear from an unexpected direction, and as casually as if only chance had brought him there.

'No doubt you'll have sold all you brought with you,' said Cadfael, encountering him thus between the stalls, clearly untroubled by business.

'Goods of quality are recognised everywhere,' said Rhodri, sharp eyes twinkling merrily. 'My lads are clearing the last few jars of honey, and the wool's long gone. But I've a half-full bottle there, if you care to share a cup at this hour? Mead, not wine, but you'll be happy with that, being a Welshman yourself.'

They sat on heaped trestles already freed from their annual use by the removal of small tradesmen who had sold out their stock, and set the bottle between them.

'And what,' asked Cadfael, with a jerk of his head towards the guarded booth, 'do you make of that affair this morning? After all that's gone before? Have we more birds of prey this way than usual, do you think? It may be they've taken fright and left the shires where there's still fighting, and we get the burden of it.'

Rhodri shook his shaggy head, and flashed his large white teeth out of the thicket in a grin. 'I would say you've had a more than commonly peaceful and well-mannered fair, myself—apart from the misfortunes of two merchants only. Oh, tonight's the last night, and there'll be a few drunken squabbles and a brawl or two, I daresay, but what is there in that? But chance has played no part in what has happened to Thomas of Bristol. Chance never goes hounding one man for three days through hundreds of his fellows, yet never grazes one of the others.'

'It has more than grazed Euan of Shotwick,' remarked Cadfael dryly.

'Not chance! Consider, brother! Earl Ranulf of Chester's eyes and ears comes to a Shropshire fair and is killed. Thomas of Bristol, from a city that holds by Earl Robert of Gloucester, comes to the same fair, and is killed the very night of his coming. And after his death, everything he brought with him is turned hither and yon, but precious little stolen, from all I hear.' And certainly he had a way of hearing most of what was said within a mile of him, but at least he had made no mention of the violation of Master Thomas's coffin. Either that had not reached his ears, and never would, or else he had been the first to know of it, and would be the last ever to admit it. The parish door was always open, no need to set root in the great court or pass the gatehouse. 'Something Thomas brought to Shrewsbury is of burning interest to somebody, it seems to me, and the somebody failed to get hold of it from man, barge or stall. And the next thing that happens is that Euan of Shotwick is also killed in the night, and all his belongings ransacked. I would not say but things were stolen there. They may have learned enough for that, and his goods are small and portable, and why despise a little gain on the side? But for all that—No, two men from opposite ends of a divided country, meeting midway, on important private business? It could be so! Gloucester's man and Chester's man.'

'And whose,' wondered Cadfael aloud, 'was the third man?'

'The third?'

'Who took such an interest in the other two that they died of it. Whose man would he be?'

'Why, there are other factions, and every one of them needs its intelligencers. There's the king's party—they might well feel a strong interest if they noted Gloucester's man and Chester's man attending the same fair midway between. And not only the king—there are others who count themselves kings on their own ground, besides Chester, and they also need to know what such a one as Chester is up to, and will go far to block it if it threatens their own profit. And then there's the church, brother, if you'll take it no offence is meant to the Benedictines. For you'll have heard by now that the king has dealt very hardly with some of his bishops this last few weeks, put up all manner of clerical backs, and turned his own brother and best ally, Bishop Henry of Winchester, who's papal legate into the bargain, into a bitter enemy. Bishop Henry himself might well have a finger in thi pie, though I doubt if he can have had word of things afoot here in time, being never out of the south. But Lincoln, or Worcester— all such lords need to know what's going on, and for men of influence there are always plenty of bully-boys for hire, who'll do the labouring work while their masters sit inviolable at home.'

And so, thought Cadfael, could wealthy men sit inviolable here in their stalls, in full view of hundreds, while their hired bully-boys do the dirty work. And this black Welshman is laying it all out for me plain to be seen, and taking delight in it, too! Cadfael knew when he was being deliberately teased! What he could not be quite sure of was whether this was the caprice of a blameless but mischievous man, or the sport of a guilty one taking pleasure in his own immunity and cleverness. The black eyes sparkled and the white teeth shone. And why grudge him his enjoyment, if something useful could yet be gleaned from it? Besides, his mead was excellent.

'There must,' said Cadfael thoughtfully, 'be others here from Cheshire, even some from close to Ranulf's court. You yourself, for instance, come from not so far away, and are knowledgeable about those parts, and the men and the mood there. If you are right, whoever has committed these acts knew where to look for the thing they wanted, once they gave up believing that it was still among the effects of Thomas of Bristol. Now how would they be able to choose, say, between Euan of Shotwick and you? As an instance, of course! No offence!'

'None in the world!' said Rhodri heartily. 'Why, bless you! The only reason I know myself is because I *am* myself, and know I'm not in Ranulf of Chester's employ. But *you* can't know that, not certainly, and neither can any other. There's a small point, of course—Thomas of Bristol, I doubt, spoke no Welsh.'

'And you no English,' sighed Cadfael. 'I had forgotten!'

'There was a traveller from down towards Gloucester stayed overnight at Ranulf's court not a month ago,' mused Rhodri, twinkling happily at his own omniscience, 'a jongleur who got unusual favour, for he was called in to play a stave or two to Ranulf and his lady in private, after they left the hall at night. If Earl Ranulf has an ear for music, it's the first I've heard of it. It would certainly need more than a French virelai to fetch him in for his father-in-law's cause. He would want to know what were the prospects of success, and what his reward might be.' He slanted a radiant smile along his shoulder at Cadfael, and poured out the last of the mead. 'Your health, brother! You, at least, are delivered from the greed for gain. I have often wondered, is there a passion large enough to take its place? I am still in the world myself, you understand.'

'I think there might be,' said Cadfael mildly. 'For truth, perhaps? Or justice?'

TWO

THE GAOLER UNLOCKED THE DOOR OF PHILIP'S CELL SOMEWHAT BE-
fore noon, and stood back to let the provost enter. Father and
son eyed each other hard, and though Geoffrey Corviser
continued to look grimly severe, and Philip obdurate and
defiant, nevertheless the father was mollified and the son
reassured. By and large, they understood each other pretty
well.

'You are released to my warranty,' said the provost shortly.
'The charge is not withdrawn, not yet, but you're trusted to
appear when called, and until then, let's hope I may get some
sensible work out of you.'

'I may come home with you?' Philip sounded dazed; he
knew nothing of what had been going on outside, and was
unprepared for this abrupt release. Hurriedly he brushed himself down, all too aware that he presented no very savoury
spectacle to walk through the town at the provost's side.
'What made them change their mind? There's no one been
taken for the murder?' That would clear him utterly in Emma's
eyes, no doubts left.

'Which murder?' said his father grimly. 'Never mind now,
you shall hear, once we have you out of here.'

'Ay, stir yourself, lad,' advised the goodhumoured warder,
jingling his keys, 'before they change their minds again. The
rate things are happening at this year's fair, you might find
the door slammed again before you can get through it.'

Philip followed his father wonderingly out of the castle.
The noon light in the outer ward fell warm and dazzling upon
him, the sky was a brilliant, deep blue, like Emma's eyes
when she widened them in anxiety or alarm. It was impossible not to feel elated, whatever reproaches might still await

him at home; and hope and the resilience of youth blossomed in him as his father recounted brusquely all that had happened while his son fretted in prison without news.

'Then there have been two attacks upon Mistress Vernold's boat and booth, her goods taken, her men assaulted?' He had quite forgotten his own bedraggled appearance, he was striding towards home with his head up and his visage roused and belligerent, looking, indeed, very much as he had looked when he led his ill-fated expedition across the bridge on the eve of the fair. 'And no one seized for it? Nothing done? Why, she herself may be in danger!' Indignation quickened his steps. 'For God's sake, what's the sheriff about?'

'He has enough to do breaking up unseemly riots by you and your like,' said his father smartly, but could not raise so much as a blush from his incensed offspring. 'But since you want to know, Mistress Vernold is in the guest-hall of the abbey, safe enough, in the care of Hugh Beringar and his lady. You'd do better to be thinking about your own troubles, my lad, and mind your own step, for you're not out of the wood yet.'

'What did I do that was so wrong? I went only one pace beyond what you did yourself the day before.' He did not even sound aggrieved about being judged hard, he made that brief defence only absently, his mind all on the girl. 'Even in the guest-hall she may not be out of reach, if this is all some determined plot against her uncle and all his family.' In the death of one more tradesman at the fair he showed less interest, shocking though it was, since it seemed to have little or nothing to do with the vindictive catalogue of offences against Master Thomas and all his possessions. 'She spoke so fairly,' he said. 'She would not have me accused of worse than I did.'

'True enough! She was a fine, honest witness, no denying it. But no business of yours now, she's well cared for. It's your mother you need to be thinking of, she's been in a fine taking over you all this while, and now they're looking in other directions for the one who did the killing—with one eye still on you, though, mind!—she'll likely take some sweetening. One way or another, you'll get a warm welcome.'

Philip was far beyond minding that, though as soon as he

entered the house behind the shoemaker's shop he did indeed get a warm welcome, not one way or another, but both ways at once. Mistress Corviser, who was large, handsome and voluble, looked round from her fireside hob, uttered a muted shriek, dropped her ladle, and came billowing like a ship in full sail to embrace him, shake him, wrinkle her nose at the prison smell of him, abuse him for the damage to his best cotte and hose, box his ears for laughing at her tirade, exclaim lamentably over the dried scar at his temple, and demand that he sit down at once and let her crop the hair that adhered to the matted blood, and clean up the wound. By far the easiest thing to do was to submit to all, and let her talk herself out.

'The trouble and shame you've put us to, the heartaches you've cost me, wretch, you don't deserve that I should feed you, or wash and mend for you. The provost's son in prison, think of our mortification! Are you not ashamed of yourself?' She was sponging away the encrusted blood, and relieved to find so insignificant a scar remaining; but when he said blithely: 'No, mother!' she pulled his hair smartly.

'Then you should be, you good-for-nothing! There, that's not so bad. Now I hope you're going to settle down to work, and make up for all the trouble you've made for us, instead of traipsing about the town egging on other people's sons to mischief with your wild ideas . . .'

'They were the same ideas father and all the guild merchant had, mother, you should have scolded them. And you ask those who're wearing my shoes whether there's much amiss with my work.' He was a very good workman, in fact, as she would have asserted valiantly if anyone else had cast aspersions on his diligence and ability. He hugged her impulsively, and kissed her cheek, and she put him off impatiently, with what was more a slap than a caress. 'Get along with you, and don't come moguing me until you're cleared of the worse charge, and have paid your fine for the riot. Now come and eat your dinner!'

It was an excellent dinner, such as she produced on festivals and saints' days. After it, instead of shedding the clothes he had worn day and night in his cell, he shaved carefully, made a bundle of his second-best suit, and left the house with it under his arm.

'*Now* where are you going?' she demanded inevitably.

'To the river, to swim and get clean again.' They had a garden upstream, below the town wall, as many of the burgesses had, for growing their own fruit and vegetables, and there was a small hut there, and a sward where he could dry in the sun. He had learned to swim there, shortly after he learned to walk. He did not tell her where he was going afterwards. It was a pity he would have to present himself in his second-best coat, but in this hot summer weather perhaps he need not put it on at all; in shirt and hose most men look the same, provided the shirt is good linen and well laundered.

The water was not even cold in the sandy shallow by the garden, but after his meal he did not stay in long, or swim out into deep water. But it was good to feel like himself again, cleansed even of the memory of his failure and downfall. There was a still place under the bank where the water hung almost motionless, and showed him a fair image of his face, and the thick bush of red-brown hair which he combed and straightened with his fingers. He dressed as carefully as he had shaved, and set off back to the bridge, and over it to the abbey. The town's grievance, which he had had on his mind the last time he came this way, was quite forgotten; he had other important business now on the abbey side of Severn.

'There's one here,' said Constance, coming in from the great court with a small, private smile on her lips, 'who asks to speak with Mistress Vernold. And not a bad figure of a young fellow, either, though still a thought coltish about the legs. He asked very civilly.'

Emma had looked up quickly at the mention of a young man; now that she had gone some way towards accepting what had happened, and coming to terms with a disaster which, after all, she had not caused, she had been remembering words Ivo had used, almost disregarded then in her shocked daze, but significant and warming now.

'Messire Corbière?'

'No, not this time. This one I don't know, but he says his name is Philip Corviser.'

'I know him,' said Aline, and smiled over her sewing. 'The provost's son, Emma, the boy you spoke for in the sheriff's court. Hugh said he would see him set free today. If there's one soul can say he has done no evil to you or any these last two days, he's the man. Will you see him? It would be a kindness.'

Emma had almost forgotten him, even his name, but she recalled the plea he had made for her belief in him. So much had happened between. She remembered him now, unkempt, bruised and soiled, pallid-sick after his drunkenness, but still with a despairing dignity. 'Yes, I remember him. Of course I'll see him.'

Philip followed Constance into the room. Fresh from the river, with damp hair curling thickly about his head, shaven and glowing and in fierce earnest, but without the aggression of the manner she had first seen in him, this was a very different person from the humiliated prisoner of the court. The last look he had given her, chin on shoulder, as he was dragged out. . . . yes, she saw the resemblance there. He made his reverence to Aline, and then to Emma.

'Madam, I am released on my father's bail. I came to say my thanks to Mistress Emma for speaking so fairly for me, when I had no right to expect goodwill from her.'

'I'm glad to see you free, Philip,' said Aline serenely, 'and looking none the worse. You will like to speak with Emma alone, I daresay, and company other than mine may be good for her, for here we talk nothing but babies.' She rose, folding her sewing carefully to keep the needle in view as she carried it. 'Constance and I will sit on the bench by the hall door, in the sun. The light is better there, and I am no such expert needlewoman as Emma. You can be undisturbed here.'

Out she went, and they saw a ray of sun from the open outer door sparkle in her piled gold hair, before Constance followed, and closed the door between. The two of them were left, gazing gravely at each other.

'The first thing I wanted to do with freedom,' said Philip, 'was to see you again, and thank you for what you did for me. As I do, with all my heart. There were some who bore witness there who had known me most of my life, and surely had no grudge against me, and yet testified that I had been the first to strike, and done all manner of things I knew I had not done. But you, who had suffered through my act, though God knows I never willed it, you spoke absolute truth for me. It took a generous heart and a fair mind to do so much for an unknown whom you had no cause to love.' He had not chosen that word, it had come naturally in the commonplace phrase, but when he heard it, it raised a blush like fire in his own face, faintly reflected the next moment in hers.

'All I did was to tell the truth of what I had seen,' she said. 'So should we all have done, it's no virtue, but an obligation. It was shame that they did not. People do not think what it is they are saying, or trouble to be clear about what they have seen. But that's all by now. I'm very glad they've let you go. I was glad when Hugh Beringar said they must, taking into account what has been happening, for which you certainly can bear no blame. But perhaps you have not heard. . . .'

'Yes, I have heard. My father has told me.' Philip sat down beside her in the place Aline had vacated, and leaned towards her earnestly. 'There is some very evil purpose against you and yours, surely, how else to account for so many outrages? Emma, I am afraid for you . . . I fear danger threatening even you. I'm grieved for your loss, and all the distress you've suffered. I wish there might be some way in which I could serve you.'

'Oh, but you need not be troubled for me,' she said. 'You see I am in the best and kindest hands possible, and tomorrow the fair will all be over, and Hugh Beringar and Aline will help me to find a safe way to go home.'

'Tomorrow?' he said, dismayed.

'It may not be tomorrow. Roger Dod will take the barge down-river tomorrow, but it may be that I must stay a day or two more. We have to find a party going south by Gloucester, for safe-conduct, and with some other women for company. It may take a day or two.'

Even a day or two would be gold; but after that she would be gone, and he might never see her again. And still, confronted by this cause for unhappiness on his own part, he could only think of her. He could not rid himself of the feeling that she was threatened.

'In only two days, see how many ill things have happened,

and always close to you, and what may not still happen in a day or two more? I wish you were safe home this moment,' he said passionately, 'though God knows I'd rather lose my right hand than the sight of you.' He was not even aware that that same right hand had taken possession of her left one, and was clasping it hard. 'At least find me some way of serving you before you go. If nothing more, tell me you know that I never did harm to your uncle . . .'

'Oh, yes,' she said warmly, 'that I can, most willingly. I never did truly believe it. You are no such person, to strike a man dead by stealth. I never thought it. But still we don't know who did it! Oh, don't doubt me, I'm sure of *you*. But I wish it could be shown clear to the world, for your sake.'

It was said very prettily and sincerely, and he took it to his heart gratefully, but it was said out of generous fellow-feeling, and nothing deeper, and he was gallingly sure of it while he hugged at least the kindness to him.

'For mine, too,' she said honestly, 'and for the sake of justice. It is not right that a mean murderer should escape his due, and it does aggrieve me that my uncle's death should go unpaid for.'

Find me some way of serving you, he had said; and perhaps she had. There was nothing he would not have undertaken for her; he would have lain over the threshold of any room in which she was, like a dog on guard, if she had needed it, but she did not, she was cared for by the sheriff's own deputy and his lady, and they would watch over her until they saw her safely on her way home. But when she spoke of the unknown who had slipped a dagger in her uncle's back, her great eyes flared with the angry blue of sapphires, and her face grew marble-clear and taut. Her complaint was his commission. He would achieve something for her yet.

'Emma,' he began in a whisper, and drew breath to commit himself deep as the sea.

The door opened, though neither of them had heard the knock; Constance put her head into the room.

'Messire Corbière waits to see you, when you are free,' she said, and withdrew, but left the door ajar. Evidently Messire Corbière ought not to be kept waiting long.

Philip was on his feet. Emma's eyes had kindled at the

name like distant stars, forgetting him. 'You may remember him,' she said, still sparing a morsel of her attention for Philip, 'the young gentleman who came to help us on the jetty, along with Brother Cadfael. He has been very kind to me.'

Philip did remember, though his bludgeoned senses at the time had seen everything distorted; a slender, elegant, assured lordling who leaped a rolling cask to catch her in his arm at the water's edge, and further, to be just to him, had appeared in the sheriff's court and borne out Emma's honest story— even if he had also produced his falconer to testify to the silly threats Philip had been indulging in, drunk as he was, later that evening. Testimony Philip did not dispute, since he knew he had been incapable of clear thought or positive recollection. He recalled his disgusting self, and smarted at the thought. And the young lord with the bright gold crest and athlete's prowess had showed so admirable by contrast.

'I'll take my leave,' said Philip, and allowed her hand to slip out of his, though with reluctance and pain. 'For the journey, and always, I wish you well.'

'So do I you,' she said, and with unconscious cruelty added: 'Will you ask Messire Corbière to come in?'

Never in his life until then had Philip been required to draw himself to his full stature, body and mind. His departure was made with a dignity he had not dreamed he could achieve, and meeting Corbière face to face in the hall, he did indeed bid him within, at Mistress Emma's invitation, very civilly and amiably, while he burned with jealousy inwardly. Ivo thanked him pleasantly, and if he looked him over, did so with interest and respect, and with no apparent recollection of ever having seen him in less acceptable circumstances.

No one would have guessed, thought Philip, marching out into the sunshine of the great court, that a working shoemaker and a landed lord rubbed shoulders there. Well, he may have several manors in Cheshire and one in Shropshire, and be distant kin of Earl Ranulf, and welcome at his court; but I have something I can try to do for her, and I have a craft as honourable as his noble blood, and if I succeed, whether she comes my way or no, she'll never forget me.

* * *

Brother Cadfael came in at the gatehouse after some hours of fruitless prowling about the fair and the riverside. Among hundreds of men busy about their own concerns, the quest of a gashed sleeve, or one recently and hastily mended, is much the same as hunting one straw in a completed stack. His trouble was that he knew no other way to set about it. Moreover, the hot and settled weather continued unbroken, and most of those about the streets and the stalls were in their shirt-sleeves. There was a point there, he reflected. The glover's dagger had drawn blood, therefore it had reached the skin, but never a thread of white or unbleached linen had it brought away with the sliver of brown cloth. If the intruder had worn a shirt, he had worn it with sleeves rolled up, and it had emerged unscathed, and could now cover his graze, and if the wound had needed one, his bandage. Cadfael returned to tend the few matters needing him in his workshop, and be ready for Vespers in good time, more because he was at a loss how to proceed than for any other reason. An interlude of quiet and thought might set his wits working again.

In the great court his path towards the garden happened to cross Philip's from the guest-hall to the gatehouse. Deep in his own purposes, the young man almost passed by unnoticing, but then he checked sharply, and turned to look back.

'Brother Cadfael!' Cadfael swung to face him, startled out of just as deep a preoccupation. 'It is you!' said Philip. 'It was you who spoke for me, after Emma, in the sheriff's court. And I knew you then for the one who came to help me to my feet and out of trouble, when the sergeants broke up the fight on the jetty. I never had the chance to thank you, brother, but I do thank you now.'

'I fear the getting you out of trouble didn't last the night,' said Cadfael ruefully, looking this lanky youngster over with a sharp eye, and approving what he saw. Whether it was time spent in self-examination in the gaol, or time spent more salutarily still in thinking of Emma, Philip had done a great deal of growing up in a very short time. 'I'm glad to see you about again among us, and none the worse.'

'I'm not clear of the load yet,' said Philip. 'The charge still stands, even the charge of murder has not been withdrawn.'

'Then it stands upon one leg only,' said Cadfael heartily,

135

'and may fall at any moment. Have you not heard there's been another death?'

'So they told me, and other violence, also. But surely this last bears no connection with the rest? Until this, all was malice against Master Thomas. This man was a stranger, and from Chester.' He laid a hand eagerly on Cadfael's sleeve. 'Brother, spare me some minutes. I was not very clear in my wits that night, now I need to know—all that I did, all that was done to me. I want to trace every minute of an evening I can barely piece together for myself.'

'And no wonder, after that knock on the head. Come and sit in the garden, it's quiet there.' He took the young man by the arm, and turned him towards the archway through the pleached hedge, and sat him down on the very seat, had Philip known it, where Emma and Ivo had sat together the previous day. 'Now, what is it you have in mind? I don't wonder your memory's hazy. That's a good solid skull you have on you, and a blessedly thick thatch of hair, or you'd have been carried away on a board.'

Philip scowled doubtfully into distance between the roses, hesitated how much to say, how much to keep painfully to himself, caught Brother Cadfael's comfortably patient eye, and blurted: 'I was coming now from Emma. I know she is in better care than I could provide her, but I have found one thing, at least, that might still be done for her. She wants and needs to see the man who killed her uncle brought to justice. And I mean to find him.'

'So does the sheriff, so do all his men,' said Cadfael, 'but they've had little success as yet.' But he did not say it in reproof or discouragement, but very thoughtfully. 'So, for that matter, do I, but I've done no better. One more mind probing the matter could just as well be the mind that uncovers the truth. Why not? But how will you set about it?'

'Why, if I can prove—*prove!*—that I did not do it, I may also rub up against something that will lead me to the man who did. At least I can make a start by trying to follow what happened to me that night. Not only for my own defence,' he said earnestly, 'but because it seems to me that I gave cover to the deed by what I had begun, and whoever did it may have had me and my quarrel in mind, and been glad of the opening I made for him, knowing that when murder came of the night, the first name that would spring to mind would be mine. So whoever he may be, he must have marked my comings and goings, or I could be no use to him. If I had been with ten friends throughout, I should have been out of the reckoning, and the sheriff would have begun at once to look elsewhere. But I was drunk, and sick, and took myself off alone to the river for a long time, so much I do know. Long enough for it to have been true. And the murderer knew it.'

'That is sound thinking,' agreed Cadfael approvingly. 'What, then, do you mean to do?'

'Begin from the riverside, where I got my clout on the head, and follow my own scent until I get clear what's very unclear now. I do remember what happened there, as far as you hauling me out of the way of the sheriff's men, and then being hustled away between two others, but my legs were grass and my wits were muddied, and I can't for my life recall who they were. It's a place to start, if you knew them.'

'One of them was Edric Flesher's journeyman,' said Cadfael. 'The other I've seen, though I don't know his name, a big, sturdy young fellow twice your width, with tow-coloured hair . . .'

'John Norreys!' Philip snapped his fingers. 'I seem to recall him later in the night. It's enough, I'll begin with them, and find out where they left me, and how—or where I shook them off, for so I might have done, I was no fit company for Christians.' He rose, draping his coat over one shoulder. 'That whole evening I'll unravel, if I can.'

'Good lad!' said Cadfael heartily. 'I wish you success with all my heart. And if you're going to be threading your way through a few of the ale-houses of the Foregate, as you seem to have done that night, keep your eyes open on my behalf, will you? If you can find your murderer, you may very well also be finding mine.' Carefully and emphatically he told him what to look for. 'An arm raising a flagon, or spread over a table, may show you what I'm seeking. The left sleeve sliced open for a hand's-length from the cuff of a russet-brown coat, that was sewn with a lighter linen thread. It would be on the underside of the arm. Or where arms are bared, look for the long scratch the knife made when it slit the sleeve, or for the binding that might cover it if it still bleeds. But if you find him, don't challenge him or say word to him, only bring me, if you can, his name and where to find him again.'

'This was the glover's slayer?' asked Philip, marking the details with grave nods of his brown head. 'You think they may be one and the same?'

'If not the same, well known to each other, and both in the same conspiracy. Find one, and we shall be very close to the other.'

'I'll keep a good watch, at any rate,' said Philip, and strode away purposefully towards the gatehouse to begin his quest.

THREE

AFTERWARDS BROTHER CADFAEL PONDERED MANY TIMES OVER what followed, and wondered if prayer can even have a retrospective effect upon events, as well as influencing the future. What had happened had already happened, yet would he have found the same situation if he had not gone straight into the church, when Philip left him, with the passionate urge to commit to prayer the direction of his own efforts, which seemed to him so barren? It was a most delicate and complex theological problem, never, as far as he knew, raised before, or if raised, no theologian had ventured to write on the subject, probably for fear of being accused of heresy.

Howbeit, the urgent need came over him, since he had lost some offices during the day, to recommit his own baffled endeavours to eyes that saw everything, and a power that could open all doors. He chose the transept chapel from which Master Thomas's coffin had been carried that morning, resealed into sanctity by the Mass sung for him. He had time, now, to kneel and wait, having busied himself thus far in anxious efforts like a man struggling up a mountain, when he knew there was a force that could make the mountain bow. He said a prayer for patience and humility, and then laid that by, and prayed for Emma, for the soul of Master Thomas, for the child that should be born to Aline and Hugh, for young Philip and the parents who had recovered him, for all who suffered injustice and wrong, and sometimes forgot they had a resource beyond the sheriff.

Then it was high time for him to rise from his knees, and go and see to his primary duty here, whatever more violent matters clamoured for his attention. He had supervised the herbarium and the manufactory derived from it, for sixteen years, and his remedies were relied upon far beyond the abbey walls; and though Brother Mark was the most devoted and uncomplaining of helpers, it was unkind to leave him too long alone with such a responsibility. Cadfael hastened towards his workshop with a lightened heart, having shifted his worries to broader shoulders, just as Brother Mark would be happy to do on his patron's arrival.

The heavy fragrance of the herb-garden lay over all the surrounding land, after so many hours of sunshine and heat, like a particular benediction meant for the senses, not the soul. Under the eaves of the workshop the dangling bunches of dried leafage rustled and chirped like nests of singing birds in waves of warmed air, where there was hardly any wind. The very timbers of the hut, dressed with oil against cracking, breathed out scented warmth.

'I finished making the balm for ulcers,' said Brother Mark, making dutiful report, and happily aware of work well done. 'And I have harvested all the poppy-heads that were ripe, but I have not yet broken out the seed, I thought they should dry in the sun a day or two yet.'

Cadfael pressed one of the gre heads between his fingers, and praised the judgement. 'And the angelica water for the infirmary?'

'Brother Edmund sent for it half an hour ago. I had it ready. And I had a patient,' said Brother Mark, busy stacking away on a shelf the small clay dishes he used for sorting seeds, 'earlier on, soon after dinner. A groom with a gashed arm. He said he did it on a nail in the stables, reaching down harness, though it looked like a knife-slash to me. It was none too clean, I cleansed it for him, and dressed it with some of your goose-grass unguent. They were gambling with dice up there in the loft last night, I daresay it came to a fight, and somebody drew on him. He'd hardly admit to that.' Brother Mark dusted his hands, and turned with a smile to report for the sum of his stewardship. 'And that's all. A quiet afternoon, you need not have worried.' At sight of Cadfael's face his brows went up comically, and he asked in surprise: 'Why are you staring like that? Nothing there, surely, to open your eyes so wide.'

My mouth, too, thought Cadfael, and shut it while he reflected on the strangeness of human effort, and the sudden rewards that fell undeserved. Not undeserved, perhaps, in this case, since this had fallen to Brother Mark, whose modesty made no demands at all.

'Which arm was gashed?' he asked, further baffling Brother Mark, who naturally could not imagine why that should matter.

'The left. From here, the outer edge of the wrist, down the underside of the forearm. Almost to the elbow. Why?'

'Had he his coat on?'

'Not when I saw him,' said Mark, smiling at the absurdity of this catechism. 'But he had it over his sound arm. Is that important?'

'More than you know! But you shall know, later, I am not playing with you. Of what colour was it? And did you see the sleeve that should cover that arm?'

'I did. I offered to stitch it for him—I had little to do just then. But he said he'd already cobbled it up, and so he had, very roughly, and with black thread. I could have done better for him, the original was unbleached linen thread. The colour? Reddish dun, much like most of the grooms and men-at-arms wear, but a good cloth.'

'Did you know the man? Not one of our own abbey servants?'

'No, a guest's man,' said Brother Mark, patient in his bewilderment. 'Not a word to his lord, he said! It was one of Ivo Corbière's grooms, the older one, the surly fellow with the beard.'

Gilbert Prestcote himself, unescorted and on foot, had taken an afternoon turn about the fairground to view the public peace with his own eyes, and was in the great court on his way back to the town, conferring with Hugh Beringar, when Cadfael came in haste from the garden with his news. When the blunt recital was ended, they looked at him and at each other with blank and wary faces.

'Corbière's within at this moment,' said Hugh, 'and I gather from Aline has been, more than an hour. Emma has him dazed, I doubt if he's had any other thought, these last two days. His men have been running loose much as they pleased, provided the work was done. It could be the man.'

'His lord has the right to be told,' said Prestcote. 'Households grow lax when they see the country torn, and their betters flouting law. There's nothing been said or done to alarm this fellow, I take it? He has no reason to make any move? And surely he values the shelter of a name like Corbière.'

'No word has been said to any but you,' said Cadfael. 'And the man may be telling the truth.'

'The tatter of cloth,' said Hugh, 'I have here on me. It should be possible to match or discard.'

'Ask Corbière to come,' said the sheriff.

Hugh took the errand to himself, since Ivo was a guest in his rooms. While they waited in braced silence, two of the abbey's men-at-arms came in at the gatehouse with unstrung long-bows, and Turstan Fowler between them with his arbalest, the three of them hot, happy and on excellent terms. On the last day of the fair there were normally matches of many kinds, wrestling, shooting at the butts along the river meadows, long-bow against cross-bow, though the long-bow here was usually the short bow of Wales, drawn to the breast, not the ear. The six-foot weapon was known, but a rarity. There were races, too, and riding at the quintain on the castle tiltyard. Trade and play made good companions, and especially good profits for the ale-houses, where the winners very soon parted with all they had won, and the losers made up their losses.

These three were wreathed together in argumentative amity, passing jokes along the line; each seemed to be vaunting his own weapon. They had strolled no more than halfway across the court when Hugh emerged from the guest-hall with Ivo beside him. Ivo saw his archer crossing towards the stable-yard, and made him an imperious signal to stay.

There was no fault to be found with Turstan's service since his disastrous fall from grace on the first evening; motioned to hold aloof but remain at call, he obeyed without question, and went on amusing himself with his rivals. He must have done well at the butts, for they seemed to be discussing his arbalest, and he braced a foot in the metal stirrup and drew the string to the alert for them, demonstrating that he lost little in speed against their instant arms. No doubt the dispute between speed and range would go on as long as both arms survived. Cadfael had handled both in his time, as well as the eastern bow, the sword, and the lance of the mounted man. Even at this grave moment he spared a long glance for the amicable wrangle going on a score of paces away.

Then Ivo was there among them, and shaken out of his easy confidence and grace. His face was tense, his dark eyes large and wondering under the proudly raised auburn brows and golden cap of curls. 'You wanted me, sir? Hugh has not been specific, but I took it this was urgent matter.'

'It is a matter of a man of yours,' said the sheriff.

'My men?' He shook a doubtful head, and gnawed his lip. 'I know of nothing . . . Not since Turstan drank himself stiff and stupid, and he's been a penitent and close to home ever since, and he did no harm then to any but himself, the dolt. But they all have leave to go forth, once their work's done. The fair is every man's treat. What's amiss concerning my men?'

It was left to the sheriff to tell him. Ivo paled visibly as he listened, his ruddy sunburn sallowing. 'Then my man is suspect of the killing I brushed arms with—Good God, this very morning! That you may know, his name is Ewald, he comes from a Cheshire manor, and his ancestry is northern, but he never showed ill traits before, though he is a morose man, and makes few friends. I take this hard. I brought him here.'

'You may resolve it,' said Prestcote.

'So I may.' His mouth tightened. 'And will! About this hour I appointed to ride, my horse has had little exercise here, and he'll be bearing me hence tomorrow. Ewald is the groom who takes care of him. He should be saddling him up in the stables about this time. Shall I send for him? He'll be expecting my summons. No!' he interrupted his own offer, his brows contracting. 'Not send for him, go for him myself. If I sent Turstan, there, you might suspect that a servant would stand by a servant, and give him due warning. Do you think he has not been watching us, this short while? And do you think this colloquy has the look of simple talk among us?'

Assuredly it had not. Turstan, dangling his braced bow, had lost interest in enlightening his rivals, and they, sensing that there was something afoot that did not concern them, were drawing off and moving away, though with discreet backward glances until they vanished into the grange court.

'I'll go myself, said Ivo, and strode away towards the stable-yard at a great pace. Turstan, hesitant, let him pass, since he got no word out of him in passing, but then turned and hurried on his heels, anxiously questioning. For a little way he followed, and they saw Ivo turn his head and snap some hasty orders at his man. Chastened, Turstan drew back and returned towards the gatehouse, and stood at a loss.

Some minutes passed before they heard the sharp sound of hooves on the cobbles of the stable-yard, brittle and lively. Then the tall, dusky bay, glowing like the darkest of copper and restive for want of work, danced out of the yard with the stocky, bearded groom holding his bridle, and Ivo stalking a yard or so ahead.

'Here is my man Ewald,' he said shortly, and stood back, as Cadfael noted, between them and the open gateway. Turstan Fowler drew nearer by discreet inches, and silently, sharp eyes flicking from one face to another in quest of understanding. Ewald stood holding the bridle, uneasy eyes narrowed upon Prestcote's unrevealing countenance. When the horse, eager for action, stirred and tossed his head, the groom reached his left hand across to take the bridle, and slid the right one up to the glossy neck, caressing by rote, but without for an instant shifting his gaze.

'My lord says your honour has something to ask me,' he said in a slow and grudging voice.

Under his left forearm the cobbled mend in his sleeve

showed plainly, the cloth puckered between large stitches, and the end of linen thread shivered in sun and breeze like a gnat dancing.

'Take off your coat,' ordered the sheriff. And as the man gaped in real or pretended bewilderment: 'No words! Do it!'

Slowly Ewald slipped out of his coat, somewhat awkwardly because he was at pains to retain his hold on the bridle. The horse had been promised air and exercise, and was straining towards the gate, the way to what he desired. He had already shifted the whole group, except Cadfael, who stood mute and apart, a little nearer the gate.

'Turn back your sleeve. The left.'

He gave one wild glance round, then lowered his head like a bull, set his jaw, and did it, his right arm through the bridle as he turned up the coarse homespun to the elbow. Brother Mark had bound up the gash in a strip of clean linen over his dressing. The very cleanness of it glared.

'You have hurt yourself, Ewald?' said Prestcote, quietly grim.

He has his chance now, thought Cadfael, if he has quick enough wit, to change his story and say outright that he took a knife-wound in a common brawl, and told Brother Mark the lie about a nail simply to cover up the folly. But no, the man did not stop to think; he had his story, and trusted it might still cover him. Yet if Mark, on handling the wound, could tell a cut from a tear, so at the merest glance could Gilbert Prestcote.

'I did it on a nail in the stables, my lord, reaching down harness.'

'And tore your sleeve through at the same time? It was a jagged nail, Ewald. That's stout cloth you wear.' He turned abruptly to Hugh Beringar. 'You have the slip of cloth?'

Hugh drew out from his pouch a folded piece of vellum, and opened it upon the insignificant strip of fabric, that looked like nothing so much as a blade of dried grass fretted into fibres and rotting at the edge. Only the wavy tendril of linen thread showed what it really was, but that was enough. Ewald drew away a pace, so sharply that the horse backed off some yards towards the gateway, and the groom turned and took both hands to hold and soothe the beast. Ivo had to spring hurriedly backwards to avoid the dancing hooves.

'Hand here your coat,' ordered Prestcote, when the bay was appeased again, and willing to stand, though reluctantly.

The groom looked from the tiny thing he had recognised to the sheriff's composed but unrelenting face, hesitated only a moment, and then did as he was bid, to violent effect. He swung back his arm and flung the heavy cotte into their faces, and with a leap was over the bay's back and into the saddle. Both heels drove into the glossy sides, and a great shout above the pricked ears sent the horse surging like a flung lance for the gateway.

There was no one between but Ivo. The groom drove the bay straight at him, headlong. The young man leaped aside, but made a tigerish spring to grasp at the bridle as the horse hurtled by, and actually got a hold on it and was dragged for a moment, until the groom kicked out at him viciously, breaking the tenuous hold and hurling Ivo out of the way, to fall heavily and roll under the feet of the sheriff and Hugh as they launched themselves after the fugitive. Out at the gateway and round to the right into the Foregate went Ewald, at a frantic gallop, and there was no one mounted and ready to pursue, and for once the sheriff was without escort or archers.

But Ivo Corbière was not. Turstan Fowler had rushed to help him to his feet, but Ivo waved him past, out into the Foregate, and heaving himself breathlessly from the ground, with grazed and furious face, ran limping after. The little group of them stood in the middle of the highroad, helplessly watching the bay and his rider recede into distance, and unable to follow. He had killed, and he would get clear away, and once some miles from Shrewsbury, he could disappear into forest and lie safe as a fox in its lair.

In a voice half-choked with rage, Ivo cried: 'Fetch him down!'

Turstan's arbalest was still braced and ready, and Turstan was used to jumping to his command. The quarrel was out of his belt, fitted and loosed, in an instant, the thrum and vibration of its flight made heads turn and duck and women shriek along the Foregate.

Ewald, stooped low over the horse's neck, suddenly jerked

violently and reared up with head flung high. His hands slackened from the reins and his arms swung lax on either side. He seemed to hang for a moment suspended in air, and then swung heavily sidewise, and heeled slowly out of the saddle. The bay, startled and shocked, ran on wildly, scattering the frightened vendors and buyers on both sides, but his flight was uncertain now, and confused by this sudden lightness. He would not go far. Someone would halt and soothe him, and lead him back.

As for the groom Ewald, he was dead before ever the first of the appalled stallholders reached him, dead, probably, before ever he struck the ground.

FOUR

'HE WAS MY VILLEIN,' ASSERTED IVO STRENUOUSLY, IN THE ROOM in the gatehouse where they had brought and laid the body, 'and I enjoy the power of the high justice over my own, and this one had forfeited life. I need make no defence, for myself or my archer, who did nothing more than obey my order. We have all seen, now, that this fellow's wound is no tear from a nail, but the stroke of a dagger, and the fret you took from the glover's blade matches this sleeve past question. Is there doubt in any mind that this was a murderer?'

There was none. Cadfael was there with them in the room, at Hugh's instance, and he had no doubts at all. This was the man Euan of Shotwick had marked, before he himself died. Moreover, some of Euan of Shotwick's goods and money had been found among the sparse belongings Ewald had left behind him; his saddle-roll held a pouch of fine leather full of coins, and two pairs of gloves made for the hands of girls, presents, perhaps, for wife or sister. This was certainly a murderer. Turstan, who had shot him down, obviously did not consider himself anything of the kind, any more than one of Prestcote's archers would have done, had he been given the order to shoot. Turstan had taken the whole affair stolidly, as none of his business apart from his duty to his lord, and gone away to his evening meal with an equable appetite.

'I brought him here,' said Ivo bitterly, wiping smears of blood from his grazed cheek. 'It is my honour he has offended, as well as the law of the land. I had a right to avenge myself.'

'No need to labour it,' said Prestcote shortly. 'The shire has been saved a trial and a hanging, which is to the good, and I don't know but the wretch himself might prefer this way out. It was a doughty shot, and that's a valuable man of yours. I never thought it could be done so accurately at that distance.'

Ivo shrugged. 'I knew Turstan's quality, or I would not have said what I did, to risk either my horse or any of the hundreds about their harmless business in the Foregate. I don't know that I expected a death . . .'

'There's only one cause for regret,' said the sheriff. 'If he had accomplices, he can never now be made to name them. And you say, Beringar, that there were probably two?'

'You're satisfied, I hope,' said Ivo, 'that neither Turstan nor my young groom Arald had any part with him in these thefts?'

Both had been questioned, he had insisted on that. Turstan had been a model of virtue since his one lapse, and the youngster was a fresh-faced country youth, and both had made friends among the other servants and were well liked. Ewald had been morose and taciturn, and kept himself apart, and the revelation of his villainy did not greatly surprise his fellows.

'There's still the matter of the other offences. What do you think? Was it this man in all of them?'

'I cannot get it out of my mind,' said Hugh slowly, 'that Master Thomas's death was the work of one man only. And without reason or proof, by mere pricking of thumbs, I do not believe it was this man. For the rest—I don't know! Two, the merchant's watchman said, but I am not sure he may not be increasing the odds to excuse his own want of valour—or his very good sense, however you look at it. Only one, surely, would enter the barge in full daylight, no doubt briskly, as if he had an errand there, something to fetch or something to bestow. Where there were two, this must surely be one of them. Who the other was, we are still in the dark.'

After Compline Cadfael went to report to Abbot Radulfus all that had happened. The sheriff had already paid the necessary courtesy visit to inform the abbot, but for all that Radulfus would expect his own accredited observer to bring another viewpoint, one more concerned with the repute and the standards of a Benedictine house. In an order which held moderation in all things to be the ground of blessing, immoderate things were happening.

Radulfus listened in disciplined silence to all, and there was no telling from his face whether he deplored or approved such summary justice.

'Violence can never be anything but ugly,' he said thoughtfully, 'but we live in a world as ugly and violent as it is beautiful and good. Two things above all concern me, and one of them may seem to you, brother, a trivial matter. This death, the shedding of this blood, took place outside our walls. For that I am grateful. You have lived both within and without, what must be accepted and borne is the same to you, within or without. But many here lack your knowledge, and for them, and for the peace we strive to preserve here as refuge for others beside ourselves, the sanctity of this place is better unspotted. And the second thing will matter as deeply to you as to me: Was this man guilty? Is it certain he himself had killed?'

'It is certain,' said Brother Cadfael, choosing his words with care, 'that he had been concerned in murder, most likely with at least one other man.'

'Then harsh though it may be, this was justice.' He caught the heaviness of Cadfael's silence, and looked up sharply. 'You are not satisfied?'

'That the man took part in murder, yes, I am satisfied. The proofs are clear. But what is justice? If there were two, and one bears all, and the other goes free, is that justice? I am certain in my soul that there is more, not yet known.'

'And tomorrow all these people will depart about their own

148

affairs, to their own homes and shops, wherever they may be. The guilty and the innocent alike. That cannot be the will of God,' said the abbot, and brooded a while in silence. 'Nevertheless, it may be God's will that it should be taken out of our hands. Continue your vigil, brother, through the morrow. After that others, elsewhere, must take up the burden.

Brother Mark sat on the edge of his cot, in his cell in the dortoir, with his elbows on his knees and his head in his hands, and grieved. From a child he had lived a hard life, privation, brutality and pain were all known to him as close companions until he came into this retreat, at first unwilling. But death was too monstrous and too dark for him, coming thus instant in terror, and without the possibility of grace. To live misused, ill-fed, without respite from labour, was still life, with a sky above it, and trees and flowers and birds around it, colour and season and beauty. Life, even so lived, was a friend. Death was a stranger.

'Child, it is with us always,' said Cadfael, patient beside him. 'Last summer ninety-five men died here in the town, none of whom had done murder. For choosing the wrong side, they died. It falls upon blameless women in war, even in peace at the hands of evil men. It falls upon children who never did harm to any, upon old men, who in their lives have done good to many, and yet are brutally and senselessly slain. Never let it shake your faith that there is a balance hereafter. What you see is only a broken piece from a perfect whole.'

'I know,' said Brother Mark between his fingers, loyal but uncomforted. 'But to be cut off without trial . . .'

'So were the ninety-four last year,' said Cadfael gently, 'and the ninety-fifth was murdered. Such justice as we see is also but a broken sherd. But it is our duty to preserve what we may, and fit together such fragments as we find, and take the rest on trust.'

'And unshriven!' cried Brother Mark.

'So went his victim also. And he had neither robbed nor killed, or if he had, only God knows of it. There has many a man gone through that gate without a safe-conduct, who will reach heaven ahead of some who were escorted through with absolution and ceremony, and had their affairs in order.

Kings and princes of the church may find shepherds and serfs preferred before them, and some who claim they have done great good may have to give place to poor wretches who have done wrong and acknowledge it, and have tried to make amends.'

Brother Mark sat listening, and at least began to hear. Humbly he recognised and admitted the real heart of his grievance. 'I had his arm between my hands, I saw him wince when I cleansed his wound, and I felt his pain. It was only a small pain, but I felt it. I was glad to help him, it was pleasure to anoint the cut with balm, and wrap it clean, and know he was eased. And now he's dead, with a cross-bow bolt through him . . .' Briefly and angrily, Brother Mark brushed away tears, and uncovered his accusing face. 'What is the use of mending a man, if he's to be broken within a few hours, past mending?'

'We were speaking of souls,' said Cadfael mildly, 'not mere bodies. And who knows but your touch with ointment and linen may have mended to better effect the one that lasts the longer? There's no arrow cleaves the soul. But there may be balm for it.

FIVE

HEAD-DOWN ON HIS OWN TRACES, PHILIP HAD RUN HIS FRIEND John Norreys to earth at last at the butts by the riverside, where the budding archers of the town practised, and together they hunted out Edric Flesher's young journeyman from the yard behind his master's shop. Philip's odyssey on the eve of the fair had begun with these two, who had had him bundled into their arms by Brother Cadfael when the sheriff's men descended on the Gaye.

By their own account, they had hauled him away through

the orchards and the narrow lanes behind the Foregate, avoiding the highroad, and sat him down in the first booth that sold drink, to recover his addled wits. And very ungrateful they had found him, as soon as the shock of his blow on the head began to pass, and his legs were less shaky under him.

Furious with himself, he had turned his ill-temper on them, snarled at them, said John tolerantly, that he was capable of looking after himself, and they had better go and warn some of the other stalwarts who had rushed on along the Foregate overturning stalls and scattering goods, before the officers reached them. Which they had taken good-humouredly enough, knowing his head was aching villainously by that time, and had followed him for a while at a discreet distance as he blundered away through the fairground, until he turned on them again and ordered them away. They had stood to watch him, and then shrugged and left him to his own devices, since he would have none of them.

'You had your legs again,' said John reasonably, 'and since you wouldn't let us do anything for you, we thought best to let you go your own way. Let alone, you wouldn't go far, but if we followed, you might do who knows what, out of contrariness.'

'There was another fellow who looked after you a thought anxiously,' said the butcher's man, thinking back, 'when we left that booth with you. Came out after us, and set off the same way you took. He thought you were already helpless drunk, I fancy, and might need helping home.'

'That was kind in him,' said Philip, stiffening indignantly, and meaning that it was damned officious of whoever it was. 'That would be what hour? Not yet eight?'

'Barely. I did hear the bell for Compline shortly after, over the wall. Curious how it carries over all the bustle between.' In the upper air, so it would; people in the Foregate regulated their day by the office bells.

'Who was this who followed me? Did you know him?'

They looked at each other and hoisted indifferent shoulders; among the thousands at a great fair the local people are lost. 'Never seen him before. Not a Shrewsbury man. He may not have been following, to call it that, at all, just heading the same way.'

They told him exactly where he had left them, and the direction he had taken. Philip made his way purposefully to the spot indicated, but in that busy concourse, spreading along the Foregate and filling every open space beyond, he was still without a map. All he knew was that before nine, according to the witness in the sheriff's court, he had been very drunk and still drinking in Wat's tavern, and blurting out hatred and grievance and the intent of vengeance against Master Thomas of Bristol. The interval it was hard to fill. Perhaps he had made his way there at once, and been well advanced in drink before the stranger noted his threats.

Philip gritted his teeth and set off along the Foregate, so intent on his own quest that he had no ears for anything else, and missed the news that was being busily conveyed back and forth through the fair, with imaginative variations and considerable embellishments before it reached the far corner of the horse-fair. It was news more than two hours old by then, but Philip had heard no word of it, his mind was on his own problem. All round him stalls were being stripped down to trestle and board, and rented booths being locked up, and the keys delivered to abbey stewards. Business was almost put away, but the evening was not yet outworn, there would be pleasure after business.

Walter Renold's inn lay at the far corner of the horse-fair, not on the London highroad, but on the quieter road that bore away north-eastwards. It was handy for the country people who brought goods to market, and at this hour it was full. It went against the grain with Philip even to order a pot of ale for himself while he was on this desperate quest, but alehouses live by sales, and at least he was so formidably sober now that he could afford the indulgence. The pot-boy who brought him his drink was hardly more than a child, and he did not remember the tow hair and pock-marked face. He waited to speak with Wat himself, when there was a brief interlude of calm.

'I heard they'd let you go free,' said Wat, spreading brawny arms along the table opposite him. 'I'm glad of it. I never thought you'd do harm, and so I told them when they asked. When was it they loosed you?'

'A while before noon.' Hugh Beringar had said he should

152

eat his dinner at home, and so he had, though at a later hour than usual.

'So nobody could point a finger at you over the latest ill-doings. Such a fair as we've had! Good weather and good sales, and good attendance all round, even good behaviour,' said Wat weightily, considering the whole range of his experience of fairs. 'And yet two merchants murdered, the second of them a northern man found only this morning broken-necked in his stall. You'll have heard about that? When did we ever have such happenings! It's not the lads of Shrewsbury, I said when they asked me, that get up to such villainies, you look among the incomers from other parts. We're decent folk hereabouts!'

'Yes, I know of that,' said Philip. 'But it's not that death they pointed at me, it's the first, the Bristol merchant . . .' North and south had met here, he reflected, fatally for both. Now why should that be? Both the victims strangers from far distances, where some born locally were as well worth plundering.

'This one they could hardly charge to your account,' said Wat, grinning broadly, 'even if you'd been at large so early. It's all past and gone. You hadn't heard? There was a grand to-do along the Foregate, a few hours ago. The murderer's found out red-handed, and made a break for his freedom on his lord's horse, and kicked his lord into the dust on the way. And he's shot down dead as a storm-struck tree, at his lord's orders. A master's shot, they say. The glover's soon avenged. And you'd not heard of it?'

'Not a word! The last I heard they were looking for a man who might have a slit sleeve to show, and a gash in his arm. When was this, then?' It seemed that Brother Cadfael must have found his man, unaided, after all.

'Not an hour before Vespers it must have been. All I heard was the shouting at the abbey end of the Foregate. But they tell me the sheriff himself was there.'

About five in the afternoon, perhaps less than an hour after Philip had left Brother Cadfael and gone back into the town to look for John Norreys. A short hunt that had been, no need any longer for him to cast a narrowed eye at men's sleeves wherever he went. 'And it's certain they got the right man?'

'Certain! The merchant had marked him, and they say there were goods and money from the glover's stall found in his pack. Some groom called Ewald, I heard . . .'

A mere sneak-thief, then, who had gone too far. Nothing there to bear on Philip's own quest. He was free to concentrate his mind once again, and even more intently, upon his own pilgrimage. It had begun as a penitential exercise, but was gradually abandoning that aspect. Certainly he had made a fool of himself, but the original impulse on which he had acted, and roused others to act, had not been so foolish, after all, and was nothing to be ashamed of. Only when it collapsed about him in ruins had he thrown good sense to the winds, and indulged his misery like a sulking child.

'Now if only I could find out as certainly who it was did for Master Thomas! It was that night there was grave matter urged against me, and I will own I laid myself open. It's all very well being let out on my father's bail, but no one has yet said I'm clear of the charge. The rest I'll pay my score for, but I want to prove I never did the merchant any violence. I know I was here that night—the eve of the fair, you'll remember? From what hour? I've no recollection of times, myself. According to his men, master Thomas was alive until a third of the hour past nine.'

'Oh, you were here, no question!' Wat could not help grinning at the memory. 'There was noise enough, we were busy, but you made yourself heard! No offence, lad, who hasn't made a fool of himself in his cups from time to time? It can't have been more than a quarter after eight when you came in, and I doubt you'd had much, up to then.'

Only a quarter after the hour of Compline—then he must have come straight here after shaking off his friends. Not straight, perhaps that was an inappropriate word, but weavingly and unsteadily, though at that rate not calling anywhere else on the way. It was a natural thing to do, to hurry clean through the thick of the fair, and put as much ground as possible between himself and his solicitous companions before calling a halt.

'I tell you what, boy,' said the expert kindly, 'if you'd taken it slowly you'd have been sober enough. But you had to rush the matter. I doubt I've ever seen a fellow put so much down in the time, no wonder your belly turned against it.'

It was not cheering listening, but Philip swallowed it doggedly. Evidently he had been as foolish as he had been dreading, and the archer's account of his behaviour had not been at all exaggerated.

'And was I yelling vengeance against the man who struck me? That's what they said of me.'

'Well, now, I wouldn't go so far as that, and yet it's not too far off the mark, either. Let's say you were not greatly loving him, and no wonder, we could all see the dunt he'd given you. Arrogant and greedy you called him, and a few other things I don't recall, and mark your words, you kept telling us, pride like his was due for a disastrous fall, and soon. That must be what they had in mind who witnessed against you. I never heard word of any going to this hearing from my tavern, not until afterwards. Who were they that testified, then?'

'It was one man,' said Philip. 'Not that I can blame him, it seems he told no lies—indeed, I never thought he had, I know I was the world's fool that night.'

'Why, bless you, lad, with a cracked head a man's liable to act like one cracked, he has the right. But who's this one man? What with all the incomers at the fair, I had more strangers than known customers all these evenings.'

'It was a man attending one of the abbey guests,' said Philip. 'Turstan Fowler, they said his name was. He said he was here drinking, and went from ale to wine, and then to strong liquor—it seems he ended as drunk as I was myself, they took him up helpless later, and slung him into a cell at the abbey overnight. A well-set-up fellow, but slouching and unkempt when I saw him in the court. About thirty-five years old, at a guess, sunburned, a bush of brown hair. . . .'

Wat shook his head, pondering the description. 'I don't know him, not by that, though I've got a rare memory for faces. An ale-house keeper has to have. Ah, well, if he's a stranger he'd no call to give false witness, I suppose he was but honest, and put the worst meaning on your bletherings for want of knowing you.'

'What time was it when I left here?' Philip winced even at

155

the recollection of that departure, sudden and desperate, with churning stomach and swimming head, and both hands clamped hard over his grimly locked jaw. Barely time to weave a frantic way across the road and into the edge of the copse beyond, where he had heaved his heart out, and then blundered some distance further in cover towards the orchards of the Gaye, and collapsed shivering and retching into the grass, to pass into a sodden sleep. He had not dragged himself out of it until the small hours.

'Why, reckoning from Compline, I'd say an hour had passed, it would be about nine of the clock.'

Thomas of Bristol had set out from his booth to return to his barge only a quarter of an hour or so later. And someone, someone unknown, had intercepted him on the way, dagger in hand. No wonder the law had looked so narrowly at Philip Corviser, who had reason to resent and hate, and had blundered out of sight and sound of other men around that time, after venting his grievance aloud for all to hear.

Wat rose to go and cope with the custom that was overwhelming his two potboys, and Philip sat brooding with his chin on his fist. Most of the flares must be out by now along the Foregate, most of the stalls packed up and ready for departure. Another balmy summer night, heaven dropping fat blessings on the abbey receipts and the profits of trade, after a lost summer of warfare and a winter of uncertainty. And the town walls still unrepaired, and the streets still broken!

The door stood propped wide on the warm, luminous twilight, and the traffic in and out was brisk. Youngsters came with jugs and pitchers to fetch for their elders, maids tripped in for a measure of wine for their masters, labourers and abbey servants wandered in to slake their thirst between spells of work. Saint Peter's Fair was drawing to its contented and successful close.

Through the open door came a fresh-faced youngster in a fine leather jerkin, and on his heels a sturdy, brown-faced man at least fifteen years older, in the same good livery. It took Philip a long moment of staring to recognise Turstan Fowler, sober, well-behaved, in good odour with his lord and all the world. Still longer to cause him to reflect afresh how he himself must have looked, drunk, if the difference could stretch so far. He watched the little potboy serve them. Wat was busy with others, and the room was full. The end of the fair was always a busy time. Another day, and these same hours would hang heavy and dark.

Philip never quite knew why he turned his head away, and hoisted a wide shoulder between himself and Ivo Corbière's men. He had nothing against either of them, but he did not want to be recognised and condoled with, or congratulated on his release, or in any way, sympathetic or not, have public attention called to him. He kept his shoulder hunched between, and was glad to have the room so full of people, and most of them strangers.

'Fairs are good business,' remarked Wat, returning to his place and plumping down on the bench with a sigh of pleasure, 'but I wish we could spread them round the rest of the year. My feet are growing no younger, and I've hardly been off them an hour in all, the last three days. What was it we were saying?'

'I was trying to describe for you the fellow who reported me as threatening revenge,' said Philip. 'Cast a look over yonder now, and you'll see the very man. The two in leather who came in together—the elder of the two.'

Wat let his sharp eyes rove, and surveyed Turstan Fowler with apparent disinterest, but very shrewdly. 'Slouching and hangdog, was he? Smart as a new coat now.' His gaze returned to Philip's face. 'That's the man? I remember *him* well enough. I seldom forget a man's face, but his name and condition I'd no way of knowing.'

'He can't have looked quite so trim that evening,' said Philip, 'seeing he owned to being well soused. He was lost to the world two hours later, by his own tale.'

'And he said he got it all here?' Wat's eyes had narrowed thoughtfully.

'So he said. ''Where I got my skinful'' is what he said.'

'Well, let me tell you something interesting, friend . . .' Wat leaned confidentially across the table. 'Now I see him, I know how I saw him the last time, for if you'll credit me, he looked much as he looks now. And what's more, now I know of the connection he had with you and your affairs, I can recall small things that happened that night, things I never gave a thought to before, and neither would you have done. He was in here twice that evening, or rather, he was in the doorway once, before he came over the threshold later. In that doorway he stood, and looked round him, a matter of ten minutes or so after you came in. I made nothing of it that he gave you a measuring sort of look, for well he might, you were in full cry then. But look at you he did, and weighed you up, and went away again. And the next we saw of him, it might be half an hour later, he came in and bought a measure of ale, and a big flask of strong geneva liquor, and sat supping his ale quietly, and eyeing you from time to time —as again well he might, it was about then you were greenish and going suspicious quiet. But do you know when he drank up and left, Philip, lad? The minute after you made for the door in a hurry. And his flask under his arm, unopened. Drunk? *Him?* He was stone cold sober when he went out of here.'

'But he took the juniper liquor with him,' pointed out Philip, reasonably. 'He was drunk enough two hours later, there were several of them to swear to that. They had to carry him back to the abbey on a trestle-board.'

'And how much of the juniper spirit did they find remaining? Did they ever mention that? Did they find the flask at all?'

'I never heard mention of it,' owned Philip, startled and doubtful. 'Brother Cadfael was there, I could ask him. But why?'

Wat laid a kindly if patronising hand on his shoulder. 'Lad, it's easy to see you never went beyond wine or ale, and if you'll heed me you'll leave the strong stuff to strong stomachs. I said a large flask, and large I meant. There was a quart of geneva spirits in that bottle! If any man drank that dry in two hours, it wouldn't be dead drunk they'd be carrying him away, it would be plain dead. Or if he did live to tell of it, it wouldn't be the next day, nor for several after. Sober as the sheriff himself was that fellow when he went out of here on your heels, and why he should want to lie about it is more than I can say, but lie about it he did, it seems. Now you tell me why a man should go to some pains to convict himself of a debauch he never even had, and get himself slung into a cell for recompense. Unless,' added Wat, considering the problem with lively interest, 'it was to get himself out of something worse.'

The elder potboy, a freckled lad born and bred in the Foregate, came by with a cluster of empties in either hand, and paused to nudge Wat in the ribs with an elbow, and lean to his ear.

'Do you know who you have there, master?' A jerk of his head indicated the two in leather jerkins. 'The young one's fellow-groom to the one that got a bolt through him along the Foregate a while ago. And the other—Will Wharton just told me, and he was close by and saw it all!—that's the fellow who loosed the bolt! His comrade in the same service, mark! Should he be here and in such spirits the same night? That's a stronger stomach than mine. "Fetch him down!" says the master, and down the fellow fetches him, sharp and cool. You'd have thought his hand would have shook too much to get near the target, but no!—thump between the shoulders and through to the breast, so Will says. And that's the very man that did it, supping ale like any Christian.'

They were both of them staring at him open-mouthed, and turned away only to stare again, briefly and intently, at Turstan Fowler sitting at ease with his tankard, sturdy legs splayed under the table. It had never even occurred to Philip to ask in whose service the dead malefactor was employed, and perhaps Wat would not have known the name if he had asked. He would have mentioned it else.

'That's the man? You're sure?' pressed Philip.

'Will Wharton is sure, and he helped to pick up the poor devil who was killed.'

'Turstan Fowler? The falconer to Ivo Corbière? And Corbière ordered him to shoot?'

'The name I don't know, for neither did Will. Some young lord at the abbey guest-hall. Very handsome sprig, yellow-haired, Will says. Though it's no great blame to him for wanting a murderer and thief stopped in his tracks, granted, and any road, the man had just stolen his horse, and kicked him off into the dust when he tried to halt him. And I suppose when a lord orders, his man had better jump to obey. Still, it's a grim thing to work side by side with a man maybe months and years, and then to be told, strike him dead! And

159

to do it!' And the potboy rolled up his eyes and loosed a long, soft whistle, and passed on with his handful of tankards, leaving them so sunk in reconsideration that neither of them had anything to say.

But there could not be anything in it of significance for him, surely? Philip looked back briefly as he left the inn, and Turstan Fowler and the young groom were sitting tranquilly with their ale, talking cheerfully with half a dozen other sober drinkers around them. They had not noticed him, or if they had, had not recognised him, and neither of them seemed to have anything of grave moment on his mind. Strange, though, how this same man seemed to be entangled in every untoward episode, never at the centre of things yet always somewhere in view.

As for the matter of the flask of juniper spirits, what did it really signify? The man had been picked up too drunk to talk, no one had looked round for his bottle, it might well have been left lying, still more than half-full, if the stuff was as potent as Wat said, and some scavenger by night might have picked it up and rejoiced in his luck. There were a dozen ways of accounting for the circumstances. And yet it was strange. Why should he have said he was drunk before he left Wat's inn, if he had really left it cold sober? More to the point, why should he have left so promptly on Philip's heels? Yet Wat was a good observer.

The tiny discrepancies stuck like barbs in Philip's mind. It was far too late to trouble anyone else tonight, Compline was long over, the monks of Shrewsbury, their guests, their servants, would all be in their beds or preparing to go there, except for the few lay stewards who had almost completed their labours, and would be glad enough to make a modestly festive night of it. Moreover, his parents would be vexed that he had abandoned them all the day, and he could expect irate demands for explanations at home. He had better make his way back.

All the same, he crossed the road and made for the copse, as on the night he was repeating, and found some faint signs of his wallow still visible, dried into the trampled grass. Then back towards the river, avoiding the streets, keeping to the cover of woodland, and there was the sheltered hollow where he had slept off the worst of his orgy, before gathering himself up stiffly and hobbling back to the town. There was enough lambent starlight to see his way, and show him the scuffled and flattened grasses.

But no, this was not the place! Here there was a faint, trodden path, and he had certainly moved much deeper into the bushes and trees, down-river, hiding even from the night. This glade looked very like the other, but it was not the same. Yet someone or something, large as a man, had lain here, and not peacefully. Surely more than one pair of feet had ploughed the turf. A pair of opportunist lovers, enjoying one of the traditional pleasures of the fair? Or another kind of struggle? No, hardly a struggle, though something had been dragged downhill towards the river, which was just perceptible as a gleam between the trees. There was a patch of bare soil, dry and pale as clay, between the spreading roots of the birch-tree against which he leaned, and ribbons of dropped bark littered it. The largest of them showed curiously dark instead of silvery, like the rest. He stooped and picked it up, and his fingertips recoiled from the black, encrusted stain. In the grass, if he searched by daylight, there might well be other such blots.

In looking for the place of his own humiliation, he had found something very different, the place where Master Thomas had been killed. And below, from that spur of grass standing well above the undermined bank, his body had been thrown into the river.

AFTER THE FAIR

ONE

Brother Cadfael came out from Prime, next morning, to find Philip hovering anxiously in the great court, fidgeting from one foot to the other as if the ground under him burned, and so intent and grim of face that there was no doubting the urgency of what he had to impart. At sight of Cadfael he came bounding alongside to lay a hand on his sleeve.

'Will you come with me to Hugh Beringar? You know him, he'll listen if you vouch for me. I didn't know if he'd be stirring this early, so I waited for you. I think I've found the place where Master Thomas was killed.'

It was certainly not what he had been looking for, and came as a total irrelevance for a moment to Brother Cadfael, who checked and blinked at an announcement so unexpected. 'You've done *what?*'

'It's true, I swear it! It was so late last night, I couldn't pester anyone with it then, and I've not been there by daylight— but someone bled there—someone was dragged down to the water—'

'Come!' said Cadfael, recovering. 'We'll go together.' And he set out at a brisk trot for the guest-hall, Philip's long strides keeping easy pace with him. 'If you're right . . . He'll want you to show the place. Can you find it again with certainty?'

'I can, you'll see why.'

Hugh came out to them yawning, in shirt and hose, but wide awake and shaven all the same. 'Speak low!' he said, finger on lip, and softly closed the door of his rooms behind him. 'The women are still asleep. Now, what is it? I know better than to turn away anyone who comes with Brother Cadfael's warranty.'

Philip told only what was needful. For his own personal need there would be time later. What mattered now was the glade in the edge of the woods, beyond the orchards of the Gaye.

'I was following my own scent, last night, and I made too short a cast at the way I took down to the river. I came on a place in the trees there—I can find it again—where some heavy thing had lain, and been dragged down to the water. The grass is flattened where he lay, and combed downhill where he was dragged, and for all the three days between, it still shows the traces. I think there are also spots of blood.'

'The merchant of Bristol?' asked Hugh, after an instant of startled silence.

'I think so. Daylight may show for certain.'

Hugh turned to drain his morning ale in purposeful haste, and demolish the end of oatcake he had been eating. 'You slept at home? In the town?' He was brushing his black crest hastily as he talked, tying the laces of his shirt and reaching for his cotte. 'And came to me rather than to the sheriff! Well, no harm, we're nearer than he, it will save time.' Sword and sword-belt he left lying, and thrust his feet into his shoes. 'Cadfael, you'll be missing breakfast, take these cakes with you, and drink something now, while you may. And you, friend, have you eaten?'

'No escort?' said Cadfael.

'To what end? Your eyes and mine are all we require here, and the fewer great boots stamping about the sward, the better. Come, before Aline wakes, she has a bird's hearing, and I'd rather have her rest. Now, Philip, lead! You're on your home turf, take us the quickest way.'

Aline and Emma were at breakfast, resigned to Hugh's sudden and silent departures, when Ivo came asking admittance. Punctilious as always, he asked for Hugh.

'But as that husband of mine has already gone forth somewhere on official business,' said Aline, amused, 'and as it's certainly you he really wants to see, shall we let him in? I felt sure he would not go away without paying his respects to you yet again. He has probably been exercising his wits to find a way of ensuring it shan't be the last time, either. He was

166

hardly at his best last night, and no wonder, after so many shocks, and grazed and bruised from his fall.'

Emma said nothing, but her colour rose agreeably. She had risen from her bed with a sense of entering a life entirely new, and more her own to determine than ever it had been before. By this hour Master Thomas's barge must be well down the Severn on its way home. She was relieved of the necessity of avoiding Roger Dod's grievous attentions, and eased of the sense of guilt she felt in doing him what was probably the great wrong of fearing and distrusting his intentions towards her. Her belongings were neatly packed for travelling, in a pair of saddle-bags bought at the fair, for whatever was to become of her now, she would be leaving the abbey today. If no immediate escort offered for the south, she would go home with Aline, to await whatever arrangements Hugh could make for her, and in default of any other trustworthy provision, he himself had promised her his safe-conduct home to Bristol.

The bustle of departure filled the stable-yard and the great court, and half the rooms in the guest-hall had already been vacated. No doubt Turstan Fowler and the young groom were also assembling their lord's purchases and effects, and saddling up the bay horse, returned to the abbey by an enterprising errand-boy who had been lavishly rewarded, and their own shaggy ponies. Two of them! The third would be on a leading rein.

Emma felt cold when she remembered what had befallen the rider of the third pony, and the things he had done. So sudden a death filled her with horror. But the man had done murder, and had not scrupled to ride down his own lord when he was unmasked. It was unreasonable to blame Ivo for what had happened, even if his order had not been given in an understandable rage at the misuse of his patronage and the assault upon his own person. Indeed, Emma had been touched, the previous evening, when the very vehemence with which Ivo had defended his action had so clearly betrayed his own doubts and regrets. It had ended in her offering reassurance and comfort. It was a terrible thing in itself, she thought, to have the power of life and death over your fellowmen, whatever crimes they might have committed.

If Ivo had lacked something of his normal balance and confidence last night, he had certainly regained them this morning. His grooming was always immaculate, and his dress, however simple, sat upon his admirable body with a borrowed elegance. It had been hateful to him to be spilled into the dust, and rise limping and defaced before a dozen or more witnesses. This morning he had made sure of his appearance, and wore even the healing grazes on his left cheek like ornaments; but as soon as he entered, Emma saw that he was still limping after his fall.

'I'm sorry to have missed your husband,' he said as he came into the room where they were sitting, 'but they tell me he's already gone forth. I had a scheme to put to him for approval. Dare I put it to you, instead?'

'I'm already curious,' said Aline, smiling.

'Emma has a problem, and I have a solution. I've been thinking about it ever since you told me, Emma, two days ago, that you would not be returning to Bristol with the barge, but must find a safe escort south by road. I have no right at all to advance any claim, but if Beringar will consent to trust you to me . . . You need to get home, I'm sure, as quickly as you can.'

'I must,' said Emma, eyeing him with wondering expectation. 'There are so many things I must see to there.'

Ivo addressed himself very earnestly to Aline. 'I have a sister at Stanton Cobbold who is determined to take the veil, and the convent of her choice has consented to take her. And by luck it happens that she wished to join a Benedictine house, and the place is the priory at Minchinbarrow, which is some few miles beyond Bristol. She is waiting for me to take her there, and to tell the truth, I've been delaying to give her time to change her mind, but the girl's set on her own way. I'm satisfied she means it. Now if you'll confide Emma to my care, as I swear you may with every confidence, for it will be my pleasure to serve her, then why should not she and Isabel travel down very comfortably together? I have men enough to provide a safe guard, and naturally I should myself be their escort. That's the plan I wanted to put to your husband, and I hope he would have felt able to fall in with it and give his approval. It's great pity he is not here—'

'It sounds admirable,' said Aline, wide-eyed with pleasure, 'and I'm sure Hugh would feel completely happy in trusting Emma to your care. Had we not better ask Emma herself what she has to say?'

Emma's flushed face and dazzled smile were speaking for her. 'I think it would be the best possible answer, for me,' she said slowly, 'and I'm most grateful for so kind a thought. But I must really go as soon as possible, and your sister—you said, you wanted her to have time to be sure . . .'

Ivo laughed, a little ruefully. 'I've already reached the point of giving up the hope of persuading her to stay in the world. Never fear that you may be forcing Isabel's hand, ever since she was accepted she has been trying to force mine. And if it's what she wants, who am I to prevent? She has everything ready, it will give her only pleasure if I come home to say that we can start tomorrow. If you're willing to trust yourself to me alone for the few miles to Stanton Cobbold, and sleep under our roof tonight, we can be on our way in the morning. We can provide you horse and saddle, if you care to ride, or a litter for the pair of you, as you please.'

'Oh, I can ride,' she said, glowing. 'It would be a delight.'

'We would try and make it so. *If*,' said Ivo, turning his grazed smile almost diffidently upon Aline, 'if I may have your approval, and my lord Beringar's. I would not presume without that. But since this is a journey I must make, sooner or later, and Isabel insists the sooner the better, why not take advantage of it to serve Emma's need, too?'

'It would certainly solve everything very happily,' agreed Aline. And there could be no doubt, thought Emma, bolstering her own dear wish with the persuasion of virtue, that Aline would be relieved and happy if Hugh could be spared a journey, and she several days deprived of his company. 'Emma knows,' said Aline, 'that she may choose as she thinks best, for both you and we, it seems, are equally at her service. As for approval, why, of course I approve, and so, I'm sure, would Hugh.'

'I wish he would put in an appearance,' said Ivo, 'I should be the happier with his blessing. But if we are to go, I think we should set out at once. I know I said all's ready with

Isabel, but for all that we may need to make the most of this day.'

Emma wavered between her desire and her regret at leaving without making her due and grateful farewell to Hugh. But it was gain for him, great gain, to be rid of the responsibility he had assumed, and so securely as this promised. 'Aline, you have been the soul of kindness to me, and I leave you with regret. But it is better to spare an extra journey, in such times, and then, Hugh has been kept so busy on my account already, and you've seen so little of him these days. . . . I should like to go with Ivo, if you'll give me your blessing. Yet I hate to go without thanking him properly . . .'

'Don't fret about Hugh, he will surely think you wise to take advantage of so kind and fortunate an offer. I will give him all the pretty messages you're thinking of. Once I lose sight of him, now, I never know when he'll return, and I'm afraid Ivo is right, you may yet need every moment of the day, or certainly Isabel may. It's a great step she's taking.'

'So I've told her,' he said, 'but my sister has the boldness of mind to take great steps. You won't mind, Emma, riding pillion behind me, the few miles we have to go today? At home we'll find you saddle and horse and all.'

'Really,' said Aline, eyeing the pair of them with a small and private smile, 'I begin to be envious!'

He sent the young groom to fetch out her saddle-bags. Their light weight was added to the bales of Corbière's purchases on the spare pony, her cloak, which she certainly would not need on so fine a day, folded and stowed away with the bags. It was like setting out into a new world, sunlit and inviting, but frighteningly wide. True, she had solemn duties waiting for her in Bristol, not least the confession of a failure, but for all that, she felt as if she had almost shed the past, and could be glad of the riddance, and was stepping into this unknown world unburdened and unguarded, truly her own mistress.

Aline kissed her affectionately, and wished them both a happy journey. Emma cast frequent glances towards the gate-house until the last moment, in case Hugh should appear, but he did not; she had still to leave her messages to Aline for delivery. Ivo mounted first, since the bay, as he said, was in a skittish mood and inclined to play tricks, and then turned to give her a steady, sustaining hand as Turstan Fowler hoisted her easily to the pillion.

'Even with two of us up,' said Ivo over his shoulder, smiling, 'this creature can be mettlesome when he's fresh out. For safety, hold me fast about the waist, and close your hands on my belt—so, that's well!' He saluted Aline very gracefully and courteously. 'I'll see she reaches Bristol safely. I promise!'

He rode out at the gatehouse in shirt-sleeves, just as he had ridden in, his men, now two only, at his heels, and the pack-pony trotting contentedly under his light load. Emma's arms easily spanned Ivo's slenderness, and the feel of his spare, strong body was warm and muscular and vital through the fine linen. As they threaded the Foregate, now emptying fast, he laid his own left hand over her clasped ones, pressing them firmly against his flat middle, and though she knew he was simply assuring himself that her hold was secure, she could not help feeling that it was also a caress.

She had laughed and shaken her head over Aline's romantic fantasies, refusing to believe in any union between landed nobility and trade, except for mutual profit. Now she was not so sure that wisdom was all with the sceptics.

The hollow where the big, heavy body had lain still showed at least the approximate bulk of Master Thomas's person, and round about it the grass was trodden, as though someone, or perhaps more than one, had circled all round him as he lay dead. And so they surely had, for here he must have been stripped and searched, the first of those fruitless searches Brother Cadfael had deduced from the events following. Out of the hollow, down to the raised bank of the river, went the track by which he had been dragged, the grass, growing longer as it emerged from shade, all brushed in one direction.

Nor was there any doubt about the traces of blood, meagre though they were. The sliver of birch bark under the tree showed a thin crust, dried black. Careful search found one or two more spots, and a thin smear drawn downhill, where it seemed the dead man had been turned on his back to be hauled the more easily down to the water.

'It's deep here,' said Hugh, standing on the green hillock above the river, 'and undercuts the bank, it would take him well out into the current. I fancy the clothes went after him at once, we may find the rest yet. One man could have done it. Had they been two, they would have carried him.'

'Would you say,' wondered Cadfael, 'that this is a reasonable way he might take to get back to his barge? He'd know his boat lay somewhat down-river from the bridge, I suppose he might try a chance cut through from the Foregate, and overcast by a little way. You see the end of the jetty, where the barge tied up, is only a small way upstream from us. Would you say he was alone, and unsuspecting, when he was struck down?'

Hugh surveyed the ground narrowly. It was not the scene of a struggle, there was the flattened area of the body's fall, and the trampling of feet all round its stillness. The brushings of the grass this way and that were ordered, not the marks of a fight.

'Yes. There was no resistance. Someone crept behind, and pierced him without word or scruple. He went down and lay. He was on his way back, preferring the byways, and came out a little downstream of where he aimed. Someone had been watching and following him.'

'The same night,' said Philip flatly, 'someone had been watching and following *me*.'

He had their attention at once, both of them eyeing him with sharp interest. 'The same someone?' suggested Cadfael mildly.

'I haven't told you my own part,' said Philip. 'It went out of my head when I stumbled on this place, and guessed at what it meant. What I set out to do was to find out just what I did that night, and prove I never did murder. For I'd come to think that whoever intended this killing had his eye on me from the start. I came from that riot on the jetty, with my head bleeding and my mood for murder, I was a gift, if I could but be out of sight and mind when murder was done.' He told them everything he had discovered, word for word. By the end of it they were both regarding him with intent and frowning concentration.

'The man Fowler?' said Hugh. 'You're sure of this?'

'Walter Renold is sure, and I think him a good witness. The man was there to be seen, I pointed him out, and Wat told me what he'd seen of him that night. Fowler looked in, saw and heard the condition I was in, and went away again for it might be as much as half an hour, says Wat. Then he came back, took one measure of ale to drink, and bought a big flask of geneva spirit.'

'And left with it unopened,' Brother Cadfael recalled, 'as soon as you took yourself off with your misery into the bushes. No need to blush for it now, we've all done as foolishly once or twice in our lives, many of us have bettered it. And the next that's known of him,' he said, meeting Hugh's eyes across the glade, 'is two hours later, when we discover him lying sodden-drunk under a store of trestles by the Foregate.'

'And Wat of the tavern swears he was sober as a bishop when he quit the inn.'

'And I would swear by Wat's judgment,' said Philip stoutly. 'If any man drank that flagon dry in two hours, he says, it would be the death of him, or go very near. And Fowler was testifying in court next day, and little the worse for wear.

'Good God!' said Hugh, shaking his head. 'I stooped over him, I pulled back the cloak from his shoulders. The fellow reeked. His breath would have felled an ox. Am I losing my wits?'

'Or was it rather the reek you loosed by moving the cloak? I begin to have curious thoughts,' said Cadfael, 'for I fancy that juniper liquor was bought for his outside, not his inside.'

'A costly freak,' mused Hugh, 'the price such liquors are. Cheap enough, though, if it bought him immunity from all suspicion of a thing that could have cost him a deal higher. What was the first thing I said?—more fool I! By the look of him, I said, he must have been here some hours already. And where did he go from there? Safely into an abbey punishment cell, and lay there overnight. How could he be guilty of anything but being a drunken sot? Children and drunken men are the world's only innocents! If murder was done that night, who was to look at a man who had put himself out of the reckoning from the time Master Thomas was last seen alive to the time when his body was brought back to Shrewsbury?'

173

Cadfael's mind had probed even beyond that point, though nothing beyond was yet clear. 'I have a fancy, Hugh, to look again at the place where we picked up that sodden carcase, if it can be found. Surely an honest drunk should have had his bottle lying beside him for all to see. But I remember none. If we missed it, and some stray scavenger found it by night, still half-full or more, well and good. But if by any chance it was hidden—so that no questions need ever be asked about how much had been drunk, and what manner of head could have borne it—would that be the act of a simple sot? He would not walk through the fairground stinking as he did, whether from outside or in. His baptism was there, where we found him tucked away. So should his bottle have been.'

'And if he was neither simple nor a sot that night, Cadfael, how do you read his comings and goings? He looked in at the tavern, took note of this lad's state, listened to his complaints, and went away—where?'

'As far as Master Thomas's booth, perhaps, to make sure the merchant was there, busy about his wares, and likely to be busy for a while longer? And so back to the tavern to keep watch on Philip, so handy a scapegoat, and so clearly on the way to ending the evening blind and deaf. And afterwards, when he had followed him far enough into the copse to know he was lost to the world, back to dog Master Thomas's footsteps as he made his way back to the barge. Made his way, that is, as far as this place.'

'It is all conjecture,' said Hugh reasonably.

'It is. But read it so, and it makes sense.'

'Then back with his flask of spirits ready, to slip unseen into a place withdrawn and private, and become the wretched object we found. How long would it take, would you say, to kill his man, search and strip him, in vain, as it seems, and drag him down to the river?'

'Counting the time spent following him unseen, and returning unnoticed to the fairground after all was done, more than an hour of those two hours lost between drunk and sober. No,' said Cadfael sombrely, 'I do not think he spent any of that time drinking.'

'Was it he, also, who boarded the barge? But no, that he

174

could not, he was at the sheriff's court. Concerning the merchant of Shotwick, we already know his slayer.'

'We know one of them,' said Cadfael. 'Can any of these matters be separated from the rest? I think not. This pursuit is all one.'

'You do grasp,' said Hugh, after a long moment of furious thought, 'what it is we are saying? Here are these two men, one proven a murderer, the other suspect. And yesterday the one of them fetched down the other to his death. Coldly, expertly . . . Before we say more,' said Hugh abruptly, casting a final glance about the glade, 'let's do as you suggested, look again at the place where we found him lying.'

TWO

PHILIP, WHO WAS LEARNING HOW TO LISTEN AND BE SILENT, FOL-lowed at their heels all the way back through the orchards and gardens of the Gaye. Neither of them found fault with his persistence. He had earned his place, and had no intention of being put off. All the larger boats were already gone from the jetty. Soon the labourers would begin dismantling the boards and piers until the following year, and stowing them away in the abbey storehouses. Along the Foregate stalls were being taken down and stacked for removal, while two of the abbey carts worked their way along from the horse-fair towards the gatehouse.

'More than halfway along, I remember,' said Hugh, 'and well back from the roadway. There were few lights, most of the stalls here were for the country people who come in by the day. Somewhere in this stretch.'

There had been trestles stacked that night, and canvas awnings leaning against them ready for use. This morning there were also piles of trestles and boards, ready now to be put away for the next fair. They surveyed all the likely area, but to lay a finger on the exact place was impossible. One of the collecting carts had reached this stretch, and two lay servants were hoisting the heaped planks aboard, and stacking the trestles one within another in high piles. Cadfael watched as the ground was gradually cleared.

'You've found some unexpected discards,' he commented, for a corner of the cart carried a small pile of odd objects, a large shoe, a short cotte, bedraggled but by no means old or ragged, a child's wooden doll with one arm missing, a green capuchon, a drinking-horn.

'There'll be many more such, brother,' said the carter, grinning, 'before the whole ground's cleared. Some will be claimed. I fancy some child will want to know where she lost her doll. And the cotte is good stuff, some young gentleman took a drop too much, and forgot to collect that when he moved on. The shoe's as good as new, too, and a giant's size, somebody may sneak in, shamefaced, to ask after that. I hope he had not far to go home with only one. But it wasn't a rowdy night—not like many a last night I've seen.' He slid powerful arms under a stack of trestles, and hoisted them bodily. 'You'd hardly credit where we found that flagon there.'

His nod indicated the front of the cart, to which Cadfael had hitherto devoted no attention. Slung by a thin leather thong from the shaft hung a flattened glass bottle large enough to hold a quart. 'Stuck on top of the canvas over one of the country stalls. An old woman who sells cheeses had the stall, I know her, she comes every year, and seeing she's not so nimble nowadays, we put up the stall for her the night before the fair opened. The bottle all but brained Daniel here, when we took it down, this morning! Fancy tossing a bottle like that away as if it had no value! He could have got a free drink at Wat's if he'd taken it back, whoever he was.'

His armful of trestles thumped into the cart, and he turned to heave a stack of boards after it.

'It came from Wat's tavern then, did it?' asked Cadfael, very thoughtfully gazing.

'It has his mark on the thong. We all know where they belong, these better vessels. But they're not often left for us.'

176

And where was the stall where this one was left?' asked Hugh over Cadfael's shoulder.

'Not ten yards back from where you're standing.' They could not resist looking back to measure, and it would do. It would do very well. 'The odd thing is, the old woman swore, when she came to put out her wares, that there was a stink of spirits about the place. Said she could smell it in her skirts at night, as if she'd been wading in it. But after the first day she forgot about it. She's half-Welsh, and has a touch of the strange about her, I daresay she imagined it.'

Cadfael would have said, rather, that she had a keen nose, and some knowledge of the distilling of spirits, and had accurately assessed the cause of her uneasiness. Somewhere in the grass close to her stall, he was now certain, a good part of that quart of liquor had been poured out generously over clothing and ground, no wonder the turf retained it. A taste of it, perhaps, to scent the breath and steady the mind, might have gone down a throat; but no more, for the mind had been steady indeed, when strangers stooped over its fleshly habitation, and sniffed at its flagrant drunkenness. Strangers, all but one! Cadfael began to see what could hardly be called light, for he was looking into a profound darkness.

'It so happens,' he said, 'that we have some business with Walter Renold. Will you let us take your bottle back to him? You shall have the credit for it with him.'

'Take it, brother,' agreed the carter cheerfully, unleashing the bottle from the shaft. 'Tell him Rychart Nyall sent it. Wat knows me.'

'Nothing in it, I suppose, when you found it?' hazarded Cadfael, hefting the fated thing in one hand.

'Never a drop, brother! Fair-goers may abandon the bottle, but they make sure of what's inside before they fall senseless!'

The boards were stowed, the stripped ground lay trampled and naked, the cart moved on. It would take no more than a handful of days and the next summer showers, and all the green, fine hair would grow again, and the bald clay coil into ringlets.

'It's mine, surely,' said Wat, receiving the bottle into a large hand. 'The only one of its kind I'm short. Who buys

177

this measure of spirits, even at a fair? Who has the money to afford it? And who chooses it afore decent ale and wine? Not many! I've known men desperate to sink their souls fast, at whatever cost, but seldom at a fair. They turn genial at fairs, even the sad fellows get the wind of it, and mellow. I marvelled at that one, even when he asked for it and paid the price, but he was plainly some lord's servant, he had his orders. He had money, and I sell liquor. But yes, if it's of worth to you, that same fellow Philip here knows of, that's the measure he bought.'

A retired corner of Wat's large taproom was as good a place as any to sit down and think before action, and try to make sense of what they had gathered.

'Wat has just put words to it,' said Cadfael. 'We should have been quicker to see. He was plainly some lord's servant, he had his orders, he had money. One man from a lord's household suborned to murder by an unknown, one such setting out on his own account to enrich himself by murder and theft, that I could believe in. But two? From the same household? No, I think not! They never strayed from their own manor. They served but one lord.'

'Their own? *Corbière?*' whispered Philip, the breath knocked out of him by the enormity of the implications. 'But he . . . The way I heard it, the groom tried to ride him down. Struck him into the dust when he tried to stop him. How can you account for that? There's no sense in it.'

'Wait! Take it from the beginning. Say that on the night Master Thomas died, Fowler was sent out to deal with him, to get possession of whatever it is someone so much desires. His lord has spied out the land, told him of a handy scapegoat who may yet be useful, given him money for the drink that will put him out of the reckoning when the deed is done. The man would demand immunity, he must be seen to be out of the reckoning. His lord keeps in close touch, joins us when we go forth to look for the missing merchant. Recollect, Hugh, it was *Corbière*, not we, who discovered his truant man. We had passed him by, and that would not have done. He must be found, must be seen to be so drunk as to have been helpless and harmless some hours, and must then be manifestly under lock and key many hours more. Ten murders could have been committed that night, and no one would ever have looked at Turstan Fowler.'

'All for nothing,' pointed out Hugh. 'Sooner or later he had to tell his master that murder had been done in vain. Master Thomas did not carry his treasure on him.'

'I doubt if he found that out until morning, when he had his man let out of prison. Therefore he brought Fowler to lay evidence that made sure the finger was pointed at Philip here, and while we were all blamelessly busy at the sheriff's hearing, sent his second man to search the barge. And again, vainly. Am I making sense of it thus far?'

'Sound enough,' said Hugh sombrely. 'The worst is yet to come. Which man, do you suppose, did the work that day?'

'I doubt if they ever involved the young one. Two were enough to do the business. The groom Ewald, I think. Those two were the hands that did all. But they were not the mind.'

'That same night, then, they broke into the booth, and made their search there, and still without success. The next night came the attack that killed Euan of Shotwick.' Hugh said no word of the violation of Master Thomas's coffin. 'And, as I remember you argued, once more in vain. So far, possible enough. But come to yesterday's thorny business. For God's sake, how can sense be made of that affair? I was there watching the man, I saw him change colour, I swear it! Shock and anger and affronted honour, he showed them all. He would not send for the groom, for fear a fellow-servant might warn him, he would fetch him himself. He placed himself between his man and the gate, he risked maiming or worse, trying to halt his flight. . . .'

'All that,' agreed Cadfael heavily, 'and yet there is sense in it all, though a more abominable sense even than you or I dreamed of. Ewald was in the stables, there was no escape for him unless he could break out of our walls. Corbière came at the sheriff's bidding, and was told all. His man was detected past denying, and driven into a corner, he would pour out everything he knew, lay the load on his lord. Consider the order in which everything happened from that moment. Fowler had been at the butts, and had his arbalest with him. Corbière set off to summon Ewald from the stables, Turstan made to follow him, yes, and some words were exchanged that sent him back. But what words? They were too distant to be heard. Nor could we guess what was said in the stable-yard. We waited—you'll agree?—several minutes before they came. Long enough for Corbière to tell the groom how things stood, bid him keep his head, promise him escape. Bring the horse, *I* will ensure that only I stand between you and the gate, pick your moment, mount and away. Lie up in hiding—doubtless at his manor—and you shan't be the loser. But make it clear that I have no part in this—attack me, make it good for your part, I will make it good for mine. And so he did—the finest player of a part that ever I saw. He set himself between Ewald and the gate, and between them they used the lively horse to edge us all that way. He made a gallant grab at the rein, and took a heavy fall, and the groom was clear.'

They were both gazing at him in mute fascination, wide-eyed.

'Except that his lord had one more trick to play,' said Cadfael. 'He had never intended to let him go. Escape was too great a risk, he might yet be taken, and open his mouth. "Fetch him down!" said Corbière, and Turstan Fowler did it. Without compunction, like master, like man. A dangerous mouth—dangerous to both of them—closed at no cost.'

There was a long moment of appalled silence. Even Beringar, whose breadth of mind could conceive, though with detestation, prodigies of evil and treachery, was shocked out of words. Philip stared aghast, huge of eye, and came slowly to his feet. His experience was narrow, local and decent, it was hard to grasp that men could be monsters.

'You mean it! You believe it! But this man—he visits her, he pays court to her! And you say there was something he wanted from her uncle, and has missed getting—not on his body, not in his barge, not in his booth—Where is there left, but with Emma? And we delay here!'

'Emma is with my wife,' said Hugh reasonably, 'in the abbey guest-hall, what harm can come to her there?'

'What harm?' cried Philip passionately. 'When you tell me we are dealing not with men, but with devils?' And he whirled on the heel of a trodden shoe and ran, out of the tavern and arrow-straight along the road towards the Foregate, long legs flashing.

Cadfael and Hugh were left regarding each other mutely across the table, but for no more than a moment. 'By God,' said Hugh then, 'we learn of the innocents! Come on, we'd best make haste after. The lad's shaken me!'

Philip came to the guest-hall out of breath. With chest heaving from his running he asked for Aline, and she came out, smiling but alone.

'Why, Philip, what's the matter?' Then she thought she knew, and was sorry for a lovesick boy who came too late even to take a dignified farewell, and receive what comfort a few kind words, costing nothing, could provide him. 'Oh, Philip, I am sorry you've missed her, but they could not linger, it was necessary to leave in good time. She would have wished me to say her goodbye to you, and wish you . . .' The words faded on her lips. 'Philip, what is it? What ails you?'

'Gone?' he said, hard and shrill. 'She's gone? *They*, you said! Who? *Who* is gone with her?'

'Why, she left with Messire Corbière, he has offered to escort her to Bristol with his sister, who goes to a convent there. It seemed a lucky chance . . . *Philip!* What have I said? What is wrong?' He had let out a great groan of fury and anguish, and even reached a hand to grip her wrist.

'Where? Where is he taking her? *Now, today!*'

'To his manor of Stanton Cobbold for tonight—his sister is there. . . .'

But he was gone, the instant she had named the place, running like a purposeful demon, and not towards the gatehouse, but across the court to the stable-yard. There was no time to ask leave of any man, or respect any man's property, whatever the consequences. Philip took the best-looking horse he saw ready to hand, which by luck—Philip's luck, not the owner's!—stood saddled and waiting for departure, on a tether in the yard. Before Aline, bewildered and frightened, reached the doorway of the hall, Philip was already out of the gate, and a furious groom was haring across the court in voluble and hopeless pursuit.

* * *

Since the nearest way to the road leading south towards Stretton and Stanton Cobbold was to turn left at the gate, and left again by the narrow track on the near side of the bridge, Brother Cadfael and Hugh Beringar, hastening along the Foregate, saw nothing of the turmoil that attended Philip's departure. They came to the gatehouse and the great court without any intimation that things could have gone amiss. There were still guests departing, the normal bustle of the day after the fair, but nothing to give them pause. Hugh made straight for the guest-hall, and Cadfael, following hard on his heels, was suddenly arrested by a large hand on his shoulder, and a familiar, hearty voice hailing him in amiable Welsh.

'The very man I was looking for! I come to make my farewells, brother, and thank you for your companionship. A good fair! I'm off to my boat now, and away home with a handsome profit.'

Rhodri ap Huw beamed merrily from within the covert of his black beard and thorn-bush of black hair.

'Far from a good fair to two, at least, who came looking for a profit,' said Cadfael ruefully.

'Ah, but in cash, or some other currency? Though it all comes down to cash in the end, cash or power. What else do men labour for?'

'For a cause, perhaps, now and then one. You said yourself, I remember, no place like one of the great fairs for meeting someone you'd liefer not be seen meeting. Nowhere so solitary as the middle of a market place!' And he added mildly: 'I daresay Owain Gwynedd himself may have had his intelligencers here. Though they'd need to have good English,' he said guilelessly, 'to gather much profit from it.'

'They would so. No use employing me. I daresay you're right, though. Owain needs to have forward information as much as any man, if he's to keep his princedom safe, and add a few more miles to it here and there. Now I wonder which of all these traders I've rubbed shoulders with will be making his report in Owain's ear!'

'And what advice he'll be giving him,' said Cadfael.

Rhodri stroked his splendid beard, and his dark eyes twinkled. 'I think he might take him word that the message Earl Ranulf expected from the south—who knows, maybe even from overseas—will never be delivered, and if he wants to get the best out of the hour, he should be aiming to enlarge his rule away from Chester's borders, for the earl will be taking no risks, but looking well to his own. Owain would do better to make his bid in Maelienydd and Elfael, and let Ranulf alone.'

'Now I come to think,' mused Cadfael, 'it would be excellent cover for Owain's intelligencers to ask the help of an interpreter in these parts, and be seen to need him. Tongues wag more freely before the deaf man.'

'A good thought,' approved Rhodri. 'Someone should suggest it to Owain.' Though there was every indication that the prince of Gwynedd needed no other man's wits to fortify his own, but had been lavishly endowed by God in the first place. Cadfael wondered how many other tongues this simple merchant knew. French, almost certainly enough for his purposes. Flemish, possibly a little, he had undoubtedly travelled in Flanders. It would be no surprise if he knew some Latin, too.

'You'll be coming to Saint Peter's Fair next year?'

'I may, brother, I may, who knows! Will you come forth again and speak for me, if I do?'

'Gladly. I'm a Gwynedd man myself. Take my greetings back with you to the mountains. And good speed on the way!'

'God keep you!' said Rhodri, still beaming, and clapped him buoyantly on the shoulder, and set off towards the riverside.

Hugh had no sooner set foot in the hall when Aline flew into his arms, with a cry of relief and desperation mingled, and began to pour into his ears all her bewilderment and anxiety.

'Oh, Hugh, I think I must have done something terrible! Either that, or Philip Corviser has gone mad. He was here asking after Emma, and when I told him she was gone he rushed away like a madman, and there's a merchant from Worcester in the stables accusing him of stealing his horse and making off with it, and what it all means I daren't guess, but I'm afraid . . .'

Hugh held her tenderly, dismayed and solicitous. 'Emma's

gone? But she was coming home with us. What happened to change it?'

'You know he's been paying attentions to her . . . He came this morning asking for you—he said he has a sister who is entering the nunnery at Minchinbarrow, and since he must escort her there, and it's barely five miles from Bristol, he could as well take Emma home in his sister's company. He said they'd sleep overnight at his manor, and set off tomorrow. Emma said yes, and I thought no wrong, why should I? But the very name has sent Philip off like a man demented . . .'

'Corbière?' demanded Hugh, holding her off by the shoulders to peer anxiously into her face.

'Yes! Yes, Ivo, of course—but what's so wrong in that? He takes her to his sister at Stanton Cobbold—I thought it ideal, so did she, and you were not here to say yes or no. Besides, she is her own mistress . . .'

True, the girl had a will of her own, and liked the man who had made the offer, and was flattered at being singled out for his favours. Even for the sake of her own independence she would have chosen to go, and Hugh, had he been present, would not then have known or suspected enough to prevent. He tightened his arms comfortingly round his trembling wife, his cheek pressed against her hair. 'My love, my heart, you could not have done anything but what you did, and I should have done the same. But I must go after. No questions now, you shall know everything later. We'll bring her back—there'll be no harm done. . . .'

'It's true, then!' whispered Aline, her breath fluttering against his throat. 'There's reason to fear harm? I've let her go into danger?'

'You could not stop her. She chose to go. Think no more of your part, you played none—how could you know? Where's Constance? Love, I hate to leave you like this . . .'

He was thinking, of course, like all men, she thought, that any grievous upset to his wife in this condition was a potential upset to his son. That roused her. She was not the girl to keep a man dancing anxious attention on her, even if she had a wife's claim on him, when he was needed more urgently elsewhere. She drew herself resolutely out of his arms.

'Of course you must leave me. I've taken no harm, and

shall take none. Go, quickly! They have a good three hours start of you, and besides, if you delay, Philip may run his head into trouble alone. Send quickly for what men you can muster, and I'll go see what I can do to placate the merchant whose horse has been borrowed . . .' He was loath, all the same, to let go of her. She took his head between her hands, kissed him hard, and turned him about, just as Cadfael came in at the hall door.

'She's gone with Corbière,' said Hugh, conveying news in the fewest words possible. 'Bound for his one Shropshire manor. The boy's off after them, and so must I. I'll send word to Prestcote to have a guard follow as fast as may be. You'll be here to take care of Aline . . .'

Aline doubted that, seeing the spark flare up in Brother Cadfael's bright and militant eye. Hastily she said: 'I need no one to nurse me. Only go—both of you!'

'I have licence,' said Cadfael, clutching at virtue to cover his ardour. 'Abbot Radulfus gave me the charge of seeing that his guest came to no harm under his roof, and I'll stretch that to extend beyond his roof, and make it good, too. You have a horse to spare, Hugh, besides that raw-boned dapple of yours. Come on! It's a year since you and I rode together.'

THREE

THE MANOR OF STANTON COBBOLD LAY A GOOD SEVENTEEN MILES from Shrewsbury, in the south of the shire, and cheek by jowl with the large property of the bishops of Hereford in those parts, which covered some nine or ten manors. The road lay through the more open and sunlit stretches of the Long Forest, and at its southernmost fringe plunged in among the hump-backed hills at the western side of a long, bare ridge that ran for some miles. Here and there a wooded valley backed into its bare flank, and into one of these Corbière turned, along a firm cart-track. It was the height of the early afternoon then, the sun at its highest, but even so the crowding trees cast sudden chill and shadow. The bay horse had worked off his high spirits, and went placidly under his double burden. Once in the forest they had halted briefly, and Ivo had produced wine and oat-cakes as refreshment on the journey, and paid Emma every possible delicate attention. The day was fair, the countryside strange to her and beautiful, and she was embarked on an agreeable adventure. She approached Stanton Cobbold with only the happiest anticipation, flattered by Ivo's deference, and eager to meet his sister.

A rivulet ran alongside the track, coming down from the ridge. The path narrowed, and the trees closed in.

'We are all but home,' said Ivo over his shoulder; and in a few minutes more the rising ground opened before them into a narrow, level plot enclosed before with a wooden stockade. Within, the manor house backed solidly into the hillside, trees at its back, trees shutting it in darkly at either end. A boy came running to open the gate for them, and they rode into the enclosure. Barns and byres lined the stockade within. The manor itself showed a long undercroft of stone, buttressed, and pierced with two doors wide enough for carts, and a living floor above, also of stone for most of its length, where the great hall and the kitchens and pantries lay, but at the right, stone gave place to timber, and stone mullions to wooden window-frames and stout shutters; and this wooden living apartment was taller than the stone portion, and seemed to have an additional floor above the solar. A tall stone stair led up to the hall door.

'Modest enough,' said Ivo, turning his head to smile at her, 'but it has room and a welcome for you.'

He was well served. Grooms came running before the horse had halted, a maid appeared in the hall doorway, and began to flutter down to meet them.

Ivo kicked his feet free of the stirrups, swung a leg nimbly over the horse's bowing head, and leaped down, waving Turstan Fowler aside, to stretch up his arms to Emma and lift her down himself. Her slight weight gave him no trouble, he held her aloft for a long moment to prove it, laughing, before he set her down.

'Come, I'll take you up to the solar.' He put off the maid with a nick of his hand, and she stood aside and followed them demurely up the steps, but let them go on without her when they reached the hall. The thick stone walls struck inward with a palpable chill. The hall was large and lofty, the high ceiling smoke-stained, but now, in the summer, the huge fireplace was empty and cold. The mullioned windows let in air far more genial than that within, and a comforting light, but they were narrow, and could do little to temper the oppression of the room. 'Not my most amiable home,' said Ivo with a grimace, 'but in these Welsh borders we built for defence, not for comfort. Come up to the solar. The timber end was built on later, but even there this is a chill, dark house. Even on summer evenings we need some firing.'

A short staircase at the end of the hall led up to a broad gallery and a pair of doors. 'The chapel,' he said, indicating that on the left. 'There are two small bedchambers above, dark, since they look into the hillside and the trees at close quarters. And in here, if you'll forgive me while I attend to your baggage and mine, and see the horses stabled, I'll rejoin you shortly.'

The solar into which he led her contained a massive table, a carved bench, cushioned chairs, tapestries draping the walls, and rugs on the floor, and was a place of some comfort and elegance, if also somewhat dim and cold, chiefly by reason of the looming hillside and the shrouding trees, and the narrow windows that let in so little of the day, and so filtered through heavy branches. Here there was no fireplace, the only chimney serving the hall and the kitchens; but the centre of the floor was set with large paving stones to make a hearth proof against cinders, and on this square a brazier burned, even on this summer day. Charcoal and wood glowed, discreetly massed, to give a central spark of comfort without smoke. Summer sunlight failed to warm through the arm's-length thickness of the stone walls below, and here the sun, though confronted only with friendly timber, hardly ever reached.

Emma went forward into the room and stood looking about

her curiously. She heard Ivo close the door between them, but it was only a very small sound in a large silence.

She had expected his sister to appear immediately on his return, and felt a pang of disappointment, though she knew it was unreasonable. He had sent no word ahead, how could the girl have known? She might, with good reason, be out walking on the open hill in the full summer warmth, or she might have duties elsewhere. When she did come, it would be to the pleasure of having her brother home, and with a visitor of her own sex and approximate age, into the bargain, and to hear that she was to have her will without further delay. Yet her absence was a disappointment, and his failure to remark on it or apologise for it was a check to her eagerness.

She began to explore the room, interested in everything. Her own city home was cushioned and comfortable by comparison, though no less dark and shut in, if not among trees, among the buildings the trees provided. She was aware that she had been born to comparative wealth, but wealth concentrated into one commodious and well-furbished dwelling, whereas this border manor represented only perhaps a tenth of what Ivo possessed, without regard to the land attached to all those manors. He had said himself that this was not the most genial of his homes, yet it held sway over she could not guess how many miles of land, and how many free tenants and unfree villeins. It was another world. She had looked at it from a distance, and been dazzled, but never to blindness.

She felt a conviction suddenly that it was not for her, though whether she was glad or sorry remained a mystery.

All the same, there was knowledge and taste here beyond her experience. The brazier was a beautiful thing, a credit to the smith who made it; on three braced legs like saplings, the fire-basket a trellis of vine-leaves. If it had a fault, it was that it was raised rather too high, she thought, to be completely stable. The cushions of the chairs were of fine embroidery of hunting scenes, though dulled by use and friction and the touch of slightly greasy fingers. On a shelf built under the table there were books, a psalter, a vellum folder of music, and a faded treatise with strange diagrams. The carving of chairs and table and bench-ends was like live plants growing. The tapestries that covered all the walls between windows and

door were surely old, rich, wonderfully worked, and once had
had glorious colours that showed still, here and there, in the
protected folds; but they were smoke-blackened almost beyond
recognition, rotted here and there into tinder. She parted a
fold, and the hound, plunging with snarling jaws and stretched
paws between her fingers, disintegrated into powdery dust,
and floated on the air in slow dissolution. She let fall the
threads she held, and retreated in dismay. The very dust on
her palms felt like ash.

She waited, but nobody came. Probably the time she waited
was not as long as she supposed, by no means as long as it
felt to her, but it seemed an age, a year of her life.

In the end, she thought she might not be offending by
wandering along the gallery into the chapel. She might at
least hear if there was any activity below. Ivo had bought
Flemish tapestries for his new Cheshire manor, he might well
be unbaling them and delighting in their fresh colours. She
could forgive a degree of neglect in such circumstances.

She set her hand to the latch of the door, and trustingly
lifted it. The door did not give. She tried it again, more
strongly, but the barrier remained immovable. No doubt of it,
the door was locked.

What she felt first was sheer incredulity, even amusement,
as if some foolish accident had dropped a latch and shut her
in by mistake. Then came the instinctive wish of every creature locked in, to get out; and only after that the flare of alarm
and the startled and furious reappraisal, in search of understanding. No mistake, no! Ivo's own hand had turned the key
on her.

She was not the girl to fall into a frenzy and batter on the
door. What good would that do? She stood quite still with the
latch in her hand, while her wits ran after truth as fiercely as
the hound in the tapestry after the hart. She was here in an
upstairs room, with no other door, and windows not only
narrow for even her slender body to pass through, but high
above ground, by reason of the slope. There was no way out
until someone unlocked the door.

She had come with him guilelessly, in good faith, and he
turned into her gaoler. What did he want of her? She knew
she had beauty, but suddenly was certain he would not go to

such trouble on that account. Not her person, then, and there was only one thing in her possession for which someone had been willing to go to extremes. Deaths had followed it wherever it passed. One of those deaths a servant of his had helped to bring about, and he had dealt out summary justice. A sordid attack for gain, a theft that accidentally ended in murder, and the stolen property found to prove it! She had accepted that as everyone had accepted it. To doubt it was to see beyond into a pit too black to be credited, but she was peering into that darkness now. It was Ivo, and no other, who had caged her.

If she could not pass through the windows, the letter she carried could, though that would be to risk others finding it. Its weight was light, it would not carry far. All the same, she crossed to the windows and peered out through the slits at the slope of grass and the fringe of trees below; and there, sprawled at ease against the bole of a beech with his arbalest beside him, was Turstan Fowler, looking up idly at these very windows. When he caught sight of her face between the timbers of the frame, he grinned broadly. No help there.

She withdrew from the window, trembling. Quickly she drew up, from its resting-place between her breasts, the small, tightly-rolled vellum bag she had carried ever since Master Thomas had hung it about her neck, before they reached Shrewsbury. It measured almost the length of her hand, but was thin as two fingers of that same hand, and the thread on which it hung was of silk, cobweb-fine. It did not need a very large hiding-place. She coiled the silk thread about it, and rolled it carefully into the great swathe of blue-black tresses coiled within her coif of silken net, until its shape was utterly shrouded and lost. When she had adjusted the net to hold it secure, and every strand of hair lay to all appearances undisturbed, she stood with hands clasped tightly to steady them, and drew in long breaths until the racing of her heart was calmed. Then she put the brazier between herself and the door, and looking up across the room, felt the heart she had just steeled to composure leap frantically in her breast.

Once again she had failed to hear the key turn in the lock. He kept his defences well oiled and silent. He was there in the doorway, smiling with easy confidence, closing the door behind him without taking his eyes from her. She knew by the motion of his arm and shoulder that he had transferred the key to the inner side, and again turned it. Even in his own manor, with his household about him, he took no risks. Even with no more formidable opponent than Emma Vernold! It was, in its way, a compliment, but one she could have done without.

Since he could not know whether she had or had not tried the door, she chose to behave as if nothing had happened to disturb her. She acknowledged his entrance with an expectant smile, and opened her lips to force out some harmless enquiry, but he was before her.

'Where is it? Give it to me freely, and come to no harm. I would advise it.'

He was in no hurry, and he was still smiling. She saw now that his smile was a deliberate gloss, as cold, smooth and decorative as a coat of gilt. She gazed at him wide-eyed, the blank, bewildered stare of one suddenly addressed in an unknown tongue. 'I don't understand you! What is it I'm to give you?'

'Dear girl, you know only too well. I want the letter your uncle was carrying to Earl Ranulf of Chester, the same he should have delivered at the fair, by prior agreement, to Euan of Shotwick, my noble kinsman's eyes and ears.' He was willing to go softly with her, since time was now no object, he even found the prospect amusing, and was prepared to admire her playing of the game, provided he got his own way in the end. 'Never tell me, sweet, that you have not even heard of any such letter. I doubt if you make as good a liar as I do.'

'Truly,' she said, shaking her head helplessly, 'I understand you not at all. There is nothing else I could say to you, for I know nothing of a letter. If my uncle carried one, as you claim, he never confided in me. Do you suppose a man of business takes his womenfolk into his confidence over important matters? You're mistaken in him if you believe that.'

Corbière came forward an idle pace or two into the room, and she saw that no trace of his limp remained. The brazier had burned into a steady, scarlet glow, the light from it reflected like the burnish of sunset along the waving gold of his hair. 'So I thought,' he agreed, and laughed at the memory. 'It took me a long time, too long, to arrive at you, my lady. *I* would not have trusted a woman, no. . . . But Master Thomas, it seems, had other ideas. And I grant you, he had an unusual young woman to deal with. For what it's worth, I admire you. But I shall not let that stand in my way, believe me. What you hold is too precious to leave me any scruples, even if I were given to such weaknesses.'

'But I don't hold it! I can't give you what I have not in my possession. How can I convince you?' she demanded, with the first spurt of impatience and indignation, though she knew in advance that she was wasting all pretences. He knew.

He shook his head at her, smiling. 'It is not in your baggage. We've taken apart even the seams of your saddle-bags. Therefore it is here, on your person. There is no other possibility. It was not on your uncle, it was neither in his barge nor in his booth. Who was left but you? You, and Euan of Shotwick, if I had somehow let a messenger slip through my guard. You, I knew, would keep, and come tamed to my hand—but for a sudden qualm I had, that you might have sent it back in Thomas's coffin for safe-keeping, but that was to overrate you, my dear, clever as you are. And Euan never received it. Who was then left, but you? Not his crew—all of them far too simple, even if he had not had orders to keep strict secrecy, as I know he had. I doubt if he told even you what was in the letter.'

It was true, she had no idea of its contents. She had simply been given it to wear and guard, as the obvious innocent who would never come under suspicion of being anyone's courier, but its importance had been impressed upon her most powerfully. Lives, her uncle had said, hung upon its safe delivery, or, failing that, its safe return to the sender. Or, in the last resort, its total destruction.

'I am tired of telling you,' she said forcefully, 'that you are wrong in supposing that I know anything about it, or believe it ever existed but in your imagination. You brought me here, my lord, on the pretext of providing me the companionship of your sister, and conducting us both to Bristol. Do you intend to do as you promised?'

He threw his head back and laughed aloud, the red glow

dancing on his fine cheekbones. 'You would not have come with me if there had not been a woman in the story. If you behave sensibly now you may yet meet, some day, the only sister I have. She's married to one of Ranulf's knights, and keeps me informed of what goes on in Ranulf's court. But devil a nun she'd ever have made, even if she were not already a wife. But send you safe home to Bristol—yes, that I'll do, when you've given me what I want from you. And what I will have!' he added with a snap, and his shapely, smiling lips thinned and tightened into a sword-blade.

There was a moment, then, when she almost considered obeying him, and giving up what she had kept so obstinately through so many shocks. Fear was a reality by this time, but so was anger, all the more fierce because she was so resolutely suppressing it. He came a step towards her, his smile as narrow as a cat's bearing down on a bird, and she moved just as steadily to keep the brazier between them; that also amused him, but he had ample patience.

'I don't understand,' she said, frowning as if she had begun to feel genuine curiosity, 'why you should set such store on a letter. If I had it, do you think I should refuse it to you, when I'm in your power? But why does it matter to you so much? What can there be in a mere letter?'

'Fool girl, there can be life and death in a letter,' he said, condescending to her simplicity, 'wealth, power, even land to be won or lost. Do you know what that single packet could be worth? To King Stephen, his kingdom entire! To me, maybe, an earldom. And to a number of others, their necks! For I think you must know, for all your innocence, that Robert of Gloucester has his plans made to bring the Empress Maud to England, and make a fight of it for her claim to the throne, and has been touting through his agents here to get Earl Ranulf's support for her cause when they do land. My noble kinsman has a hard head, and has demanded proof of the strength of that cause before he lifts a hand or stirs a foot to commit himself. Names, numbers, every detail, if I know my Ranulf, they've been forced to set down in writing for him. All the tale of the king's enemies, the names of all those who pay him lip service now but are preparing to betray him. There could be as many as fifty names on the list, and it will serve, believe me, for Ranulf's ruin no less, since if his name is not there, he had reached the point of considering adding it. What will not King Stephen give, to have that delivered into his hand? All committed to writing, it may be even the date they plan to sail, and the port where they hope to land. All his enemies cut off before they can forgather, a prison prepared for Maud before ever she sets foot ashore. That, my child, is what I propose to offer to the king, and never doubt but I shall get my price for it.'

She stood staring at him with drawn brows and shocked eyes across the brazier, and felt her blood chill in her veins and all her body grow cold. And he was not even a partisan! He had killed, or procured others to kill for him, three times already, not for a cause, but coldly and methodically for his own gain and advancement. He cared nothing at all for which of them wore the crown, Stephen or Maud. If he could have got his hands rather on information of value to Maud, and felt that she was likely to prevail and reward him well, he would have betrayed Stephen and all his supporters just as blithely.

For the first time she was terrified, the weight of all those imperilled lives lay upon her heart like a great stone. She had no doubt that his estimate of what would be in the letter must be very close to the truth, close enough to destroy a great many men who adhered to the same side her uncle had served with devotion. He had been a passionate partisan, and it had cost him his life. Now, unless she could bring about a miracle, the message he had carried would cost many more lives, bloodshed, bereavement, ruin. And all for the enrichment and advancement of Ivo Corbière! She had followed and supported Master Thomas as a matter of family loyalty. Now that meant nothing any longer, and all she felt was a desperate desire to avoid more killing, not to betray any man on either side of the quarrel to his enemies on the other. To help every fugitive, to hide every hunted man, to keep the wives unwidowed and the children still fathered, was better by far than to fight and kill either for Stephen or for Maud.

And she would not let him have them! Whatever the cost, he should not tread his way unscathed to his earldom over other men's faces.

'I have nothing against you,' Corbière was saying, confident and at ease. 'Give me the letter, and you shall reach Bristol in safety, and not be the loser. But don't think I'll scruple to pay you in full, either, if you thwart me.'

She stood fixed and still, her hands cupping her face, as though pressing hard to contain fear. The tips of her fingers worked unseen under the edge of her tissue net into the coils of her hair, feeling for the little cylinder of vellum, but face to face with her he saw no movement at all.

'Come, you are not so attractive to me that you need fear rape,' he said, disdainfully smiling, 'provided you are sensible, but for all that, it would be no hardship to me to strip you with my own hands, if you are obstinate. It might even give me pleasure, if the act proves stimulating. Give, or have it taken from you by force. You should know by now that I let no man stand in my way, much less a little shopkeeper's girl of no account.'

Of no account! No, she had never been of any account to him, never for a moment, only of use in his ruthless pursuit of his own ambitious interests. Still she stood as if frozen, except that when he advanced upon her at leisure, his smile now wolfish and hungry, she circled inch by inch to keep the brazier between them. Its heart was a red glow. She stood close, as if only that core of warmth gave her some comfort and protection; and suddenly she tore down the coil of her hair and clawed out the letter, tearing off her silken net with it in her haste. She dared not simply cast it into the fire, it might roll clear or be too easily retrieved. She made a desperate lunge, and thrusting it deep into the heart of the glow, held it there for an agonised moment, snatching back burned fingers with a faint cry that sounded half of pain and half of triumph.

He uttered a bellow of rage, and lunged as quickly to snatch it out again, but the net had flared at a touch, tiny worms of fire climbed to lick his hand, and all he touched of the precious letter, before he recoiled, was the wax of the seal, which had melted at once, and clung searingly to his fingers as he wrung them and whined with pain. She heard herself laughing, and could not believe she was the source of the sound. She heard him frantically cursing her, but he was too intent on recovering his prize to turn upon her then. He tore off his cotte, wrapped a corner of the skirt about his hand, and leaned to grasp again at the glowing cylinder thrust upright in the fire-basket. And he would get it, defaced and incomplete, perhaps, but enough for his purpose. The outer covering was not yet burned through everywhere. He should not have it, she would not bear it! She stooped as he snatched at it, clutched with her good hand at the leg of the brazier, and overturned it over his ankles and feet.

He screamed aloud and leaped back. Glowing coals flew, cascading over the floor, starting a brown furrow, a flurry of smoke and a stink of burning wool across the nearest rug, and reached the tinder-dry skirts of the tapestries on the wall between the two windows. There was a strange sound like a great indrawn breath, and an instant serpent of flame climbed the wall, and after it a tree of fire grew, thickened, put out lightning branches on all sides, enveloped all the space between the windows, and coursed both ways like hounds at fault, to reach the dusty hangings on the neighbouring walls. A brittle shell of fire encased the room before Emma could even stir from her horrified stillness. She saw the huntsmen and huntresses in the tapestries blaze for an instant into quivering life, the hounds leap, the forest trees shimmer in fierce light, before they disintegrated into glittering dust. Smoke rose from a dozen burning fragments over half the floor, and vision dimmed rapidly.

Somewhere in that abrupt hell beyond the hearth, Ivo Corbière, shirt and hair aflame, a length of blazing tapestry fallen upon him, rolled and shrieked in agony, the sounds he made tearing her senses. Behind her one wall of the room was still clean, but the circling flames were licking round both ways towards it.

There was a rug untouched at her back, she dragged it up and tried to reach the burning man with it, but smoke thickened quickly, stinging and blinding her eyes, and flashing tongues of fire jetted out of the smoke and drove her back. She flung the rug, in case he could still clutch at it and roll himself in its smothering folds, but she knew then that it was too late for anyone to help him. The room was already thick with smoke, she clutched her wide sleeve over mouth and nostrils, and drew back from the awful screaming that shrilled in her ears. And he had the key of the room on him! No hope of reaching him now, no hope of recovering the key. The room was ablaze, timber at window and wall and floor began to cry out in loud cracks and splitting groans, spurting strange jets of flame.

Emma drew back, shielding her face, and hammered at the door, shrieking for help against the furious sounds of the fire. She thought she heard cries somewhere below, but distantly. She knotted her hands in the tapestries on either side the door, where the flames had not yet reached, tore the rotting fabric down, rolled it up tightly to resist sparks, and hurled it into the furnace on the other side of the room. Let the door, at least, remain passable. All the hangings that were not yet burning she dragged down. Her seared hand she had forgotten, she used it as freely as the other. All those other lives, surely, were safe enough, no one was ever going to read the letter that had failed to reach Ranulf of Chester. Even that fearful life shut in this room with her must be all but over, the sounds were almost lost in the voice of the fire. A busy, preoccupied voice, not unlike the obsessed hum of the fairground. She had a life to lose, too. She was young, angry, resolute, she would not lose it tamely. She hammered at the door, and called again. No one came. She heard no voices, no hasty footsteps on the stairs to the gallery, nothing but the singing of the fire, mounting steadily from a hum to a roar, like a rioting crowd, but better harmonised, the triumphant utterance of a single will.

Emma stooped to the keyhole, and called through it as long as breath and strength lasted. She could neither see nor think by then, all about her was gathering blackness, and a throttling hand upon her throat. From stooping she sank to her knees, and from her knees sagged forward along the base of the door, and lay there with mouth and nose pressed against the gap that let in a thread of clean air. After a while she was not aware of anything, even of breathing.

FOUR

PHILIP LOST HIMSELF BRIEFLY IN THE TANGLE OF SMALL VALLEY tracks that threaded the hills, after leaving the Long Forest, and was forced to hunt out a local man from the first assart he came to, to put him on the road for Stanton Cobbold. The region he knew vaguely, but not the manor. The cottar gave him precise instructions, and turning to follow his own pointing, saw the first thin column of smoke going up into a still sky, and rapidly thickening and darkening as he stared at it.

'That could be the very place, or near it. The woods are dry enough for trouble. God send they can keep it from the house, if some fool's set a spark going . . .'

'How far is it?' demanded Philip, wildly staring.

'A mile and over. You'd best . . .' But Philip was gone, heels driving into his stolen horse's sides, off at a headlong gallop. He kept his eyes upon that growing, billowing column of smoke more often than upon the road, and took risks on those little-used and eccentric paths, that might have fetched him down a dozen times if luck had not favoured him. With every minute, the spectacle grew more alarming, the red of flames belching upward spasmodically against the black of smoke. Long before he reached the manor, and came bursting out of the trees towards the stockade, he could hear the bursting of beams, splitting apart in the heat with louder reports than any axe-blow. It was the house, not the forest.

The gate stood open, and within, frantic servants ran confusedly, dragging out from hall and kitchen whatever belongings they could, salvaging from the stables and byres, dangerously near to the wooden part of the house, terrified and shrieking horses, and bellowing cattle. Philip stared aghast at the tower of smoke and flames that engulfed one end of the

198

house. The long stone building of hall and undercroft would stand, though as a gutted shell, but the timbered part was already a furnace. Confused men and screaming maids ran about distractedly and paid him no heed. The disaster had overtaken them so suddenly that they were half out of their wits.

Philip kicked his feet out of the stirrups which were short for him, but which he had never paused to lengthen, and vaulted from the horse, leaving it to wander at will. One of the cowmen blundered across his path, and Philip seized him by the arm and wrenched him round to face him.

'Where's your lord? Where's the girl he brought here today?' The man was dazed and slow to answer; he shook him furiously. 'The girl—what has he done with her?'

Gaping helplessly, the man pointed into the pillar of smoke. 'They're in the solar—my lord as well . . . It's there the fire began.'

Philip dropped him without a word, and began to run towards the stair to the hall door. The man howled after him: 'Fool, it's the hob of hell in there, nothing could live in it! And the door's locked—he had the key with him . . . You'll go to your death!'

Nothing of this made any impression upon Philip, until mention of the locked door checked him sharply. If there was no other way in, by a locked door he would have to enter. He cast about him at all the piles of hangings and furnishings and utensils they had dragged out into the courtyard, for something he could use to break through such a barrier. The kitchen had been emptied, there were meat-choppers and knives, but, better still, there was a pile of arms from the hall. One of Corbière's ancestors, it seemed, had favoured the battle-axe. And these craven creatures of the household had made no attempt to use so handy a weapon! Their lord could roast before they would risk a burned hand for him.

Philip went up the stone steps three at a time, and into the black and stifling cavern of the hall. The heat, after all, was not so intense here, the stone walls were thick, and the floor, too, was laid with stones over the great beams of the undercroft. The worst enemy was the smoke that bit acrid and poisonous into his throat at the first breath. He spared the few moments it took to tear off his shirt and bind it round his face to cover nose and mouth, and then began to grope his way at reckless speed along the wall towards the other end of the hall, whence the heat and the fumes came. He did not think at all, he did what he had to do. Emma was somewhere in that inferno, and nothing mattered but to get her out of it.

He found the foot of the staircase to the gallery by stumbling blindly over the first step, and went up the flight stooped low, because it seemed that the bulk of the smoke was rolling along the roof. The shape of the solar door he found by the framework of smoke pouring in a thin, steady stream all round it. The wood itself was not yet burning. He hammered and strained at the door, and called, but there was no sound from within but the crackling of the fire. No way but to go through.

He swung the axe like a berserker Norseman, aiming at the lock. The door was stout, the wood old and seasoned, but less formidable axes had felled the trees that made it. His eyes smarted, streaming tears that helped by damping the cloth that covered his mouth. The blows started the beams of the door, but the lock held. Philip went on swinging. He had started a deep crack just above the lock, so deep that he had trouble withdrawing the axe. Time after time he struck at the same place, aware of splinters flying, and suddenly the lock burst clear with a harsh, metallic cry, and the edge of the door gave, only to stick again when he had thrust it open no more than a hand's breadth. The upper part, when he groped round it, offered no resistance. He felt along the floor within, and closed his hand upon a coil of silky hair. She was there, lying along the doorway, and though the heat that gushed out at him was terrifying, yet only the smoke, not the flames, had reached her.

The opening of the door had provided a way through for the wind that fed the flames, such a brightness burned up beyond the black that he knew he had only minutes before the blaze swept over them both. Frantically he leaned to get a grasp of her arm and drag her aside, so that he could open the door for the briefest possible moment, just wide enough to lift her through, and again draw it to against the demon within.

There was a great explosion of scarlet and flame, that sent

a tongue out through the opening to singe his hair, and then he had her, the soft, limp weight hoisted on his shoulder, the door dragged to again behind them, and he was half-falling, half-running down the staircase with her in his arms, and the devil of fire had done no worse than snap at their heels. He did not even realise, until he took off his shoes much later, that the very treads of the stairs had been burning under his feet.

He reached the hall doorway with head lolling and chest labouring for breath, and had to sit down with his burden on the stone steps, for fear of falling with her. Greedily he dragged the clean outside air into him, and pulled down the smoke-fouled shirt from about his face. Vision and hearing were blurred and distant, he did not even know that Hugh Beringar and his guard had come galloping into the courtyard, until Brother Cadfael scurried up the steps to take Emma gently from him.

'Good lad! I have her. Come away down after us—lean on me as we go, so! Let's find you a safe corner, and we'll see what we can do for you both.'

Philip, suddenly shivering, and so feeble he dared not trust his legs to stand, asked in urgent, aching terror: 'Is she. . . . ?'

'She's breathing,' said Brother Cadfael reassuringly. 'Come and help me care for her, and with God's blessing, she'll do.'

Emma opened her eyes upon a clean, pale sky and two absorbed and anxious faces. Brother Cadfael's she knew at once, for it bore its usual shrewdly amiable aspect, though how he had come to be there, or where, indeed, she was, she could not yet divine. The other face was so close to her own that she saw it out of focus, and it was wild and strange enough, grimed from brow to chin, the blackness seamed with dried rivulets of sweat, the brown hair along one temple curled and brown from burning! but it had two fine, clear brown eyes as honest as the daylight above, and fixed upon her with such devotion that the face, marred as it was, and never remarkable for beauty, seemed to her the most pleasing and comforting she had ever seen. The face on which her eyes had last looked, before it became a frightful lantern of flame, had been the face of ambition, greed and murder, in a plausible shell of beauty. This face was the other side of the human coin.

Only when she stirred slightly, and he moved his position to accommodate her more comfortably, did she realise that she was lying in his arms. Feeling and awareness came back gradually, even pain took its time. Her head was cradled in the hollow of his shoulder, her cheek rested against the breast of his cotte. A craftsman's working clothes, homespun. Of course, he was a shoemaker. A shopkeeper's boy, of no account! There was much to be said for it. The stink of smoke and burning still hung about them both, in spite of Cadfael's attentions with a pannikin of water from the well. The shopkeeper's boy of no account had come into the manor after her, and brought her out alive. She had mattered as much as that to him. A little shopkeeper's girl. . . .

'Her eyes are open,' said Philip in an eager whisper. 'She's smiling.'

Cadfael stooped to her. 'How is it with you now, daughter?'

'I am alive,' she said, almost inaudibly, but with great joy.

'So you are, God be thanked, and Philip here next after God. But lie still, we'll find you a cloak to wrap you in, for you'll be feeling the cold that comes after danger. There'll be pain, too, my poor child.' She already knew about the pain. 'You've a badly burned hand, and I've no salves here. I can do no more than cover it from the air, until we get back to town. Leave your hand lie quiet, if you can, the stiller the better. How did it come that you escaped clean, but for the one hand so badly burned?'

'I put it into the brazier,' said Emma, remembering. She saw with what startled eyes Philip received this, and realised what she had said; and suddenly the most important thing of all seemed to her that Philip should not know everything, that his candid clarity should not be made to explore the use of lies, deceptions and subterfuges, no matter how right the cause they served. Some day she might tell someone, but it would not be Philip. 'I was afraid of him,' she said, carefully amending, 'and I tipped over the brazier. I never meant to start such a fire . . .'

Somewhere curiously distant from the corner of peace where she lay, Hugh Beringar and the sergeant and officers who had followed him from Shrewsbury were mustering the distracted servants in salvage, and damping down all the outhouses that were still in danger from flying sparks and debris, so that the beasts could be housed, and a roof, at least, provided for the men and maids. The fire had burned so fiercely that it was already dying down, but not for some days would the heat have subsided enough for them to sift through the embers for Ivo Corbière's body.

'Lift me,' entreated Emma. 'Let me see!'

Philip raised her to sit beside him in the clean, green grass. They were in a corner of the court, their backs against the stockade. Round the perimeter the barns and byres steamed in the early evening sun from the buckets of water which had been thrown over them. Close to the solar end, men were still at work carrying buckets in a chain from the well. There would be roofs enough left to shelter horses, cattle and people, until better could be done for them. They had the equipment of the kitchen, the stores in the undercroft might be damaged, but would not all be spoiled. In this summer weather they would do well enough, and someone must make shift to have the manor restored before the winter. All that terror, in the end, had taken but one life.

'He is dead,' she said, staring at the ruin from which she, though not he, had emerged alive.

'No other possibility,' said Cadfael simply.

He surmised, but she knew. 'And the other one?'

'Turstan Fowler? He's prisoner. The sergeant has him in charge. It was he, I believe,' said Cadfael gently, 'who killed your uncle.'

She had expected that at the approach of Beringar and the law he would have helped himself to a horse and taken to his heels, but after all, he had known of no reason why he should. No one had been accusing him when he left Shrewsbury. Everyone at the abbey ought to have taken it for granted that Emma had been duly conducted home to Bristol. Why should they question it? Why *had* they questioned it? She had much to learn, as well as much to tell. There would be time, later. Now there was no time for anything but living, and exulting in living, and being glad and grateful, and perhaps, gradually and with unpractised pleasure, loving.

'What will become of him?' she asked.

'He'll surely tell all he knows, and lay the worst blame where it belongs, on his lord.' Cadfael doubted, all the same, whether Turstan could hope to evade the gallows, and doubted whether he should, but he did not say so to her. She was deeply preoccupied at this moment with life and death, and willed mercy even to the lowest and worst in the largeness of the mercy shown to her. And that was good, God forbid he should say any word to deface it.

'Are you cold?' asked Philip tenderly, feeling her shiver in his arm.

'No,' she said at once, and turned her head a little in the hollow of his shoulder, resting her forehead against his grimy cheek. He felt the soft curving of her lips in the hollow of his throat as she smiled, and was filled with so secure a sense of possession that no one would ever be able to take her away from him.

Hugh Beringar came to them across the trampled grass of the court, even his neatness smoked and odorous.

'What can be done's done,' he said, wiping his face. 'We had better get her back to Shrewsbury, there's no provision here. I'm leaving my sergeant and most of the men here for the time being, but the place for you,' he said, smiling somewhat wearily at Emma, 'is in a comfortable bed, with your hurt properly dressed, and no need for you to think or stir until you're restored. Bristol will have to wait for you. We'll take you to Aline at the abbey, you'll be easy there.'

'No,' said Philip, with large assurance. 'I am taking Emma to my mother in Shrewsbury.'

'Very well, so you shall,' agreed Hugh, 'it's hardly a step further. But give Cadfael time at the abbey to hunt out the salves and potions he wants from his workshop, and let Aline see for herself that we've not let Emma come to any great harm. And don't forget, friend, you owe Aline something for entertaining the fellow you robbed of his horse, and guarding your back for you until you can restore him.'

Beneath his coating of soot Philip could still blush. 'True enough, I'm likely to end in gaol again for theft, but not until I've seen Emma safe lodged in my mother's care.'

Hugh laughed, and clapped him amiably on the shoulder.

204

'Nor then nor ever, while I'm in office—not unless you choose to kick the law in the teeth on some other occasion. We'll satisfy the merchant, Aline will have sweetened him into complacency, you'll find. And his horse has been rubbed down and watered and rested, while you've been otherwise occupied, and we'll take him back with us unloaded, none the worse for his adventures. There are horses enough here. I'll find you the pick of them, a steady ride fit to bear two.' He had had one eye on Emma while he had been mustering water-carriers and husbanding household effects, he knew better than to try to wrest her out of Philip's arms, or send for a horse-litter to carry her back. There were two here so joined together that only a fool would attempt to part them even for a few hours; and Hugh was no fool.

They wrapped her gently in a brychan borrowed from the salvaged bedding, rather for comfortable padding than for warmth, for the evening was still serene and mild, though she might yet suffer the cold that comes after effort is all over. She accepted everything with serenity, like one in a dream, though the pain of her hand must, they reasoned, be acute. She seemed to feel nothing but a supreme inner peace that made everything else of no account. They mounted Philip on a great, broad-backed, steady-paced gelding, and then lifted Emma up to him in her swathing blanket, and she settled into the cradle of his lap and arms and braced shoulder as though God had made her to fit there.

'And perhaps so he did,' said Brother Cadfael, riding behind with Hugh Beringar close beside him.

'So he did what?' wondered Hugh, starting out of very different considerations, for two officers brought a bound Turstan Fowler behind them.

'Direct all,' said Cadfael. 'It is, after all, a way he has.'

Halfway back towards Shrewsbury she fell asleep in his arms, nestled on his breast. For the fall of her black, smoke-scented hair he could see only the lower part of her face, but the mouth was soft and moist and smiling, and all her weight melted and moulded into the cradle of his loving body as into a marriage-bed. In her dream she had gone somewhere beyond the pain of her burned hand. It was as if she had thrust her hand into the future, and found it worth the price. The left hand, the unmarked one, lay clasped warmly round him, inside his coat, holding him close to her in her dream.

FIVE

THE SUMMER DARKNESS OF FINE NIGHTS, WHICH IS NEVER QUITE dark, showed a horse-fair deserted, no trace of the past three days but the trampled patches and the marks of trestles in the grass. All over for another year. The abbey stewards had gathered in the profits of rent and toll and tax, delivered their accounts, and gone to their beds. So had the monks of the abbey, the lay servants, the novices and the pupils. A sleepy porter opened the gate for them; and mysteriously, at the sounds of their arrival, though circumspect and subdued, the great court awoke to life. Aline came running from the guest-hall with the aggrieved merchant, now remarkably complacent, at her back, Brother Mark from the dortoir, and Abbot Radulfus's own clerk from the abbot's lodging, with a bidding to Brother Cadfael to attend there as soon as he arrived, however late the hour.

'I sent him word what was toward,' said Hugh, 'as we left. It was right he should know. He'll be anxious to hear how it ended.'

While Aline took Emma and Philip, half awake and dazedly docile, to rest and refresh themselves in the guest-hall, and Brother Mark ran to the herbarium to collect the paste of mulberry leaves and the unguent of Our Lady's mantle, known specifics for burns, and the men-at-arms went on to the castle with their prisoner, Brother Cadfael duly attended Radulfus in his study. Whether at midday or midnight, the abbot was equally wide-awake. By the single candle burning he surveyed Cadfael and asked simply: 'Well?'

'It is well, Father. We are returned with Mistress Vernold safe and little the worse, and the murderer of her uncle is in the sheriff's hands. One murderer—the man Turstan Fowler.'

'There is another?' asked Radulfus.

'There *was* another. He is dead. Not by any man's hand, Father, none of us has killed or done violence. He is dead by fire.'

'Tell me,' said the abbot.

Cadfael told him the whole story, so far as he knew it, and briefly. How much more Emma knew was a matter for conjecture.

'And what,' the abbot wished to know, 'can this communication have been, to cause any man to commit such crimes in pursuit of it?'

'That we do not know, and no man now will know, for it is burned with him. But where there are two warring factions in a land,' said Cadfael, 'men without scruples can turn controversy to gain, sell men for profit, take revenge on their rivals, hope to be awarded the lands of those they betray. Whatever evil was intended, now will never come to fruit.'

'A better ending than I began to fear,' said Radulfus, and drew a thankful sigh. 'Then all danger is now over, and the guests of our house are come to no harm.' He pondered for a moment. 'This young man who did so well for us and for the girl—you say he is son to the provost?'

'He is, Father. I am going with them now, with your permission, to see them safely home and dress their burns. They are not too grave, but they should be cleansed and tended at once.'

'Go with God's blessing!' said the abbot. 'It is convenient, for I have a message to the provost, which you may deliver for me, if you will. Ask Master Corviser, with my compliments, if he will be kind enough to attend here tomorrow morning, about the end of chapter. I have some business to transact with him.'

Mistress Corviser had undoubtedly been fulminating for hours about her errant son, a good-for-nothing who was no sooner bailed out of prison than he was off in mischief somewhere else until midnight and past. Probably she had said at least a dozen times that she washed her hands of him, that he was past praying for, and she no longer cared, let him go to the devil his own way. But for all that, her husband could not get her to go to bed, and at every least sound that might be a footstep at the door or in the street, steady or staggering, she flew to look out, with her mouth full of abuse but her heart full of hope.

And then, when he did come, it was with a great-eyed girl in his arm, a thick handful of his curls singed off at one temple, the smell of smoke in his coat, his shirt in tatters, a monk of Saint Peter's at his heels, and a look of roused authority and maturity about him that quite overcame his draggled and soiled state. And instead of either scolding or embracing him, she took both him and the girl by the hand and drew them inside together, and went about seating, feeding, tending them, with only few words, and those practical and concerned. Tomorrow Philip might be brought to tell the whole story. Tonight it was Cadfael who told the merest skeleton of it, as he cleansed and dressed Emma's hand, and the superficial burns on Philip's brow and arm. Better not make too much of what the boy had done. Emma would take care of that, later; his mother would value it most of all from her.

Emma herself said almost nothing, islanded in her exhaustion and bliss, but her eyes seldom left Philip, and when they did, it was to take in with deep content the solid, dark furnishings and warm panelling of this burgess house, so familiar to her that being accepted here was like coming home. Her rapt, secret smile was eloquent; mothers are quick to notice such looks. Emma had already conquered, even before she was led gently away to the bed prepared for her, and settled there by Mistress Corviser with all the clucking solicitude of a hen with one chick, with a posset laced with Brother Cadfael's poppy syrup to make sure that she slept, and forgot her pain.

'As pretty a thing as ever I saw,' said Mistress Corviser, coming back softly into the room, and closing the door between. She cast a fond look at her son, and found him asleep in his chair. 'And to think that's what he was about, while I was thinking all manner of bad things about him, who should have known him better!'

'He knows himself a deal better than he did a few days ago,' said Cadfael, repacking his scrip. 'I'll leave you these pastes and ointments, you know how to use them. But I'll come and take a look at her later tomorrow. Now I'll take my leave, I confess I'm more than ready for my own bed. I doubt if I shall hear the bell for Prime tomorrow.'

In the yard Geoffrey Corviser was himself stabling the horse from Stanton Cobbold with his own. Cadfael gave him the abbot's message. The provost raised sceptical eyebrows. 'Now what can the lord abbot want with me? The last time I came cap in hand to chapter, I got a dusty answer.'

'All the same,' advised Cadfael, scrubbing thoughtfully at his blunt brown nose, 'in your shoes I think I'd be curious enough to come and see. Who knows but the dust may have settled elsewhere by this time!'

It was no wonder if Brother Cadfael, though he did manage to rise for Prime, took advantage of his carefully chosen place behind a pillar to doze his way through chapter. He was so sound asleep, indeed, that for once he was in danger of snoring, and at the first melodious horn-call Brother Mark took fright, and nudged him awake.

The provost had obeyed the abbot's invitation to the letter, and arrived only at the very end of chapter. The steward of the grange court had just announced that he was in attendance when Cadfael opened his eyes.

'What can the provost be here for?' whispered Mark.

'He was asked to come. Do I know why? Hush!'

Geoffrey Corviser came in in his best, and made his reverence respectfully but coolly. He had no solid cohort at his back this time, and to tell the truth, though he may have felt some curiosity, he was attaching very little importance to this encounter. His mind was on other things. True, the problems of the town remained, and at any other time would have taken foremost place in his concern, but today he was proof against public cares by reason of private elation in a son vindicated and praised, a son to be proud of.

'You sent for me, Father Abbot. I am here.'

'I thank you for your courtesy in attending,' said the abbot mildly. 'Some days ago, master Provost, before the fair, you came with a request to me which I could not meet.'

The provost said not a word; there was none due, and he felt no need to speak at a loss.

'The fair is now over,' said the abbot equably. 'All the rents, tolls and taxes have been collected, and all have been delivered into the abbey treasury, as is due by charter. Do you endorse that?'

'It is the law,' said Corviser, 'to the letter.'

'Good! We are agreed. Right has therefore been done, and the privilege of this house is maintained. That I could not infringe by any prior concession. Abbots who follow me would have blamed me, and with good reason. Their rights are sacrosanct. But now they have been met in full. And as abbot of this house, it is for me to determine what use shall be made of the monies in our hold. What I could not grant away in imperilment of charter,' said Radulfus with deliberation, 'I can give freely as a gift from this house. Of the fruits of this year's fair, I give a tenth to the town of Shrewsbury, for the repair of the walls and repaving of the streets.'

The provost, enlarged in his family content, flushed into startled and delighted acknowledgement, a generous man accepting generosity. 'My lord, I take your tenth with pleasure and gratitude, and I will see that it is used worthily. And I make public here and now that no part of the abbey's right is thereby changed. Saint Peter's Fair is your fair. Whether and when your neighbour town should also benefit, when it is in dire need, that rests with your judgment.'

'Our steward will convey you the money,' said Radulfus, and rose to conclude a satisfactory encounter. 'This chapter is concluded,' he said.

SIX

AUGUST CONTINUED BLESSEDLY FINE, AND ALL HANDS TURNED gladly to making sure of the harvest. Hugh Beringar and Aline set off with their hopes and purchases for Maesbury, as did the merchant of Worcester for his home town, a day late, but well compensated with a fee for the hire of his horse in an emergency, on the sheriff's business, and a fine story which he would retail on suitable occasions for the rest of his life. The provost and council of Shrewsbury drafted a dignified acknowledgement to the abbey for its gift, warm enough to give proper expression to their appreciation of the gesture, canny enough not to compromise any of their own just claims for the future. The sheriff put on record the closure of a criminal affair, as related to him by the young woman who had been lured away on false pretences, with the apparent design of stealing from her a letter left in her possession, but of the contents of which she was ignorant. There was some suspicion of a conspiracy involved, but as Mistress Vernold had never seen nor been told the significance of what she held, and as in any case it was now irrevocably lost by fire, no further action was necessary or possible. The malefactor was dead, his servant, self-confessed a murderer at his master's orders, awaited trial, and would plead that he had been forced to obey, being villein-born and at his lord's mercy. The dead man's overlord had been informed. Someone else, at the discretion of the earl of Chester, would take seisin of the manor of Stanton Cobbold.

Everyone drew breath, dusted his hands, and went back to work.

Brother Cadfael went up into the town on the second day, to tend Emma's hand. The provost and his son were at work together, in strong content with each other and the world. Mistress Corviser returned to her kitchen, and left leech and patient together.

'I have wanted to talk to you,' said Emma, looking up earnestly into his face as he renewed the dressing. 'There must be one person who hears the truth from me, and I would rather it should be you.'

'I don't believe,' said Cadfael equably, 'that you told the sheriff a single thing that was false.'

'No, but I did not tell him all the truth. I said that I had no knowledge of what was in the letter, or even for whom it was intended, or by whom it was sent. That was true, I had no such knowledge of my own, though I did know who brought it to my uncle, and that it was to be handed to the glover for delivery. But when Ivo demanded the letter of me, and I span out the time asking what could be so important about a letter, he told me what he believed to be in it. King Stephen's kingdom stood at stake, he said, and the gain to the man who provided him the means to wipe out his enemies would stretch as wide as an earldom. He said the empress's friends were pressing the earl of Chester to join them, and he would not move unless he had word of all the other powers her cause could muster, and this was the promised despatch, to convince him his interest lay with them. As many as fifty names there might be, he said, of those secretly bound to the empress, perhaps even the date when Robert of Gloucester hopes to bring her to England, even the port where they plan to land. All these sold in advance to the king's vengeance, life and limb and lands, he said, and the earl of Chester with them, who had gone so far as to permit this approach! All these offered up bound and condemned, and *he* would get his own price for them. This is what he told me. This is what I do not know of my own knowledge, and yet in my heart and soul I do know it, for I am sure what he said was true.' She moistened her lips, and said carefully: 'I do not know King Stephen well enough to know what he would do, but I remember what he did here, last summer. I saw all those men, as honest in their allegiance as those who hold with the king, thrown into prison, their lives forfeit, their families stripped of land and living, some forced into exile . . . I saw deaths and revenges and still more bitterness if the tide should turn again. So I did what I did.'

'I know what you did,' said Brother Cadfael gently. He was bandaging the healing proof of it.

'But still, you see,' she persisted gravely, 'I am not sure if I did right, and for right reasons. King Stephen at least keeps a kind of peace where his writ runs. My uncle was absolute for the empress, but if she comes, if all these who hold with her rise and join her, there will be no peace anywhere. Whichever way I look I see deaths. But all I could think of, then, was preventing *him* from gaining by his treachery and murders. And there was only one way, by destroying the letter. Since then I have wondered. . . . But I think now that I must stand by what I did. If there must be fighting, if there must be deaths, let it happen as God wills, not as ambitious and evil men contrive. Those lives we cannot save, at least let us not help to destroy. Do you think I was right? I have wanted someone's word, I should like it to be yours.'

'Since you ask what I think,' said Cadfael, 'I think, my child, that if you carry scars on the fingers of this hand lifelong, you should wear them like jewels.'

Her lips parted in a startled smile. She shook her head over the persistent tremor of doubt. 'But you must never tell Philip,' she said with sudden urgency, holding him by the sleeve with her good hand. 'As I never shall. Let him believe me as innocent as he is himself . . .' She frowned over the word, which did not seem to her quite what she had wanted, but she could not find one fitter for her purpose. If it was not innocence she meant—for of what was she guilty?—was it simplicity, clarity, purity? None of them would do. Perhaps Brother Cadfael would understand, none the less. 'I felt somehow mired,' she said. '*He* should never set foot in intrigue, it is not for him.'

Brother Cadfael gave her his promise, and walked back through the town in a muse, reflecting on the complexity of women. She was perfectly right. Philip, for all his two years advantage, his intelligence, and his new and masterful maturity, would always be the younger, and the simpler, and—yes, she had the just word, after all!—the more innocent. In Cadfael's experience, it made for very good marriage prospects, where the woman was fully aware of her responsibilities.

On the thirtieth of September, just two months after Saint Peter's Fair, the Empress Maud and her half-brother Robert of Gloucester landed near Arundel and entered into the castle there. But Earl Ranulf of Chester sat cannily in his own palatine, minded his own business, and stirred neither hand nor foot in her cause.

ABOUT THE AUTHOR

ELLIS PETERS is a pseudonym for Edith Pargeter, author of many books under her own name. The recipient of the C.W.A. Silver Dagger Award, she is also well known as a translator of poetry and prose from the Czech. Miss Pargeter makes her home in Shropshire, England.